THE BIG HEART HEALTHY COOKBOOK

Simple Low Sodium and Low-Fat Recipes
for Beginners and Advanced Users

Lorraine Braxton

Table of Contents

Chapter 2 Beans and Legume .. 28

Chapter 3 Vegetarian and Vegan Dishes 46

Chapter 4 Seafood Recipes 67

Chapter 6 Snacks, Soups and Stews 106

Introduction

Heart disease is the number two cause of death in both men and women. It's claimed more lives than all forms of cancer combined and can take a toll on your emotional health as well. On the bright side, it is possible to survive even with cardiovascular disease by making smart lifestyle choices. By controlling weight, exercising regularly, and consuming good-for-the-heart foods like oatmeal or spinach.

Not a single source of food can make you magically healthy. What you eat is more important than what certain sources of food are. If you do not like fried, processed, packaged food and sugary snacks, then maybe it's not as much a matter of what kind of food you eat but rather how the food is used in your diet. With that said, here's a cookbook filled with delicious recipes which will guide you on how to use this fresh-from-the-ground produce and incorporate it into your meal plans for a happier, healthier lifestyle overall!

A heart-healthy diet is an eating plan that can help you minimize the negative impact of your diet on your heart health. The overall goal is to reduce sodium and fat intake. Too much sodium can increase blood sodium levels, leading to high blood pressure. High blood pressure is one of the major risk factors for coronary heart disease and other heart problems. Fat on the other hand is also the factor for coronary heart disease and other heart problems.

A heart-healthy diet consists of nutrient-rich foods, such as fruits and vegetables, lean poultry, fish, and whole grains. Eat these foods more often compared to less healthy items such as greasy or fried food as well as these unhealthy items: sweets, candy, chips, and margarine. Moreover, limit saturated fats and avoid trans fats while adding other unsaturated ones to get healthier vegetable oil. An overall goal is to help the consumer achieve the best possible parameter results for their blood pressure or lipid profile; help maintain a healthy weight for height/age

What is Heart-Healthy Diet?

A heart-healthy diet should be based on eating healthful and natural foods, particularly those that are fresh. This often translates to eating plenty of fruits and vegetables mainly, plus whole grains, seeds, nuts, and beans for protein. You should cut out greasy processed foods like snack foods and junk or fast food. Though meats may seem like they're the most natural thing on earth to eat, be aware of how much you consume – not only is meat high in fat and sodium which isn't good for you but it's also pretty bad when you don't consume enough nutrients from fresh plants too (you can get these from juices, if necessary, though watch out for added salt!). Moderation is key! Learn more about why a healthy diet is good for heart.

The Advantages of Heart Healthy Diet

A heart-healthy diet usually contains nutrient-dense foods from all major food groups, such as lean proteins, whole spices, heart-healthy fats, and fruits and vegetables of many colors. Replacing unhealthy snacks with nutritious options is another great way to promote a heart-healthy diet.

1.Heart Health

Exercising regularly and following a healthy diet plan consisting of a balanced variety of whole grains, fruits, vegetables, and proteins including fish at least twice a week such as an albacore tuna, salmon or flounder as well as low-fat dairy products like skim milk or cottage cheese are good for heart health.

2.Reduced Cancer Risk

Eating fruits, vegetables, and nuts containing antioxidants can reduce a person's risk of developing cancer. Phytochemicals found in fruits, vegetables, seeds, and nuts act as antioxidants to remove free radicals from the body which lowers the incidence of cancerous cells. Antioxidants are proven to protect the body from damage by further reducing free radicals.

3.Better Mood

Some evidence suggests a close relationship between diet and an individual's mood. Researchers found that diets with a high glycemic load may trigger increased symptoms of depression and fatigue. On the other hand, vegetables, whole fruit, and whole grains have a lower glycemic load. If you have suspicions that you might suffer from these symptoms, it's important to talk to your doctor as soon as possible so he/she can guide you towards appropriate help!

4.Improved Gut Health

The colon is full of bacteria which play an important role in digestion and metabolism. There are even some strains of bacteria that benefit the body by producing vitamins like K and B, which are associated with colon health. These good bacteria also help to fight off other harmful or bad bacteria as well as viruses. A diet made up of mostly vegetables, fruits, legumes, and whole grains provides a combination of prebiotics and probiotics that allows beneficial bacteria in your gut to flourish!

5. Improved Memory

A heart-healthy diet helps to maintain proper brain function. A 2015 study analyzed food and dietary habits to determine which foods can help reduce the risk of cognitive decline and dementia. The following was found to be helpful:
vitamin D, vitamin C, and vitamin E
omega-3 fatty acids
flavonoids and polyphenols
fish

6.Weight Loss

Maintaining a moderate healthy weight is an important part of staying healthy and staying away conditions such as:
heart disease
type 2 diabetes
poor bone density
some cancers
Healthy foods that are high in fiber and low in calories like fruits, vegetables, beans, nuts, and whole grains contain plenty of nutrients that help your heart stay healthy. A diet filled with processed foods is typically much higher in fat and sugar than more natural foods, which can make it more difficult to lose weight (and keep the weight off) without counting calories. Junk foods are also often high in sodium - a type of salt - which elevates blood pressure levels and puts stress on your heart. Researchers have determined that the best diet for people who want to shed pounds is one focused on filling up on low-calorie foods rich in protein and fiber without trying to count or otherwise restrict calories.

7.Diabetes Management

A heart-healthy diet can help a person with diabetes in managing blood glucose levels, keeping blood pressure and cholesterol within target ranges. It is necessary for people with diabetes to limit their food intake of foods with sugar and salt.

What Foods Are Recommended?

Your heart is the most crucial organ in your body! If you want it to stay functioning optimally, it needs to be fueled with lots of nutrients and all the good stuff. To accomplish this task, you need to focus on a healthy diet filled with foods that not only taste incredibly delicious but are known for their ability to help regulate your blood pressure as well as keep your heart working like clockwork too. The number of people diagnosed with heart disease and cardiac arrest has been going up over recent years so we want you to do whatever you can, if possible, to lower your risk of such things happening by eating healthy foods rich in antioxidants, fiber, minerals, and omega 3 fatty acids.
Fruits high in soluble fiber, veggies high in soluble fiber, omega-3-rich nuts/seeds, other tree nuts/seeds, rolled oats, fish and all types of legumes are heart healthy foods, and you can use spices to taste instead of salt.
Here enlisted the foods to protect your heart and keep your heart beating at its best:

1.Salmon

Omega-3 fatty acids are a type of good fat that can lower your risk of heart disease and high blood pressure. As a healthy person, you should consume two servings of foods rich in omega-3s each week. One serving is 3.5 ounces but canned salmon has enough that it doesn't necessarily have to be a main dish like the grilled salmon recipe mentioned above - you would simply need one can per serving to get your daily recommended dosage.

2.Oatmeal

Oatmeal is tasty breakfast food. It can also be used in a wide variety of recipes to bring some extra flavor and texture to your dishes. You can also make delicious cookies out of it, or you can use it as meatloaf if you mix it with turkey meat. Oatmeal is very high in fiber – a single one-cup serving contains four grams of fiber! It's such an amazing nutrient to have in our boards that will keep us full for longer without needing more meals. Plus, the other nutrients that it offers come packaged with the energy we need to explore our day ahead with enthusiasm! Don't hesitate to enjoy your bowl of oatmeal this morning!

3.Black or Kidney Beans

Bean is good for the heart! Beans are nutritious - they contain B-complex vitamins, niacin, folate magnesium, and calcium. What's more, they're also a top source of protein. Beans are so versatile! They can be used on their own as in salads or added to a meal such as soups, stews, or pasta. Strangely enough, black beans taste amazing in pita sandwiches with avocado - one of my favorite ways to make meals out of them. You can also combine nuts with kidney beans for a delicious vegetarian chili or add mashed beans to your salad for lunchtime on the go.

4.Nuts

Nuts are no longer a luxury item. They've gone mainstream in recent years and for good reason. Namely their ability to lower blood cholesterol, and reduce blood pressure and triglycerides which is important for your heart health. And some nuts like almonds contain positive nutrients that make them key contributors to overall health.

5.Almonds

Almonds are great if you're on a diet, or if you're trying to make some healthy dietary changes. Almonds are delicious by themselves and can be incorporated into almost any dish. They do contain moderate amounts of monounsaturated fats and polyunsaturated fatty acids. This is one reason why it's smart to purchase raw or dry roasted versions of almonds so that you can remain more in control of how much fat and cholesterol will be received in your daily consumption level.

6.Tuna

Tuna contains omega-3 fatty acids. Although tuna does not contain as many omega-3s like salmon, it still provides a moderately low amount of this healthy nutrient. Tuna salads are easy to make and when made light on mayonnaise can keep you feeling full until dinner time rolls around. They can also be grilled for an easy dinner that is quite tasty.

7.Tofu

Tofu is a great source of protein. Tofu is also vegetarian food, and it includes niacin, folate, calcium, magnesium, and potassium for your heart health. Some call tofu "bean curd" because it is made from pressed soybean curd. It's easy to study and can be part of almost any meal. Thinly slice firm tofu; marinate for several hours and grill or add to your favorite veggie stir-fry. Make tofu, lettuce, and tomato sandwich on whole-grain bread; use instead of meats in pasta dishes; and add slices or cubes to salads for added protein.

8.Brown Rice

Brown rice has never tasted so good. There is an abundance of ways to use brown rice and it's delicious too! It's a good source of soluble fiber (vital for a healthy digestive system) and provides calcium, manganese, vitamin B6, potassium, magnesium, and iron. Protein levels in brown rice can be improved by cooking it with beans or tofu as well as tomatoes or broccoli. You can add brown rice to stir-fries or soups!

9.Soy Milk

Soy milk is a tasty accompaniment to your breakfast bowl of whole-grain cereal. It's protein-rich and the soy proteins found in soy milk are not that different from the ones found in animal milk but it contains almost no cholesterol. Soymilk has less lactose than cow's milk so many people who experience discomfort eating or drinking other kinds of dairy products find that they can tolerate soy just fine. Soy milk is different in flavor but you will undoubtedly love the taste!

10.Blueberries

Blueberries are packed with nutrients that are part of a healthy diet, including beta carotene, lutein, vitamin C and anthocyanin. Blueberries help lower your chances of heart disease since they contain antioxidants which in addition to protecting against cancer also help lower bad cholesterol levels in your body. Blueberries are easy to eat as a healthy snack by themselves or on top of your cereal or pancakes or blend into a smoothie so they can become part of almost any dish you prepare at home.

11.Carrots

Carrots are a great source of beta carotene and have lots of the more well-known nutrients. They also have alpha and gamma carotenes – carotenoids that are associated with lower risks of some diseases like heart disease and stroke to name but two. Carrots make for a great snack on their own or paired with other foods like salads or inside muffin or tomato sauce recipes. Spinach is another food that can pack a punch when it comes to fighting heart disease, etc. because it's packed full of beta carotene, vitamins C and E, potassium, folate, calcium, and plenty of fiber.

12.Spinach

Spinach is a leafy green vegetable that is highly nutritious and has surprisingly many functions. Among other nutrients such as beta-carotene, vitamins C and E, potassium, folate, and calcium, spinach also contains fiber. It's a great base for salads and can be used on sandwiches instead of lettuce. You can also sneak some into a fruit smoothie, add it to your pizza or mix it into an egg-white omelet. Furthermore, you can use it on pasta to add some extra nutrition or you're able to make great sauces out of it alongside other vegetables that can further complement the flavor giving healthy dishes even more nutritional value!

13.Broccoli

Broccoli, like other cruciferous vegetables, is a powerhouse food for us because of its rich vitamin and mineral content - including vitamins A, Carotene-α, along with folic acid, calcium, and fiber. It's low-calorie too so it makes sense to add more servings of broccoli to your diet if you want to improve the health of your heart.

14.Sweet Potato

Sweet potatoes are healthy to eat. They contain plenty of dietary fiber and provide a good dose of vitamin A, C, and E as well as antioxidant beta-carotene. You'll also get plenty of minerals from sweet potatoes including calcium, iron, magnesium, phosphorus, potassium, and sodium. Like many vegetables, you can eat them in many different ways. You can eat the skins for an additional source of fiber when cooking or bake them whole - it doesn't matter!

15.Red Bell Peppers

Red bell peppers have a tangy taste. They are full of heart-healthy nutrients like beta-carotene and carotenoids including B-complex vitamins, folate, potassium, and fiber. Bell peppers make lovely side dishes. You can enjoy them as they are or cut them into slices to eat raw. Bell peppers also taste great grilled or roasted to accompany your main dish of choice. For a delectable dish with heart-healthy nutrients, go for red bells pepper.

16.Asparagus

Asparagus contains beta-gentian, which is a carotenoid that helps protect against cancers and cardiovascular disease. Asparagus also contains vitamin B, flavonoid and fiber. Asparagus can promote gastrointestinal motility, help digestion and increase appetite. In addition, asparagus also has certain anti-cancer effects.

17.Oranges

Oranges are a great portable snack to have on your person. They're juicy and filled with nutrients like the calcium, iron, phosphorus, antioxidant beta-kryptoxanthin, carotenoids like beta- and alpha-carotene, as well as flavones, vitamin C, vitamin B1, potassium, folate and fiber. The whole fruit is best, but in a pinch, you can also add orange slices to salads or yogurt, or even chicken dishes. Be careful though if you're going to be drinking orange juice: pound for pound it isn't nearly as beneficial compared to eating the whole fruit!

18.Tomatoes

Tomatoes are an easy and delicious way to add antioxidants to your meals. They bring a powerful flavor to any dish, but be mindful that not all tomatoes are created equal! For instance, the main antioxidant in tomatoes is lycopene. Unlike the health-restoring beta-carotene and alpha-carotene which are fat-soluble, lycopene is water-soluble and only found in red tomatoes - so remember to choose organic if you're looking for that added benefit.

19.Acorn Squash

Acorn squash is another heart-healthy food with beta-carotene and lutein (carotenoids), B-complex and C vitamins, folate, calcium, magnesium, potassium, and fiber. The flesh of this food is commonly baked to make a popular winter side dish. To make it: Simply cut the squash in half, scrape out the seeds, and fill it with brown rice and other healthy vegetables like spinach or squash before roasting.

20.Cantaloupe

Cantaloupe contains many nutrients that the human body needs physiologically, such as carotene, dietary fiber, carbohydrates, pectin, vitamin B, vitamin A, vitamin C, potassium, phosphorus and so on. You can enjoy cantaloupe any time of day or try something different by adding it to smoothies or making fresh fruit salads with it.

21.Papaya

Papayas are excellent examples of the many varieties of delicious fruits that can be eaten raw. They taste great in salads or made into smoothies, they blend well with other ingredients such as yogurt and orange juice, they may even be frozen into ice popsicles, and they make for a delectable addition to fruit salads! Papayas provide health benefits such as vitamins A and C, folate, calcium, and potassium. The papaya is best paired with heart-healthy salmon for its ability to help reduce high blood pressure and protect the cardiovascular system.

22.Dark Chocolate

Dark chocolate with 70% or higher cocoa content has a great deal of heart-healthy resveratrol and cocoa phenols in it, great for lowering blood pressure, nuts are also an interesting source for sleeping well. Everything is about moderation.

What Foods Are Not Advisable?

What you eat affects how your body functions, including your heart. Changing eating habits can help reduce your risk of having heart disease.
Here's a breakdown of foods that should be limited in the heart-healthy diet.

1.Sugar, Salt, Unhealthy Fat

Over time, high amounts of salt, sugar and refined carbs will put stress on the heart because they damage blood vessels and stiffen arteries. If you're worried about your heart getting clogged with bad food, then limit the amount of these things in your diet. But rather than have a bad focus on one thing in particular you should aim to focus on an overall healthy diet instead. You can still eat these things but only if you eat a lot of healthy fruits and vegetables as well as whole grains, lean protein, and low-fat dairy to balance everything out!

2.Bacon

More than half of bacon's calorific value can raise your blood cholesterol levels and increase your risk of heart disease and stroke. It's full of salt, which increases your blood pressure and places a strain on your cardiovascular system. In high doses, sodium (the main component in salt) can lead to a real risk of developing both stroke and heart disease. This is in addition to the preservatives used in meat products such as bacon that have been associated with these conditions too.

3.Red Meat

Eating a lot of beef, lamb and pork can raise your risk for heart disease and diabetes. They may boost your cholesterol. More recent studies point to how the bacteria in your gut break down

L-carnitine (a compound found in meat) into compounds that are toxic to our hearts in large amounts. Be mindful of your portions! Also look for lean cuts like round, sirloin, and extra-lean ground beef.

4.Baked Goods

Treats should be a rare indulgence. They're typically full of sugar and empty calories that can lead to weight gain, which is linked to high triglyceride levels, heart disease, and stroke. The main ingredient - usually white flour or sugary treats - may spike your blood sugar and leave you hungrier in no time. We recommend you make healthier treats by swapping out white flour for a whole-wheat alternative and trimming down on the amount of sugar used as well as opting for liquid plant oils instead of butter.

5.Processed Meats

Hot dogs, sausages, salami, and lunch meat comprise the worst types of meats for your heart. They're typically high in salt - except turkey. Turkey is a milder taste than salami but contains a substantial amount of sodium that isn't good for you if eaten too frequently.

6.White Rice, Bread, and Pasta

Rice, bread, and pasta soon turn into sugar in your body, which is the last thing you need. Just think about how your mom told you to not eat too much candy because it turns into fat. Whole grains - the rice should not be the only one on that list for example brown rice, oats, etc. Ultimately get as many whole grains in your diet as possible by sticking to healthy snacks such as veggies or fruit.

7.Alcohol

People who drink too much alcohol are at high risk for getting a variety of health problems involving the heart, brain, and other vital organs. The key to being healthy while still enjoying an occasional drinking session is knowing your limits as nobody should take more than they can handle.

8.Butter

Butter can raise bad cholesterol and make heart disease more likely. Thus, it may be a good idea to replace butter with olive oil or vegetable oil-based spreads, which contain heart-healthy mono- and polyunsaturated fats. It's always best to make sure you're doing things that lower your LDL cholesterol levels.

9.Fried Chicken

Deep-frying chicken is unhealthy. Frying can add a significant amount of salt, fat, calories, and other unsavory things to otherwise healthy food. There have been studies done stating that individuals who have fried foods in their diet have a higher chance of experiencing heart failure compared to those who do not.

10.Canned Soup

Soup is all about good flavor, nutrition, and most of all comfort. However, the amount of salt in canned soups is high! This is why we recommend whenever you go to make soup from scratch always use low sodium broth or simply buy a low sodium broth depending on what's best for you and your family.

4-Week Diet Plan

Week 1

Day 1:

Breakfast: Soft and Chewy Raisin Cashew Oats
Lunch: Black Bean & Quinoa Salad
Snack: Sesame Edamame
Dinner: Braised Beef with Parsley
Dessert: Banana Mango Shake

Day 2:

Breakfast: Strawberry Quinoa Breakfast Bowl
Lunch: Avocado-Tuna Sandwich
Snack: Marinated Berries with Mints
Dinner: Parmesan Orzo with Sweet Leek
Dessert: Banana Vanilla Mousse

Day 3:

Breakfast: Easy Tomato Egg Tart
Lunch: Peanut Butter Taco Salad
Snack: Roasted Chickpeas
Dinner: Veggie Chicken Bowls
Dessert: Matzo Almond and Apricot Macaroons

Day 4:

Breakfast: Easy Vanilla Almond Shake
Lunch: Toasted-Bulgur Salad
Snack: Delicious Kale Chips
Dinner: Spicy Eggplant Tagine
Dessert: Simple Blueberry Peach Crisp

Day 5:

Breakfast: Chocolate-Oatmeal Bread
Lunch: Sweet Quiche with Greens
Snack: Smoked Salmon Crudités
Dinner: Tuna Sandwich
Dessert: Brownie Bites

Day 6:

Breakfast: Apple Whole Grain Muffins
Lunch: Veggie Chickpea Pilaf
Snack: Potato Gratin Mix
Dinner: Baked Salmon Fillets
Dessert: Sweet Vanilla Cookies

Day 7:

Breakfast: Banana Pancakes
Lunch: Full-Bodied Zucchini
Snack: Pecan-Berry Pilaf
Dinner: Tomatoes & Spinach Polenta
Dessert: Easy Peach Cobbler

Week 2

Day 1:

Breakfast: Scrambled Egg and Herbs
Lunch: Cream Soup with Almond
Snack: Stuffed Dates with Nut Butter
Dinner: Garlic Mackerel Fillets
Dessert: Pecan Phyllo Tarts

Day 2:

Breakfast: Simple Puff Pastry
Lunch: Spicy Eggplant Tagine
Snack: Stewed Prunes, Pears, and Apple
Dinner: Baked Chicken with Artichoke
Dessert: Banana Ice-cream

Day 3:

Breakfast: Banana Granola
Lunch: Swiss Chard and Lentil Salad
Snack: Classic Cashew Cream
Dinner: Tomato Fish Stew
Dessert: Almond Pumpkin Pie

Day 4:

Breakfast: Garlicky Beef with Onion and Eggs
Lunch: Full-Bodied Zucchini
Snack: Citrus-Marinated Olives
Dinner: Creamy Shrimp
Dessert: Homemade Kiwi Smoothie

Day 5:

Breakfast: Breakfast Cups
Lunch: Tasty Falafel with Pinto Bean
Snack: Greek Deviled Eggs
Dinner: Coconut Salmon
Dessert: No-Oil Carrot Muffins

Day 6:

Breakfast: Baked Biscuits
Lunch: Italian Pasta with Tomatoes
Snack: Yummy Caprese Grilled Cheese
Dinner: Garlicky Pork Tenderloin
Dessert: Tasty Strawberry Shortcake

Day 7:

Breakfast: Easy Huevos Rancheros
Lunch: Tasty Falafel with Pinto Bean
Snack: Thai-style Roasted Carrots
Dinner: Creamy Shrimp
Dessert: Fruit Party Punch

Week 3

Day 1:

Breakfast: Almond Granola
Lunch: Taquitos with Black Beans
Snack: Carrot-Cranberry Muffins
Dinner: Salmon-Peaches Mix
Dessert: No-Bake Strawberry Cheesecake

Day 2:

Breakfast: Almond Apple Salad
Lunch: Sticky-Nice Rice with Cauliflower
Snack: Delicious Good Morning Grits
Dinner: Chicken Lettuce Wraps
Dessert: Brownie Bites

Day 3:

Breakfast: Basil Tomato Omelet
Lunch: Sodium-Free Herbs Chickpeas
Snack: Classic Tex-Mex Kale
Dinner: Yogurt Trout
Dessert: Simple Blueberry Peach Crisp

Day 4:

Breakfast: Banana Pancakes
Lunch: Cream Soup with Almond
Snack: Breakfast Mushroom Risotto
Dinner: Potatoes Mix Salmon
Dessert: Fruit Party Punch

Day 5:

Breakfast: Garlicky Beef with Onion and Eggs
Lunch: Tasty Falafel with Pinto Bean
Snack: Fresh Vanilla Almonds
Dinner: Scallop & Strawberry Mix
Dessert: Banana Mango Shake

Day 6:

Breakfast: Raspberry Oatmeal
Lunch: Fresh Spinach with Almond Milk
Snack: Tortilla Chips
Dinner: Veggie Chicken Bowls
Dessert: Orange Peel Cake with Icing

Day 7:

Breakfast: Veggie Frittata
Lunch: Parmesan Orzo with Sweet Leek
Snack: Pomegranate Chickpea Fatteh
Dinner: Garlic Tomato Mussels
Dessert: Vanilla Apple Cake

Week 4

Day 1:

Breakfast: Easy Apple Cinnamon Quinoa Bowl
Lunch: Creamy Cabbage with Sunflower Seeds
Snack: Marinated Berries with Mints
Dinner: Pesto Chicken Pizza
Dessert: Cool Berry Cucumber Drink

Day 2:

Breakfast: Baby Kale Breakfast Salad
Lunch: Fiber-Rich Couscous
Snack: Easy Granola Bars
Dinner: Veggie Mix & Salmon
Dessert: Vanilla Huckleberry Cake

Day 3:

Breakfast: Yummy Pumpkin English Muffins
Lunch: Spicy Eggplant Tagine
Snack: Burrata Caprese Stack
Dinner: Veggie Chicken Bowls
Dessert: Fruit Party Punch

Day 4:

Breakfast: Easy Eggs in an Avocado
Lunch: Low-Fat Lentil Salad
Snack: Salmon-Stuffed Cucumbers
Dinner:
Dessert: Banana Vanilla Mousse

Day 5:

Breakfast: Simple Lemon Chia Seed Parfaits
Lunch: Cream Soup with Almond
Snack: Roasted Potatoes and Carrots
Dinner: Herbed Chicken Kebabs
Dessert: Cranberry-Oat Crisp

Day 6:

Breakfast: Baked Mushrooms with Onion
Lunch: Quinoa Stew with Red Lentil
Snack: Lemony Beets and Onions
Dinner: Onion and Carrot Soup
Dessert: Cocoa Pudding

Day 7:

Breakfast: Scrambled Egg and Herbs
Lunch: Green Pea Pesto with Nuts
Snack: Peanut Butter Banana Sushi
Dinner: Wasabi Cod Salad
Dessert: No-Oil Carrot Muffins

Best Ever Banana Nut Muffins

Prep time: 5 minutes | Cook time: 30 minutes | Serves: 4

Olive oil nonstick cooking spray	⅛ teaspoon salt
⅔ cup sliced very ripe banana	2 egg whites, beaten
2 teaspoons granulated stevia or	¼ cup unsweetened applesauce
2 tablespoons brown sugar	½ teaspoon vanilla extract
½ teaspoon baking soda	½ cup whole-wheat pastry flour
	4 tablespoons chopped walnuts

1. Heat the oven to 375 degrees F ahead of time and lightly spray two 7-ounce ramekins with the cooking spray. 2. Mash the banana with a fork in a large bowl, leaving some lumps for texture. In the meanwhile, put the baking soda, stevia, whisk as well as baking soda together for 1 minute. 3. Put in vanilla, applesauce, egg whites and then stir until combined. Besides, put in the flour and stir with a spatula until just combined. 4. Separate the batter evenly between the ramekins, and they should be half to three-quarters full or so. Also, sprinkle the walnuts evenly over the top. 5. Bake the food for 25 to 30 minutes, or until the tops are golden brown and a toothpick inserted in the center comes out clean. 6. Let them cool for a few minutes, get away from the ramekins and keep warm.
Per Serving: Calories 159; Fat 5.23g; Sodium 264mg; Carbs 24.33g; Fiber 3.3g; Sugar 8.61g; Protein 6.1g

Ultimate Whole-Wheat Blueberry Muffins

Prep time: 5 minutes | Cook time: 23 minutes | Serves: 4

Olive oil nonstick cooking spray	¼ cup shredded zucchini
¾ cup whole-wheat flour	3 tablespoons nonfat milk or
½ teaspoon baking soda	plant-based milk
Pinch of low-sodium salt	½ teaspoon vanilla extract
2 teaspoons granulated stevia	½ cup blueberries (fresh or
or 2 tablespoons brown sugar	frozen)
2 egg whites, beaten	

1. Heat the oven to 375 degrees F and lightly spray two cups of a giant muffin pan with the cooking spray ahead of time. 2. Mix together the flour, baking salt, stevia as well as soda in a large bowl. Set it aside. 3. Put together the zucchini, vanilla, milk as well as egg whites in a small bowl. 4. Whisk the wet into the dry. Softly fold in the blueberries. 5. Separate the batter equally between the prepared muffin cups. 6. Bake the food for 19 to 23 minutes, or till a toothpick put in the center turns clean. Keep them cool for 3 minutes before eating.
Per Serving: Calories 128; Fat 0.79g; Sodium 212mg; Carbs 26.31g; Fiber 2.9g; Sugar 9.63g; Protein 5.41g

Rice Vegetable Shake

Prep time: 5 minutes | Cook time: None | Serves: 2

2 cups carrots, chopped	1 (1½-inch) piece fresh ginger,
2 cups kale, chopped	peeled
2 cups cashew milk	½ cup brown rice
2 tablespoons ground flaxseed	

1. Add the chopped kale, cashew milk, peeled ginger, chopped carrots as well as ground flaxseed in a blender. In a blender, add the chopped carrots, Blend for 1 to 2 minutes, until smooth and no lumps remain. 2. Add the ice and blend until smooth. Serve cold.
Per Serving: Calories 312; Fat 13.18g; Sodium 193mg; Carbs 37.96g; Fiber 7.4g; Sugar 18.25g; Protein 12.56g

Yummy Pumpkin English Muffins

Prep time: 1 minute | Cook time: 3 or 4 minutes | Serves: 4

Olive oil nonstick cooking spray	½ teaspoon pumpkin pie spice
½ cup gluten-free oat flour	½ teaspoon ground cinnamon
1 teaspoon baking powder	Pinch salt
4 egg whites	½ to 1 teaspoon granulated stevia
¼ cup pumpkin purée	

1. Spray two 7-ounce ramekins with the cooking spray. 2. In a medium bowl, Whisk the baking powder, pumpkin purée, egg whites, stevia, cinnamon, salt, stevia as well as oat flour until well combined. 3. Divide the batter evenly between the two ramekins. Separate the batter evenly between the two ramekins. 4. Place one ramekin in the microwave and microwave on high for 1 minute to 1 minute 30 seconds (depending on your microwave), or until set. With the second ramekin one more time. 5. Keep the muffins cool for a moment, then get away from the ramekins. Cut each English muffin in half horizontally and toast until done to your liking. Serve the spread of your choice or nut butter.
Per Serving: Calories 117; Fat 4.96g; Sodium 97mg; Carbs 11.41g; Fiber 1.6g; Sugar 0.98g; Protein 7.73g

Black Bean-Avocado Burritos

Prep time: 10 minutes | Cook time: 25 minutes | Serves: 5

1 tablespoon olive oil	black beans, drained and rinsed
1 red bell pepper, cut into strips	½ teaspoon low-sodium salt
½ medium yellow onion, chopped	1 avocado, cut into chunks
1 teaspoon ground cumin	2 teaspoons fresh lime juice
1 teaspoon dried oregano	¾ cup 0% plain Greek yogurt
1 (15-ounce) can no-salt-added	5 small whole wheat tortillas

1. Heat the oil over medium heat in a medium skillet. Add the pepper and onion and sauté for 4 to 5 minutes, until soft. 2. Stir in the cumin and oregano to coat. Transfer the vegetable mixture to a bowl to cool. 3. Mix the salt and black beans in the same skillet. Cover and simmer over low heat for 15 minutes or until the beans soften. 4. Mix the lime juice, avocado, as well as yogurt and mash together in a medium bowl. 5. Place the tortillas on a large cutting board; spread 1 tablespoon of the avocado mixture, 1 tablespoon of peppers and onions, and 3 tablespoons of black beans in each. Roll the tortillas into burritos. 6. Wrap the burritos individually in tight plastic wrap, and then place in a zip-top plastic bag. Do not forget to keep in the refrigerator.
Per Serving: Calories 266; Fat 14.07g; Sodium 229mg; Carbs 28.06g; Fiber 8.2g; Sugar 3.83g; Protein 9.27g

Easy Peach-Raspberry Smoothie

Prep time: 5 minutes | Cook time: None | Serves: 4

1½ cups plain nonfat Greek yogurt
1 cup frozen chopped mango
½ cup frozen banana slices
½ cup frozen raspberries
½ cup unsweetened almond milk
1 teaspoon vanilla extract
1 ripe peach, sliced (about ⅔ cup)
½ cup fresh raspberries
2 tablespoons sliced almonds
2 tablespoons chia seeds

1. Put in the mango, Greek yogurt, raspberries, almond milk, banana, vanilla to a blender and blend on low until the mixture reaches a soft serve consistency. 2. Scoop into two serving bowls and top each bowl with half the fresh raspberries, sliced peach, chia seeds as well as almonds. 3. Serve the meal as soon as possible.
Per Serving: Calories 227; Fat 2.91g; Sodium 55mg; Carbs 41.89g; Fiber 6.2g; Sugar 35.19g; Protein 11.13g

Delicious Red Velvet Beet and Cherry Smoothie

Prep time: 5 minutes | Cook time: None | Serves: 4

1½ cups plain nonfat Greek yogurt
1 cup unsweetened almond milk
2 tablespoons unsweetened cocoa powder
1 cup frozen cherries
⅔ cup frozen banana slices
½ cup raw peeled and chopped beets
½ cup gluten-free rolled oats
2 pitted Medjool dates
1 teaspoon vanilla extract
1 cup ice cubes

1. Combine all the in a high-speed blender and blend until smooth. 2. Pour into two tall glasses and enjoy the meal as soon as possible.
Per Serving: Calories 240; Fat 3.66g; Sodium 139mg; Carbs 45.61g; Fiber 5.6g; Sugar 32.91g; Protein 14.25g

Baby Kale Breakfast Salad

Prep time: 10 minutes | Cook time: None | Serves: 4

For the salad
4 cups baby kale
1 (7.5 ounce) jar artichoke hearts packed in water, drained
1 (15-ounce) can chickpeas, drained and rinsed
1 cup grape tomatoes, halved
2 tablespoons hemp seeds
For the dressing
¼ cup almond butter
Juice of 1 lemon
1 tablespoon low-sodium soy sauce
1 tablespoon minced garlic
1 tablespoon minced ginger
2 tablespoons water, plus more as needed

To make the salad: 1. To start with, wash and dry the baby kale. Set it aside. 2. Combine the chickpeas, tomatoes, hemp seeds as well as artichoke hearts in a medium bowl.
To make the dressing: 1. Stir together all the dressings, adding extra water as needed to get to the desired consistency in a small bowl. 2. Add the dressing to the artichoke mix, and combine until evenly coated. 3. Separate the baby kale between serving plates. Ornament half of the artichoke mixture and serve as soon as possible.
Per Serving: Calories 277; Fat 12.84g; Sodium 321mg; Carbs 34.15g; Fiber 9.9g; Sugar 10.45g; Protein 11.87g

Sweet Potato Hash

Prep time: 10 minutes | Cook time: 25 minutes | Serves: 4

For the sweet potato hash
2 teaspoons olive oil
1 garlic clove, minced
1 cup diced yellow onion
2 cups peeled and cubed sweet potatoes
1 cup canned black beans, drained and rinsed
½ teaspoon paprika
½ teaspoon ground cumin
Pinch low-sodium salt
¼ cup chopped fresh cilantro
For the guacamole
½ avocado, peeled, seeded, and mashed
Juice of ½ lime
Low-sodium salt
For the pico de gallo
½ cup diced grape tomatoes
¼ cup finely diced white onion
¼ cup chopped fresh cilantro
Low-sodium salt

To make the sweet potato hash: In a large skillet, heat the olive oil over medium heat. Add the sweet potatoes, onion, garlic, paprika, black beans salt as well as cumin. Cook for 20 to 25 minutes, stirring every few minutes until the potatoes become tender and slightly caramelized. Get away from the heat and stir in the fresh cilantro.
To make the guacamole: 1. Stir together the mashed avocado and lime juice in a small bowl. 2. Flavored with salt and then set it aside.
To make the pico de gallo: 1. In a small bowl, stir together the tomatoes, onion, and cilantro. 2. Season with salt and set it aside. 3. Stir the onion, cilantro as well as tomatoes in a small bowl. 4. Flavored with salt and then set it aside.
To assemble: 1. Spoon the sweet potato hash onto two plates, and top with the guacamole and pico de gallo. 2. Enjoy the meal as soon as possible.
Per Serving: Calories 174; Fat 8.76g; Sodium 47mg; Carbs 20.75g; Fiber 7.2g; Sugar 4.5g; Protein 5.37g

Fresh Lentil Asparagus Omelet

Prep time: 5 minutes | Cook time: 10 minutes | Serves: 4

4 eggs, whisked
1 tablespoon dried thyme
¼ cup chopped onion
1 cup chopped asparagus (about ½ pound asparagus)
½ cup canned lentils, drained
and rinsed
½ cup chopped grape tomatoes, for garnish
8 avocado slices, for garnish (optional)

1. Whisk together the thyme and the egg in a medium bowl. Set them aside. 2. Heat a small nonstick skillet over medium heat. Add the onion and asparagus and cook for 2 to 3 minutes. Add the lentils and cook for an additional 2 minutes until heated through. Lower the heat to low to keep warm. 3. Heat a medium nonstick skillet over medium heat. Repeat whisk the eggs, then add half of the eggs to the frying pan and cook for 2 to 3 minutes. 4. Spread half of the asparagus-lentil mixture on one half of the eggs. First of all, cook for 1 to 2 minutes more, then fold in the egg over the filling and cook for another 1 to 2 minutes. Get away from the pan and place on a serving plate. 5. To save the resources, you can recycle the remaining to make the second omelet. 6. Fill up with the avocado slices and chopped tomatoes (optional) and enjoy the meal as soon as possible.
Per Serving: Calories 160; Fat 8.25g; Sodium 66mg; Carbs 13.25g; Fiber 4.9g; Sugar 4.65g; Protein 9.31g

Nutty Blueberry-Avocado Smoothie

Prep time: 5 minutes | Cook time: None | Serves: 2

1 cup plain nonfat Greek yogurt
1 cup unsweetened vanilla almond milk
1 teaspoon vanilla extract
2 cups fresh baby spinach
1 cup frozen blueberries
½ cup mashed avocado
¼ cup almonds
2 tablespoons wheat germ
1 teaspoon granulated stevia (or sweetener of choice)
¼ teaspoon ground cinnamon
1 cup ice cubes

1. Combine all the in a blender and process them at high speed until smooth. 2. Pour into two tall glasses and enjoy the meal as soon as possible.
Per Serving: Calories 349; Fat 10.82g; Sodium 180mg; Carbs 45.17g; Fiber 6.4g; Sugar 33.62g; Protein 20.31g

Sweet Berry Griddle Cakes

Prep time: 15 minutes | Cook time: 10 minutes | Serves: 2

1 cup rolled oats
½ cup blueberries
½ cup strawberries, chopped
3 tablespoons fat-free plain yogurt
¼ cup unsweetened almond
milk
1 tablespoon chia seeds
1 large free-range egg
½ teaspoon ground cinnamon
2 teaspoons olive oil

1. Add the blueberries, chopped strawberries, the rolled oats, chia seeds, ground cinnamon, unsweetened almond milk, large egg, plain yogurt, 2. Heat the olive oil over medium-low heat in a large heavy bottom pan or crêpe pan. 3. Pour ¼ cup of batter into the pan and allow to cook for 4 to 5 minutes until bubbles form at the top, flip, and cook for 1 or 2 minutes, or until golden brown and no longer doughy. Do the same to the remaining batter. 4. Keep warm.
Per Serving: Calories 324; Fat 15.52g; Sodium 78mg; Carbs 50.36g; Fiber 14.2g; Sugar 10.47g; Protein 15.55g

Easy Eggs in an Avocado

Prep time: 10 minutes | Cook time: 5 minutes | Serves: 2

1 large avocado, halved, pitted, and peeled
Low-sodium salt
Freshly ground black pepper
1 tablespoon olive oil, divided
2 large eggs
3 or 4 tablespoons water
½ cup halved cherry tomatoes
¼ cup chopped fresh chives

1. Lay the avocado halves on a clean work surface, hollow-side up. Gently press the avocado down to slightly flatten the bottom so it will sit without tipping. (Keep the hollow part of the avocado intact to crack the eggs into later.) Flavored with pepper and salt. 2. In a high-sided skillet, heat ½ tablespoon of olive oil over medium-high heat. Add the avocado halves, hollow-side up. Allow the avocados to sear for 1 minute. Crack an egg into each hollow. Season the eggs with salt and pepper. Pour 3 or 4 tablespoons of water into the bottom of the pan and cover the pan with a lid. 3. Fetch the water to simmer and steam the eggs for 3 to 5 minutes, or until the egg whites have set and the yolks are firm (or set to your liking). 4. Meanwhile, mix together the chives, tomatoes, and remaining ½ tablespoon of olive oil in a medium bowl, flavored with pepper and salt. 5. Get away from the egg-stuffed to two serving plates. Top with the tomato and

chive mixture, and enjoy the meal.
Per Serving: Calories 297; Fat 26.29g; Sodium 118mg; Carbs 10.25g; Fiber 7.2g; Sugar 1.12g; Protein 8.52g

Baked Vegetable and Egg Skillet

Prep time: 5 minutes | Cook time: 7 minutes | Serves: 4

1 tablespoon olive oil
3 cups chopped mixed vegetables (such as zucchini, mushrooms, onions, bell pepper)
1 teaspoon garlic powder
Low-sodium salt
Freshly ground black pepper
4 eggs
¼ cup chopped fresh cilantro

1. Heat the broiler ahead of time. 2. Possess the olive oil in a medium baking dish or a broiler-proof. Add the vegetables and garlic powder. Season with salt and pepper, and toss gently to coat. 3. Place the skillet under the broiler on the middle oven rack for about 2 minutes, then stir and cook for about 2 more minutes. Keep the skillet under the broiler on the middle oven rack for 2 minutes or so, then mix and cook for about 2 more minutes. 4. Remove the skillet from the oven, crack the eggs over the veggies, and return to under the broiler. 5. Broil the eggs for 2 to 3 minutes until cooked to your liking. Watch closely as the eggs will cook quickly. 6. Separate the egg and vegetable mixture between two serving plates, top with the fresh cilantro, and enjoy the meal as soon as possible.
Per Serving: Calories 151; Fat 7.61g; Sodium 122mg; Carbs 15.12g; Fiber 0.2g; Sugar 4.08g; Protein 5.81g

Crispy Waffles with Cinnamon-Almond Butter

Prep time: 5 minutes | Cook time: 20 minutes | Serves: 5

¾ cup whole wheat flour
¾ cup all-purpose flour
1 teaspoon baking powder
¾ teaspoon baking soda
1 cup fat-free milk
1 tablespoon fresh lemon juice or distilled white vinegar
1 large egg, beaten
1 tablespoon 0% plain Greek yogurt
⅓ cup canola oil
Nonstick cooking spray
¾ teaspoon ground cinnamon
½ cup natural almond butter

1. Heat a waffle iron to medium heat ahead of time. 2. While the waffle iron heats up, mix with the all-purpose flour, baking powder, whole wheat flour, and baking soda in a medium bowl. 3. Combine the lemon juice and milk and let it sit for 1 minute to make "buttermilk" in a separate bowl. 4. Add the yogurt, oil as well as egg to the milk mixture and then stir together. 5. Make a well in the dry ingredients and add the wet ingredients. Stir to combine. 6. Mist the top and bottom of the waffle maker with cooking spray. Pour in ½ cup of batter and cook for 3 to 5 minutes, until golden brown. Transfer the waffle to a plate and make the remaining batter one more time. 7. Meanwhile, combine the cinnamon and almond butter in a small airtight container. Store the almond butter mixture in the refrigerator (for up to 6 months) until ready to spread on the waffles. 8. Let the waffles cool for 20 minutes, then portion out into five zip-top bags and store in the refrigerator and/or freezer.
Per Serving: Calories 443; Fat 30.04g; Sodium 224mg; Carbs 35.65g; Fiber 5.3g; Sugar 3.88g; Protein 11.91g

Easy Apple Cinnamon Quinoa Bowl

Prep time: 5 minutes | Cook time: 20 minutes | Serves: 2

½ cup uncooked quinoa
1 cup unsweetened vanilla or unflavored almond milk
1 or 2 cinnamon sticks
½ teaspoon ground cinnamon
Pinch salt

Toppings
2 tablespoons sliced almonds
1 cup chopped apple
2 tablespoons hemp seeds
Optional sweeteners: stevia, brown sugar, honey

1. In a drain and colander, rinse the quinoa thoroughly. Transfer the quinoa to a small saucepan and add the cinnamon sticks, almond milk, salt as well as ground cinnamon. 2. Bring to a high simmer, cover, and decrease the heat to low. Simmer for 15 minutes. 3. Remove the pan from the heat and let the quinoa sit for 5 minutes until the almond milk is absorbed and the quinoa has cooked through. 4. Divide the quinoa between two serving bowls. Add half the apple, hemp seeds as well as the almonds to each bowl. Add sweetener, if desired, and serve.
Per Serving: Calories 375; Fat 11.24g; Sodium 150mg; Carbs 58.54g; Fiber 6.2g; Sugar 26.15g; Protein 12.68g

Easy and Healthy Carrot Cake Overnight Oats

Prep time: 85 minutes | Cook time: None | Serves: 2

1 cup gluten-free rolled oats
1½ cups unsweetened almond milk
½ cup grated carrots
1 tablespoon maple syrup

½ teaspoon vanilla extract
1 teaspoon ground cinnamon
¼ teaspoon ground ginger
½ cup chopped walnuts
¼ cup raisins

1. Mix together the almond milk, maple syrup, carrots, oats, cinnamon, ginger, walnuts, raisins as well as vanilla in a medium bowl. 2. Divide the oat mixture between two 8-ounce Mason jars or other small, lidded containers and chill in the refrigerator for at least 8 hours, or overnight. 3. Stir and serve in the morning.
Per Serving: Calories 381; Fat 18.7g; Sodium 151mg; Carbs 61.49g; Fiber 10.8g; Sugar 2.45g; Protein 12.65g

Delicious Apricot Granola with Fresh Fruit

Prep time: 5 minutes | Cook time: 5 minutes | Serves: 2

¼ cup gluten-free rolled oats
2 tablespoons almonds
2 tablespoons walnuts
2 tablespoons ground flaxseed
¾ tablespoon olive oil
1 tablespoon maple syrup
Pinch ground cinnamon

¼ cup chopped dried apricots
1 mango, peeled and chopped
¾ cup fresh strawberries
½ cup fresh blueberries
Nonfat dairy milk or plant-based milk, for topping

1. Put the almonds, flaxseed, walnuts as well as oats into a small pan over medium heat. 2. Stir until the oats and nuts are warm, and then brown for 3 to 4 minutes. 3. Pour the olive oil into the pan and stir until mixed through. 4. Pour the maple syrup into the pan and stir until mixed through. 5. Add the cinnamon and stir, then add the dried apricots and mix until combined. 6. Take off

the heat and let it cool. 7. Peel and chop the mango, wash and slice the strawberries, and clean the blueberries. 8. Portion the granola into two serving bowls, and put the milk and fresh fruit on it. 9. Serve as soon as possible.
Per Serving: Calories 394; Fat 16.49g; Sodium 13mg; Carbs 64.75g; Fiber 11.8g; Sugar 44.88g; Protein 8.94g

Crash Red Onion, Pea, Egg and Avocado on Toast

Prep time: 5 minutes | Cook time: None | Serves: 2

2 slices whole-grain bread
½ ripe avocado, sliced
¼ cup peas (fresh or frozen and thawed)
Low-sodium salt

Freshly ground black pepper
½ red onion, thinly sliced
1 hard-boiled egg, cut in half
Fresh basil leaves, for garnish

1. Toast the bread and set it aside. 2. Crush half the avocado, put in peas in a small bowl, and crush one more time. Flavored with pepper and salt. 3. Spread the avocado-pea mixture on each slice of toast. Top equally with the remaining red onion slices, basil, egg as well as avocado slices. 4. Enjoy immediately.
Per Serving: Calories 237; Fat 11.79g; Sodium 211mg; Carbs 24.39g; Fiber 6.9g; Sugar 4g; Protein 9.9g

Healthy Spinach Wraps

Prep time: 15 minutes | Cook time: 10 minutes | Serves: 2

3 large eggs
2 large whole-grain tortillas
4 Cheddar cheese slices
2 cups spinach, divided
1 medium tomato, chopped,

divided
2 tablespoons Tomato Salsa, divided
1 tablespoon avocado oil

1. Crack the eggs into a large bowl. Beat gently with a fork. 2. Set out two plates and place a whole-wheat tortilla on each. Place 2 cheddar cheese slices down the middle of each tortilla. Top each with half of the spinach, then half of the tomato salsa and tomato. 3. In a nonstick frying over medium heat, heat the avocado oil. Add the beaten eggs and stirring occasionally until they are scrambled. 4. As soon as the eggs are done, spoon them on top of the salsa and tomatoes. 5. Gently fold in the sides of the tortillas and roll them up. 6. Place the wraps, seam-side down, in the pan, cover, and warm through for 2 to 3 minutes over medium heat, watching that they don't burn. Serve warm.
Per Serving: Calories 297; Fat 18.52g; Sodium 521mg; Carbs 21.5g; Fiber 3.3g; Sugar 6.34g; Protein 12.92g

Low- Carb Chocolate Smoothie

Prep time: 10 minutes | Cook time: None | Serves: 1-2

1 medium beet, peeled and quartered
1 tablespoon unsweetened cacao powder
2 teaspoons unsalted raw peanut

butter
½ medium banana
3 ounces' silken tofu
1 cup unsweetened almond milk

1. Mix cacao powder, the beet, banana, tofu, and almond milk, peanut butter, in a blender and blend for 1 to 2 minutes until well combined. 2. Eat your meal as soon as possible.
Per Serving: Calories 195; Fat 9g; Sodium 91mg; Carbs 21.22g; Fiber 2.8g; Sugar 13.34g; Protein 9.82g

Creamy Millet Porridge with Baked Berries

Prep time: 5 minutes | Cook time: 40 minutes | Serves: 2

For the strawberries
2 cups quartered strawberries
1 tablespoon maple syrup
For the millet
1 cup millet
1½ cups almond milk with added protein (or soy milk), plus more as needed
1½ cups water
¼ cup sliced almonds

To Make the Strawberries: 1. Heat the oven to 375 degrees F. 2. Toss the strawberries with the maple syrup, and roast for 15 to 20 minutes, or until the strawberries are soft and juicy.
To Make the Millet: 1. Add the millet and lightly baked for 3 or 4 minutes until slightly fragrant and browned in a medium skillet over medium heat. Get away from the heat and keep cool slightly. 2. Add the millet to a coffee grinder or blender and pulse until it is roughly half grain, half flour. 3. In a medium saucepan over medium-low heat, combine the millet, milk, water and simmer, stirring frequently, for 15 to 20 minutes, or until it reaches a porridge consistency and the grain pieces are soft. Once the grains taste hard, add some milk and go on to cook until the grains become tender. 4. Serve with the additional milk, sliced almonds and roasted strawberries.
Per Serving: Calories 529; Fat 5.21g; Sodium 120mg; Carbs 101.36g; Fiber 11.5g; Sugar 13.39g; Protein 19.37g

Favorite Overnight Chia Seed and Coconut Milk Pudding

Prep time: 13 minutes | Cook time: None | Serves: 2-4

½ cup chia seeds
2 cups light coconut milk
3 teaspoons honey, divided
¼ cup sliced banana
¼ cup fresh raspberries
½ tablespoon sliced almonds
½ tablespoon chopped walnuts
2 teaspoons unsweetened cocoa powder, divided

1. In a small bowl, mix the coconut milk, chia seed as well as 2 teaspoons of honey together. Portion into two glass Mason jars and refrigerate for 8 hours or overnight. 2. Take away the jars from the refrigerator and top each jar with half the raspberries, walnuts, cocoa, almonds as well as banana. Drizzle each jar with the remaining 1 teaspoon of honey, dividing it equally. 3. Enjoy immediately.
Per Serving: Calories 412; Fat 33.65g; Sodium 20mg; Carbs 27.09g; Fiber 11g; Sugar 9.32g; Protein 7.7g

Soft and Chewy Raisin Cashew Oats

Prep time: 5 minutes | Cook time: None | Serves: 4

1 cup rolled oats
1 cup unsweetened cashew milk
2 tablespoons flaxseeds
2 cups raisins
½ cup unsalted cashew nuts, chopped

1. Separate the cashew milk, rolled oats, as well as flaxseed into 4 small containers, and then mix well. Cover and place in the fridge overnight. 2. When you are going to eat, add 2 tablespoon chopped cashew nuts per serving and ½ cup of raisins may be the best choice for you.
Per Serving: Calories 217; Fat 13.52g; Sodium 31mg; Carbs 24.98g; Fiber 5.6g; Sugar 4.46g; Protein 9.65g

Strawberry Quinoa Breakfast Bowl

Prep time: 15 minutes | Cook time: 20 minutes | Serves: 4

1¾ cups water
1 cup quinoa
Pinch low-sodium salt
2 cups strawberries, sliced
½ cup unsalted cashew nuts, chopped
1 cup unsweetened cashew milk
4 teaspoons honey

1. Add the quinoa, salt as well as the water in a medium sized stockpot. Then mix to combine and allow to boil. 2. Reduce the heat to low, cover the pot, and cook for 15 minutes until the water has been absorbed. Remove from the heat and allow to stand for 5 minutes. 3. Divide ¾ cup of quinoa, sliced strawberries, chopped cashews into 4 serving bowls. Separate sliced strawberries, ¾ cup of quinoa, chopped cashews into 4 serving bowls. 4. Add in the cashew milk, and drizzle with honey. Keep cold or warm.
Per Serving: Calories 332; Fat 12.49g; Sodium 72mg; Carbs 46.34g; Fiber 5g; Sugar 13.2g; Protein 11.14g

Flaxseed Bread

Prep time: 15 minutes | Cook time: 20 minutes | Serves: 6

Nonstick cooking spray
2 tablespoons ground flaxseed
5 tablespoons unsweetened almond milk
1¼ cups rolled oats
1 teaspoon baking powder
2 tablespoons unsweetened
cacao powder
1 teaspoon ground cinnamon
1 tablespoon organic honey
1 medium banana, mashed
2 tablespoons unsalted cashew butter

1. Heat the oven to 400 degrees F. Spray a standard loaf pan with nonstick cooking spray. Place the pan in the oven. 2. In a small sized mixing bowl, add the ground flaxseed and unsweetened almond milk; allow the mixture sit for 5 minutes until it congeals. 3. Add the baking powder, rolled oats, ground cinnamon, unsweetened cacao powder, and then mix to combine in a large sized mixing bowl. 4. Add the mashed banana, the organic honey, the flaxseed mixture, cashew butter in a small sized mixing bowl, mix until well combined. 5. Add the dry into the wet and mix until fully incorporated. 6. Carefully take the loaf pan out of the oven and pour the batter into it. Bake for 20 minutes, or until a toothpick inserted comes out clean. 7. Serve warm.
Per Serving: Calories 144; Fat 6.01g; Sodium 11mg; Carbs 25.97g; Fiber 5.2g; Sugar 6.41g; Protein 5.83g

Thick and Creamy Cashew Nut Shake

Prep time: 10 minutes | Cook time: None | Serves: 1-2

2 cups spinach
1 tablespoon unsweetened cacao powder
2 teaspoons unsalted cashew butter
½ medium banana
3 ounces firm tofu
1 cup unsweetened cashew milk
¼ cup unsalted cashew nuts

1. In a blender, add the unsweetened cacao powder, firm tofu, banana, cashew milk, unsalted cashew nuts, cashew butter, and the spinach, blend on high speed for 1 to 2 minutes until smooth and no lumps remain. 2. Enjoy your meal as soon as possible.
Per Serving: Calories 306; Fat 18.31g; Sodium 88mg; Carbs 24.5g; Fiber 3.6g; Sugar 10.93g; Protein 15.76g

Yummy Honey Griddle Cakes

time: 15 minutes | Cook time: 30 minutes | Serves: 4

1¼ cups almond milk
1 cup oats and honey granola
2 tablespoons sunflower oil, divided
2 large free-range eggs
1 teaspoon vanilla extract

½ cup whole-wheat flour
1 tablespoon organic honey, plus extra for garnish
1 teaspoon baking powder
¼ teaspoon low-sodium salt
2 medium bananas, mashed

1. Add the oats, almond milk as well as honey granola in a large sized mixing bowl, 1 tablespoon of large eggs, vanilla extract, and sunflower oil, stir until well incorporated. Mix in the whole-wheat flour, organic honey, baking powder, and salt. Mix until it becomes a batter consistency. 2. Heat a large crêpe-pan over medium heat. Add the remaining 1 tablespoon of sunflower oil, tilt to coat the bottom. 3. Add ¼ cup of batter per griddle cake. Cook for 2 to 3 minutes, once the tops are bubbly and the bottoms are golden, flip, and cook for 2 minutes, or until golden. 4. Keep warm with a drizzle of honey and a drizzle of honey.
Per Serving: Calories 315; Fat 12.34g; Sodium 102mg; Carbs 52.09g; Fiber 7.1g; Sugar 18.72g; Protein 10.32g

Gluten-Free Apple Spiced Muffins

Prep time: 15 minutes | Cook time: 15 minutes | Serves: 8

1¾ cups whole-wheat flour
½ teaspoon baking powder
2 tablespoons ground cinnamon
1½ teaspoons allspice
3 large free-range eggs
¾ cup fat free plain yogurt

¾ cup unsweetened applesauce
4 tablespoons raisins
3 cups honey crisp apples, peeled, cored, and cut into bite-size pieces

1. Heat the oven to 400 degrees F. Line a muffin tin with paper liners. 2. Add the baking powder, allspice, whole-wheat flour as well as ground cinnamon in a medium sized mixing bowl, stir until well blended. 3. Add the plain yogurt, raisins, unsweetened applesauce as well as the large eggs in a large sized mixing bowl. 4. Use a hand whisk, to fold half of the dry into the wet ingredients, then fold in the remaining flour mixture. Add the apple pieces and mix until fully incorporated. 5. Spoon the batter evenly into the prepared muffin tin. Bake the batter for 15 minutes, or until a toothpick inserted comes out clean. 6. Serve warm or allow to cool completely before storing it in an airtight container.
Per Serving: Calories 317; Fat 6.5g; Sodium 416mg; Carbs 58.02g; Fiber 5.7g; Sugar 24.95g; Protein 9.03g

Cool Kidney Bean Tortilla

Prep time: 15 minutes | Cook time: 5 minutes | Serves: 2

1 cup canned kidney beans, drained and rinsed
½ ripe avocado, peeled, pitted, and diced
½ medium mango, diced
1 lime, juiced

¼ cup parsley, chopped
1 tablespoon apple cider vinegar
1 large egg, poached
2 whole-wheat tortillas

1. Add the diced avocado, kidney beans, chopped parsley, diced mango, and lime juice to a medium sized mixing bowl, and then mix to combine. 2. Fill a medium sized stockpot with water halfway and bring to a boil and add the apple cider vinegar. 3. Crack the large egg into a small sized mixing bowl. Reduce the heat to a simmer. Mix the water with a spoon to create a whirlpool.

4. After softly drop the egg inside, and then boil for 3 minutes, until the egg white has set. Take away carefully with a slotted spoon and place on a paper towel to drain. Spread the kidney bean mixture on a whole-wheat tortilla, place the poached egg on top and serve.
Per Serving: Calories 351; Fat 17.86g; Sodium 226mg; Carbs 41.75g; Fiber 9.2g; Sugar 13.32g; Protein 9.52g

Easy Tomato Egg Tart

Prep time: 20 minutes | Cook time: 20 minutes | Serves: 4

2 cups artichoke, finely chopped
⅓ cup fresh basil, chopped
1 cup grape tomatoes, halved
¾ teaspoon freshly ground black pepper

¼ cup low-moisture part-skim ricotta cheese
4 large eggs
8 large egg whites
Nonstick cooking spray

1. Heat the oven to 400 degrees F. 2. Stir the chopped basil, halved tomatoes, ricotta cheese, eggs, egg whites, chopped artichoke, and ground black pepper in a large bowl. 3. Coat a large oven-safe dish with nonstick cooking spray. Add the mixture to the pan and bake for 20 minutes, or until the eggs are cooked through, and the edges are slightly browned. Take away the oven and keep cool for 10 minutes. Separate 4 even pieces and enjoy your meal, or keep in the refrigerator for 5 to 7 days.
Per Serving: Calories 197; Fat 6.77g; Sodium 314mg; Carbs 17.13g; Fiber 4.9g; Sugar 7.49g; Protein 18.54g

Homemade Blueberry Granola

Prep time: 5 minutes | Cook time: None | Serves: 2

1 cup low-fat plain yogurt, divided
1 medium banana, sliced, divided
½ cup coconut granola, divided

¼ cup walnuts, chopped, divided
1 cup blueberries, divided

1. Portion the plain yogurt between two serving bowls. 2. Add the divided coconut granola, blueberries, chopped walnuts as well as sliced banana, into the 2 serving bowls. Keep cold before you enjoy your meal.
Per Serving: Calories 388; Fat 17.99g; Sodium 130mg; Carbs 49.84g; Fiber 5.7g; Sugar 33.19g; Protein 10.62g

Toasted Quinoa with Mixed-Berry Yogurt Parfaits

Prep time: 5 minutes | Cook time: 5 minutes | Serves: 5

½ cup quinoa
2½ cups 0% plain Greek yogurt
2 teaspoons vanilla extract

2 teaspoons maple syrup
2½ cups frozen mixed berries

1. Add the quinoa to a small skillet, and toast it, stirring frequently, for 3 minutes over medium heat or until it turns golden brown. Set aside to cool. 2. In a medium bowl, combine the yogurt, vanilla extract, and maple syrup. 3. In each of four screw-top jars or airtight containers, place 2 tablespoons of Greek yogurt mixture topped with 2 tablespoons of mixed berries in each. Repeat 3 times in each jar. Top each jar with 2 tablespoons of toasted quinoa. 4. Secure the jars and store in the refrigerator and/or freezer. Thaw in the refrigerator overnight before eating it.
Per Serving: Calories 184; Fat 1.99g; Sodium 45mg; Carbs 26.59g; Fiber 3.3g; Sugar 12.2g; Protein 14.86g

Easy Vanilla Almond Shake

Prep time: 5 minutes | Cook time: None | Serves: 2

2 cups frozen strawberries
1¾ cups vanilla almond milk
1 cup spinach, stems removed

and chopped
¼ cup unsalted almond butter
½ cup ice

1. In a blender, Add the vanilla almond milk, almond butter, chopped spinach, and the strawberries. Blend until completely smooth. 2. Add the ice and blend until smooth.
Per Serving: Calories 352; Fat 19.83g; Sodium 151mg; Carbs 40.44g; Fiber 9g; Sugar 24.65g; Protein 8.81g

Blueberry, Chia Seed, and Yogurt Pancakes

Prep time: 5 minutes | Cook time: 10 minutes | Serves: 2

1 cup rolled oats
1 cup blueberries
3 tablespoons fat-free, plain Greek yogurt
¼ cup unsweetened soymilk

1 tablespoon chia seeds
1 egg
½ teaspoon cinnamon
2 teaspoons avocado oil

1. Mix the blueberries, egg, oats, soymilk, cinnamon, yogurt, chia seeds in a medium mixing bowl and until a doughy consistency forms. 2. Heat the oil over medium-low heat in a large skillet and add the batter. Make either one large pancake that makes smaller individual pancakes or covers the entire pan 3. Cook the food for 4 to 5 minutes. Once the edges are brown, flip the pancake. To make it easier to flip, you can cut the larger pancake into 4 sections and flip them individually. 4. Cook on the opposite side for 1 or 2 minutes, until the pancake is no longer doughy. Stay warm and top with your favorite toppings.
Per Serving: Calories 276; Fat 11.99g; Sodium 57mg; Carbs 46.45g; Fiber 11.2g; Sugar 9.63g; Protein 15.18g

Apple Whole Grain Muffins

Prep time: 15 minutes | Cook time: 15 minutes | Serves: 8

1¾ cups whole wheat flour
½ teaspoon baking powder
2 tablespoons cinnamon
1½ teaspoons cardamom
3 whole eggs
¾ cup low-fat, plain Greek

yogurt
¾ cup unsweetened applesauce
3 large dates, chopped
3 cups Gala apples, peeled, cored, and cut into bite-size pieces

1. Heat the oven to 400 degrees F ahead of time. Line a muffin tin with 8 muffin liners. 2. Combine the baking powder, flour, cardamom and cinnamon in a medium mixing bowl. 3. Combine the Greek yogurt, applesauce, eggs, and dates in a large mixing bowl. 4. Using either a hand whisk or spatula, fold half of the dry into the full bowl of wet, then fold in the other half. Stir in the apple pieces until evenly distributed throughout the batter. 5. Separate the batter evenly into the prepared muffin tin. Bake for 15 minutes, or until a toothpick inserted into the center of the muffins comes out clean. 6. This dish can be kept in an airtight container in the refrigerator for more than a week. Stay warm in the increments.
Per Serving: Calories 179; Fat 3.24g; Sodium 133mg; Carbs 31.44g; Fiber 5.4g; Sugar 8.36g; Protein 8.88g

Easy-Made Overnight Blueberry Chia Pudding

Prep time: 5 minutes | Cook time: None | Serves: 5

1 cup fat-free milk
2 teaspoons maple syrup
1 cup blueberries

2 teaspoons lemon extract
½ cup chia seeds

1. In a blender, combine the milk, maple syrup, blueberries, lemon extract, and chia seeds. Blend well. 2. Divide the pudding equally between five airtight containers or screw-top jars; store in the refrigerator and/or freezer. 3. Thaw frozen pudding in the refrigerator overnight before you plan on eating it.
Per Serving: Calories 152; Fat 7.16g; Sodium 30mg; Carbs 18.13g; Fiber 8.5g; Sugar 6.98g; Protein 5.66g

Delicious Ground Flaxseed with Ginger-Cinnamon Oatmeal

Prep time: 5 minutes | Cook time: 10 minutes | Serves: 5

4½ cups water
2¼ cups rolled oats
1 teaspoon ginger paste

1 teaspoon ground cinnamon
2 teaspoons honey
2 tablespoons ground flaxseed

1. Combine the water, oats, ginger paste, cinnamon, and honey in a microwave-safe bowl. Cover the bowl and microwave for 4 minutes. 2. Remove the cooked oats from the microwave and stir in the ground flaxseed. 3. Let the oatmeal cool for 30 minutes, then portion out into five airtight containers and store in the refrigerator or freezer.
Per Serving: Calories 136; Fat 4.72g; Sodium 7mg; Carbs 32.01g; Fiber 7.9g; Sugar 3.01g; Protein 8.11g

Cheese-Broccoli Strata

Prep time: 10 minutes | Cook time: 25 minutes | Serves: 5

Nonstick cooking spray
6 slices whole wheat bread, cut into cubes
1 cup chopped broccoli
¼ medium yellow onion, chopped

4 large eggs
1 cup fat-free milk
⅓ cup shredded reduced-fat (2%) cheddar cheese
½ teaspoon freshly ground black pepper

1. Heat oven to 400 degrees F ahead of time. Mist an 8-by-8-inch baking dish with cooking spray. 2. Place the onion, broccoli, as well as cubed bread in the baking dish and stir to combine. 3. In a medium bowl, Mix the milk, pepper, cheddar as well as eggs until blended. Pour the egg mixture over the bread cubes and broccoli mixture. 4. After baking for 30 to more than 40 minutes, you will found that cubed bread turns puffy and golden brown. Let the strata cool for 30 minutes. Cut in half in one direction, then into 5 strips in the other direction (for 10 total rectangles). 5. Make five packets of 2 pieces each wrapped tightly in plastic wrap, then place them in a freezer-safe zip-top bag. 6. Whether it is keep in the refrigerator and/or freezer, all depends on you.
Per Serving: Calories 188; Fat 5.94g; Sodium 311mg; Carbs 22.11g; Fiber 2.9g; Sugar 3.09g; Protein 12.45g

Spinach Scramble with Tomatoes

Prep time: 5 minutes | Cook time: 10 minutes | Serves: 5

1 tablespoon olive oil
5 cups baby spinach, chopped
2 tablespoons diced red onion
15 grape tomatoes, quartered
1 teaspoon Italian seasoning
¼ teaspoon red pepper flakes
¼ teaspoon garlic powder
1 teaspoon low-sodium salt
5 large eggs
5 tablespoons water
Nonstick cooking spray

1. Heat the oil over medium heat in a large nonstick skillet. Add the tomatoes, spinach as well as onion, sauté them for 3 to 4 minutes, until the onion is translucent. 2. Stir in the Italian seasoning, garlic powder, salt as well as red pepper flakes, to coat the vegetables. 3. Mix together the water and eggs in a small bowl. Mist the skillet with cooking spray and pour the egg mixture over the vegetables. 4. Reduce the heat to low, and cook vegetables and eggs, stirring gently, for about 4 minutes, until the eggs are fully cooked. 5. Let the scramble cool for 10 minutes, then portion out into five airtight containers and store in the refrigerator or freezer.
Per Serving: Calories 118; Fat 7.73g; Sodium 140mg; Carbs 4.76g; Fiber 1.5g; Sugar 2.22g; Protein 7.74g

Avocado Tuna Salad

Prep time: 10 minutes | Cook time: None | Serves: 5

1 avocado, halved and pitted
Juice of 1 lemon
1 tablespoon Dijon mustard
3 tablespoons 0% plain Greek yogurt
½ teaspoon dried dill
2 (5-ounce) cans no-salt-added water-packed tuna, drained
2 celery stalks, diced
1 scallion, chopped

1. Scoop the avocado into a large bowl. Add the mustard, yogurt, dill, as well as lemon juice. Mash the avocado and mix well. 2. Add the diced celery stalks, tuna, and scallion to the avocado mixture, and stir to combine. 3. Divide some into five airtight containers and store in the refrigerator.
Per Serving: Calories 153; Fat 6.91g; Sodium 81mg; Carbs 5.24g; Fiber 3.1g; Sugar 1.12g; Protein 18.25g

Greek Yogurt Topped with Turmeric-Spiced Almonds

Prep time: 5 minutes | Cook time: 10 minutes | Serves: 2

¼ teaspoon ground turmeric
¼ teaspoon cinnamon powder
⅛ teaspoon freshly ground black pepper
¼ cup raw almonds, sliced
¼ cup raw pumpkin seeds
2 cups fat-free or low-fat plain Greek yogurt

1. Heat the oven to 425 degrees F ahead of time. Line a baking sheet with parchment paper. 2. On the baking sheet pan, mix the black pepper, cinnamon, and turmeric, with the pumpkin seeds and almonds. Spread them out once thoroughly mixed, so they do not overlap. 3. Bake the food for 5 to 8 minutes, until golden brown and fragrant. 4. If you are going to enjoy your meal, you will fill each serving bowl with 1 cup of yogurt and top with the seed mixture and nut. 5. Store nuts in an airtight container in the refrigerator for up to 5 days.
Per Serving: Calories 230; Fat 8.27g; Sodium 125mg; Carbs 11.56g; Fiber 1.3g; Sugar 8.03g; Protein 29.06g

Berry and Kale Smoothie Recipe

Prep time: 5 minutes | Cook time: None | Serve: 1

1 cup frozen mixed berries
½ cup kale
2 teaspoons creamy raw
unsalted almond butter
1 cup unsweetened soymilk
2 small dates or 1 Medjool date

1. Add all the ingredients to a blender and blend for 1 minute until they are well combined. 2. Enjoy your meal as soon as possible.
Per Serving: Calories 326; Fat 7.95g; Sodium 124mg; Carbs 60.78g; Fiber 8.4g; Sugar 45.68g; Protein 9.82g

Fresh Ginger-Mango Smoothie

Prep time: 5 minutes | Cook time: None | Serve: 1

½ cup frozen mango
1 cup spinach
½ cup low-fat, plain Greek yogurt
½ inch ginger, peeled
3 tablespoons water, as needed to thin

1. Combine the spinach, ginger, yogurt, mango in a blender. 2. Blend to your desired thickness, adding water as necessary. Enjoy your meal as soon as possible.
Per Serving: Calories 134; Fat 2.34g; Sodium 111mg; Carbs 22.27g; Fiber 2g; Sugar 20.04g; Protein 7.99g

Quinoa, Walnut and BerryBowl

Prep time: 5 minutes | Cook time: 25 minutes | Serves: 2

½ cup quinoa
1 cup unsweetened almond milk
1 teaspoon cinnamon, plus more
for coating
10 raw walnuts
1 cup strawberries, sliced

1. Heat the oven to 425 degrees F ahead of time, and line a baking sheet with parchment paper. 2. Bring the almond milk, cinnamon as well as quinoa to a boil in a medium pot. 3. Lower the heat to a simmer, cover the pot and cook for 12 minutes, or until the almond milk has been absorbed. 4. Put a dash of cinnamon and walnuts onto the prepared baking sheet and bake for 5 minutes until lightly golden. 5. Combine the walnuts and quinoa, and top with the strawberries in a serving bowl. (When storing, put the quinoa only in the refrigerator for up to 1 week. When you are going to enjoy your meal, you will add the strawberries and walnuts.)
Per Serving: Calories 410; Fat 21.4g; Sodium 55mg; Carbs 43.81g; Fiber 7g; Sugar 10.52g; Protein 14.98g

Easy Kefir Parfait

Prep time: 10 minutes | Cook time: None | Serves: 2

12 ounces' low-fat kefir
4 tablespoons Chia Berry Jam

1. Into each of two serving bowls, place half of the kefir and 2 tablespoons of chia jam, and dig in! 2. Enjoy!
Per Serving: Calories 169; Fat 0.16g; Sodium 84mg; Carbs 35.98g; Fiber 0.4g; Sugar 28.06g; Protein 5.88g

Healthy Pumpkin-Pecan Oatmeal

Prep time: 5 minutes | Cook time: None | Serves: 1

cup fat-free or low-fat plain Greek yogurt	½ cup no-sugar-added canned pumpkin puree
¼ cup oats	¼ teaspoon pumpkin spice
¼ cup unsweetened almond milk	2 teaspoons unsalted raw pecans, chopped
¼ teaspoon vanilla extract	

1. Put the oats, vanilla, yogurt, pumpkin spice, almond milk, and pumpkin in a Mason jar or medium container. Mix them well. 2. Keep it overnight in the refrigerator. Mix them in the morning one more time and top with the pecans. Usually, leftovers are good suitable for 3 days; the more the oatmeal sits, the softer the oats become.
Per Serving: Calories 291; Fat 10.63g; Sodium 130mg; Carbs 44.41g; Fiber 4.7g; Sugar 19.82g; Protein 18.99g

Chocolate-Oatmeal Bread

Prep time: 10 minutes | Cook time: 25 minutes | Serves: 6

Nonstick avocado oil cooking spray	2 tablespoons unsweetened cacao powder
2 tablespoons ground flaxseed	1 teaspoon cinnamon
5 tablespoons unsweetened organic soymilk	1 tablespoon pure maple syrup
1¼ cups rolled oats	1 banana, mashed
1 teaspoon baking powder	2 tablespoons unsalted raw almond butter

1. Heat the oven to 400 degrees F ahead of time. 2. Spray a standard (8½-by-4½-by-2½-inch) loaf pan with cooking spray or grease it with 1 teaspoon of oil spread equally on the sides. Place the pan in the oven. 3. Mix the soymilk and flaxseed in a small mixing bowl and let the mixture sit for 5 minutes, until it congeals. 4. Combine the baking powder, oats, cinnamon, cacao powder in a large mixing bowl, and mix well. In a small mixing bowl, combine the almond butter, flaxseed mixture, banana, maple syrup and mix well. Add the dry into the wet until well combined. 5. Carefully take the bread pan out of the oven and pour the mixture into it. Bake the food for 20 minutes, or until a fork inserted into the middle of the loaf comes out clean. To make the loaf stay warm might as well. Store in the refrigerator covered for up to 1 week. To rewarm, heat in the microwave in 15-second increments until warm.
Per Serving: Calories 139; Fat 6.02g; Sodium 11mg; Carbs 24.7g; Fiber 5.6g; Sugar 5.49g; Protein 5.91g

Tzatziki Dip and Swiss Chard on Whole Wheat Toast

Prep time: 10 minutes | Cook time: 15 minutes | Serves: 2

1 teaspoon avocado oil	divided
1 small onion, chopped	2 slices low-sodium whole wheat bread
2 garlic cloves, thinly sliced	1 cup Tzatziki Dip
1 bunch Swiss chard, stems diced and leaves chopped,	

1. Heat the oil over medium-low heat in a medium pot, add the garlic, Swiss chard stems, and onion. Heat for 5 minutes, until the onions become translucent and the chard stalks bleed red into the dish. 2. Add the chard leaves and cover for 5 minutes, until the leaves are wilted and the dish is fragrant. 3. Meanwhile, roast the bread until crisp. Place it on a serving plate and top each slice of bread with ½ cup of the dip and 1 cup of cooked Swiss chard.
Per Serving: Calories 190; Fat 3.91g; Sodium 239mg; Carbs 22.91g; Fiber 3g; Sugar 6.84g; Protein 16.55g

Avocado and Black Bean Tacos

Prep time: 5 minutes | Cook time: 5 minutes | Serves: 2

1 cup canned black beans, drained and rinsed	¼ cup chopped fresh cilantro
½ ripe avocado, diced	1 tablespoon rice vinegar (optional)
½ mango, diced	1 egg, poached (optional)
2 tablespoons lime juice (1 lime)	2 low-sodium whole wheat taco-size tortillas

1. Combine the avocado, lime juice, black beans, mango, and cilantro in a medium mixing bowl. Mix well. 2. If adding the egg: Fill a medium pot with water halfway and bring to a boil. Add the rice vinegar. Crack the egg into a small mixing bowl. Reduce the heat to a simmer. Stir the water with a slotted spoon to create a vortex, drop the egg inside, and cook for 3 minutes, until the white has set. Take away carefully with the slotted spoon and place on a paper towel. 3. On a tortilla, spread the black bean mixture, and then place the poached egg on top, and enjoy your meal. Besides, the black bean mixture can be kept in an airtight container for 3 days.
Per Serving: Calories 409; Fat 14.27g; Sodium 248mg; Carbs 57.65g; Fiber 16.3g; Sugar 13.19g; Protein 16.18g

No-Bake Carrot Cake

Prep time: 20 minutes | Cook time: None | Serves: 4

1 cup shredded carrots (about 2 medium carrots)	¾ cup rolled oats
	¼ cup raw walnuts
4 Medjool dates	½ teaspoon pumpkin spice

1. Line a baking sheet with parchment paper. 2. Mix the dates, walnuts, pumpkin spice as well as carrots, in a large mixing bowl for a food processor, for 3 minutes until the consistency is doughy, scraping down the sides halfway through. 3. Form the mixture into bite-size balls, place on the prepared baking sheet, and put the sheet into the freezer for 10 minutes, until the breakfast bites maintain their shape. It will be kept 5 days with an airtight container in the refrigerator.
Per Serving: Calories 155; Fat 4.63g; Sodium 20mg; Carbs 33.14g; Fiber 5.5g; Sugar 17.66g; Protein 4.51g

Cucumber Tomato Wrap with Hummus

Prep time: 10 minutes | Cook time: 0 | Serves: 1

2 tablespoons hummus	1 teaspoon lemon juice
½ tablespoon black pepper	¼ cucumber
1 whole-wheat tortilla	8 mint leaves
½ teaspoon lemon zest	¼ medium onion
1 plum tomato	1 cup bay lettuce mix

1. Spread the tortilla over a plate and then top the tortilla with the hummus. 2. Place all the remaining ingredients over the tortilla top and roll it. 3. Serve.
Per Serving: Calories 260; Fat 7g; Sodium 302mg; Carbs 44.28g; Fiber 8.2g; Sugar 14.84g; Protein 7.51g

Brussels Sprouts and Chickpea Hash

Prep time: 10 minutes | Cook time: 10 minutes | Serves: 2

½ cup canned chickpeas, reserving
2 tablespoons packing water
2 tablespoons water
¼ teaspoon freshly ground black pepper

1 tablespoon nutritional yeast
1 teaspoon chia seeds
2 teaspoons avocado oil
1 scallion, finely chopped
1 cup shaved Brussels sprouts

1. Put the chickpeas in a blender, and store water, packing water, nutritional yeast and pepper in a blender. Blend for 1 to 2 minutes, until well combined but the chickpeas still have some texture. Add the chia seeds to the mixture and let sit for about 5 minutes. 2. Heat the oil on medium heat for 1 minute or so in a medium saucepan, till the pan become hot. Then add the chickpea mixture and cook for about 3 minutes, stirring occasionally. Using a spatula, chop the formed mixture in the pan to resemble a hash. Add in the scallion and cook for 1 more minute, until the chickpea mixture is lightly browned. 3. Firstly, add the Brussels sprouts, cover, and then roast for 2 minutes, till the sprouts turn slightly wilted. Separate the mixture in half and enjoy your meal. Besides, keep in the refrigerator in an airtight container for up to 3 days.
Per Serving: Calories 274; Fat 8.19g; Sodium 291mg; Carbs 38.61g; Fiber 9.1g; Sugar 6.64g; Protein 14.28g

Asparagus, Buckwheat, and Tomato Bowl

Prep time: 10 minutes | Cook time: 25 minutes | Serves: 2

½ cup buckwheat
3 cups water
2 garlic cloves, smashed
2 teaspoons avocado oil
2 cups asparagus (about 20

spears), sliced
1 cup cherry tomatoes
1 teaspoon Mediterranean Seasoning Rub Blend

1. Bring the water, buckwheat, and garlic to boil in a saucepan, low the heat, cover the saucepan and cook for 15 minutes or so in a medium saucepan, until the buckwheat groats are opened, exposing a creamy white texture, and the majority of the water has cooked out. Do not drain the water; it will soak into and thicken the mixture as it sits. 2. Heat the asparagus, oil, cherry tomatoes, meanwhile, and the spice blend in a medium skillet on medium-low heat. Mix well and cook for 4 to 6 minutes, until the tomatoes are blistered and the asparagus is fork-tender. 3. Add the asparagus and tomatoes to the buckwheat. Mix well, separate two servings, and enjoy or keep in the refrigerator for up to 5 days.
Per Serving: Calories 128; Fat 5.09g; Sodium 120mg; Carbs 18.3g; Fiber 5.1g; Sugar 5.04g; Protein 5.28g

Super Fluffy Veggie Egg Omelet

Prep time: 10 minutes | Cook time: 10 minutes | Serves: 1-2

1 teaspoon avocado oil
1 small onion, diced
½ cup orange bell pepper, diced
2 medium eggs
2 egg whites

2 tablespoons water
1 cup packed fresh spinach
¼ teaspoon Mediterranean Seasoning Rub Blend

1. In a medium pan, heat the oil over medium heat. Add the onions and cook until translucent, about 1 minute. Add the bell peppers and cook for an additional 2 minutes. 2. Meanwhile, combine egg whites, water as well as eggs and stir together until well combined. Add the spinach and spice blend to the medium pan. Whisk and cook for 1 minute, until the spinach is wilted. Add the eggs and cook, covered, for 3 minutes until the edges are lightly browned. 3. Uncover the pan, flip, and cook for 1 to 2 minutes more, until the eggs are cooked through. 4. Serve on a plate.
Per Serving: Calories 149; Fat 6.66g; Sodium 157mg; Carbs 11.76g; Fiber 1.2g; Sugar 7.15g; Protein 10.38g

Vegan Tofu Shakshuka

Prep time: 15 minutes | Cook time: 20 minutes | Serves: 2

2 teaspoons avocado oil
1 large onion, diced
1 large red bell pepper, diced
2 large tomatoes, diced
3 tablespoons double-concentrated tomato paste
½ cup water

1 (14-ounce) package firm tofu, cut into 1-inch-thick square pieces
4 heaping tablespoons chopped fresh basil
2 teaspoons Mediterranean Seasoning Rub Blend

1. Heat the oil over medium heat in a large pot. 2. Add the bell pepper, tomatoes and the onion and cook for 2 minutes or so, till the onions are translucent. Add the tomato paste and water to the pot, stir, and cover. Cook for 5 minutes, until the peppers are fork-tender and the tomatoes are soft. 3. Add the basil, tofu, and spice blend and combine well other. Cook, covered, for another 5 to 10 minutes, until fragrant, stirring occasionally. 4. Divide among four plates and serve, or store in an airtight container in the refrigerator for up to 5 days.
Per Serving: Calories 429; Fat 22.44g; Sodium 262mg; Carbs 31.02g; Fiber 9.8g; Sugar 12.36g; Protein 35.52g

Artichoke-Tomato Crustless Quiche

Prep time: 20 minutes | Cook time: 30 minutes | Serves: 4

2 cups artichoke hearts, finely chopped
⅓ cup chopped fresh basil
1 cup cherry tomatoes, halved
¾ teaspoon freshly ground

black pepper
¼ cup part-skim ricotta cheese
4 whole eggs
8 egg whites
Avocado oil spray

1. Heat the oven to 400 degrees F ahead of time. 2. Stir the basil, pepper, artichoke hearts, tomatoes, whole eggs, egg whites as well as ricotta cheese, and combine well in a large mixing bowl. 3. Spray a large oven-safe dish with cooking spray (or evenly grease it with 1 teaspoon of avocado oil). Pour the mixture into an oven-safe pan or a frying pan and bake in the oven for 15 minutes at 400 degrees F, then increase the heat to 425 degrees F for an additional 5 minutes, until the eggs are baked through and the edges are slightly browned. 4. Firstly, remain cool for less than 10 minutes, and then separate into 4 or 8 even pieces and enjoy your meal. Besides, you can be kept in the refrigerator for 5 or 7 days.
Per Serving: Calories 220; Fat 10.24g; Sodium 268mg; Carbs 15.97g; Fiber 5.2g; Sugar 6.13g; Protein 17.72g

Scrambled Eggs with Spinach and Tomato

Prep time: 10 minutes | Cook time: 10 minutes | Serves: 1

2 eggs
1 teaspoon olive oil
1 teaspoon fresh basil
1 tomato

½ teaspoon cayenne pepper
½ cup spinach
¼ cup Swiss cheese

1. In a bowl, mix up the eggs with the Swiss cheese, basil and pepper in a bowl. 2. Cut the tomato into chunks. 3. In a fry pan, heat the oil over medium heat; add the tomatoes and sauté them for 3 minutes; add the spinach and sauté for 2 minutes; lastly, add the egg mixture and sauté them for 3 minutes. 4. Serve and enjoy.
Per Serving: Calories 298; Fat 20.86g; Sodium 163mg; Carbs 8.26g; Fiber 2.3g; Sugar 4.08g; Protein 20.1g

Oat Banana Smoothie

Prep time: 20 minutes | Cook time: 0 | Serves: 4

2 ripe bananas
½ teaspoon vanilla extract
1 cup mixed berries
¼ cup dry oats
1 cup frozen

1 tablespoon flax seed
¼ cup orange juice
1 cup no-fat yogurt
¼ cup pomegranate juice

1. Add all the ingredients to the blender and then blend them until smooth and creamy. 2. Serve and enjoy.
Per Serving: Calories 217; Fat 4.36g; Sodium 74mg; Carbs 40.33g; Fiber 3.2g; Sugar 27.32g; Protein 6.69g

Baked Kale Frittata

Prep time: 10 minutes | Cook time: 40 minutes | Serves: 6

1 tablespoon olive oil
¼ teaspoon pepper
5 ounces kale and spinach
1 cup free fat cheddar cheese

1 red bell pepper
¾ cup non-fat milk
⅓ cup scallions
12 eggs

1. Preheat the oven to 375 degrees F. Brush a casserole dish with oil. 2. In a bowl, mix up the all the ingredients except for cheddar cheese and then add the egg mixture in the oiled casserole dish. 3. Bake the food in the preheated oven for 35 minutes. 4. When the time is up, spread the cheese over food and bake for 5 minutes longer. 5. Allow the dish to cool before serving.
Per Serving: Calories 207; Fat 11.82g; Sodium 325mg; Carbs 8.01g; Fiber 1.3g; Sugar 5.01g; Protein 17.13g

Parmesan Avocado Egg Cup

Prep time: 10 minutes | Cook time: 25 minutes | Serves: 4

2 ripe avocados
4 teaspoons parmesan
1 stalks scallion

4 dashes of pepper
4 dashes of paprika
4 eggs

1. Preheat the oven to 375 degrees F. 2. Cut the avocados into pieces and then remove the seed from them. 3. Make the hole in the avocado and place them on the baking sheet. 4. Pour in one egg in the hole of one avocado and then sprinkle paprika and pepper over each egg. 5. Bake the food for 25 minutes. 6. Serve and enjoy.
Per Serving: Calories 256; Fat 19.4g; Sodium 94mg; Carbs 15.33g; Fiber 8.3g; Sugar 3.47g; Protein 9.5g

Easy Almond Oatmeal

Prep time: 20 minutes | Cook time: 0 | Serves: 1

2 tablespoons oats
1 teaspoon chia seed
½ cup low-fat milk

1 teaspoon sunflower seeds
1 tablespoon raisins
5 almond pieces

1. In a container with lid, mix up all the ingredients. 2. Put the container in the refrigerator and refrigerate the food overnight. 3. Serve as breakfast.
Per Serving: Calories 197; Fat 8.06g; Sodium 55mg; Carbs 22.71g; Fiber 4.3g; Sugar 6.98g; Protein 9.85g

Berry Oat Bran

Prep time: 5 minutes | Cook time: 2 minutes | Serves: 1

¼ cup dried cranberries
½ cup water

½ cup orange juice
⅓ cup oat bran

1. In a bowl, mix up all the ingredients. 2. Microwave the mixture for 2 minutes and serve.
Per Serving: Calories 145; Fat 2.46g; Sodium 5mg; Carbs 36.78g; Fiber 6.3g; Sugar 11.98g; Protein 6.34g

Banana Pancakes

Prep time: 25 minutes | Cook time: 5 minutes | Serves: 2

1 banana
2 eggs

Olive oil as required

1. Add the banana and eggs to the blender and then blend them well. 2. Heat the olive oil in the skillet over medium heat; pour in the batter and cook the batter for 2 minutes on each side. 3. Once done, serve and enjoy.
Per Serving: Calories 155; Fat 8.88g; Sodium 63mg; Carbs 13.79g; Fiber 1.5g; Sugar 7.38g; Protein 6.17g

Cherries Oatmeal

Prep time: 10 minutes | Cook time: 4 hours | Serves: 8

1 teaspoon cinnamon
4 cups almond milk
2 packets of stevia
⅓ cup raisins

4 cups water
⅓ cup apricot
2 cups oats
⅓ cup cherries

1. In a slow cooker, add and mix all the ingredients. 2. Cover the cooker and cook them on low for 4 hours. 3. Serve as breakfast.
Per Serving: Calories 136; Fat 3.2g; Sodium 89mg; Carbs 31.73g; Fiber 4.8g; Sugar 14.54g; Protein 5.08g

Scrambled Egg with Mushroom and Spinach

Prep time: 10 minutes | Cook time: 7 minutes | Serves: 1

1 teaspoon olive oil
1 slice of wheat toast
1 cup spinach
Pepper

2 eggs whites
½ cup mushrooms
2 tablespoons American cheese
1 egg

1. Crack the egg into a bowl and beat with cheese and egg whites, then sprinkle pepper over the mixture 2. In the skillet, heat the oil in the pan over medium heat; add the mushrooms, spinach and sauté them for 3 minutes; add the egg mixture and sauté for 4 minutes. 3. When done, serve and enjoy.
Per Serving: Calories 294; Fat 13.53g; Sodium 711mg; Carbs 21.51g; Fiber 2.8g; Sugar 5.41g; Protein 22.33g

Baked Sweet Potatoes

Prep time: 5 minutes | Cook time: 40 minutes | Serves: 4

4 sweet potatoes
¼ cup unsweetened coconut flakes

½ cup fat-free coconut
2 tablespoons maple syrup
1 medium apple

1. Preheat the oven to 400 degrees F. 2. Arrange the potatoes on the baking sheet. 3. Bake the potatoes in the oven for 40 minutes. 4. Slice the potatoes into slices and pour the remaining ingredients over them. 5. Serve.
Per Serving: Calories 221; Fat 4.99g; Sodium 90mg; Carbs 43.43g; Fiber 6.4g; Sugar 18.79g; Protein 2.66g

Simple Lemon Chia Seed Parfaits

Prep time: 15 minutes | Cook time: 0 | Serves: 4

2 cups Greek yogurt
1 cup fresh blueberries
¼ cup honey
1 cup fresh raspberries

2 tablespoons lemon juice
1 teaspoon vanilla extract
2 teaspoons lemon zest
2 tablespoons chia seeds

1. In the bowl, mix up all the ingredients except for yogurt, blueberries and raspberries. 2. Top the mixture with berries and yogurt. 3. Serve and enjoy.
Per Serving: Calories 181; Fat 2.22g; Sodium 33mg; Carbs 32.5g; Fiber 4.7g; Sugar 25.6g; Protein 10.23g

Fruits Raisins

Prep time: 10 minutes | Cook time: 10 minutes | Serves: 6

3 cups water
1 cup raisins
¾ cups bulgur's
8 ounces low-fat vanilla yogurt
¾ cup brown rice

1 granny apple smith
1 orange
1 red apple

1. Boil a pot of water over high heat; add the bulgur and rice, lower the heat and cover the pot, simmer them for 10 minutes. 2. Transfer them to bowl and allow them to cool. 3. Chop the orange and apple, then place them over the cooled grains; add the yogurt and mix well. 4. Serve.
Per Serving: Calories 180; Fat 1.35g; Sodium 31mg; Carbs 37.95g; Fiber 3.9g; Sugar 13.83g; Protein 4.65g

Roasted Eggplant with Sautéed Tomatoes and Chickpeas

Prep time: 10 minutes | Cook time: 35 minutes | Serves: 4

1 eggplant
2 tablespoons non-salt harissa paste
3 tablespoons olive oil
1 packet stevia
½ teaspoon salt
1 cup chickpeas

3 garlic cloves
1 cup water
1 onion
6 tomatoes
1 tablespoon smoked paprika
1 tablespoon cumin
1 teaspoon coconut aminos

1. Preheat the oven to 425 degrees F. 2. Rub the eggplant with salt and oil, then arrange the eggplant to the baking sheet. 3. Roast the eggplant in the preheated oven for 15 minutes. 4. Meanwhile, in a pot, heat the oil over medium heat; add the onion, garlic and sauté them for 3 minutes; add the tomatoes, paprika, cumin and sauté for 7 minutes. 5. Stir in the chickpeas, harissa paste and coconut aminos. Once done, put in more water and set to a simmer. 6. Rub with stevia and serve.
Per Serving: Calories 369; Fat 14.3g; Sodium 325mg; Carbs 51.54g; Fiber 13.5g; Sugar 16.18g; Protein 14.09g

Homemade Banana-Blueberry Pancakes

Prep time: 10 minutes | Cook time: 15 minutes | Serves: 14

1 cup wheat flour
1 cup frozen blueberries
½ cup all-purpose flour
1 teaspoon vanilla extract
2 tablespoons sugar

3 medium ripe bananas
2 teaspoons baking soda
1 cup fat-free milk
½ teaspoon salt
1 egg

1. Mix up the baking soda, flour, salt, sugar, bananas, vanilla and milk in a bowl. 2. Brush the skillet with cooking spray and then pour the mixture into the cupsful. 3. Top the mixture with the berries and sauté them until golden. 4. Pour the banana and maple syrup over it. 5. Serve and enjoy.
Per Serving: Calories 75; Fat 0.69g; Sodium 277mg; Carbs 14.9g; Fiber 1.6g; Sugar 4.04g; Protein 2.73g

Healthy Avocado Toast with Pepper Flakes

Prep time: 10 minutes | Cook time: 0 | Serves: 4

8 ounces avocado
¼ teaspoon red pepper flakes
¼ teaspoon black pepper

1 garlic clove, mashed
4 slices grain bread

1. In a bowl, mash the avocado flesh and then sprinkle the pepper over it. 2. Brown the bread slices and coat them with garlic until fragrant. 3. Top the bread slices with the mashed avocado and red pepper flake. 4. Serve and enjoy.
Per Serving: Calories 171; Fat 9.27g; Sodium 152mg; Carbs 19.56g; Fiber 5.1g; Sugar 2.24g; Protein 4.36g

Baked Sweet Potatoes with Avocado and Pita Bread

Prep time: 10 minutes | Cook time: 20 minutes | Serves: 8

2 sweet potatoes
4 pitas bread, whole-wheat
2 tablespoons olive oil
1 cup corn kernel
¾ teaspoon cumin
¼ cup red onion
1 teaspoon chili powder
¼ cup cilantro
1 avocado
¼ teaspoon salt
15 ounces black beans
3 tablespoons lime juice
2 tablespoons jalapeno

1. Preheat the oven to 375 degrees F. 2. In the baking pan, thoroughly mix the sweet potatoes with chili powder and cumin. Bake the potatoes in the preheated oven for 20 minutes 3. Mash the minced jalapeno, cumin, lime juice, chili powder, avocado in a bowl; add the remaining ingredients and rub to coat well. 4. Put in the baked sweet potatoes and coat them well. 5. Serve and enjoy.
Per Serving: Calories 342; Fat 8.47g; Sodium 169mg; Carbs 55.7g; Fiber 12.8g; Sugar 3.97g; Protein 14.73g

Baked Mushrooms with Onion

Prep time: 10 minutes | Cook time: 25 minutes | Serves: 4

Pepper
1 stalk of green onion
4 eggs
½ cup mushrooms
½ onion

1. Preheat the oven to 400 degrees F. Brush the baking dish with the olive oil. 2. In a bowl, mix up the pepper, eggs, mushrooms and onion. 3. Transfer the mixture to the oiled baking dish and bake in the oven for 20 minutes. 4. When the time is up, spread the green onion over the mixture and bake for 3 minutes longer. 5. Allow this dish to cool before serving.
Per Serving: Calories 73; Fat 4.27g; Sodium 64mg; Carbs 2.53g; Fiber 0.6g; Sugar 1.1g; Protein 6.14g

Garlicky Beef with Onion and Eggs

Prep time: 10 minutes | Cook time: 25 minutes | Serves: 4

Low-sodium salt
½ pound ground beef
¼ teaspoon pepper
1 onion
3 eggs
3 cloves garlic

1. In the oven-safe pan, sauté the ground beef for 5 minutes over medium heat; add the garlic, onion and sauté for 5 minutes, discard the fat. 2. Sprinkle salt and pepper. Spot the beef in the pan and reduce the heat. 3. In a bowl, beat the eggs and then pour over the beef, sauté for 10 minutes. 4. Transfer the pan in the oven and broil the food for 3 minutes. 5. Serve and enjoy.
Per Serving: Calories 141; Fat 6.02g; Sodium 87mg; Carbs 4.98g; Fiber 0.6g; Sugar 2.36g; Protein 16.83g

Cardamom Sour Cream Waffles

Prep time: 10 minutes | Cook time: 15 minutes | Serves: 7

¾ all-purpose flour
1 teaspoon vanilla extract
¾ cup wheat flour
1 tablespoon butter
1 teaspoon baking powder
¾ low-fat sour cream
½ cup brown sugar
1 teaspoon cardamom
1 cup far free milk
¾ teaspoon baking soda
2 eggs
½ teaspoon Cinnamon
¼ teaspoon salt

1. Mix up the all-purpose flour, wheat flour, baking powder, baking soda, cinnamon, cardamom and salt in a bowl. 2. Combine the brown sugar, vanilla, butter, milk, sour cream and eggs in another bowl. 3. Combine dry and liquid ingredients. 4. Sauté the mixture in the preheated waffle iron until golden according to the package directions. 5. Serve and enjoy.
Per Serving: Calories 207; Fat 3.37g; Sodium 273mg; Carbs 38.68g; Fiber 0.9g; Sugar 17.21g; Protein 5.36g

Sautéed Eggplant with Pepper Flakes

Prep time: 25 minutes | Cook time: 20 minutes | Serves: 4

1 eggplant
¼ cup dry breadcrumbs
1 garlic clove
¼ cup low-fat ricotta cheese
1 tablespoon olive oil
¼ cup low-fat parmesan cheese
Low-sodium salt
¼ cup water
¼ teaspoon pepper flakes
2 tablespoons shredded pepper jack cheese

1. Cut the eggplant into 5 pieces. 2. In a bowl, mix up the ricotta, pepper, parmesan cheese and pepper jack cheese. 3. In the pan, heat the olive oil over medium heat; add the eggplant pieces and sauté for 2 minutes; add the garlic and sauté for 2 minutes; add the pepper flakes, salt and sauté for 4 minutes. 4. Minimize the heat and sauté for 4 minutes longer until soft. 5. Add in the marinara sauce and cook for 8 minutes, stirring constantly; add the cheese mixture and cook until brown. 6. Serve and enjoy.
Per Serving: Calories 217; Fat 6.35g; Sodium 610mg; Carbs 16.79g; Fiber 5.5g; Sugar 7.24g; Protein 24.64g

Delicious Veggie Pepper Tortillas

Prep time: 15 minutes | Cook time: 20 minutes | Serves: 4

4 tortillas
2 tomatillos
1 cup low-fat mozzarella cheese
1 jalapeno pepper
1 onion
1 refried beans
2 cups cilantro
4 eggs
Juice of 1 lime
3 cups frozen brown potatoes
Black pepper

1. Preheat the broiler. 2. Arrange the red onion, tomatillos, jalapeno and onion to the baking sheet. 3. Broil the food in the broiler for 5 minutes until tender. 4. In a blender, blend the broiled vegetables in the blender and blend by adding water and pepper. 5. In the skillet over medium heat, sauté the potatoes for 10 minutes until brown, transfer the potatoes to a plate. 6. Still in the skillet, scramble the eggs for 1 minute over medium heat; Transfer the eggs to a bowl and clean the skillet with a paper towel. 7. Add the beans to the skillet and sauté for 3 minutes. 8. Put the beans in the center of each tortilla and then top them with the blended vegetables, cheese, potatoes and eggs; fold the lower edge of the tortilla and roll-up. 9.Enjoy.
Per Serving: Calories 428; Fat 14.76g; Sodium 667mg; Carbs 52.46g; Fiber 6.2g; Sugar 5.54g; Protein 22.34g

Egg Covered Veggie and Beef

Prep time: 15 minutes | Cook time: 40 minutes | Serves: 4

1 green bell pepper	8 ounces ground beef
1 onion, cut into the shape to your liking	3 garlic cloves
	¼ teaspoon pepper
4 eggs	Low-sodium salt

1. Preheat the oven to 400 degrees F. 2. In the skillet, heat the oil over medium heat; add the ground beef and sauté for 5 minutes; add the garlic, onion and sauté them for 3 minutes; add the bell pepper and sauté for 3 minutes longer. 3. Sprinkle salt and pepper over the food, discard the fat and then transfer them to the baking pan. 4. Add the eggs over the food and then bake them in the oven for 25 minutes. 5. Allow this dish to rest before serving.
Per Serving: Calories 161; Fat 7.09g; Sodium 103mg; Carbs 5.97g; Fiber 0.7g; Sugar 2.83g; Protein 18.4g

Eggs, Onion and Spinach Casserole

Prep time: 20 minutes | Cook time: 15 minutes | Serves: 2

Low-sodium salt	1 tablespoon olive oil
¼ cup low-fat mayonnaise cheese	4 eggs
¼ teaspoon pepper	1 onion, cut to your liking
½ cup spinach	1 teaspoon garlic powder

1. Preheat the oven to 400 degrees F. 2. Mix up the eggs, onion, garlic powder, mayonnaise, salt and pepper in a bowl. 3. Brush the baking tray with the oil and then add the egg mixture and spinach in the bottom. 4. Bake the food in the oven for 15 minutes. 5. When done, allow the food to rest for 10 minutes before serving.
Per Serving: Calories 271; Fat 18.79g; Sodium 264mg; Carbs 8.51g; Fiber 1.3g; Sugar 3.64g; Protein 16.92g

Lasagna and Beef with Spinach

Prep time: 20 minutes | Cook time: 70 minutes | Serves: 4

½ teaspoon black pepper	1 bunch scallion
¼ cup parsley leaves	1 cup low-fat mozzarella cheese
8 ounces lasagna noodles	¼ cup whole-wheat all-purpose flour
10 ounces spinach	
6 ounces ground beef	½ teaspoon nutmeg
½ cup low-sodium parmesan cheese	2 cups skim milk

1. Cook the noodles according to the directions on the package and then remove the salt and oil. 2. Transfer the cooked lasagna to the colander and wash with cool water. Set aside for later use. 3. In the skillet, heat the oil over medium heat; add the ground beef and sauté for 5 minutes until brown; add the scallion whites and sauté for 5 minutes, then spread the flour over the beef until absorbed. 4. Pour in the milk until it starts thickening, cook with the sauce for 2 minutes. 5. Spray the baking dish, pour the sauce in the bottom and arrange the cooked lasagna in layer; add the remaining meat sauce, spinach, cheese mixture, pepper and scallion green over the noodles. 6. Cover the dish with foil and keep it in the refrigerator. 7. Preheat the oven to 350 degrees F. 8. Cook the dish in the preheated oven for 45 minutes. 9. Once done, allow it to cool, sprinkle with parsley leaves and serve.
Per Serving: Calories 377; Fat 16.12g; Sodium 628mg; Carbs 24.69g; Fiber 4g; Sugar 8.75g; Protein 34.99g

Scrambled Egg and Herbs

Prep time: 10 minutes | Cook time: 10 minutes | Serves: 4

6 eggs	1 tablespoon Fresh chives
1 teaspoon olive oil	½ teaspoon fresh tarragon leaves
¼ cup skim milk	
¼ teaspoon black pepper	2 tablespoon parsley leaves

1. In a bowl, add the milk, eggs, tarragon, parsley and chives, mix them well. 2. In the skillet, heat the oil over medium heat; pour in the egg mixture and cook for 7 minutes, stir constantly. 3. Serve and enjoy.
Per Serving: Calories 98; Fat 6.59g; Sodium 89mg; Carbs 1.47g; Fiber 0.1g; Sugar 1.02g; Protein 7.79g

Sautéed Red Potatoes and Peppers

Prep time: 20 minutes | Cook time: 20 minutes | Serves: 8

5-pound red potatoes	1 green bell pepper
½ teaspoon basil	½ teaspoon cayenne pepper
4 garlic cloves	1 red bell pepper
½ teaspoon rosemary	1 teaspoon coconut aminos
1 onion	Olive oil
½ teaspoon pepper	

1. In the skillet, heat the olive oil over medium heat; add the garlic, onion, potatoes, coconut aminos and sauté for 5 minutes. 2. Cover the skillet and let the food cook for 8 minutes, stir occasionally. 3. Remove the cover, add the remaining ingredients and then sauté for 7 minutes over high heat. 4. Serve and enjoy.
Per Serving: Calories 227; Fat 2.16g; Sodium 53mg; Carbs 48.16g; Fiber 5.4g; Sugar 4.86g; Protein 5.88g

Simple Puff Pastry

Prep time: 30 minutes | Cook time: 20 minutes | Serves: 8

8-ounce low-fat cheese	2 tablespoons ricotta cheese, part skim milk
1 egg	
⅓ cup sugar	1 tablespoon lemon zest
2 sheets frozen pastry	1 teaspoon vanilla extract
2 egg yolks	

1. Spray the baking sheet with oil. 2. In a mixer, mix the sugar, cheese and then shake in the lemon zest, eggs yolk, vanilla extract and ricotta cheese. 3. On the floured board, place the puff pastry and then use a knife to cut them into the sheet. 4. Place the cheese in the center of each sheet, apply the egg on all sides and fold them to stick firmly. 5. Apply the egg wash over the top of all the pastries and arrange them to the sheet pan. 6. Put the pie in the refrigerator for 15 minutes. 7. Preheat the oven to 390 degrees F. 8. When the time is up, bake the pastries in the oven for 20 minutes until brown.
Per Serving: Calories 163; Fat 8.34g; Sodium 564mg; Carbs 10.92g; Fiber 0.2g; Sugar 4.48g; Protein 10.35g

Egg Avocado Cup

Prep time: 15 minutes | Cook time: 15 minutes | Serves: 4

2 avocados, cut in half and remove the seeds
¼ teaspoon black pepper
4 eggs
¼ cup low-fat parmesan cheese
1 teaspoon garlic powder
1 teaspoon pepper
4 dash low-sodium salt

1. Preheat the oven to 400 degrees F. 2. Arrange the avocado halves to the baking sheet and crack one egg in one hole, then sprinkle pepper, salt, and garlic powder. 3. Bake the food in the oven for 15 minutes. 4. When the time is up, place the cheese on the top and allow them to sit for 5 minutes in the oven. 5. Serve and enjoy.
Per Serving: Calories 257; Fat 20.74g; Sodium 135mg; Carbs 10.75g; Fiber 7g; Sugar 1.47g; Protein 10.24g

Fruits Cups

Prep time: 10 minutes | Cook time: 0 | Serves: 6

4 cups fresh fruit
¼ teaspoon almond extract
¾ cup mandarin orange
½ teaspoon orange zest
1 tablespoon honey

1. Divide the fruits between the bowls evenly. 2. Top each bowl of fruits with the extract, honey, yogurt, orange zest and honey. 3. Serve and enjoy.
Per Serving: Calories 75; Fat 0.18g; Sodium 7mg; Carbs 19.64g; Fiber 2g; Sugar 17.36g; Protein 0.89g

Scrambled Eggswith Smoked Salmon

Prep time: 15 minutes | Cook time: 10 minutes | Serves: 6

¼ pound smoked salmon
3 cups spinach   6 eggs
8 blades fresh chives
½ cup skim milk
1 tablespoon olive oil
¼ teaspoon black pepper

1. Cut the smoked salmon into small slices. 2. In a bowl, beat the eggs and mix with the skim milk; put in the chives and rub them with pepper and egg mixture. 3. In a large skillet, heat the oil over medium heat; add the spinach, egg mixture, salmon slices and sauté them until well. 4. Arrange the salmon slices on the top for garnish; enjoy.
Per Serving: Calories 129; Fat 7.88g; Sodium 165mg; Carbs 3.64g; Fiber 0.4g; Sugar 2.86g; Protein 10.56g

Lean Beef and Egg Hash

Prep time: 20 minutes | Cook time: 15 minutes | Serves: 4

8 ounces lean beef (slices)
4 slices of low-fat cheddar cheese
1 onion
¼ teaspoon black pepper
1 bell pepper
1 tablespoon olive oil
4 eggs
2 medium potatoes

1. In the pan over medium heat, sauté the beef for 3 minutes or until brown. 2. Add the potatoes, onion and sauté them for 7 minutes. Remove the pan from the heat 3. In the skillet, heat the olive oil over medium heat; add the eggs and sprinkle them with black pepper; top the hash with the cheese and melt for 1 minute longer. 4. Serve and enjoy.
Per Serving: Calories 375; Fat 12.98g; Sodium 369mg; Carbs 36.83g; Fiber 4.7g; Sugar 3.49g; Protein 28.25g

Simple Raisin Oatmeal

Prep time: 5 minutes | Cook time: 0 | Serves: 1

½ cup rolled oats
¼ teaspoon cinnamon
½ cup fat-free milk
1 teaspoon honey
2 tablespoon raisins

1. In a jar, add all the ingredients and mix them well. 2. Place the jar in the refrigerator and refrigerate the food overnight. 3. Serve as breakfast.
Per Serving: Calories 185; Fat 3.54g; Sodium 67mg; Carbs 44.32g; Fiber 7.7g; Sugar 13.11g; Protein 12.41g

Easy Huevos Rancheros

Prep time: 10 minutes | Cook time: 10 minutes | Serves: 2

2 eggs
1 handful cilantro
2 eggs whites
1 tablespoon jalapeño
½ cup onion
1 teaspoon olive oil
½ lime juice

1. In a bowl, beat the eggs white and jalapeno. 2. In a non-stick pan, heat the oil over medium heat; add the onion and sauté for 3 minutes; add the cilantro and sauté for 2 minutes; add the egg mixture and sauté for 1 minute longer. 3. Serve and enjoy.
Per Serving: Calories 119; Fat 6.61g; Sodium 132mg; Carbs 5.15g; Fiber 0.6g; Sugar 1.81g; Protein 9.65g

Carrot Raisins Muffins

Prep time: 10 minutes | Cook time: 20 minutes | Serves: 4

2 eggs
½ cup raisins
½ cup skim milk
2 teaspoons baking powder
⅓ cup carrots
½ cup wheat flour
¼ cup brown sugar

1. Preheat the oven and prepare the muffin cups. 2. In a bowl, mix up all the ingredients until flour is moistened. 3. Divide the batter into the muffin cups and bake them in the oven for 20 minutes. 4. Once done, serve and enjoy.
Per Serving: Calories 167; Fat 2.31g; Sodium 57mg; Carbs 31.65g; Fiber 0.7g; Sugar 17.86g; Protein 5.45g

Baked Biscuits

Prep time: 10 minutes | Cook time: 10 minutes | Serves: 4

⅓ cup low-fat milk   1 cup low sodium easy baking mix

1. Preheat the oven to 450 degrees F. 2. In a bowl, add the low sodium baking mix; make the well in the middle and pour in the milk, mix and form the mixture to the shape to your liking. 3. Brush the baking pan with the oil and then place the shaped mixtures on it. 4. Bake the mixture in the oven for 10 minutes until golden brown.
Per Serving: Calories 67; Fat 0.44g; Sodium 63mg; Carbs 29.14g; Fiber 1.3g; Sugar 1.05g; Protein 0.74g

Veggie Frittata

Prep time: 10 minutes | Cook time: 20 minutes | Serves: 4

1 teaspoon olive oil
4 eggs
2 teaspoons garlic
1 cup kale
1 cup mushroom

1. In the pan, heat the oil over medium heat; add garlic, mushrooms and sauté for 2 to 5 minutes; add the kale and sauté for 4 minutes until wilted. 2. Crack into the eggs and reduce the heat to low heat, stir well and sauté for 10 minutes with a shut top. 3. Transfer the frittata to a plate and allow it to sit for 5 minutes. 4. Slice and serve.
Per Serving: Calories 82; Fat 5.44g; Sodium 65mg; Carbs 1.91g; Fiber 0.4g; Sugar 0.74g; Protein 6.53g

Scrambled Eggs with Spinach and Onion

Prep time: 10 minutes | Cook time: 10 minutes | Serves: 4

4 eggs
1 teaspoon olive oil
4 eggs white
½ teaspoon garlic
½ cup almond milk
2 cups spinach
¼ teaspoon pepper
¼ onion

1. In a bowl, mix up the eggs, eggs white, garlic, almond milk and pepper. 2. In the fry pan, heat the olive oil over medium heat; add the onion and sauté for 3 minutes; add the spinach and sauté for 3 minutes; pour in the egg mixture and sauté for 4 minutes longer. 3. When done, serve and enjoy.
Per Serving: Calories 112; Fat 6.04g; Sodium 144mg; Carbs 3.42g; Fiber 0.5g; Sugar 2.3g; Protein 10.67g

Basil Tomato Omelet

Prep time: 10 minutes | Cook time: 10 minutes | Serves: 6

1 teaspoon olive oil
2 Roma tomatoes
6 eggs
1 cup fresh basil
¼ cup skim milk
1 teaspoon coconut amino
¼ teaspoon pepper

1. In a bowl, mix up the eggs, skim milk, coconut amino and pepper. 2. In the skillet, heat the oil over medium heat; add the tomatoes and sauté for 2 minutes; add the basil leaves and sauté for 2 minutes; pour in the egg mixture and cook for 5 minutes longer. 3. When done, serve and enjoy.
Per Serving: Calories 83; Fat 5.05g; Sodium 83mg; Carbs 3.03g; Fiber 0.4g; Sugar 1.5g; Protein 6.42g

Garlicky Cauliflower and Eggs

Prep time: 10 minutes | Cook time: 15 minutes | Serves: 4

1 teaspoon olive oil
¼ teaspoon pepper
3 cloves garlic
1 onion
1 head cauliflower
4 eggs

1. In a blender, blend the garlic and cauliflower and then transfer them to the bowl, and drain the excess water. 2. In another bowl, beat eggs and pepper. 3. In the pan, heat the oil over medium heat; add the onion and sauté for 5 minutes until tender; add the cauliflower mixture and sauté for 5 minutes or until tender; add the egg mixture and sauté for 5 minutes longer. 4. When done, serve and enjoy.
Per Serving: Calories 105; Fat 5.54g; Sodium 84mg; Carbs 7.19g; Fiber 1.9g; Sugar 2.76g; Protein 7.3g

Feta Artichoke Frittata

Prep time: 10 minutes | Cook time: 25 minutes | Serves: 8

1 can artichoke hearts
2 tablespoons parsley
2 red peppers, cut and remove the seeds
4-ounce low-fat feta cheese
¼ cup green onion
¼ teaspoon pepper
8 eggs

1. In a bowl, beat the eggs and pepper. 2. Preheat the oven to 400 degrees F. Sprinkle cooking spray over the baking dish. 3. Place the onion and red peppers on the bottom of the baking dish and then top them with the artichoke; cover the dish with foil. 4. Bake the food for 15 minutes; when the time is up, remove the foil and top the food with egg mixture and cheese, bake for 10 minutes longer. 5. Once done, allow it to cool before garnishing with parsley and serving.
Per Serving: Calories 123; Fat 7.35g; Sodium 194mg; Carbs 3.86g; Fiber 1.4g; Sugar 1.21g; Protein 10.47g

Banana Granola

Prep time: 15 minutes | Cook time: 30 minutes | Serves: 16

3 cups rolled oats
2 teaspoon cinnamon
1-¼ cups pecans
¾ cup walnut
1 banana
¼ cup coconut oil
2 teaspoon vanilla extract
⅓ cup maple syrup

1. Preheat the oven to 350 degrees F. Cover the baking sheet with parchment paper. 2. In a bowl, mix up the cinnamon, walnuts, oats and flax seeds. 3. In the saucepan, heat the vanilla extract and maple syrup over low heat. 4. Remove the saucepan from the heat and add in the mashed banana. 5. Mix the banana mixture and oats thoroughly. 6. In the baking sheet, pour the mixture and cook them in the preheated oven for 30 minutes. 7. When the time is up, serve and enjoy.
Per Serving: Calories 176; Fat 12.69g; Sodium 2mg; Carbs 19.63g; Fiber 4.1g; Sugar 5.57g; Protein 4.43g

Blueberry Wheat Bread

Prep time: 15 minutes | Cook time: 30 minutes | Serves: 6

6 slices of wheat bread
¼ cup brown sugar
2 eggs
1 cup fat-free milk
2 teaspoons cinnamon
½ cups blueberries
1 lemon zest

1. Preheat the oven to 350 degrees F. Spray the muffin tins with the cooking spray. 2. In a bowl, mix up the cinnamon, eggs, lemon, milk and ⅓ of the brown sugar; add the bread slices and ¼ cup of the blueberries. 3. Fill the muffin tins with the mixture. 4. Mix up cinnamon and the ⅓ of the brown sugar, then top the muffin tins with them. 5. Bake the food in the oven for 22 minutes. 6. While baking, in the saucepan, mix the remaining brown sugar, blueberries, and the lemon zest over medium heat to make the syrup, mashing the blueberries. 7. Serve the cakes with the syrup on the top.
Per Serving: Calories 159; Fat 2.48g; Sodium 192mg; Carbs 28.25g; Fiber 1.9g; Sugar 14.11g; Protein 6.52g

Almond Granola

Prep time: 10 minutes | Cook time: 20 minutes | Serves: 12

½ cups rolled oats
1 teaspoon cinnamon
¼ cup hulled raw almonds
¼ cup unsweetened yogurt
¼ cup sliced sunflower seeds

¼ cup raisins
¼ cup honey
2 teaspoons vanilla
2 tablespoons vegetable oil

1. Preheat the oven to 325 degrees F. Cover the baking sheet with parchment paper. 2. In a bowl, mix up the oats, coconut, sunflower seeds, almonds and cinnamon; add the honey, oil and vanilla, mix them well. 3. Pour the mixture over the parchment paper and bake them in the oven for 20 minutes until brown. 4. When done, allow the granola to cool and pour the yogurt over it. 5. Serve and enjoy.
Per Serving: Calories 74; Fat 4.22g; Sodium 3mg; Carbs 9.51g; Fiber 1g; Sugar 6.27g; Protein 1.5g

Raspberry Oatmeal

Prep time: 10 minutes | Cook time: 25 minutes | Serves: 6

3 cups fat-free milk
1 teaspoon cinnamon
2 cups rolled oats
1 teaspoon vanilla extract

2 tablespoons brown sugar
1 cup raspberries
2 tablespoons walnuts

1. In the saucepan, heat the milk over medium heat; add the oats, cinnamon, vanilla and sauté them for 5 minutes. 2. Transfer the oatmeal mixture to the muffin cups. 3. Cool the muffin cups in the refrigerator for 20 minutes. 4. After adding walnuts, raspberries, and brown sugar, allow them to broil for 1 minute until golden. 5. Serve.
Per Serving: Calories 168; Fat 4.11g; Sodium 67mg; Carbs 34.37g; Fiber 6.6g; Sugar 11.92g; Protein 10.51g

Eggs in Purgatory

Prep time: 15 minutes | Cook time: 40 minutes | Serves: 4

1 tablespoon olive oil
4 slices of roasted pepper
½ yellow onion
3 cloves garlic
1 tablespoon tomato paste
2 wheat pitas

3 teaspoons paprika
28 ounce tomatoes
4 eggs
⅛ teaspoon salt
¼ cup parsley
3 cups fresh spinach

1. In the skillet, heat the oil over medium heat; add the onion and sauté for 2 minutes or until softened; add the garlic and tomatoes, sauté them for 3 minutes. 2. Sauté in the onion until softened, put in the garlic and tomatoes, and cook for 3 minutes. 3. Cook in the salt, potatoes, and tomatoes by setting o the simmer and then minimize the heat and cook for 30 minutes. 4. Mix the parsley and spinach and prepare the tomato mixture with a wooden spoon. 5. Put the egg over it and cook with the cover until heat through the eggs white. 6. Apply the garnishing by putting the parsley over it.
Per Serving: Calories 208; Fat 9.1g; Sodium 418mg; Carbs 25g; Fiber 6g; Sugar 10.2g; Protein 10.8g

Eggs in Sweet Potato Nests

Prep time: 10 minutes | Cook time: 20 minutes | Serves: 6

1-pound sweet potatoes
¼ teaspoon low-sodium salt
2 tablespoons olive oil

12 eggs
¼ teaspoon black pepper

1. Preheat the oven to 400 degrees F. Brush the muffin tins with some oil. 2. In a bowl, mash the potatoes. 3. In the skillet, heat the oil over medium heat; add the mashed potatoes and sauté for 5 minutes until soft. 4. Divide the potato mixture between muffin tins and sprinkle cooking spray over it. 5. Bake the food in the oven for 5 minutes until brown thoroughly. 6. When the time is up, add the eggs with salt and pepper to the potato nest, then bake for 15 minutes longer. 7. When done, allow the food to cool for 5 minutes. 8. Serve and enjoy.
Per Serving: Calories 198; Fat 13.26g; Sodium 508mg; Carbs 7.44g; Fiber 4g; Sugar 0.37g; Protein 12.95g

Almond Apple Salad

Prep time: 10 minutes | Cook time: 0 | Serves: 8

4 tart green apples
8 ounces nonfat vanilla yogurt
¼ cup slivered almonds

¼ cup cherries
¼ cup cranberries

1. In a bowl, mix up the green apples, almonds, cherries and cranberries, then pour the yogurt over it. 2. Serve and enjoy.
Per Serving: Calories 67; Fat 0.24g; Sodium 18mg; Carbs 16.45g; Fiber 2.3g; Sugar 13.1g; Protein 1.4g

Banana Bran Muffins

Prep time: 10 minutes | Cook time: 25 minutes | Serves: 12

2 eggs
⅓ cup walnuts
⅔ cup brown sugar
½ cup chocolate chips, lower fat
1 cup ripe banana
½ teaspoon cinnamon

1 cup buttermilk
¼ teaspoon low-sodium salt
1 cup unprocessed wheat bran
½ teaspoon baking soda
¼ cup canola oil
¾ cup vanilla extract

1. Preheat the oven to 400 degrees F. Spray the muffin cups with some cooking oil. 2. In a bowl, mix up the eggs, vanilla, buttermilk, brown sugar, bran and oil. 3. In another bowl, mix up the walnuts, banana, all-purpose flour, salt, baking powder and baking soda, then stir in the egg mixture and add the chocolate chips. 4. Transfer the mixture to the muffin cups and then bake the food in the oven for 25 minutes. 5. When done, serve and enjoy.
Per Serving: Calories 215; Fat 8.32g; Sodium 134mg; Carbs 27.04g; Fiber 3g; Sugar 19.15g; Protein 3.31g

Berry Almond Tortilla

Prep time: 10 minutes | Cook time: 0 | Serves: 1

1 tortilla
2 tablespoons slice almond
2 teaspoons strawberry

½ cup fresh strawberries
2 tablespoons low-fat ricotta cheese

1. Top the tortilla with ricotta cheese; arrange the fruits over it and spread the almond. 2. Roll it properly and wrap it in the foil. Enjoy.
Per Serving: Calories 215; Fat 8.32g; Sodium 134mg; Carbs 27.04g; Fiber 3g; Sugar 19.15g; Protein 3.31g

Breakfast Cups

Prep time: 10 minutes | Cook time: 25 minutes | Serves: 12

Cooking spray
Black pepper
¼ cup bell pepper
3 cups hash browns
¼ cup onion

5 slices of turkey bacon
3 tablespoons fat-free margarine
1 cup egg substitute
1 cup low-fat cheddar cheese

1. Preheat the oven to 400 degrees F. Grease the muffin tin with cooking spray. 2. In a bowl, mix up the salt, pepper and hash browns. 3. Arrange the mixture into the muffin cups evenly and then bake them in the oven for 15 minutes. 4. In the second bowl, mix up the egg, bell pepper and salt. 5. Cut the bacon into slices and spot over the mixture; add the egg mixture to the muffin cups, then bake the food for 15 minutes longer. 6. Serve and enjoy with cheese on the top.
Per Serving: Calories 163; Fat 8.45g; Sodium 324mg; Carbs 14.86g; Fiber 8.45g; Sugar 1.19g; Protein 6.99g

Multigrain Pancakes with Berry-Apple Sauce

Prep time: 10 minutes | Cook time: 30 minutes | Serves: 4

Cooking spray
1 cup strawberries
½ cup all-purpose flour
¼ cup apple juice
¼ cup wheat pastry
¼ cup cornmeal

1 tablespoon canola oil
1 tablespoon baking powder
1 cup nonfat buttermilk
1 egg
¼ teaspoon baking soda
¼ teaspoon salt

1. Grease the non-stick pan with the cooking spray. 2. In a large bowl, mix up the salt, sugar, baking powder and baking soda. 3. In another bowl, mix up the canola oil and buttermilk, then blend the liquid with the salt mixture. 4. Spot the pan over the heat and put the batter in it, cook the food until golden on both sides. 5. In the saucepan over the heat, add the apple and strawberries to make the sauce. 6. Once the sauce is ready, allow it to cool. 7. Top the pancake with the sauce and enjoy.
Per Serving: Calories 239; Fat 7.79g; Sodium 323mg; Carbs 34.9g; Fiber 2.4g; Sugar 6.89g; Protein 8.32g

Zesty Rice with Cuban Black Beans

Prep time: 20 minutes | Cook time: 2.5 hours | Serves: 4

For the black beans:
1-pound black beans, soaked overnight
1 large onion, peeled and diced
1 medium tomato, chopped
3 medium carrots, peeled and diced
1 red bell pepper, seeded and diced
2 bay leaves
3 cloves garlic, peeled and minced
3 celery stalks, diced
2 tablespoons ground cumin
2 tablespoons minced oregano
1 cup finely chopped cilantro

stems
2 tablespoons apple cider vinegar
½ teaspoon freshly ground white or black pepper
3 tablespoons chopped cilantro leaves
Salt
For the cilantro rice:
1 cup brown rice
2 tablespoons finely chopped cilantro leaves
1 tablespoon low-sodium light brown miso paste

To make the black beans: 1. Add and boil the beans, onion, cumin, garlic, bay leaves, celery, carrots, oregano, red pepper, cilantro stems, and 5 cups of water in a large pot. 2. Simmer and cook the food for 90 minutes, place ¼ of the beans, and mash them in another bowl, and then put them back to the pot. 3. Add and stir the apple cider vinegar, cilantro leaves, pepper, and tomato. When the beans are done, serve the dish with salt. Remove the bay leaves.
To make the cilantro rice: 1. Cook to boil the rice and the miso paste and 2 cups of water in a large saucepan. Turn down the heat to simmer for 20 minutes, with a lid. Lower the heat and continue to simmer for another 30 minutes, fluff the rice and whisk in the cilantro leaves. 2. Divide the rice into 4 plates and garnish with the beans.
Per Serving: Calories 642; Fat 4g; Sodium 221mg; Carbs 123g; Fiber 24g; Sugar 9g; Protein 31g

Easy Drop Biscuits

Prep time: 25 minutes | Cook time: 10 minutes | Serves: 12

2 cups flour
1 cup milk
1 tablespoon low-sodium

baking soda
½ cup unsalted butter
2 tablespoon sugar

1. Preheat the oven to 450 degrees F. 2. Slice the butter. 3. In a bowl, mix up the flour, baking soda, sugar and butter, then mix in the milk. 4. Brush the baking pan with the oil and then transfer the mixture to it. 5. Bake the food in the oven for 10 minutes until golden. 6. When done, serve and enjoy.
Per Serving: Calories 133; Fat 6.31g; Sodium 14mg; Carbs 17.28g; Fiber 2.2g; Sugar 2.41g; Protein 3.59g

Burritos with Beans

Prep time: 15 minutes | Cook time: 8 hours | Serves: 6

2 15-ounce cans black beans, drained and rinsed
¼ cup salsa
2 15-ounce cans diced tomatoes
½ cup corn, fresh, frozen, or canned
1 cup brown rice
2 tablespoons taco seasoning
2 chipotle peppers in adobo sauce, finely chopped

1 teaspoon ground cumin
1 teaspoon salt
2½ cups vegetable broth
½ cup lentils
12 whole wheat tortillas
Additional toppings, such as more salsa, avocado or guacamole, and black olives

1. To make the filling: put and mix the beans, salsa, tomatoes, corn, rice, taco seasoning, chipotles, cumin, salt, and broth in a slow cooker, cook on low for 6-8 hours, with a lid, or on high for 3-4 hours. Cook until 40 minutes left, add the lentil, and cook to boil the beans into tender. Once absorbed the water, the rice would be tender. 2. Spread the tortillas and put about ⅓ to ½ cup of the filling on each tortilla. 3. Lay out the filling to the center of the tortilla, fold each end about 1½ inches over the point edge of the beans. And roll up the tortilla along the long edge. 4. Pile up and garnish with more avocado, salsa or guacamole, and black olives. 5. Serve the food!
Per Serving: Calories 499; Fat 11g; Sodium 1496mg; Carbs 88g; Fiber 16g; Sugar 9g; Protein 15g

Time-Saving Oatmeal

Prep time: 10 minutes | Cook time: 0 | Serves: 4

1 cup rolled oats
Skim milk
½ cup whole-wheat bran flakes
½ cup raisins
¼ cup hulled sunflower seeds
¼ cup walnuts

1. In a bowl, mix up all the ingredients except for the milk. 2. Add the milk and enjoy, or you can eat them directly.
Per Serving: Calories 197; Fat 9.78g; Sodium 28mg; Carbs 30.68g; Fiber 7.8g; Sugar 8.61g; Protein 9.71g

Tasty Wrap with Pea

Prep time: 10 minutes | Cook time: 15 minutes | Serves: 4

4 ounces cremini mushrooms, cleaned, stemmed, and cut into ¼-inch thick slices
1 15-ounce can low-salt black-eyed peas, drained and rinsed
5 tablespoons grape seed or olive oil
2 tablespoons fresh basil or
parsley, minced
½ teaspoon wheat-free tamari
2 garlic cloves, minced
½ red onion, chopped
1 avocado, sliced
4 large lettuce leaves or spelt bread
¼ teaspoon dried thyme

1. Place a large skillet over medium heat and heat the oil in the skillet. 2. Add and cook the mushrooms and thyme for 2-3 minutes, stirring frequently, till browned. Add red onion and garlic and cook for 2 minutes, till fragrant and softened. Turn off the heat. 3. In a large bowl, add the black-eyed peas and mash it with a spoon or a masher, leave some peas intact. Mix the mushroom mixture, basil or parsley, and tamari. Cook the mixture into four patties. 4. Adjust the heat to medium-high heat, cook the oil until hot in a sauté pan, add and fry the patties for 5-6 minutes per side till browned. 5. Garnish bread or lettuce leaves with the red onion and avocado. Serve the dish!
Per Serving: Calories 477; Fat 26g; Sodium 96mg; Carbs 53g; Fiber 22g; Sugar 20g; Protein 18g

Edamame & Rice

Prep time: 15 minutes | Cook time: 20 minutes | Serves: 4

2 potatoes, peeled and diced
4 cups edamame
3 cups cooked brown rice
1 cup chopped tarragon
1 lime, quartered
1 red bell pepper, seeded and diced
2 jalapeño peppers, diced (for
less heat, remove the seeds)
5 cloves garlic, smashed and skin removed
1 teaspoon ground nutmeg
Salt and freshly ground black pepper to taste
1½ teaspoons oregano, toasted

1. Add and sauté the potatoes, red pepper, and jalapeño peppers in a large saucepan over medium heat, for 7-8 minutes. 2. To prevent the vegetable from sticking to the pan, add water 1 to 2 tablespoons at a time. Stir in the cumin, garlic, and oregano, cook for 3 minutes. 3. Add and whisk the edamame and 1 cup of water, cook for 10 minutes. Add some water as needed. 4. Add the salt and pepper to taste. Pour the rice, serve the dish with the tarragon and lime wedges.
Per Serving: Calories 461; Fat 10g; Sodium 21mg; Carbs 74g; Fiber 14g; Sugar 6g; Protein 24g

Homemade Fava Beans

Prep time: 10 minutes | Cook time: 2½ hours | Serves: 4

1½ pounds dried fava beans, soaked for 8 to 10 hours
1 medium red onion, peeled and finely chopped
5 olives, seeded and diced
3 cloves garlic, peeled and
minced
1 teaspoon ground thyme
1 tablespoon red wine vinegar
Salt to taste
fresh sage

1. After draining and rinsing the beans, put them to a large pot. Pour enough water to top the beans by 4 inches, and then boil over high heat. Lower the heat to medium and cook with a lid, till beans are softened, for 1½ to 2 hours. 2. When simmering the beans, you can add and stir the onion in another pan, adjust to medium heat to cook for 8-10 minutes, till the onion becomes browned. Add and stir in the garlic, thyme, red wine vinegar, and olives and cook for over 5 minutes. Set aside. 3. Once the beans done, the food need draining roughly, pour the onion mixture to the beans Mix them completely, drizzle the salt. Decorate with fresh sage to serve the dish!
Per Serving: Calories 170; Fat 2g; Sodium 97mg; Carbs 33g; Fiber 13g; Sugar 17g; Protein 14g

Green Herbed Spring Peas

Prep time: 10 minutes | Cook time: 15 minutes | Serves: 6

1 tablespoon unsalted non-hydrogenated plant-based butter
½ zucchini, diced
1 cup store-bought low-sodium vegetable broth
3 cups fresh shelled peas
1 bay leaf

1. Place a skillet over medium heat and add the butter until melted. 2. Stir and sauté zucchini for 2 -3 minutes. Then the onion should be translucent. 3. Pour the broth, lower the heat. 4. Add and stir the peas and bay leaf, cover and cook for 7-10 minutes, till the peas become tender. Discard the bay leaf. 5. Garnish with coastal creole shrimp.
Per Serving: Calories 65; Fat 2g; Sodium 86mg; Carbs 10g; Fiber 3g; Sugar 5g; Protein 3g

Black Bean Spread with Maple Syrup

Prep time: 10 minutes | Cook time: 0 minute | Serves: 5

4 cups cooked black beans, or 2 15-oz. cans, drained and rinsed
6 cloves garlic, smashed and skin removed
Zest of 1 lemon and juice of 2 lemons
1 tablespoon maple syrup
3 teaspoons mint
Salt to taste

1. In a blender, put and mix the beans, garlic, lemon zest and juice, mint, maple syrup, salt, and 1 cup of water, pulse completely, till it becomes smooth and creamy. 2. To reach a smooth consistency, you can add more water.
Per Serving: Calories 52; Fat 0.2g; Sodium 2mg; Carbs 11g; Fiber 2.4g; Sugar 3g; Protein 2.4g

Black Beans and Citrus Quinoa

Prep time: 15 minutes | Cook time:20 minutes | Serves: 4

1½ cups quinoa, rinsed and drained
2 cups cooked black beans, or 1 15-ounce can, drained and rinsed
1½ teaspoons grated ginger
1½ teaspoons cumin seeds, toasted and ground
2 tablespoons balsamic vinegar
Zest and juice of 1 orange
4 green onions, white and green parts, thinly sliced
Salt and freshly ground black pepper

1. Place a medium pot with a lid over high heat to boil 3 cups of water, and then add the quinoa. Turn down the heat to medium-low, cook the quinoa with a lid, till tender for 15-20 minutes. 2. In a large bowl, add the quinoa and cumin, ginger, black beans, orange zest and juice, vinegar, and green onions. Mix them well. Serve with the salt and pepper if you like.
Per Serving: Calories 294; Fat 4g; Sodium 10mg; Carbs 53g; Fiber 8g; Sugar 1.5g; Protein 11g

Fast-Cook Chickpea Caponata

Prep time: 15 minutes | Cook time: 30 minutes | Serves:4

1 medium eggplant, stemmed and diced
2 ripe Roma tomatoes, diced
2 cups cooked chickpeas, drained and rinsed
1 medium yellow onion, peeled and diced
2 celery stalks, chopped
½ cup Kalamata olives, pitted and coarsely chopped
3 tablespoons capers
3 tablespoons red wine vinegar
¼ cup golden raisins
½ cup chopped basil
¼ cup pine nuts, toasted, optional
Salt and freshly ground black pepper

1. Place a large saucepan over medium heat and cook the onion and celery for about 10 minutes. 2. To keep the vegetable from sticking to the pan, add 1 tablespoon water at a time, add the tomatoes, eggplant, and chickpeas. Cook for 15 minutes with a lid. 3. Add and stir the red wine vinegar, olives, capers, raisins, and pine nuts and cook for over 5 minutes. 4. Turn off the heat and add the basil. Season with salt and pepper.
Per Serving: Calories 304; Fat 10g; Sodium 297mg; Carbs 46g; Fiber 13g; Sugar 18g; Protein 11g

Savory Garbanzo Beans

Prep time: 5 minutes | Cook time: 15 minutes | Serves: 4

2 pounds Garbanzo beans
2 tablespoons extra-virgin olive oil
Sea salt
Freshly ground black pepper
Juice of ½ lemon

1. Set the oven to 400 ℉ in advance. 2. Use aluminum foil to line a baking sheet. 3. In a large mixing bowl, mix the beans with the canola oil, and then sprinkle with the salt and pepper. 4. Put the beans on the baking pan in a single layer. 5. Bake the beans for 10-12 minutes, till caramelized and soft. 6. Mix the beans with lemon juice, plate it on each dish.
Per Serving: Calories 918; Fat 20g; Sodium 55mg; Carbs 143g; Fiber 28g; Sugar 24g; Protein 46g

Palatable Salad with Sprouts and Cabbage

Prep time: 10 minutes | Cook time: 10 minutes | Serves: 4

For the sprouts:
½ cup whole mung beans
½ teaspoon turmeric
¼ teaspoon salt
For the salad:
2 medium potatoes, skin on
½ cup blueberries, diced
½ cup cabbage, finely chopped
¼ cup peach, diced
¼ cup basil, finely chopped
2 tablespoons tahini
1 tablespoon white wine vinegar
1 teaspoon ground allspice
1 teaspoon ground fennel
1 teaspoon salt

To sprout the mung beans: 1. Soak the mung beans in 1 cup of filtered water overnight. Drain the beans. Spread a clean, damp cloth in a large bowl, wrap them in the cloth. Put the bowl to a cool place away from sun, dampen the cloth every 6 hours. The beans will sprout to about 0.5-centimeter sprouts in 12 hours. 2. As the beans have already sprouted, clean them. Boil the sprouts in 2 cups of water, add the turmeric and salt, cook for 10 minutes, till the sprouts are just tender. Drain the sprouts and put aside.
To make the salad: 1. Cut the potatoes in half, pour the water to a medium saucepan and cover. 2. Set the medium heat to boil the potato, simmer for 10 minutes or till soft. Drain the potatoes to cool, peel and cut into ½-inch cubes. 3. Plate the potatoes in a large bowl, add and stir the drained sprouts, blueberries, cabbage, peach, basil, tahini, white wine vinegar, allspice, fennel, and salt. 4. Mix them completely, serve the dish.
Per Serving: Calories 240; Fat 5g; Sodium 753mg; Carbs 47g; Fiber 6g; Sugar 12g; Protein 6g

Fresh Spinach with Almond Milk

Prep time: 15 minutes | Cook time: 30 minutes | Serves: 4

2 pounds fresh spinach, chopped
2 cups cooked chickpeas, drained and rinsed
1 medium yellow onion, peeled and diced small
1 jalapeño pepper, minced
3 cloves garlic, peeled and minced
1 large tomato, finely chopped
1 cup unsweetened plain almond

milk
1 tablespoon grated ginger
2 teaspoons ground cumin
1 teaspoon ground coriander
1 teaspoon turmeric
1 teaspoon fenugreek
1 teaspoon crushed red pepper flakes, or to taste
Salt

1. Place a large saucepan over medium-high heat and sauté the onion in the saucepan. 2. To prevent the vegetable from sticking to the pan, add water 1 to 2 tablespoons at a time. Lower the heat to cook the jalapeño pepper, coriander, ginger, cumin, garlic, turmeric, fenugreek, and crushed red pepper flakes. 3. Stir frequently, for 4 minutes. Add and cook the tomato for 5 minutes, and then add the spinach, almond milk, and chickpeas. 4. Lower the heat and cover with a lid, and then cook for 10 minutes. Sprinkle the salt, serve the dish!
Per Serving: Calories 605; Fat 38g; Sodium 334mg; Carbs 50g; Fiber 19g; Sugar 11g; Protein 28g

Green Pea Pesto with Nuts

Prep time: 5 minutes | Cook time: 0 minute | Serves: 4

¼ cup extra-virgin olive oil
½ cup fresh green peas
½ cup grated Parmesan cheese
¼ cup fresh basil leaves

¼ cup pine nuts
2 garlic cloves, minced
¼ teaspoon sea salt

1. Except the oil, put all the remaining in a blender or food processor, pulse together to smooth. 2. When running the machine, you can slowly add the olive oil, and combine for 1- 2 minutes.
Per Serving: Calories 246; Fat 23g; Sodium 431mg; Carbs 6g; Fiber 1g; Sugar 1g; Protein 6g

Taquitos with Black Beans

Prep time: 15 minutes | Cook time: 30 minutes | Serves: 4

4 cups cooked black beans, or 2 15-ounce cans, drained and rinsed
1 large yellow onion, peeled and diced small
4 cloves garlic, peeled and minced
2 teaspoons cumin seeds, toasted and ground

2 chiles in adobo sauce, minced, or 2 teaspoons ancho chile powder
Zest and juice of 2 oranges
20 to 24 corn tortillas
2 cups fresh tomato salsa
1 batch tofu sour cream
1 batch not-so-fat guacamole
Salt

1. In a large saucepan, before setting the medium heat, put and sauté the onion for 8-10 minutes. To prevent the vegetable from sticking to the pan, add water 1 to 2 tablespoons at a time 2. Add and cook the garlic and cumin orange zest and juice, chiles, and black beans, for several minutes. Add salt to season. 3. Place the mixture in a food processor, puree until smooth and slightly chunky 4. Place a nonstick skillet over medium-low heat, add the tortillas and cook for 3-4 minutes, and turn occasionally until the tortillas are soften. 5. Using a kitchen towel to wrap the tortillas, repeating the rest of tortillas. 6. Spread 3 tablespoons of the black bean mixture over half of each tortilla, rolling up. For another part, roll up from the bean-filled. Repeat with the rest of tortillas. 7. Cook to heat the taquitos in a 200°F (95°C) oven for 10 to 15 minutes. Enjoy the dish with tofu sour cream, guacamole, and salsa.
Per Serving: Calories 380; Fat 6g; Sodium 78mg; Carbs 74g; Fiber 12g; Sugar 8g; Protein 12g

Sodium-Free Herbs Chickpeas

Prep time: 5 minutes | Cook time: 56 minutes | Serves: 6

1-pound dried chickpeas
2 bay leaves
Fresh herbs, like parsley,

thyme, rosemary, etc. cut into 3-inch pieces and tied together with kitchen twine

1. Clean and rinse the chickpeas, put them in the electric pressure cooker. Pour 8 cups of water, and add the lay leaves and the herbs. Cover with a lid and lock. 2. Seal the pressure valve. 3. Cook on high pressure for 35 minutes. 4. Once the cooking has done, hit Cancel. Allow the pressure to release naturally for 20 minutes, then quick release any remaining pressure. 5. Unlock and take off the lid, discard the herb bundle and bay leaves. 6. Plate the chickpeas into air-tight containers, cover with the cooking liquid, and then let cool.
Per Serving: Calories 288; Fat 5g; Sodium 18mg; Carbs 48g; Fiber 9g; Sugar 8g; Protein 15.5g

Zesty Soup with Pinto Beans

Prep time: 10 minutes | Cook time: 180 minutes | Serves: 8

6 cups water
4-5 white onions
2 cups dried pinto beans
2 large cloves of garlic, whole

1 bay leaf
1 large jalapeno pepper, top cut off
1 tablespoon sea salt

1. Add and boil the pinto beans, pepper, onions, water, bay leaf and garlic. Sprinkle with the sea salt. Lower the heat to simmer for 2-3 hours. Check and whisk every 30-40 minutes, if needed, add water. 2. Serve the dish!
Per Serving: Calories 195; Fat 1g; Sodium 884mg; Carbs 36.5g; Fiber 9g; Sugar 4g; Protein 11g

Savory Sauté with Potato, Corn and Squash

Prep time: 10 minutes | Cook time:16 minutes | Serves: 4

2 potatoes, peeled and diced
3 medium cucumbers, cut into ½-inch rounds
4 yellow squash, cut into ½-inch rounds
2 cups corn kernels (from about 3 ears)

2 navy beans, or 1 15-ounce can, drained and rinsed
1 tablespoon apple cider
1 teaspoon rosemary
1 cup sage, finely chopped
Salt and freshly ground black pepper to taste

1. Add and sauté the potatoes in a large saucepan, adjust the heat to medium to cook for 7-8 minutes. Add water 1 to 2 tablespoons at a time to prevent the pan from sticking. 2. Add and cook to stir the cucumbers, squash, corn, nutmeg, and beans for 8 minutes, turn off the heat. 3. Add and stir the apple cider and sage, and then drizzle the salt and red pepper. 4. Serve and enjoy!
Per Serving: Calories 238; Fat 3g; Sodium 167mg; Carbs 50g; Fiber 12g; Sugar 10g; Protein 9g

Easy Cooking Red Lentil

Prep time: 10 minutes | Cook time: 30 minutes | Serves: 4

2 cup red lentils, rinsed
1 large yellow onion, peeled and diced
2 cloves garlic, peeled and minced
1 teaspoon turmeric
1 tablespoon cumin seeds, toasted and ground

1 tablespoon coriander seeds, toasted and ground
½ teaspoon crushed red pepper flakes
1 bay leaf
1 tablespoon grated ginger
Zest of 1 lemon
Salt

1. Place a large saucepan over medium heat and add the onion to cook for 10 minutes. 2. To prevent the onion from sticking to the pan, add water 1 to 2 tablespoons at a time, add the garlic, ginger, bay leaf, turmeric, coriander, cumin, and crushed red pepper flakes and cook for over 1 minute. 3. Increase the heat to high and bring 4 cups of water to a boil and the lentils. Reduce the heat to medium, cook in the pan for 20-25 minutes, with a lid. 4. Sprinkle with salt, and then add the lemon zest. Serve the dish!
Per Serving: Calories 380; Fat 3g; Sodium 12mg; Carbs 68g; Fiber 12g; Sugar 2g; Protein 24g

Delicious Salad with Red Bean Date

Prep time:10 minutes | Cook time: 0 minute | Serves: 4

4 cups cooked red beans, or 2 15-ounce cans, drained and rinsed
1 cup dates, halved and seeded
1 tablespoon mint, minced
1 taro, peeled, halved, and diced
½ cup finely chopped parsley

½ teaspoon cayenne pepper
3 tablespoons Greek yogurt
2 cloves garlic, crushed
1 teaspoon dry thyme
1 tablespoon raisins
Salt and freshly ground black pepper to taste

1. Put and add all the ingredients in a large bowl. Mix them completely. Chill for 1 hour. 2. Serve the dish!
Per Serving: Calories 170; Fat 1g; Sodium 12mg; Carbs 40g; Fiber 6g; Sugar 25g; Protein 4g

Garlic Cannellini Beans and Veggie Mix

Prep time: 10 minutes | Cook time: 10 minutes | Serves: 4

3 tablespoons extra-virgin olive oil
1-pound mixed greens (such as mustard greens, kale, collard greens, and chard), coarsely chopped
1 (15-ounce) can cannellini beans, rinsed and drained
3 tablespoons water or chicken

broth
½ small red onion, finely chopped
2 large cloves garlic, minced
¼ teaspoon chile pepper flakes
⅛ teaspoon sea salt
⅛ teaspoon cracked black pepper
½ tablespoon lemon zest
½ cup toasted pine nuts

1. After washing the vegetables, drain them completely. 2. Place a large sauté pan over medium heat to cook the oil. Add and cook the onion for 1 minute, and then add the garlic and chile pepper flake. When the garlic shows fragrant, add the vegetables, and sprinkle the salt and pepper. 3. Reduce a bit of heat. Stir occasionally. 4. Pour the water or broth, cover a lid for cooking 3 minutes. 5. After that, add the beans and cook for additional 2 minutes to heat the beans well. 6. Plate the food, garnish with the toasted pine nuts.
Per Serving: Calories 550; Fat 20g; Sodium 547mg; Carbs 72g; Fiber 28g; Sugar 3g; Protein 27g

Escarole, Parsnips & White Beans

Prep time: 10 minutes | Cook time: 30 minutes | Serves: 4

1 large head escarole, soaked in cool water, rinsed well, and chopped
4 cups cooked cannellini beans, or two 15-ounce (425 g) cans, drained and rinsed
1 medium yellow onion, peeled

and diced
2 large parsnips, peeled and diced
4 cloves garlic, peeled and minced
Salt and freshly ground black pepper

1. In a large skillet, add and put the onion, adjust the heat to medium to sauté for 5 minutes. 2. To prevent the vegetable from sticking to the pan, add water 1 to 2 tablespoons at a time. 3. Put and cook the parsnips and garlic for 4 minutes. 4. Add and cook the escarole for 15 minutes. 5. Add and cook the beans for over 5 minutes, and then sprinkle the salt and pepper. Serve the dish!
Per Serving: Calories 346; Fat 15.6g; Sodium 1988mg; Carbs 48.7g; Fiber 24.6g; Sugar 9.4g; Protein 10g

Pinto Beans with Avocado

Prep time: 6 minutes | Cook time: 1 minute | Serves: 4

1 (15-ounce) can pinto beans, drained and rinsed
2 bell peppers, cored and chopped
1 cup corn kernels (cut from 1 to 2 ears or frozen and thawed)

Salt
Freshly ground black pepper
Juice of 2 limes
1 tablespoon olive oil
1 avocado, chopped

1. Put and mix the beans, bell peppers, corn, salt, and pepper in a large bowl. 2. Squeeze fresh lime juice and whisk in olive oil. 3. Chill the mixture in the refrigerator for 30 minutes. 4. Add avocado to the food. Serve the dish!
Per Serving: Calories 233; Fat 12g; Sodium 247mg; Carbs 28g; Fiber 8.5g; Sugar 3g; Protein 7g

Sweet Rice Pudding

Prep time: 15 minutes | Cook time: 50 minutes | Serves: 2

5 ½ cups whole milk, divided
½ cup packed light brown sugar
2 teaspoons pure vanilla extract
ground cinnamon, for garnish
½ teaspoon kosher salt

½ cup Jasmine rice
1 tablespoon butter

1. Place a large pot over medium heat to boil 5 cups milk, sugar, and salt. Stir frequently. 2. Once the milk has done, stir in the rice and reduce the heat to low to cook for 45-50 minutes, till the rice is tender and the stew becomes thick. 3. Turn off the heat, add and stir the rest of 12 cups of milk, butter, vanilla, and salt. Sprinkle with cinnamon. Serve the dish!
Per Serving: Calories 852; Fat 28g; Sodium 935mg; Carbs 124g; Fiber 1g; Sugar 88g; Protein 24g

Fava Bean Ratatouille with Roma Tomato

Prep time:15 minutes | Cook time: 40 minutes | Serves: 4

2 potatoes, peeled and diced
1 large eggplant, stemmed and cut into ½-inch dice
1 medium carrot, diced
2 cups cooked fava beans, or one 15-ounce can, drained and rinsed
2 Roma tomatoes, chopped

1 red bell pepper, seeded and diced
2 cloves garlic, peeled and finely chopped
¼ cup tarragon, finely chopped
Salt and freshly ground black pepper to taste

1. Place a large saucepan over medium heat and add the potatoes to cook for 7 to 8 minutes. 2. To prevent the potatoes from sticking to the pan, add water 1 to 2 tablespoons at a time, stir and cook the carrot, garlic, fava beans, and tomatoes, for over 5 minutes. 3. Reduce the heat, cook and stir the food occasionally, for 15 minutes, or till the vegetable becomes soft. 4. Turn off the heat, add and stir the tarragon, sprinkle the salt and pepper.
Per Serving: Calories 215; Fat 0.7g; Sodium 33mg; Carbs 48g; Fiber 10.6g; Sugar 10.5g; Protein 7g

Low-Sodium Broth with White Bean

Prep time: 15 minutes | Cook time: 55 minutes | Serves: 4

1 medium yellow onion, peeled and finely diced
1 celery stalk, finely diced
1 medium carrot, peeled and finely diced
1½ cups pearled barley
2-inch piece orange peel

1 cinnamon stick
3 cups low-sodium vegetable broth
2 cups cooked navy or other white beans, or one 15-ounce (425 g) can, drained and rinsed
¼ cup finely chopped dill

1. In a large saucepan, add and mix the onion, celery, and carrot. Set the medium heat to sauté them for 7-8 minutes. 2. To prevent the vegetable from sticking to the pan, add water 1 to 2 tablespoons at a time. Add and boil the orange peel, barley, cinnamon stick, and vegetable stock over high heat. 3. Reduce the heat to medium, and cook the food for 35 minutes. Add the beans to cook for 10 minutes, till softened. Add and stir in the dill.
Per Serving: Calories 540; Fat 3g; Sodium 750mg; Carbs 111g; Fiber 27g; Sugar 11g; Protein 20g

Black-Eyed Cucumber Zuppa

Prep time: 15 minutes | Cook time: 20 minutes | Serves: 4

1½ cups cooked black-eyed peas
½ cup uncooked quinoa
½ cup leeks (white and light green parts), finely chopped and rinsed
½ cup cucumber
2 medium taros, chopped

⅛ teaspoon turmeric
¼ teaspoon ground rosemary
¼ teaspoon salt
Dash fenugreek seeds
3 cloves garlic, peeled and minced
Freshly ground black pepper to taste

1. Add and boil the black-eyed peas, quinoa, and fenugreek seeds to a pot with 3 cups of water. 2. Add the garlic and leeks, and stir them together. Adjust the heat to medium to cook, for 10 to 15 minutes. 3. After pouring 1½ cups of water, the taros, turmeric, rosemary, and salt, simmer for about 5-7 minutes over medium heat, till the quinoa and black-eyed peas are tender. 4. Add the cucumber and stir the food, drizzle the black pepper. Serve the dish!
Per Serving: Calories 167; Fat 2g; Sodium 157mg; Carbs 32g; Fiber 5g; Sugar 3.7g; Protein 6.3g

Button Mushrooms Risotto

Prep time: 15 minutes | Cook time: 20 minutes | Serves: 2

8 cups low-sodium chicken or vegetable broth
1 tablespoon extra-virgin olive oil
1 onion, finely chopped
2 tablespoons butter, divided
2 cups Arborio rice
½ cup white wine
1 cup freshly grated Parmesan
¾ cup frozen peas, thawed

2 tablespoons chopped fresh parsley
2 cloves garlic, minced
1 pound button mushrooms, sliced
1 bay leaf
4 sprigs of thyme leaf, removed
kosher salt
Freshly ground black pepper

1. Place a medium saucepan over medium heat to cook the chicken broth. After that, reduce the heat to low. 2. In a large saucepan or Dutch oven, heat the oil. Add the onion and cook until the onion becomes transparent, for 5 minutes. 3. Add 1 tablespoon butter, garlic, mushrooms, bay leaf, and thyme, and cook for over 4 minutes, till the mushrooms are tender, sprinkle with salt and pepper. Place the mixture to the pot. 4. Scoop out and melt the rest of the butter in the saucepan, rapidly stir in the Arborio rice, and cook for 2 minutes until it smells slightly toasted. Stir occasionally. 5. Add and cook 1 cup hot broth, whisk in the rice, till liquid has been absorbed completely. 6. Continue to add 1 cup of the rest of the broth at a time. Whisk the mixture till shows creamy. 7. Mix the mushrooms mixture with rice. 8. Add and combine the Parmesan, decorate with parsley. Serve hot!
Per Serving: Calories 1596; Fat 53g; Sodium 807mg; Carbs 276g; Fiber 55g; Sugar 17g; Protein 76g

Zesty Rice Soup with Lemon Chicken

Prep time: 15 minutes | Cook time: 20 minutes | Serves:4

1 tablespoon extra-virgin olive oil
1 pound chicken, cut into ½"cubes
kosher salt
Freshly ground black pepper
1 cup cooked white rice
2 green onions, thinly sliced

Juice and zest of 1 lemon
1 clove garlic, minced
1 onion, chopped
2 carrots, diced
2 celery stalks, diced
5 cups low-sodium chicken stock

1. Place a large saucepan over medium-high heat. Heat the oil in the saucepan. Sprinkle with salt, pepper, and half of the lemon zest to season the chicken. 2. Both sides of the chicken need to be browned for 5 minutes. After 2-3 minutes, add the garlic, onion, and sauté, scraping the bottom of the pan. Drizzle the season with salt and pepper. Add and cook the carrots and celery for 5 minutes. 3. Add the chicken stock, lemon juice, and cooked rice, and then cook them for 5 minutes. Sprinkle with the green onions. 4. Garnish with the rest of the lemon zest, serve the dish!
Per Serving: Calories 306; Fat 12.7g; Sodium 219mg; Carbs 22g; Fiber 2g; Sugar 3.6g; Protein 28g

Peanut Butter Taco Salad

Prep time: 10 minutes | Cook time: 5 minutes | Serves: 6

For the salad:
4 corn tortillas
6 cups chopped spinach
1½ cups zucchini, seeded and diced
1½ cups pineapple, peeled and diced
1½ cups cauliflower florets, chopped
1 15-ounce can black beans, drained and rinsed
1 15-ounce can lima beans, drained and rinsed
3 ears corn, kernels removed (about 2 cups)

For the dressing:
1 15-ounce can cannellini beans, drained and rinsed
2 cups parsley, leaves and tender stems
1 cup scallion
¼ cup peanut butter
1 4-ounce can radish, diced
2 tablespoons low-sodium soy sauce
1 teaspoon nutmeg
¼ teaspoon chili powder
2 cloves garlic, crushed
Zest and juice of 2 limes

To make the salad: 1. Slice the corn tortillas, line the slices on a small baking sheet, toast for 3-5 minutes, or till crispy. 2. Line the spinach in a large bowl, add with the zucchini, pineapple, cauliflower, black beans, lima beans, and corn. Put aside.
To make the dressing: 1. In a food processor, add and mix the cannellini beans, scallion, parsley, peanut butter, radish, peanut butter, chili powder, nutmeg, garlic, lime zest and juice, and 1 cup of water. Pulse until smooth. 2. Top with the tortilla strips, and then drizzle with the dressing. Serve the dish!
Per Serving: Calories 288; Fat 6.5g; Sodium 483mg; Carbs 51g; Fiber 11g; Sugar 15.6g; Protein 13g

Fresh Greens Paella

Prep time: 15minutes | Cook time: 20 minutes | Serves: 4

4 tablespoons extra-virgin olive oil, divided
2 medium zucchinis
8 ounces sliced mushrooms
Kosher salt
½ small yellow onion, finely chopped
3 cloves garlic, finely chopped
3 ½ cups vegetable broth
Chopped fresh parsley for serving

Lemon wedges, for serving
1 teaspoon smoked paprika
Pinch saffron threads (optional)
1 (14-ounce) can chopped tomatoes
1 ½ cups short-grain paella rice (such as Bomba rice)
1 cup fresh or frozen peas
1 cup Piquillo peppers, sliced (or roasted red peppers)
5 ounces baby spinach

1. Set the 425 °F for the oven. 2. Adjust the heat to medium and add 2 tablespoons of oil in a 12-inch cast-iron. 3. Add and cook the zucchini and mushrooms, stir frequently, for 3 minutes, after that sprinkle the salt and pepper. Mix and cook, frequently whisking, for 8-10 minutes. Plate the food to another bowl. 4. Return the skillet over the heat to heat 2 tablespoons of olive oil, sprinkle the salt and pepper in the skillet. Cook and stir for 3 - 5 minutes, till softened. 5. Add the garlic, onion, smoked paprika, and saffron, cook and stir for 30 seconds. Add and mix the tomatoes with rice. Add the peas, piquillo peppers, and spinach with the zucchini combination. 6. Add and boil the broth and ¾ teaspoon salt. Cook for 20-22 minutes, without a lid. 7. Then adjust the heat to medium to cook the rice for 2-3 minutes, till crispy. Garnish with lemon wedges and parsley. Serve the dish!
Per Serving: Calories 468; Fat 9g; Sodium 772mg; Carbs 85g; Fiber 10g; Sugar 8g; Protein 14g

Appetizing Fried Rice with Veggie

Prep time: 15 minutes | Cook time:10 minutes | Serves: 2

3 tablespoons sesame oil, divided
3 large eggs
1 tablespoon peeled and minced ginger (from a 1" piece)
4 cups cooked long grain rice (preferably leftover)
¾ cup frozen peas

3 tablespoons low-sodium soy sauce
Kosher salt
2 carrots, diced
3 green onions, thinly sliced, white and green parts divided
3 cloves garlic, minced

1. Place a big cast-iron skillet over high heat and add 1 tablespoon of oil until it is heated up. 2. Add and cook the egg, 2 tablespoons of water, and a hefty pinch of salt, for 30 seconds. Frequently whisk, till form big soft curds. Place on a platter. 3. Adjust the heat to high to cook 2 tablespoons of oil, carrots, and green onion whites, for 2 4. minutes. Stir for 1 minutes, till the garlic and ginger are aromatic. 5. Add and cook the rice, peas, and cooked eggs, pour the soy sauce and simmer, constantly stirring, for 1 minute. Drizzle the salt and pepper, mix the rest of green onions. Serve the dish!
Per Serving: Calories 797; Fat 31.5g; Sodium 941mg; Carbs 105g; Fiber 11g; Sugar 5g; Protein 24g

Delicious Chicken Rice

Prep time: 15 minutes | Cook time: 15 minutes | Serves: 2

⅓ cup fresh orange juice
¼ cup extra-virgin olive oil, divided
2 tablespoons fresh lime juice
½ teaspoon garlic powder
½ teaspoon oregano
3 tablespoons lime juice
1 tablespoon chopped fresh cilantro
Cooked white rice
Shredded romaine
Canned black beans, drained

Lime wedges
Sriracha
½ teaspoon ground cumin
½ teaspoon paprika
1-pound boneless skinless chicken breasts
kosher salt
Freshly ground black pepper
1 ½ cups canned pineapple
½ small red onion, finely chopped
1 clove garlic, minced

1. In a medium mixing bowl, add and whisk the orange juice, 2 tablespoons of olive oil, lime juice, garlic powder, oregano, cumin, and paprika. Add and toss in the chicken breasts to cover all sides. Covered with plastic wrap, put the food to refrigerator, chill for 15 minutes or up to 2 hours. 2. Prepare the tropical salsa: 3. In a medium mixing basin, add and mix the pineapple, red onion, garlic, lime juice, and cilantro. Sprinkle with salt. Place them to refrigerator. 4. Place a large skillet over medium heat and add the remaining olive oil. Heat up well. 5. Then rub salt and pepper over each side of the chicken breast. 6. Add to the pan and then cook for 5 minutes per side. Turn off the heat and set aside for 10 minutes, slice or cut into strips or cubes. 7. Enjoy the food with lettuce, black beans, and pineapple salsa. If you like, drizzle with Sriracha and squeeze lime juice over the top.
Per Serving: Calories 674; Fat 33g; Sodium 109mg; Carbs 42g; Fiber 3g; Sugar 32g; Protein 53g

Caramelized Beef and Rice Bowl

Prep time: 15 minutes | Cook time: 20 minutes | Serves: 2

1 tablespoon vegetable oil
1 pound ground beef (preferably 80 percent lean meat)
1 tablespoon grated ginger
1 tablespoon minced garlic, from about four cloves
Freshly ground black pepper, to taste
Cooked rice for serving
3 tablespoons soy sauce

2 tablespoons agave syrup (or any sweetener you prefer)
2 tablespoons sesame oil
Kosher salt, to taste
Optional toppings:
chopped scallion greens or cilantro,
toasted sesame seeds,
sliced radishes, cucumbers, red onions, or tomatoes

1. Place a large skillet over medium heat and add the vegetable oil. 2. When the oil is heated, add the ground beef and cook to broken them into little 2- inch clumps with a little space between piece in advance. 3. Cook each side of the chicken for 2 minutes or more, or until browned. 4. Cut the beef into tiny pieces, cook the food until the beef could not show pink, for 1 minute. 5. Add and mix the ginger and garlic. Cook for 30 seconds. Add and whisk in the soy sauce and agave syrup. Scrape up any black pieces off the bottom of the pan. 6. Remove the skillet from the heat. 7. Sprinkle the food with salt and pepper. 8. Serve the food with cooked rice.
Per Serving: Calories 828; Fat 57g; Sodium 922mg; Carbs 16.5g; Fiber 0.3g; Sugar 12g; Protein 59.5g

Palatable Onion Rice

Prep time:15 minutes | Cook time: 20 minutes | Serves: 4

6 tablespoons butter
1 tablespoon extra-virgin olive oil
2 large onions, divided (about 1 ½ lb.)
1 ¼ teaspoons kosher salt
3 cups low-sodium beef broth
Freshly shredded Gruyère, for serving

Lemon wedges, for serving
6 cloves garlic, minced
1 tablespoon fresh thyme leaves, plus more for garnish
1 teaspoon freshly ground black pepper
¼ cup white wine (optional)
2 cups basmati rice, rinsed and drained

1. Place a large saucepan over medium heat and add 3 tablespoons butter and the olive oil. Heat them up until the butter has melted. 2. Add and cook the onion for 35-40 minutes, till the onion becomes caramelized, put the food to another basin. 3. After melting 1 tablespoon of butter, add and stir garlic, thyme, and pepper, for 1 minute. Cook enough until the wine has completely evaporated. 4. Melt the rest of two tablespoons of butter, whisk the rice till it is toasted, for 3-4 minutes. Put 34% the caramelized onion back to saucepan, the rest of it need to be mixed. 5. Boil the broth, and then reduce the heat with a lid. Simmer for 18 minutes, till the rice is tender. 6. Before taking away the lid, set the food aside for 5 minutes, softly fluff the rice. 7. Top with the leftover caramelized onions, Gruyère, additional thyme, and a squeeze of lemon. Serve the dish!
Per Serving: Calories 716; Fat 17g; Sodium 956mg; Carbs 112g; Fiber 6g; Sugar 9g; Protein 17g

Best-Ever Paella with Savory Chicken

Prep time: 15 minutes | Cook time: 20 minutes | Serves: 8

1 ½ pounds boneless skinless chicken breasts, cut into 1" pieces
½ pound chorizo, sliced
kosher salt
Freshly ground black pepper
1 cup short-grain rice
½ pound medium shrimp
1 ½ cups frozen peas
Freshly chopped parsley for

garnish
Lemon wedges, for serving
1 15-ounce can dice tomatoes
1 large onion, chopped
4 cloves garlic, minced
2 teaspoons paprika
Pinch of cayenne pepper
2 cups low-sodium chicken broth
⅓ cup dry white wine

1. Place a large skillet over medium heat and heat up oil in the skillet. 2. Place the chicken on one side and the chorizo on the other. Sprinkle the chicken with salt and pepper, and cook for 10 minutes or until the chicken is browned. 3. In a large slow cooker, add and cook the browned chicken-chorizo combination, rice, tomatoes, onion, garlic, paprika, and cayenne pepper, sprinkle with the salt and pepper. Pour and mix the chicken broth and white wine. 4. Cook and cover on high, for 1 ½-2 hours. 5. After removing the cover, add and mix the shrimp and frozen pea. Continue to cook for 10 minutes, till the shrimp becomes pink and the peas are warm. 6. Garnish with parsley. Serve with lemon wedges. Serve the dish!
Per Serving: Calories 410; Fat 15.7g; Sodium 731mg; Carbs 29g; Fiber 3g; Sugar 2g; Protein 36.6g

Spice Jollof Rice

Prep time: 15 minutes | Cook time: 1 hour 20 minutes | Serves: 4

Cooking Spray
1 Scotch bonnet or habanero pepper
3 medium tomatoes
1 medium onion, ½ chopped; other sliced and set aside
3 red bell peppers, cored, chopped
1 cup chicken stock or water, or if necessary
⅓ cup vegetable oil
1 tablespoon onion powder
1 teaspoon freshly ground black pepper

1 tablespoon tomato paste
2 cups long-grain rice, rinsed and strained until the water ran clear
2 tablespoons unsalted butter
1 teaspoon kosher salt
2 bay leaves
1 teaspoon curry powder
1 teaspoon sweet or smoky paprika
1 tablespoon dried thyme
½ teaspoon ground ginger
1 tablespoon garlic powder

1. Set the 350°F to the oven in advance. 2. Coat a 9-by-13-inch baking dish with cooking spray. 3. In a blender, add tomatoes, Scotch bonnet pepper, diced onions, and bell peppers,1 cup of stock. Blend until smooth. Boil the food in a big saucepan, and then reduce the heat to low to simmer 10-20 minutes, or until the liquid is reduced to 2 to 2 ½ cups. 4. In a separate big pan, adjust the heat to medium to cook the oil, add and cook the cut onion for 2-3 minutes. Sprinkle with salt. 5. Adjust the heat to medium. In a large mixing bowl, combine and cook the bay leaves, curry powder, paprika, dried thyme, ginger, garlic powder, onion powder, and black pepper, for 3 minutes. Stir in tomato paste for additional 2 minutes. 6. Add and whisk in the reduced tomato-pepper-Scotch bonnet combination, for 10-12 minutes. 7. Add and boil 1 cup of the stock for 1- 2 minutes. 8. In a mixing bowl, add and combine the rice and butter, sprinkle with salt and pepper. 9. Put the mixture in a greased dish! 10. Using foil to cover the baking dish, bake for 40 -50 minutes. 11. After 30 minutes, check the rice and add more water, if the rice is still firm or dry, add more water. 12. Fluff the rice, serve the dish!
Per Serving: Calories 625; Fat 25.6g; Sodium 718mg; Carbs 90g; Fiber 7g; Sugar 7.6g; Protein 11g

Sweet Custards with Roasted-Buckwheat

Prep time: 15 minutes | Cook time: 1 hour | Serves: 1

1 ½ ounces soba-cha or roasted-buckwheat tea
12 ounces heavy cream
3 ounces sugar
Whipped cream for garnish
Pinch kosher salt
6 large egg yolks

1. Set the 300 °F to the oven in advance. 2. In a large pot, add and boil the water. And then, in a medium saucier or saucepan, add and combine cream and soba-cha together. 3. Adjust the heat to medium to simmer the food. To prevent burning, use a rubber or silicone spatula to swirl and scrap the bottom of cooker regularly. 4. Turn off the heat and put the food aside to rest for 5 minutes. 5. Prepare a heatproof measuring cup, make sure the infused cream dry, push down on the soba-cha to extract the liquid, discard the soba-cha. After that, add enough fresh cream to the infused cream to make 1 ½ cups total. Sprinkle with a bit of salt. 6. In a clean medium saucier or saucepan, whisk egg yolks with sugar. Add hot infused cream into the mixture as whisking occasionally. 7. By using a rubber or silicone spatula to stir and scrap the bottom and sides of the saucepan, till the custard registers 140°F (60°C) on an instant-read thermometer. 8. Carefully sieve the custard, putting it to the ramekins, and then transfer it to the baking sheet. 9. By using the aluminum foil to cover the baking dish finely, remember to leave a tiny space in the foil, and then place it in the oven. 10. Slowly and carefully add and pour the prepared boiling water into a baking dish, till water comes halfway up the ramekin edges. Seal the foil and bake the custards for 30-45 minutes, or until just set. 11. Take off the dish, let the custards cool in the water bath for about 1 hour without adding cold water. After that, cover the plastic wrap and chill for over 3 hours. 12. It is proper to store the food for 5 days in the refrigerator. Add the whipped cream and a few stray toasted buckwheat seeds. Serve the dish!
Per Serving: Calories 917; Fat 76g; Sodium 91mg; Carbs 49g; Fiber 0g; Sugar 46.6g; Protein 11.6g

Basmati Rice with Toasted Cashews

Prep time: 15 minutes | Cook time: 30 minutes | Serves: 4

4 tablespoons ghee or butter
30 curry leaves (optional)
1 large red onion, diced, divided
6 cloves garlic, minced
1 inch fresh ginger, finely minced
2 ½ tablespoons yellow curry powder
1 cup peas (optional)
toasted cashews, for serving
cilantro, for serving
freshly sliced red chilis, for
serving
yogurt, for serving
2 teaspoons cumin seeds
1 teaspoon ground coriander
¼ teaspoon ground cayenne
¾ teaspoon freshly ground black pepper
1 ¼ teaspoons kosher salt
2 cups basmati rice, rinsed and drained
3 cups low-sodium chicken or vegetable broth

1. In a large saucepan, adjust the heat to medium to melt the ghee, once they show translucent and crispy. Set aside. 2. Add most of the onion to the saucepan and save ¼ cup for topping. Cook for 4 minutes, or until semi-translucent. 3. Add and stir the garlic and ginger for 30 seconds, cook and stir frequently, for 4 or more minutes. 4. Whisk occasionally for 4 minutes, and then boil the

broth over low heat with a lid. Simmer for 10 minutes, till the rice is tender. 5. Remove the covered pot from the heat and set it aside for 5 minutes, take away the lid. Softly fluff the rice and mix the peas. 6. Top with cashews, cumin seeds, cayenne, fresh chili, leftover red onions, cilantro, crispy curry leaves, and yogurt for each plate. Serve the dish!
Per Serving: Calories 406; Fat 26g; Sodium 936mg; Carbs 52g; Fiber 20g; Sugar 9.8g; Protein 14g

Healthy Bulgur Salad with Walnuts

Prep time: 15 minutes | Cook time: 30 minutes | Serves: 2

3 scallions, white and green parts
1 cup bulgur wheat
½ cup chopped walnuts
¼ cup freshly squeezed lemon juice
½ teaspoon salt
2 ½ teaspoons agave nectar
¼ cup extra virgin olive oil
Freshly ground black pepper
½ small head radicchio
½ cup chopped fresh parsley leaves
½ cup chopped dried apricots
½ cup chopped fresh mint leaves

1. Boil a large pot of water. Sprinkle the bulgur and salt in a medium bowl, cover the 1-¼ cup boiling water. And then cover the bowl with plastic wrap, set aside for 25-30 minutes, till all the water has been absorbed. 2. Mix the cooked bulgur with the other ingredients, sprinkle with salt and pepper, serve the dish!
Per Serving: Calories 576; Fat 41g; Sodium 624mg; Carbs 51g; Fiber 11g; Sugar 21g; Protein 9g

Spelt Salad with Cremini Mushrooms

Prep time: 15 minutes | Cook time: 20 minutes | Serves: 4

½ cup plus 1 tablespoon extra-virgin olive oil, divided
1 pound cremini mushrooms, diced
1 large (12-ounce) leek, diced
6 cups cooked whole grain spelled (from about 24 ounces dry)
2 small Persian cucumbers quartered lengthwise, then sliced crosswise into ¼-inch pieces
½ cup minced flat-leaf parsley
¼ cup minced chives
Espelette pepper powder, for garnish (optional)
2 medium cloves garlic, thinly sliced
¼ cup plus two tablespoons cider vinegar
1 teaspoon picked thyme leaves, minced
Kosher salt and freshly ground black pepper

1. Place a large pan over medium-high heat and add 3 tablespoons oil. Heat up. 2. Add and cook the mushrooms, add the water has evaporated about 5 minutes. Sprinkle with the salt and pepper, simmer the food, till leek garlic, and thyme are tender, about 4 minutes. 3. Put the food in a large mixing bowl, add ¼ cup cider vinegar. Set aside for 15 minutes. 4. In a large mixing basin, add and mix the spelled cucumbers and mushroom-leek combination. Sprinkle with salt and pepper, whisk in the remaining olive oil, 2 tablespoons cider vinegar, parley, and chives. 5. Top with Espelette pepper, plate the salad. Serve the dish!
Per Serving: Calories 1111; Fat 15.5g; Sodium 244mg; Carbs 235g; Fiber 28g; Sugar 6.8g; Protein 27g

Toasted-Bulgur Salad

Prep time: 15 minutes | Cook time: 20 minutes | Serves: 6

3 lemons, cut into wedges
½ cup sugar
1 cup bulgur wheat
1 ¾ cups water
½ teaspoon kosher salt
8 ounces smoked trout
4 radishes (about 6 ounces), halved and thinly sliced
½ teaspoon lemon zest
½ cup plus 1 tablespoon extra-virgin olive oil
Kosher salt and freshly ground

pepper
½ small red onion
1 medium Granny Smith apple
1 cup loosely packed flat-leaf parsley leaves
Freshly ground black pepper
2 tablespoons fresh juice from 1 lemon
1 tablespoon reserved lemon soaking syrup

1. In a heat-proof basin, place each lemon segment, slightly tearing the food into ½-inch pieces. 2. In a small pot, add and combine sugar and ½ cup water. Adjust the heat to high to boil the food, and then lower the heat and stir, till the sugar has dissolved. Pouring the syrup over the lemon slices, set the food aside to rest for 45 minutes. 3. In a medium pan, adjust the heat to high to roast the bulgur, turn regularly, until nutty-smelling, for 3 minutes. Place in a medium heatproof bowl. 4. In a small saucepan, boil the rest of 1 ¼ cups water and ½ teaspoon salt. Cover and pour the boiling water over the bulgur, standing for 20 minutes. Fluff the food, and then cover a lid, cool the food for 30 minutes. 5. In a large mixing basin, add and toss the fish, radish, onion, apple, and parsley with the cold bulgur. Drain the lemon segments and save 1 tablespoon of the lemon soaking syrup for the dressing. Add and mix the salad with the drained lemon slices. 6. In a medium mixing dish, add and combine lemon juice, 1 tablespoon reserved syrup, and lemon zest. Pour the olive oil and whisk in salt and pepper. 7. Add salt and pepper to season the salad. Chill or serve at room temperature.
Per Serving: Calories 306; Fat 15g; Sodium 282mg; Carbs 34g; Fiber 6g; Sugar 21g; Protein 12g

Tasty Farro with Parmigiano-Reggiano Cheese

Prep time: 15 minutes | Cook time: 30 minutes | Serves: 2

2 tablespoons extra-virgin olive oil, plus more for drizzling
1 ½ cups farro
2 medium shallots, thinly sliced
4 large eggs, poached or fried
Parmigiano-Reggiano cheese, for shaving (optional)

Chili sauce, for serving (optional)
3 medium cloves garlic, minced
1 large bunch Lacinato (Tuscan) kale
2 tablespoons red wine vinegar

1. Wash the kale and remove the tough stems and finely chop the leaves. 2. In a saucepan, add and boil the salted water, and then add the farro. Lower the heat and simmer for 20 minutes, till the farro is tender but not mushy. Drain and set aside. 3. In a large skillet, set the medium heat to cook the oil. Cook the shallots for 4 minutes, till the food becomes tender. 4. Add and cook the garlic for 30 seconds. Cook and occasionally stir the food, till the kale is wilted, for 4 minutes. Add and toss farro and vinegar, till the farro has warmed completely, drizzle the salt and pepper. 5. Put the greens and grains into four dishes, sprinkle the salt and pepper. 6. Top with egg, serve the dish! (if you like, garnish with shaved Parmesan.)
Per Serving: Calories 696; Fat 26g; Sodium 215mg; Carbs 88g; Fiber 10.6g; Sugar 12g; Protein 31.5g

Special Farro Salad

Prep time: 15 minutes | Cook time: 20 minutes | Serves: 4

2 medium cloves garlic, minced
3 tablespoons red wine vinegar
⅓ cup extra-virgin olive oil
Kosher salt and freshly ground black pepper
10 ounces farro
4 cups water
1 small white or yellow onion, quartered
1 medium clove garlic smashed
1 ½ tablespoons minced, fresh lemon thyme or regular thyme
3 ounces crumbled blue cheese

¼ cup pine nuts, lightly toasted
Freshly ground black pepper
1 medium carrot, peeled and cut into large chunks
2 teaspoons kosher salt, plus more for seasoning
1 medium tomato, chopped
1 small seedless cucumber, finely chopped
¼ cup chopped fresh basil
¼ cup minced, fresh flat-leaf parsley

1. In a small bowl, add and mix the vinaigrette, sprinkle with the salt and pepper. 2. Add and boil the farro, water, onion, garlic, carrot, and 2 tablespoons salt in a medium saucepan over medium-high heat. 3. Reduce the heat, partially cover and simmer the food over medium-low heat for 20 minutes, till the farro is tender. Drain and discard the onion, garlic and carrot, chill the food. 4. Put the rest of salad ingredients into the chilled farro softly. 5. Add a few teaspoons of vinaigrette at a time, sprinkle the salt and pepper into the food, if you like, you could add more vinaigrette. Serve the dish!
Per Serving: Calories 584; Fat 31g; Sodium 1433mg; Carbs 61g; Fiber 4g; Sugar 5g; Protein 16g

Sautéed Blini with Buckwheat

Prep time: 15 minutes | Cook time: 15 minutes | Serves: 2

1 cup buckwheat flour
½ cup all-purpose flour
2 tablespoons unsalted butter, melted
2 large eggs, separated
1 tablespoon vegetable oil
Chilled caviar or smoked

salmon
Sour cream or crème fraiche
2 teaspoons sugar
½ teaspoon kosher salt
½ teaspoon baking powder
¼ teaspoon baking soda
2 cups buttermilk

1. Heat the oven to 50°F (65°C) or its lowest feasible setting in advance. 2. In a medium mixing basin, add and whisk all-purpose flour, buckwheat flour, sugar, kosher salt, baking powder, and baking soda. 3. In a mixing dish, separately add and mix the buttermilk, melted butter, egg yolks, and vegetable oil. 4. Add and stir the buttermilk into the dry ingredients, mix to narrowly incorporated. 5. In a small bowl, whisk eggs whites, till show firm peaks. Add and fold the egg white into the batter softly, till narrowly incorporated. 6. Heat a large nonstick skillet over medium heat for 5 minutes (or use an electric griddle set to 350°F/177°C). 7. Spread a bit of vegetable oil in the skillet with a paper towel. Put the silver dollar pancake–sized circles of batter (approximately 2 ½ inches in diameter) in the skillet 8. Cook for 2 minutes, or till bubbles show the blini, or the sides are light golden brown. 9. After flipping the blini, cook for additional 2 minutes. 10. Using a clean chicken towel to wrap blini, put the towel on a wire rack, keeping warm in the oven. Repeat the process, till the batters are gone. 11. Traditionally, Blinis could be served with sour cream, chilled caviar or smoked salmon, and traditional accompaniments such as finely minced shallots, sliced chives, and chopped hard-boiled eggs.
Per Serving: Calories 625; Fat 24g; Sodium 1295mg; Carbs 81g; Fiber 7g; Sugar 16g; Protein 25.6g

Zesty Wild Rice Salad

Prep time: 15 minutes | Cook time: 50 minutes | Serves: 1

1 cup wild rice, rinsed
1 teaspoon kosher salt
2 tablespoons apple cider vinegar
¾ teaspoon orange zest and 2 tablespoons juice from one orange

1 teaspoon honey
Freshly ground black pepper
½ cup dried cranberries
¾ cup pecans, toasted and coarsely chopped
2 scallions, finely sliced
2 tablespoons extra-virgin olive oil

1. In a saucepan, add and boil the rice, salt and 3 ½ cups water. Lower the heat, cover, till the rice is soft, for 50 minutes. Put the rice to a sieve and drain any other water, set aside to cool. 2. In a large mixing bowl, add and mix the rice, cranberries, pecans, scallions, olive oil, vinegar, orange zest, orange juice, and honey. Sprinkle the salt and pepper. Serve the dish!
Per Serving: Calories 1446; Fat 82g; Sodium 2347mg; Carbs 159g; Fiber 18g; Sugar 31g; Protein 31g

Homemade Red Beans and Brown Rice

Prep time: 5 minutes | Cook time: 50 minutes | Serves: 2

½ cup dry brown rice
1 (15-ounce, 425g) can red beans, drained and rinsed
1 cup water, plus ¼ cup
1 tablespoon ground cumin

Juice of 1 lime
4 handfuls fresh spinach
Optional toppings: avocado, chopped tomatoes, plain Greek yogurt, onions

1. In the pot, add the brown rice and 1 cup of water, then bring to a boil; when boiled, cover the pot and lower the heat, then simmer the rice for 30 to 40 minutes (or cook the rice according to the package directions). 2. While simmering, in the skillet, add the beans, cumin, lime juice and ¼ cup of water, bring to a boil and reduce to a simmer; cook the food for 5 to 7 minutes until most of the liquid is absorbed. 3. Once the liquid is mostly gone, remove from the heat and add the spinach. Cover the skillet and let spinach wilt slightly for 2 to 3 minutes. 4. Serve the dish with the rice and the topping you like.
Per Serving: Calories 321; Fat 8.58g; Sodium 358mg; Carbs 49.67g; Fiber 14.4g; Sugar 8.11g; Protein 22.88g

Sautéed Veggie with Brown Rice

Prep time: 15 minutes | Cook time: 7 minutes | Serves: 2

2 cups cooked brown rice, fully cooled
1 bunch baby bok choy, trimmed and chopped
½ medium yellow onion, peeled and diced
½ medium red bell pepper, seeded and diced
3 cloves garlic, peeled and

minced
¼ cup Chinese Brown Sauce
2 tablespoons dry sherry, optional
½ teaspoon crushed red pepper flakes
4 green onions (white and green parts), thinly sliced

1. In the skillet over high heat, sauté the onion and red pepper for 4 minutes, adding 1 tablespoon of water at a time to prevent sticking. 2. Add the baby bok choy and sauté for 3 minutes; add the garlic, Chinese Brown Sauce, sherry, crushed red pepper

flakes and brown rice, then cook them until heated through. 3. Serve and enjoy.
Per Serving: Calories 314; Fat 2.12g; Sodium 465mg; Carbs 67.31g; Fiber 7.9g; Sugar 10.83g; Protein 8.51g

Authentic Cornmeal Polenta

Prep time: 5 minutes | Cook time: 40 minutes | Serves: 4-6

1½ cups coarse cornmeal
¾ teaspoon salt

5 cups of water

1. Cook the cornmeal for 30 minutes until the mixture is thick and creamy, stirring constantly. In the saucepan, add the water and bring to a boil. 2. Stir in the cornmeal, a little at a time. 3. When done, season with the salt and serve
Per Serving: Calories 145; Fat 0.69g; Sodium 297mg; Carbs 31.18g; Fiber 1.5g; Sugar 0.63g; Protein 2.79g

Brown Rice Pilaf with Golden Raisins

Prep time: 5 minutes | Cook time: 15 minutes | Serves: 6

1 tablespoon extra-virgin olive oil
1 cup chopped onion (about ½ medium onion)
1 teaspoon ground cumin
½ teaspoon ground cinnamon
½ cup shredded carrot (about 1 medium carrot)

1¾ cups 100% orange juice
2 cups instant brown rice
¼ cup water
½ cup shelled pistachios
1 cup golden raisins
Chopped fresh chives (optional)

1. In the saucepan, heat the oil over medium-high heat; add the onion and sauté for 5 minutes; add the carrot, cumin, cinnamon and sauté them for 1 minute longer. 2. Add the orange juice, rice and water, then bring to a boil; cover the pan and reduce the heat to medium-low. 3. Simmer the food for 7 minutes or until the rice is cooked through and the liquid is absorbed. 4. Stir in the pistachios, raisins and chives (optional), serve and enjoy.
Per Serving: Calories 266; Fat 6.66g; Sodium 40mg; Carbs 49.95g; Fiber 5g; Sugar 8.4g; Protein 5.35g

Italian Rice and Peas

Prep time: 10 minutes | Cook time: 35 minutes | Serves: 4

2 tablespoons extra-virgin olive oil
1 onion, chopped
1 cup brown rice
2 cups frozen baby peas

⅛ teaspoon salt
2½ cups water, divided
¼ teaspoon dried mint leaves
2 tablespoons grated Parmesan cheese

1. In the saucepan, heat the olive oil over medium heat; add the onion and sauté for 2 to 3 minutes until tender. 2. Stir in the rice until the rice is coated with the oil. Sprinkle with the salt, add 1 cup of water and then stir for 5 to 10 minutes until the water is absorbed. 3. Add another ½ cup of water and stir for 5 minutes longer until it's absorbed, then add the remaining 1 cup of water, cover the pan and simmer for about 20 minutes, stirring occasionally, until the rice is tender. 4. Add the peas, mint and sauté for 3 to 5 minutes, until the peas are hot and tender. 5. Sprinkle with the cheese, serve and enjoy.
Per Serving: Calories 327; Fat 4.87g; Sodium 216mg; Carbs 59.92g; Fiber 7g; Sugar 1.6g; Protein 11.23g

Bulgur Pilaf with Walnuts

Prep time: 15 minutes | Cook time: 25 minutes | Serves: 4

1 medium yellow onion, peeled and diced	2 cups bulgur
2 cloves garlic, peeled and minced	½ cup golden raisins
1 cinnamon stick	½ cup dried unsulfured apricots, chopped (see more on sulfites and sulfur dioxide)
2 teaspoons ground coriander	
3½ cups low-sodium vegetable broth	2 green onions (white and green parts), thinly sliced
½ cup walnuts, toasted and coarsely chopped	Salt and freshly ground black pepper

1. In the saucepan over medium-high heat, sauté the onion for 7 to 8 minutes or until golden, adding 1 tablespoon of water to prevent sticking. 2. Add the garlic and sauté for 1 minute; add the coriander, apricots, raisins, bulgur, cinnamon stick and the stock, then increase the heat to high and bring to boil. 3. When boiled, reduce the heat to medium and cover the pan, wait for 15 minutes until the bulgur is tender. 4. Remove from the heat, pick out the cinnamon stick, and stir in the green onions. 5. Season with salt and pepper. Garnished with the chopped walnuts and serve.
Per Serving: Calories 303; Fat 7.72g; Sodium 279mg; Carbs 57.69g; Fiber 9g; Sugar 28.93g; Protein 8.15g

Chicken Cubes with Brown Rice

Prep time: 10 minutes | Cook time: 5 minutes | Serves: 4

2 cups cooked brown rice	½ cup (120 ml) chicken broth
1 tablespoon coconut oil	1 teaspoon salt
2 scallions, sliced	½ teaspoon ground ginger
1 cup cooked chicken, cut into ½-inch cubes	1 teaspoon toasted sesame oil
	1 teaspoon coconut aminos
4 ounces (113 g) snow peas, strings removed	

1. In the pan, melt the coconut oil over high heat; add the cooked brown rice and chicken cubes, sauté them for 2 minutes. 2. Add the salt, snow peas, chicken broth, ginger and then cover the pan, lower the heat to low and wait for 3 minutes until the snow peas turn bright green. Remove the pan from the heat. 3. Stir in the coconut aminos, sesame oil and scallions, serve and enjoy.
Per Serving: Calories 248; Fat 10.31g; Sodium 734mg; Carbs 25.42g; Fiber 2.7g; Sugar 1.82g; Protein 13.23g

Brown Basmati Rice with Berries

Prep time: 10 minutes | Cook time: 35 minutes | Serves: 4

1 cup brown basmati rice	½ cup shaved coconut, divided
2 dates, pitted and chopped	1 cup water
1 cup fresh blueberries, or raspberries, divided	1 cup coconut milk
¼ cup toasted slivered almonds, divided	1 teaspoon salt

1. In the saucepan, heat the basmati rice, water, coconut milk, salt and date pieces over high heat. 2. Stir until the mixture comes to a boil; when boiled, lower the heat to simmer and wait for 20 to 30 minutes until the rice is tender. 3. Divide the rice among 4 bowls, top each bowl of rice with the blueberries, almonds and coconut milk. Enjoy.
Per Serving: Calories 268; Fat 20.69g; Sodium 625mg; Carbs 27.14g; Fiber 9g; Sugar 8.99g; Protein 5.9g

Barley Risotto in Vegetable Broth

Prep time: 5 minutes | Cook time: 25 minutes | Serves: 6

1 tablespoon extra-virgin olive oil	2 cups uncooked pearl barley
	½ cup dry white wine
1 cup freshly grated Parmesan cheese (about 4 ounces, 113 g), divided	¼ teaspoon freshly ground black pepper
	¼ teaspoon kosher or sea salt
4 cups low-sodium or no-salt-added vegetable broth	Fresh chopped chives and lemon wedges, for serving (optional)
1 cup chopped yellow onion (about ½ medium onion)	

1. In the saucepan, add the broth and bring to a simmer. 2. In the stockpot, heat the oil over medium-high heat; add the onion and sauté for 8 minutes; add the barley and sauté for 2 minutes until the barley is toasted. 3. Add the wine and cook for about 1 minute, or until most of the liquid evaporates. 4. Place 1 cup of warm broth into the pot, cook and stir for 2 minutes, or until most of the liquid is absorbed; add the remaining broth to the pot 1 cup at a time and cook until each cup of broth is absorbed before adding the next cup, about 2 minutes at a time. The last addition of broth will take a bit longer to absorb, about 4 minutes. 5. Remove the pot from the heat, add salt, pepper and ½ cup of cheese. Serve with the remaining cheese, the chives and lemon wedges (optional).
Per Serving: Calories 371; Fat 6.52g; Sodium 494mg; Carbs 65.02g; Fiber 11.5g; Sugar 6.18g; Protein 15.63g

Porcini Mushroom Risotto

Prep time: 15 minutes | Cook time: 50 minutes | Serves: 3-4

1 ounce dried porcini mushrooms soaked for 30 minutes in 1 cup of water that has just been boiled	3 cloves garlic, peeled and minced
	1½ cups pearled barley
	½ cup dry white wine
3 large shallots, peeled and finely diced	3 to 4 cups low-sodium vegetable broth
8 ounces cremini mushrooms, sliced	¼ cup nutritional yeast, optional
2 sage leaves, minced	Salt and freshly ground black pepper

1. Drain the porcini mushrooms, reserving the liquid. Chop the mushrooms finely and set aside. 2. In the saucepan over medium heat, sauté the shallots for 4 to 5 minutes, adding 1 tablespoon of water at a time to prevent sticking. 3. Add the cremini mushrooms and sauté for 5 more minutes, let the mushrooms brown by adding little water; add the sage, barley, garlic, and white wine and cook for 1 minute. 4. Add 2 cups vegetable stock and the 1 cup of reserved porcini soaking liquid and boil them over high heat. 5. When boiled, lower the heat to medium and cover the pan, cook the food for 25 minutes; stir in the chopped porcini mushrooms and nutritional yeast. 6. Season with salt and pepper and serve immediately.
Per Serving: Calories 274; Fat 2.46g; Sodium 1270mg; Carbs 53.1g; Fiber 9.3g; Sugar 10.82g; Protein 12.76g

Mushroom Polenta

Prep time: 30 minutes | Cook time: 15 minutes | Serves: 4-6

1 batch Basic Polenta, kept warm
1 ounce (28 g) porcini mushrooms, soaked for 30 minutes in 1 cup of water that has just been boiled, and coarsely chopped
1 shallot, peeled and minced
2 cloves garlic, peeled and minced
1-pound wild mushrooms, thinly sliced
Chopped parsley
Salt and freshly ground black pepper

1. In the saucepan, sauté the shallot and garlic for 5 minutes over a medium-low heat, adding 1 tablespoon of water at a time to prevent sticking. 2. Add the porcini mushrooms and their soaking liquid and the wild mushrooms. Cook until the mushrooms about 10 minutes are tender. Season with salt and pepper. 3. Divide the polenta among 4 serving plates, top with some of the mushrooms and garnish with parsley. Enjoy.
Per Serving: Calories 64; Fat 0.64g; Sodium 11mg; Carbs 11.78g; Fiber 1.9g; Sugar 1.96g; Protein 3.63g

Tomato and Eggplant Polenta

Prep time: 15 minutes | Cook time: 1 hour | Serves: 6-8

1 large red bell pepper, seeded and diced
1 large yellow onion, peeled and diced
2 large eggplants (about 3 pounds, 1.4 kg), stemmed and diced
2 large tomatoes, diced
8 cloves garlic, peeled and minced
1 cup chopped basil
1 batch Basic Polenta, kept warm
Salt and freshly ground black pepper

1. Preheat the oven to 350 degrees F. 2. In the saucepan, sauté the onion for 10 minutes over medium heat, adding 1 tablespoon of water at a time to prevent sticking. 3. Add eggplant, red bell pepper and garlic, cover the pan and cook for 15 minutes, stirring occasionally, adding more water as needed. 4. Mix in the tomatoes, salt and pepper, cook for 10 minutes longer. Add the basil. 5. Spoon the mixture into a baking dish and then top the mixture with the polenta; bake the food for 30 minutes. 6. When done, serve and enjoy.
Per Serving: Calories 85; Fat 0.61g; Sodium 114mg; Carbs 19.03g; Fiber 5.7g; Sugar 7.26g; Protein 2.91g

Veggie Chickpea Pilaf

Prep time: 15 minutes | Cook time: 1 hour | Serves: 4

1 large eggplant, stemmed and cut into ½-inch cubes
2 cups cooked chickpeas, or one 15-ounce (425 g) can, drained and rinsed
2 cups (480 ml) low-sodium vegetable broth
1 cup brown basmati rice
1 large yellow onion, peeled and diced small
6 cloves garlic, peeled and minced
2 jalapeño peppers, seeded and minced
1 tablespoon cumin seeds, toasted and ground
1 tablespoon ground coriander
1 teaspoon turmeric
½ cup finely chopped cilantro
¼ cup finely chopped mint
½ cup finely chopped basil
Salt

1. In the saucepan, boil the vegetable stock; add the rice and bring the mixture back to a boil over high heat; when boiled, lower the heat to medium and cover the pan, then wait for 45 minutes or until the rice is tender. 2. In another saucepan over medium heat, sauté the onion for 7 to 8 minutes, adding 1 tablespoon of water at a time to prevent sticking; add the garlic, turmeric, cumin, jalapeño peppers, coriander, eggplant and sauté them for 12 minutes until the eggplant is tender. 3. Mix in the cooked rice, chickpeas, mint, and basil. Season with salt and garnish with the cilantro. Enjoy.
Per Serving: Calories 235; Fat 8.75g; Sodium 379mg; Carbs 39.91g; Fiber 13.5g; Sugar 12.22g; Protein 11.84g

Garlicky Adzuki Beans Pilaf

Prep time: 15 minutes | Cook time: 15 minutes | Serves: 4

4 cups cooked wild rice blend
2 cups cooked adzuki beans, or one [15-ounce (425 g)] can, drained and rinsed
2 medium leeks (white and light green parts), diced and rinsed
4 green onions (white and green parts), thinly sliced
2 cloves garlic, peeled and minced
¾ teaspoon Berbere Spice Blend
Zest of 1 orange
Salt and freshly ground black pepper

1. In the saucepan, sauté the leeks for 10 minutes over medium heat, adding 1 tablespoon of water at a time to prevent sticking. 2. Add the garlic and cook for 2 minutes; add the berbere spice and cook for 30 seconds. Stir in the beans, wild rice, and orange zest and season with salt and pepper. 3. Cook the mixture until heated through. 4. Garnish with the green onions and serve.
Per Serving: Calories 229; Fat 0.87g; Sodium 18mg; Carbs 48.82g; Fiber 5.3g; Sugar 5.25g; Protein 8.72g

Lentils, Rice and Macaroni with Tomato

Prep time: 15 minutes | Cook time: 2 hours | Serves: 6

1 cup green lentils, rinsed
1 cup medium-grain brown rice
3 large tomatoes, diced small
1 cup whole-grain elbow macaroni, cooked, drained, and kept warm
1 large onion, peeled and minced
4 cloves garlic, peeled and minced
1 teaspoon ground cumin
1 teaspoon ground coriander
½ teaspoon ground allspice
½ teaspoon crushed red pepper flakes
2 tablespoons tomato paste
1 tablespoon brown rice vinegar
Salt

1. In the pot, add the lentils and 3 cups of water, then bring to boil over high heat; when boiled, reduce the heat to medium, cover the pot and wait for 40 to 45 minutes. 2. Drain any excess water from the lentils, season with salt and set aside. 3. In another saucepan, add the brown rice and 2 cups of water, cover the pan and bring the liquid to a boil over high heat; when boiled, lower the heat to medium and cook for 45 minutes longer. 4. Heat the skillet over high heat and then reduce the heat to medium; sauté the onion for 15 minutes, adding 1 tablespoon of water at a time to prevent sticking; add the garlic and sauté for 3 to 4 minutes longer. 5. Add the allspice, cumin, coriander, red pepper flakes, tomato paste and cook for 3 minutes; add the fresh tomatoes and sauté for 15 minutes or until the tomatoes start to break down. Season with the salt. 6. In a serving bowl, mix the lentils, cooked macaroni, rice, tomato mixture and brown rice vinegar, enjoy.
Per Serving: Calories 209; Fat 1.64g; Sodium 414mg; Carbs 43.46g; Fiber 3.9g; Sugar 4.08g; Protein 6.92g

Pineapple Pea Rice in Chinese Brown Sauce

Prep time: 15 minutes | Cook time: 6 minutes | Serves: 4

2 8-ounce cans pineapple chunks, drained (about 1½ cups)
4 cups cooked brown rice, fully cooled
1 medium yellow onion, peeled and thinly sliced
1 serrano chile, sliced into thin rings
4 cloves garlic, peeled and minced
½ cup Chinese Brown Sauce
½ cup cooked peas, thawed if frozen
½ cup cashews, toasted
½ cup cilantro, chopped

1. In the skillet over high heat, sauté the onion and chile for 4 to 5 minutes, adding 1 tablespoon of water at a time to prevent sticking. 2. Add the garlic and sauté for 30 seconds; add the Chinese brown sauce and cook for 30 seconds. 3. Mix in the rice, peas, pineapple, cilantro and cashews, cook them until heated through. 4. When done, serve and enjoy.
Per Serving: Calories 371; Fat 9.74g; Sodium 237mg; Carbs 64.83g; Fiber 6.1g; Sugar 9.69g; Protein 8.53g

Red Pepper and Asparagus Rice

Prep time: 15 minutes | Cook time: 6 minutes | Serves: 2

½ pound asparagus, trimmed and cut into 1-inch pieces
½ medium yellow onion, peeled and thinly sliced
½ medium red bell pepper, seeded and julienned
3 cups cooked brown rice, fully cooled
¼ cup Chinese brown sauce
Zest and juice of 1 lemon
3 tablespoons minced jalapeño pepper

1. In the skillet over high heat, sauté the onion, asparagus and red pepper for 4 to 5 minutes, adding 1 tablespoon of water at a time to prevent sticking. 2. Add the Chinese brown sauce, lemon zest and juice, jalapeño pepper and cook for another minute; add the brown rice and cook until heated through. 3. When done, serve and enjoy.
Per Serving: Calories 404; Fat 3.06g; Sodium 466mg; Carbs 85.29g; Fiber 10g; Sugar 10.26g; Protein 12.44g

Lentils and Rice with Onions

Prep time: 15 minutes | Cook time: 2 hours | Serves: 4

1½ cups green lentils, rinsed
¾ cup brown basmati rice
3 large yellow onions, peeled and diced
¾ teaspoon ground cinnamon
½ teaspoon ground allspice
Salt and freshly ground black pepper

1. In the pot, add the lentils and 5 cups of water, boil them over high heat; when boiled, lower the heat to medium and simmer for 30 minutes; add the cinnamon and allspice and cook for another 15 to 20 minutes. 2. In another medium saucepan, bring 1½ cups of water to a boil; add the rice and bring the pot to a boil again over high heat; reduce the heat to medium and cover the pan, then wait for 45 minutes. 3. In the skillet over high heat, sauté the onions for 10 minutes, adding 1 tablespoon of water at a time to prevent sticking; lower the heat to medium-low and continue cooking about 10 minutes. 4. Add the lentils and rice to the onions, mix them well and then season with salt and pepper. Serve and enjoy.
Per Serving: Calories 149; Fat 4.93g; Sodium 9mg; Carbs 28.85g; Fiber 7.4g; Sugar 4.98g; Protein 6.87g

Bean and Brown Rice Casserole

Prep time: 15 minutes | Cook time: 40 minutes | Serves: 4

3 cloves garlic, peeled and minced
1 large yellow onion, peeled and diced
1 red bell pepper, seeded and diced
1 tablespoon cumin seeds, toasted and ground
2 teaspoons ancho chile powder
2 cups cooked brown rice
2 cups cooked black beans, or one 15-ounce can, drained and rinsed
1 batch No-Cheese Sauce
Chopped cilantro
3 ears corn, kernels removed (about 2 cups)
2 medium zucchini, cut into ½-inch dice

1. Preheat the oven to 350 degrees F. 2. In the saucepan over medium heat, sauté the onion and red pepper for 7 to 8 minutes or until the onion starts to brown, adding 1 tablespoon of water at a time to prevent sticking. 3. Add the garlic and sauté for 4 minutes; add the cumin and chile powder, cook them for another 30 seconds. 4. Remove from the heat. Combine the cooked rice, black beans, zucchini, corn, and No-Cheese Sauce. 5. Spoon the mixture into a baking dish and then bake the mixture in the preheated oven for 25 minutes until bubbly. 6. Garnish with the cilantro, serve and enjoy.
Per Serving: Calories 240; Fat 2.09g; Sodium 260mg; Carbs 51.85g; Fiber 6.7g; Sugar 5.89g; Protein 7.78g

Hearty Sweet Potato and Cauliflower Pilaf

Prep time: 15 minutes | Cook time: 1 hour 15 minutes | Serves: 4

3 to 3½ cups (720 ml-840 ml) low-sodium vegetable broth
1½ cups brown basmati rice
1 large cinnamon stick
½ small head cauliflower, cut into florets
2 cloves garlic, peeled and minced
2 whole cloves
2 cardamom pods
1 medium yellow onion, peeled
and cut into ½-inch dice
1 medium carrot, peeled and cut into ½-inch dice
1 medium sweet potato, peeled and cut into ½-inch dice
1 cup peas, thawed if frozen
½ cup chopped cilantro
1 large pinch saffron, soaked in 3 tablespoons hot water
low-sodium salt

1. In the pot, boil 3 cups of the vegetable stock and then add the rice, cloves, cinnamon stick and cardamom pods. Bring the mixture back to a boil over high heat, then lower the heat to medium and cover the pot, let them cook for 45 minutes until the rice is tender. 2. Check the rice for tenderness and add more stock, if needed. Remove the cloves, cinnamon stick and cardamom pods. 3. In the saucepan over medium-high heat, sauté the onion for 7 to 8 minutes or until the onion is tender and starting to brown, adding 1 tablespoon of water at a time to prevent sticking. 4. Add the sweet potato, carrot and cook for 10 minutes; add the cauliflower, garlic and cook for 6 to 7 minutes longer, until the cauliflower is tender. 5. Add the peas, cilantro, salt, saffron and its soaking liquid, mix well. 6. Serve the dish with the cook rice.
Per Serving: Calories 241; Fat 10.16g; Sodium 141mg; Carbs 44.27g; Fiber 13.5g; Sugar 10.67g; Protein 9.66g

Healthy Vegetables and Brown Rice

Prep time: 5 minutes | Cook time: 10 minutes | Serves: 4

1 teaspoon onion powder
⅓ cup garlic vinegar
1½ tablespoons dark molasses
2 whole eggs plus 4 egg whites, lightly beaten

1 cup frozen edamame
1 teaspoon olive oil
1 cup frozen mixed vegetables
2 cups cooked brown rice

1. In a glass jar, mix up the garlic vinegar, molasses and onion powder. 2. In the skillet, heat 1 teaspoon of olive oil over medium-high heat; add the eggs and egg whites, cook them for 1 minute or until the eggs set and then cut eggs with a spatula into small pieces. 3. Add the frozen mixed vegetables and frozen edamame, cook them for 4 minutes, stirring frequently. 4. Add the brown rice and sauce over the vegetable-and-egg mixture and cook for 5 minutes longer or until heated through. 5. Serve and enjoy.
Per Serving: Calories 272; Fat 6.25g; Sodium 113mg; Carbs 38.86g; Fiber 5.9g; Sugar 8.64g; Protein 14.46g

Lemony Pea and Barley Salad

Prep time: 10 minutes | Cook time: 20 minutes | Serves: 4

1 ounce dried porcini mushrooms soaked for 30 minutes in 1 cup of water that has just been boiled
3 large shallots, peeled and finely diced
8 ounces cremini mushrooms, sliced
2 sage leaves, minced

3 cloves garlic, peeled and minced
1½ cups pearled barley
½ cup dry white wine
3 to 4 cups low-sodium vegetable broth
¼ cup nutritional yeast, optional
Salt and freshly ground black pepper

1. In the saucepan, bring water to a boil in a saucepan; add the barley and cover the pan, then simmer them for 10 minutes until the water is absorbed. 2. Turn off the heat and let the barley rest for 5 minutes. 3. Rinse the barley under cold water and mix it with the peas, parsley, onion, olive oil and lemon juice. 4. Season with sea salt and freshly ground pepper, serve and enjoy.
Per Serving: Calories 119; Fat 3.56g; Sodium 75mg; Carbs 19.22g; Fiber 4.5g; Sugar 0.91g; Protein 3.57g

Basic Polenta with Mushroom-Onion Sauce

Prep time: 15 minutes | Cook time: 30 minutes | Serves: 6

1 batch Basic Polenta, refrigerated about 2 to 3 hours
½ medium yellow onion, peeled and diced small
1 pound (454 g) cremini or button mushrooms, thinly sliced
3 cloves garlic, peeled and minced
½ teaspoon ground nutmeg
1 cup dry white wine

1 tablespoon minced thyme
½ cup Kalamata olives, pitted and chopped
1 batch No-Cheese Sauce
Chopped parsley
Zest and juice of 1 lemon
Salt and freshly ground black pepper

1. Preheat the oven to 350 degrees F. 2. Slice the polenta into 6 rectangles and cut each piece in half on the diagonal to form triangles, then arrange them to the baking pan. 3. Bake the food in the preheated oven for 15 minutes or until heated through. 4. In the saucepan over medium heat, sauté the onion and mushrooms for 7 to 8 minutes, adding 1 tablespoon of water at a time to prevent sticking. 5. Add the thyme, garlic and nutmeg, sauté them for 2 minutes; add the wine and then simmer until the liquid is reduced by half. 6. Mix in the lemon zest and juice, No-Cheese Sauce and olives, simmer them for 5 minutes. Season with salt and pepper. 7. In the center of each serving plate, put 2 polenta triangles and spoon some of the sauce over the polenta; garnish with the parsley and enjoy.
Per Serving: Calories 159; Fat 9.7g; Sodium 407mg; Carbs 16.44g; Fiber 6g; Sugar 2.58g; Protein 9.66g

Berries Salad

Prep time: 10 minutes | Cook time: 1 hour 50 minutes | Serves: 4

2½ cups wheat berries, soaked overnight
¼ cup plus 2 tablespoons maple syrup
¼ cup peanut milk
2 avocados, peeled, seeded and diced

½ cup chopped tarragon
1 cooked taro
½ cup fruit-sweetened dried raspberries
2 tablespoons minced parsley
Salt and freshly ground black pepper to taste

1. In the saucepan, boil 5 cups of water and then stir in the wheat berries. 2. Return to a boil over high heat, then lower the heat to medium and cover the pan, cook the berries for 1-¾ hours or until the wheat berries are softened. 3. Drain off the excess water from the pan and rinse the berries until cool. 4. In a large bowl, mix up the other ingredients and add in the cooled wheat berries, blend them well and then chill for 1 hour. 5. Enjoy.
Per Serving: Calories 585; Fat 15.94g; Sodium 24mg; Carbs 102.23g; Fiber 12.1g; Sugar 20.53g; Protein 11.11g

Vegetable Mix and Brown Basmati Rice

Prep time: 15 minutes | Cook time: 1 hour | Serves: 4-6

2 cups brown basmati rice
2 teaspoons turmeric
1 teaspoon ground coriander
1 teaspoon ground cumin
½ teaspoon ground cinnamon
½ teaspoon ground cardamom
low-sodium salt
For the vegetables:
2 teaspoons ground coriander
1 teaspoon whole cumin seeds, toasted and ground

1 medium yellow onion, peeled and diced
2 stalks broccoli, cut into florets
1 small head cauliflower, cut into florets (about 3 cups)
2 medium carrots, peeled and thinly sliced
6 cloves garlic, peeled and minced
2 tablespoons grated ginger
½ cup golden raisins
¼ cup sliced almonds, toasted

To make the rice: 1. In the saucepan, boil 4 cups of water; add the rice and bring the liquid back to a boil over high heat. 2. Lower the heat to medium, cover the pan and cook the rice for 40 minutes. 3. Stir in the cardamom, turmeric, coriander, cumin, cinnamon, salt and cook for 5 longer until the rice is tender.
To make the vegetables: 1. In a larger pan, sauté the onion for 8 minutes over medium heat, adding 1 tablespoon of water at a time to prevent sticking. 2. Add the cauliflower, broccoli, carrots and sauté them for 8 to 10 minutes until the vegetables are tender. 3. Add the garlic, cumin, coriander, ginger and sauté for 5 minutes longer. 4. Add the raisins, cooked rice, and almonds, season with additional salt if needed and enjoy.
Per Serving: Calories 210; Fat 8.9g; Sodium 31mg; Carbs 39.48g; Fiber 10.8g; Sugar 10.45g; Protein 8.45g

Quinoa Apricots Pilaf

Prep time: 15 minutes | Cook time: 15 minutes | Serves: 4

2 shallots, peeled and diced small
1 medium red bell pepper, seeded and diced small
¼ cup pistachios, toasted
4 cups cooked quinoa, made with 4 cups low-sodium vegetable broth

¾ cup dried unsulfured apricots, chopped
3 tablespoons chopped mint
Zest and juice of 1 orange
½ teaspoon crushed red pepper flakes
Low-sodium salt

1. In the saucepan, sauté the shallots and red bell pepper for 10 minutes over medium heat, adding 1 tablespoon of water at a time to prevent sticking. 2. Add the quinoa, mint, orange zest and juice, apricots and crushed red pepper flakes and sauté them for 5 minutes until heated through; season with the low-sodium salt. 3. Garnish with the pistachios and serve.
Per Serving: Calories 345; Fat 7.25g; Sodium 231mg; Carbs 61.72g; Fiber 8.3g; Sugar 18.58g; Protein 11.1g

Herbed Chicken Thighs

Prep time: 10 minutes | Cook time: 8 hours | Serves: 6

6 bone-in, skin-on chicken thighs
1 cup uncooked brown rice
3 cups (720 ml) poultry broth
1 teaspoon garlic powder
1 teaspoon ground cumin
1 teaspoon dried oregano

2 onions, chopped
1 (14-ounce) can diced tomatoes and peppers, drained
¼ teaspoon sea salt
⅛ teaspoon cayenne pepper

1. In the slow cooker, mix up all the ingredients. 2. Let the food cook on low for 8 hours. 3. Remove the skin from the chicken, then serve.
Per Serving: Calories 347; Fat 8.55g; Sodium 901mg; Carbs 39.62g; Fiber 5.3g; Sugar 9.93g; Protein 23.91g

Orange Chicken Breasts with Brown Rice

Prep time: 15 minutes | Cook time: 10 minutes | Serves: 2

2 (4-ounce) boneless, skinless chicken breasts
½ cup coarsely chopped shiitake mushroom
1 tablespoon sesame oil
1 tablespoon extra-virgin olive oil
½ teaspoon grated orange zest

1 large clove garlic, minced
¼ teaspoon ground ginger
¼ cup chopped white onion
¼ teaspoon grated lemon zest
¼ teaspoon cracked black pepper
Juice of ½ orange
4 cups spinach
1 cup cooked brown rice

1. Remove the fat from the chicken breast and cut the chicken breast into small cubes. 2. In a medium saucepan, heat sesame oil and olive oil over medium heat; add the mushrooms, onions and garlic, sauté them for 1 minute; 3. Add the chicken cubes and then sprinkle with pepper, ginger, orange zest and lemon zest to taste, cook them for about 4 to 5 minutes until the chicken is browned; pour the orange juice, stir the chicken and scrape off the bottom of the pan to add flavor. 4. Add the spinach and then remove the pot from the heat, immediately cover the pan and let the spinach steam for 3 to 4 minutes. 5. Divide the cooked brown rice into two serving plates or bowls, add the dish over the rice and enjoy.

Per Serving: Calories 491; Fat 18.8g; Sodium 519mg; Carbs 30.87g; Fiber 3.8g; Sugar 3.74g; Protein 53.04g

Onion Millet Loaf

Prep time: 15 minutes | Cook time: 1 hour | Serves: 6

2½ cups low-sodium vegetable stock or water
¾ cup millet
1 large yellow onion, peeled and diced small
4 cloves garlic, peeled and minced
1 tablespoon sage
1 tablespoon thyme
½ teaspoon freshly ground black

pepper
⅛ teaspoon ground nutmeg
2 tablespoons mellow white miso, dissolved in ¼ cup hot water
¼ cup nutritional yeast, optional
¼ to ¾ cup Tomato Sauce
½ cup low-sodium ketchup, optional
Low-sodium salt

1. Preheat the oven to 350 degrees F. 2. In the saucepan, boil the vegetable stock over high heat; add the millet and bring the mixture back to a boil, then lower the heat to medium and cover the pan, cook for 20 minutes until the millet is tender. Set aside for later use. 3. In another pan, sauté the onion for 7 to 8 minutes over medium heat, adding 1 tablespoon of water at a time to prevent sticking; add the garlic, thyme, sage, nutmeg, and black pepper and cook for another minute; add the nutritional yeast, miso, and ¼ cup of tomato sauce and mix well. 4. Mix in the millet and season with salt. 5. Spoon the mixture into a nonstick loaf pan and press it firmly into the pan, top with another ½ cup of tomato sauce and then bake the food in the oven for 30 minutes. 6. When done, let the food rest for 10 minutes before slicing.
Per Serving: Calories 175; Fat 1.66g; Sodium 436mg; Carbs 34.22g; Fiber 4.4g; Sugar 8.87g; Protein 7.4g

Palatable Pasta with Greens and Beans

Prep time: 30 minutes | Cook time: 5-10 minutes | Serves: 5

For the pasta
½ teaspoon salt
8 ounces uncooked linguine
1 tablespoon extra-virgin olive oil
2 garlic cloves, minced
1 bunch Swiss chard, trimmed, stems chopped, leaves sliced into thin ribbons
1 (15-ounce) can no-salt-added

white beans, rinsed and drained
Zest and juice of 1 lemon (about 3 tablespoons juice)
¼ cup grated Parmesan cheese
Freshly ground black pepper
For the sauce
1 cup part-skim ricotta cheese
¾ cup chopped walnuts
¼ cup grated Parmesan cheese
1 garlic clove, peeled

1. Pour the water into a large pot till it is full. Add the salt to boil. Cook the linguine to al dente base on the package directions. Spoon out ½ cup of the pasta cooking water, then drain the pasta, leave it in the colander. 2. Take the pot back to the stovetop and set medium heat to cook, add and sauté the olive oil, garlic, and chard stems for 2-3 minutes. And then add the chard leaves. Cook just till wilted or 2 minutes. 3. To make the sauce, blend and mix the ricotta cheese, walnuts, Parmesan cheese, and garlic in a food processor or blender. Gently add the reserved ½ cup of cooking water to thin the sauce. 4. Put the pasta and sauce and white beans to the pot. Stir and heat completely. 5. Add the lemon zest and juice. Top with the Parmesan cheese and pepper. Serve the dish.
Per Serving: Calories 329; Fat 16.29g; Sodium 513mg; Carbs 38.39g; Fiber 5.5g; Sugar 25.53g; Protein 12.88g

Slow-Cooked Turkey with Wild Rice

Prep time: 10 minutes | Cook time: 8 hours | Serves: 6

1-pound boneless, skinless turkey thighs, cut into 1-inch chunks
1 cup uncooked wild rice
1 cup fresh or frozen cranberries
Zest and juice of 1 orange
1 onion, chopped
3 cups poultry broth
1 teaspoon garlic powder
1 teaspoon dried thyme
½ teaspoon sea salt
¼ teaspoon freshly ground black pepper

1. In the slow cooker, mix up all the ingredients except for the orange juice. 2. Cover and cook them on low for 8 hours. 3. Stir in the fresh orange juice and serve.
Per Serving: Calories 297; Fat 2.5g; Sodium 754mg; Carbs 49.15g; Fiber 2.2g; Sugar 23.79g; Protein 21.24g

Lemony Sweet Potato and Barley Pilaf

Prep time: 15 minutes | Cook time: 55 minutes | Serves: 4

3½ cups (840 ml) low-sodium vegetable broth
1½ cups pearled barley
1 large sweet potato (about ¾ pound, 340 g), peeled and diced small
1 medium onion, peeled and chopped
2 cloves garlic, peeled and minced
¼ cup minced tarragon
zest and juice of 1 lemon
low-sodium salt and freshly ground black pepper

1. Sauté the onion in the large saucepan over medium heat for 6 minutes, adding 1 tablespoon of water at a time to prevent sticking. 2. Add the garlic and sauté for 3 minutes; add the vegetable stock, barley and bring them to boil over high heat, then lower the heat to medium and cover the pan, let the food cook for 30 minutes. 3. When the time is up, add the sweet potato and cook for 15 minutes longer until the potato and barley are tender. 4. Turn off the heat, stir in the tarragon and lemon zest and juice, season with salt and pepper. Serve and enjoy.
Per Serving: Calories 364; Fat 1.74g; Sodium 147mg; Carbs 80.43g; Fiber 15g; Sugar 11.25g; Protein 10.88g

Brown Rice and Veggie in Thai Red Curry Paste

Prep time: 15 minutes | Cook time: 7 minutes | Serves: 2

2 cups cooked brown rice, fully cooled
½ medium yellow onion, peeled and cut into ½-inch strips
2 medium carrots, peeled and cut into matchsticks
2 cups shiitake mushrooms, trimmed and thinly sliced
4 teaspoons Thai red curry paste
¼ cup slivered almonds, toasted, optional
4 green onions (white and green parts), chopped
2 large leeks (white and light green parts), thinly sliced and rinsed
Salt and freshly ground black pepper

1. Heat the skillet over high heat; add and sauté the leeks, onion,

mushrooms and carrots for 5 to 6 minutes, adding 1 tablespoon of water at a time to prevent sticking. 2. Stir in the curry paste and cook for 30 seconds more. Add the green onions, almonds, and rice and cook until heated through. 3. Season with salt and pepper, serve and enjoy.
Per Serving: Calories 372; Fat 3.58g; Sodium 95mg; Carbs 79.52g; Fiber 12.7g; Sugar 14.58g; Protein 9.62g

Vegan Black Bean Soup

Prep time: 10 minutes | Cook time: 8-10 hours | Serves: 6

1-pound dried black beans
2 (14-ounce) cans no-salt-added diced tomatoes
3 cups low-sodium vegetable broth
½ red onion, diced
1 green bell pepper, seeded and diced
1 poblano pepper, seeded and diced
2 jalapeño peppers, seeded and diced
3 tablespoons red wine vinegar
6 garlic cloves, minced
1½ tablespoons chili powder
2 teaspoons ground cumin
½ teaspoon dried oregano
½ teaspoon salt
½ teaspoon freshly ground black pepper
2 bay leaves

1. In the large bowl, add the beans and 2 quarts of water, soak the beans overnight at room temperature. Next day, drain the rinse the beans. 2. In the slow cooker, add all the ingredients. 3. Cover and cook on high for 8 to 10 hours, then remove the bay leaves. 4. Stir and serve hot.
Per Serving: Calories 336; Fat 2.38g; Sodium 344mg; Carbs 63.24g; Fiber 16.6g; Sugar 10.85g; Protein 19.93g

Slow-cooked White Beans with Vegetables

Prep time: 5 minutes | Cook time: 7-8 hours | Serves: 8

1-pound white beans, soaked overnight
4 cups low-sodium vegetable broth
1 (6-ounce) can no-salt-added tomato paste
1 cup water
3 carrots, diced
1 sweet onion, diced
2 red, orange, yellow, or green bell peppers, diced
¼ cup low-sodium ketchup
¼ cup dry cooking sherry
¼ cup low-sodium tamari
¼ cup cider vinegar
2 tablespoons sugar
1 tablespoon dried marjoram
1 tablespoon dried thyme
2 teaspoons freshly ground black pepper
1 tablespoon cornstarch

1. Drain and rinse the beans. 2. In the slow cooker, combine all the ingredients except for the cornstarch. 3. Cover and cook the food on low for 7 to 8 hours; during the last 15 minutes of cooking time, stir in the cornstarch. 4. When the broth thickens, serve and enjoy.
Per Serving: Calories 105; Fat 0.92g; Sodium 112mg; Carbs 23.51g; Fiber 4.2g; Sugar 13.69g; Protein 3.52g

Hearty Wheat Berry–Edamame Pilaf

Prep time: 5 minutes | Cook time: 6-8 hours | Serves: 12

1 cup wheat berries
1 cup wild rice
4 cups low-sodium vegetable broth
2 cups frozen shelled edamame
1 medium red bell pepper, chopped

1 red onion, finely chopped
4 garlic cloves, minced
1 tablespoon extra-virgin olive oil
1 teaspoon dried thyme
Freshly ground black pepper

1. Rinse and drain the wheat berries and wild rice. 2. In the slow cooker, mix up all the ingredients. 3. Cover and cook the food on low for 6 to 8 hours on low until the liquid is absorbed. 4. Serve and enjoy with a green salad.
Per Serving: Calories 142; Fat 2.56g; Sodium 60mg; Carbs 24.92g; Fiber 4.1g; Sugar 4.13g; Protein 7.16g

Creole Black-Eyed Peas with Tomatoes

Prep time: 5 minutes | Cook time: 7-8 hours | Serves: 8

6 cups low-sodium vegetable broth
1-pound dried black-eyed peas
6 celery stalks, chopped
2 medium tomatoes, diced
1 (4-ounce) can diced jalapeño peppers
1 onion, diced

6 garlic cloves, minced
1 or 2 canned chipotle peppers in adobo sauce, chopped
1 tablespoon freshly squeezed lemon juice
1 tablespoon Creole seasoning, or more to taste

1. In the slow cooker, combine all of the ingredients. 2. Cover and cook on low for 7 to 8 hours. 3. Serve and you can enjoy this dish with the cooked brown rice.
Per Serving: Calories 85; Fat 0.86g; Sodium 198mg; Carbs 17g; Fiber 3.6g; Sugar 9.64g; Protein 4.25g

Navy Bean Soup with Ham

Prep time: 10 minutes | Cook time: 8-10 hours | Serves: 8

1-pound dried navy beans
2 cups low-sodium chicken broth
1 (15-ounce) can no-salt-added diced tomatoes
8 ounces 98% fat-free, reduced-sodium ham, finely diced
3 celery ribs, diced
3 carrots, diced
1 onion, diced

3 garlic cloves, minced
1½ teaspoons onion powder
1 teaspoon dried parsley
1 teaspoon dried sage
1 teaspoon garlic powder
1 bay leaf
½ teaspoon freshly ground black pepper
½ teaspoon salt

1. In the large bowl, add the beans and 2 quarts of water, soak the beans overnight at room temperature. Next day, drain the rinse the beans. 2. In the slow cooker, add the beans and cover them with the other ingredients. 3. Cover and cook the food on low for 8 to 10 hours. 4. Use the back of a spoon to mash some of the beans against the sides of the slow cooker and stir them back into the soup, creating a creamier texture. 5. Serve hot.
Per Serving: Calories 81; Fat 1.83g; Sodium 551mg; Carbs 10.17g; Fiber 3.3g; Sugar 3.7g; Protein 7.67g

Slow-Cooked Navy Beans

Prep time: 10 minutes | Cook time: 7-8 hours | Serves: 8

1-pound dry navy beans, soaked overnight
6 cups water
1 large sweet onion, diced
1 medium yellow bell pepper, diced
½ cup low-sodium ketchup
¼ cup maple syrup
2 tablespoons molasses

1 tablespoon extra-virgin olive oil
1 teaspoon dried mustard
¼ teaspoon garlic powder
2 teaspoons smoked paprika
1 tablespoon apple cider vinegar
Freshly ground black pepper

1. Drain and rinse the soaked beans. 2. In the slow cooker, combine all the ingredients except for vinegar and pepper. 3. Cover and cook on low for 7 to 8 hours. 4. Stir in the vinegar and season with the pepper just before serving.
Per Serving: Calories 276; Fat 1.81g; Sodium 39mg; Carbs 54.11g; Fiber 9.6g; Sugar 17.24g; Protein 13.54g

Onion, Carrot and Lima Bean Casserole

Prep time: 5 minutes | Cook time: 7-8 hours | Serves: 8

1-pound dried lima beans, soaked overnight
1 (28-ounce) can no-salt-added tomatoes, diced
1 cup finely chopped sweet potato
1 medium carrot, finely

chopped
1 onion, finely chopped
4 garlic cloves, minced
1 tablespoon dried mustard
½ teaspoon freshly ground black pepper
2 cups water

1. Rinse the soaked beans in cold water and then drain. 2. In the slow cooker, combine all the ingredients; be certain that the water fully covers the ingredients and you can add more if needed. 3. Cover and cook the food on low for 7 to 8 hours. 4. Serve warm.
Per Serving: Calories 51; Fat 0.68g; Sodium 43mg; Carbs 11.06g; Fiber 4g; Sugar 5.59g; Protein 2.16g

Red Beans with Lime Wedges

Prep time: 5 minutes | Cook time: 7-8 hours | Serves: 8

1 cup dried red beans, soaked overnight
4 cups low-sodium chicken broth
1 (14.5-ounce) can light coconut milk
1½ cups long-grain basmati white rice
1 large onion, finely diced

2 garlic cloves, minced
1 teaspoon red pepper flakes
½ teaspoon coconut extract (optional)
1 to 2 tablespoons freshly squeezed lime juice
2 limes, cut into wedges, for serving

1. Drain and rinse the soaked beans. 2. In the slow cooker, mix up all the ingredients except for the lime juice and lime wedges. 3. Cover and cook the beans for 7 to 8 hours on low. 4. When the time is up, stir in the lime juice. 5. With the lime wedges on the side, enjoy this dish.
Per Serving: Calories 354; Fat 13.48g; Sodium 50mg; Carbs 49.24g; Fiber 5.5g; Sugar 3.44g; Protein 11.55g

Black Beans and Vegetables Casserole

Prep time: 10 minutes | Cook time: 6-7 hours | Serves: 8

1-pound dried black beans, picked over and rinsed	1 green bell pepper, chopped
3 cups water	1 large onion, chopped
2 cups low-sodium vegetable broth	6 garlic cloves, minced
1 (14.5-ounce) can no-salt-added diced tomatoes	2 bay leaves
	1 teaspoon ground cumin
1 (4-ounce) can chopped green chiles (more or less to taste)	1 teaspoon dried oregano
	Freshly ground black pepper
	2 tablespoons freshly squeezed lime juice (optional)

1. Combine all the ingredient except for the lime juice in the slow cooker. 2. Cover and cook on low for 6 to 7 hours, until the beans are tender. 3. Discard the bay leaves and add the lime juice (optional) before serving.
Per Serving: Calories 234; Fat 1.3g; Sodium 81mg; Carbs 44.39g; Fiber 1g; Sugar 6.01g; Protein 13.96g

Ranch-Style Pinto Beans with Onion

Prep time: 10 minutes | Cook time: 7-8 hours | Serves: 8

1-pound dried pinto beans, soaked overnight	1 tablespoon ancho chili powder
5 cups low-sodium beef broth	1 teaspoon chili powder
1 cup low-sodium tomato sauce	1 teaspoon apple cider vinegar
1 medium white onion, diced	1 teaspoon ground cumin
1 jalapeño pepper, seeded, and finely diced	1 packed teaspoon brown sugar
	1 teaspoon smoked paprika
4 garlic cloves, minced	½ teaspoon dried oregano
	Freshly ground black pepper

1. Drain and rinse the soaked beans. 2. In the slow cooker, combine all the ingredients except for the pepper. 3. Cover and cook the food on low for 7 to 8 hours, when done, the beans should be tender and the liquid should have thickened slightly. 4. Season with the pepper and serve warm.
Per Serving: Calories 155; Fat 4.68g; Sodium 90mg; Carbs 23.86g; Fiber 3g; Sugar 4.86g; Protein 8.5g

Quinoa and Vegetables with Basil

Prep time: 10 minutes | Cook time: 6-7 hours | Serves: 8

2 cups quinoa, rinsed and drained	1 cup fresh green beans, chopped
4 cups or low-sodium vegetable broth	2 garlic cloves, minced
	Freshly ground black pepper
1 medium onion, chopped	1 teaspoon chopped fresh basil, for garnish
1 medium red bell pepper, chopped	
2 medium carrots, chopped	

1. In the slow cooker, stir all the ingredients except for the basil to combine. 2. Cover and cook the food on low for 6 to 7 hours, until the vegetables are tender and the liquid is absorbed into the quinoa. 3. Garnish the dish with the fresh basil and enjoy.
Per Serving: Calories 203; Fat 3.19g; Sodium 84mg; Carbs 37.07g; Fiber 5.1g; Sugar 5.66g; Protein 7.91g

Garlic Veggie Lentils

Prep time: 15 minutes | Cook time: 7-8 hours | Serves: 8

3 cups dried lentils	2 leeks, chopped
5 cups low-sodium vegetable broth	8 garlic cloves, minced
	2 large carrots, chopped
1 (28-ounce) can no-salt-added diced tomatoes	2 bay leaves
	1 teaspoon dried thyme
1 large onion, chopped	Freshly ground black pepper

1. Discard any stones or impurities among the lentils and then rinse them under cold water in a fine-mesh strainer. 2. In the slow cooker, mix up the lentils with the broth, carrots, diced tomatoes, onion, leeks, garlic, bay leaves, thyme and pepper. 3. Cover and cook the food on low for 7 to 8 hours until the lentils are tender and the sauce has thickened. 4. Discard the bay leaf before serving.
Per Serving: Calories 112; Fat 1.1g; Sodium 119mg; Carbs 24.05g; Fiber 4.6g; Sugar 9.69g; Protein 5.81g

Tasty Chickpea Risotto

Prep time: 10 minutes | Cook time: 6-7 hours | Serves: 8

5 cups low-sodium vegetable broth	small pieces
	4 garlic cloves, minced
2 cups hulled barley, rinsed	1 teaspoon dried thyme
1 (15-ounce) can chickpeas, drained and rinsed	1½ tablespoons freshly squeezed lemon juice
1 cup water	⅓ cup grated Parmesan cheese
3 carrots, minced	4 tablespoons chopped fresh parsley, for garnish (optional)
1 onion, finely chopped	
½ head cauliflower, cut into	

1. In addition to the lemon juice, Parmesan cheese and parsley, combine all the ingredients in the slow cooker. 2. Cover and cook the food on low for 6 to 7 hours, until the barley is tender and has absorbed most of the liquid. 3. When done, stir in the Parmesan cheese and lemon juice; garnish with the parsley and enjoy.
Per Serving: Calories 298; Fat 3.19g; Sodium 260mg; Carbs 59.75g; Fiber 12.1g; Sugar 9.71g; Protein 10.84g

Wild Rice with Mushrrom and Pecans

Prep time: 10 minutes | Cook time: 6-8 hours | Serves: 8

3 cups wild rice, rinsed and drained	2 cups sliced mushrooms
	2 garlic cloves, minced
1 tablespoon extra-virgin olive oil	1 teaspoon dried thyme
	Freshly ground black pepper
6 cups low-sodium vegetable broth	½ cup chopped pecans
	1 tablespoon fresh rosemary
¾ cup finely chopped shallots	

1. Add the wild rice and oil to the slow cooker and stir until the grains are well coated. 2. Add the other ingredients except for the pecans and rosemary and stir well. 3. Cover and cook the food on low for 6 to 8 hours; when done, the rice should be tender. 4. Stir in the pecans and fresh rosemary, serve and enjoy.
Per Serving: Calories 307; Fat 6.5g; Sodium 125mg; Carbs 54.73g; Fiber 5.6g; Sugar 7.65g; Protein 11.45g

Multi-Type Beans

Prep time: 10 minutes | Cook time: 7-8 hours | Serves: 8

6 cups low-sodium vegetable broth
1 (15-ounce) can lima beans, drained and rinsed
1 (14.5-ounce) can fire-roasted tomatoes
1 cup dried kidney beans, soaked overnight
1 cup dried pinto beans, soaked overnight

1 large sweet onion, chopped
1 medium red bell pepper, chopped
½ cup low-sodium ketchup
⅓ cup loosely packed brown sugar
1 tablespoon Dijon mustard
1 tablespoon apple cider vinegar
Freshly ground black pepper

1. Combine all the ingredients in the slow cooker. 2. Cover and cook on low for 7 to 8 hours, when done, the beans should be tender. 3. Serve warm.
Per Serving: Calories 235; Fat 2.34g; Sodium 346mg; Carbs 45.42g; Fiber 8.7g; Sugar 17.2g; Protein 10.97g

Simple Northern Beans

Prep time: 10 minutes | Cook time: 7-8 hours | Serves: 8

6 cups water
1-pound dried great northern beans
2 celery ribs, chopped
1 large onion, chopped

4 garlic cloves, minced
2 bay leaves
¼ teaspoon freshly ground black pepper

1. Rinse the beans well and pick them over. Discard any small stones among the beans. 2. Combine all the ingredients in the slow cooker and stir, then cover and cook the food on low for 7 to 8 hours; when done, the beans should be tender. 3. Freeze the beans in airtight containers, use them when you need them.
Per Serving: Calories 207; Fat 0.73g; Sodium 33mg; Carbs 38.53g; Fiber 12.3g; Sugar 2.43g; Protein 12.89g

Bulgur and Lentils

Prep time: 10 minutes | Cook time: 7-8 hours | Serves: 8

1 cup lentils
6 cups low-sodium vegetable broth
4 medium tomatoes, chopped with juices (about 3 cups)
2 cups bulgur wheat
1 large onion, chopped
4 garlic cloves, minced

1 teaspoon ground cumin
2 tablespoons pitted, chopped Kalamata olives
2 ounces crumbled reduced-fat feta cheese
Chopped fresh mint (optional)

1. Discard any debris among the lentils, then rinse and drain them well. 2. In the slow cooker, mix up the lentils with the broth, tomatoes, bulgur wheat, onion, garlic and cumin. 3. Cover and cook on low for 7 to 8 hours, when done, the lentils and bulgur should be tender. 4. Garnish with the olives, feta cheese and fresh mint (optional) before serving.
Per Serving: Calories 127; Fat 2.71g; Sodium 193mg; Carbs 23.06g; Fiber 4.3g; Sugar 8.12g; Protein 5.91g

Herbed Mushroom Rice

Prep time: 10 minutes | Cook time: 6-7 hours | Serves: 8

4 cups low-sodium beef broth
2 cups water
2 cups long-grain brown rice
1 (15-ounce) can chickpeas, drained and rinsed
1 cup sliced button mushrooms
1 cup sliced baby portobello mushrooms

½ cup dried shiitake mushrooms
¼ cup dry cooking sherry
4 garlic cloves, minced
1 tablespoon extra-virgin olive oil
1 teaspoon dried thyme
1 teaspoon dried rosemary
Freshly ground black pepper

1. In the slow cooker, mix up all the ingredients. 2. Cover the cooker and cook the food on low for 6 to 7 hours, until the rice is tender. 3. When done, serve and enjoy.
Per Serving: Calories 324; Fat 5.91g; Sodium 134mg; Carbs 57.87g; Fiber 4.9g; Sugar 3.31g; Protein 12.49g

Farro Pea Risotto

Prep time: 10 minutes | Cook time: 6-7 hours | Serves: 8

5 cups low-sodium vegetable broth
2 cups whole farro
2 cups frozen peas
1 cup sliced button mushrooms
1 large leek, white and light green parts only, halved and thinly sliced

4 garlic cloves, minced
1 tablespoon extra-virgin olive oil
Freshly ground black pepper
⅓ cup grated Parmesan cheese
½ cup fresh parsley, chopped

1. In the slow cooker, combine all the ingredients except for the parsley and cheese. 2. Cover the cooker and cook the food on low for 6 to 7 hours; when done, the farro and vegetables should be tender. 3. Stir in the Parmesan cheese and garnish with the parsley before serving.
Per Serving: Calories 257; Fat 3.18g; Sodium 187mg; Carbs 50.62g; Fiber 10.1g; Sugar 5.36g; Protein 9.01g

Easy Lemony Risotto

Prep time: 10 minutes | Cook time: 5½-6½ hours | Serves: 8

5 cups low-sodium chicken broth
2 cups medium-grain brown rice
1 cup water
4 garlic cloves, minced
4 shallots, minced
1 tablespoon extra-virgin olive

oil
1 teaspoon dried thyme
½ cup fresh grated Parmesan cheese
2 teaspoons lemon zest
1 tablespoon freshly squeezed lemon juice
Freshly ground black pepper

1. In the slow cooker, mix up the short-grain brown rice with the stock, water, garlic, shallots, olive oil and thyme. 2. Cover the cooker and cook the food on low for 5 to 6 hours, until the rice is tender. 3. Add the Parmesan cheese, lemon zest and lemon juice, stir well and cook on low for 20 minutes more. 4. When the time is up, season with the pepper and serve hot.
Per Serving: Calories 236; Fat 4.69g; Sodium 176mg; Carbs 40.61g; Fiber 1.9g; Sugar 1.09g; Protein 8.61g

Chapter 3 Vegetarian and Vegan Dishes

Vitamin-Rich Sandwich

Prep time: 15 minutes | Cook time: None | Serves: 2

2 teaspoons red wine vinegar
1 teaspoon extra-virgin olive oil
¼ teaspoon ground cumin
⅓ cup shredded carrot (about 1 carrot)
2 tablespoons hummus, divided

4 slices whole-grain multigrain bread
½ avocado, sliced
6 (½-inch-thick) jarred roasted red peppers, drained well
4 green lettuce leaves

1. Mix the vinegar, oil, and cumin in a regular bowl, add and toss the carrot, put the dish aside and marinate for 10 minutes. 2. Scoop 1 tablespoon of hummus and spread it on each of two slices of bread. 3. Slice the avocado and add it between the other two pieces of bread. Put the roasted peppers and lettuce onto the top of them. 4. Add the carrot on top of the lettuce after drain it. The sandwiched is done and enjoy it.
Per Serving: Calories 418; Fat 14.98 g; Sodium 900 mg; Carbs 59 g; Fiber 14g; Sugar 16 g; Protein 15 g

Pizza Toast with Fresh Sprout

Prep time: 22 minutes | Cook time: 10 minutes | Serves: 2

1 tablespoon canola or sunflower oil
4 slices sprouted-grain bread
2 tablespoons extra-virgin olive oil
½ teaspoon stir-in garlic paste
½ cup shredded mozzarella

cheese
½ cup cherry tomatoes, thinly sliced, divided
¼ cup fresh basil leaves, stacked, rolled, and thinly sliced, divided

1. Set the oven to 400°F in advance. 2. Sprout or brush a single layer of canola or sunflower oil on a baking sheet. Put the bread and spread it out on the sheet. Toast for 2½ minutes, turn the bread and toast for over 2½ minutes. 3. At the same time, put and mix the olive oil and garlic paste in a small bowl. 4. Take out the toast, sprout or brush a little bit garlic oil on each slice of bread, add some mozzarella to each slice. Decorate the food with half of cherry tomatoes and basil. 5. Bake for about 5 minutes till the cheese is melted and crust starts to brown.
Per Serving: Calories 480; Fat 28g; Sodium 548mg; Carbs 41g; Fiber 8g; Sugar 0g; Protein 17g

Black Bean & Quinoa Salad

Prep time: 25 minutes | Cook time: 0 minutes | Serves: 4

For the salad
¾ cup uncooked quinoa
1 (15-ounce) can no-salt-added black beans, rinsed and drained
1 large tomato, chopped
½ red bell pepper, chopped
½ cup chopped red onion
1 cup frozen corn kernels (they will thaw by the time the salad is ready)

1 cup chopped fresh cilantro
⅔ cup crumbled or cubed feta cheese
For the dressing
3 tablespoons extra-virgin olive oil
2 tablespoons red wine vinegar
2 garlic cloves, minced
2 teaspoons chili powder
¼ teaspoon low-sodium salt

1. Base on the package to cook the quinoa. 2. At the same time, add and mix olive oil, vinegar, garlic, chili powder, and salt in a big bowl. 3. Add and mix the black beans, tomato, bell pepper, onion, corn, and cilantro into the dressing, and whisk to coat well. 4. As the quinoa is cooked done, add and toss the salad, put the fete cheese on its top. 5. Serve the dish at once or it is proper to refrigerate to get better flavor.
Per Serving: Calories 311; Fat 12.95g; Sodium 370mg; Carbs 38.76g; Fiber 6g; Sugar 5.08g; Protein 11.23g

Swiss Chard and Lentil Salad

Prep time: 30 minutes | Cook time: 10 minutes | Serves: 4

For the salad
¾ cup uncooked quinoa
½ cup salted shelled pumpkin seeds
1 bunch Swiss chard
1 cup blackberries
1 cup canned lentils, rinsed and drained
⅓ cup crumbled goat cheese
For the dressing

3 tablespoons extra-virgin olive oil
3 tablespoons freshly squeezed lemon juice (about 1 lemon)
2 teaspoons honey
¼ teaspoon salt
¼ teaspoon freshly ground black pepper

1. Base on the package to cook the quinoa. Prepare an empty bowl to chill. 2. Cook the quinoa as toast the pumpkin seeds for 3-4 minutes in a small, dry skillet. Pay attention to in case it is burned. Once it becomes brown, take the food out and slide it onto a plate. 3. Meanwhile, trim the chard stems and pile up the leaves, and then slice thinly and lightly. 4. Add and mix the olive oil, lemon juice, honey, salt, and pepper in a small bowl. 5. As the quinoa is done, put it to the chilled bowl, cook for 5 minutes. Decorate the chard to the quinoa, add and toss the dressing to coat completely. 6. Gradually add the blackberries, lentils, goat cheese, and toasted pumpkin seeds. Lightly mix.
Per Serving: Calories 336; Fat 17.34g; Sodium 353mg; Carbs 34.69g; Fiber 5.7g; Sugar 5.38g; Protein 14.17g

Low-Fat Lentil Salad

Prep time: 20 minutes | Cook time: 0 | Serves: 3

For the dressing
3 tablespoons apple cider vinegar
2 tablespoons extra-virgin olive oil
1 teaspoon water
1 teaspoon Dijon mustard
¼ teaspoon salt
¼ teaspoon freshly ground black pepper

For the salad
1 (15-ounce) can lentils, rinsed and drained
1 red bell pepper, seeded and chopped
½ cup frozen corn kernels, thawed
½ cup chopped snap peas
½ cup diced Jarlsberg cheese
¼ cup chopped fresh cilantro

1. Mix the vinegar, oil, water, mustard, salt, and pepper in a big bowl. 2. Put the lentils, bell pepper, corn, snap peas, cheese, and cilantro in the bowl, toss them well.
Per Serving: Calories 233; Fat 14g; Sodium 374mg; Carbs 19g; Fiber 2g; Sugar 2g; Protein 9g

Quinoa with Amazing Chile-Stuffed Tomatoes

Prep time: 10 minutes | Cook time: 25 minutes | Serves: 2

2 large tomatoes
½ teaspoon sea salt
1 teaspoon olive oil
½ sweet onion, chopped
1 teaspoon minced garlic
½ chili (such as jalapeño or serrano) pepper, minced
½ cup fresh or frozen corn kernels
1 cup cooked quinoa
1 tablespoon chopped fresh cilantro
1 teaspoon freshly squeezed lime juice
½ teaspoon ground cumin
Pinch freshly ground black pepper
2 tablespoons grated Parmesan

1. Cut the top off tomatoes. Scoop out the insides of the tomatoes, carefully keeping the shell intact. Roughly dice the half of tomatoes, and reserve the rest of tomatoes. Add some salt into the inside of the shells and then turn upside down on paper towels for drain the juice, for 30 minutes. After that, turn over the tomatoes and transfer them in a small skillet. 2. Set the 350°F to heat the oven in advance. 3. Adjust the heat to medium to cook the olive oil in a big skillet, add and sauté the onion, garlic, and chili for 2 minutes, till become softened. Put the corn and chopped tomatoes pulp and cook them for 1 minute. Add the remaining ingredients to the skillet and mix to combine. 4. Distribute the vegetable-quinoa mixture evenly between the tomatoes. 5. Roast for 20 minutes to heat the filling and tomatoes. 6. Serve hot.
Per Serving: Calories 267; Fat 5.4g; Sodium 665mg; Carbs 46.88g; Fiber 7g; Sugar 11.66g; Protein 10.16g

Fast-Cook Penne Pasta

Prep time: 10 minutes | Cook time: 0 | Serves: 4

½ cup fresh basil
¼ cup pine nuts
2 garlic cloves, chopped
¼ cup extra-virgin olive oil
¼ cup grated Parmesan cheese
Juice of ½ lemon
½ teaspoon sea salt
¼ teaspoon red pepper flakes
8 ounces' whole-wheat penne pasta, cooked according to package instructions and drained

1. Mix and combine the basil, pine nuts, garlic, olive oil, Parmesan cheese, lemon juice, and salt in a blender or food processor, pulse for 20 seconds till they are well chopped. 2. Toss the hot pasta. Serve the dish.
Per Serving: Calories 198; Fat 14.85g; Sodium 664mg; Carbs 12.88g; Fiber 2.2g; Sugar 2.35g; Protein 5.16g

Edamame-Quinoa Salad with Slivered Almonds

Prep time: 20 minutes | Cook time: 5 minutes | Serves: 3

For the salad
½ cup uncooked quinoa
1 (5-ounce) package baby kale
1 medium carrot, peeled and grated
1 (11-ounce) can no-sugar-added mandarin orange segments, drained
1 cup frozen shelled edamame,
thawed
⅓ cup slivered almonds
For the dressing
2 tablespoons canola or sunflower oil
2 tablespoons rice vinegar
1½ tablespoons reduced-sodium soy sauce
1 teaspoon minced fresh ginger

1. Base on the package to cook the quinoa. 2. To make the dressing, mix the oil, vinegar, soy sauce, and ginger in a large bowl. 3. Trim the kale. Add and combine the kale, carrot, and mandarins in a large salad bowl. 4. Once the quinoa had done, add the edamame and cover it. Set aside for a 5 minutes to steam. 5. Add and toss the quinoa, edamame, and dressing to the salad bowl. Decorate food with almonds. 6. Serve warm or chilled.
Per Serving: Calories 332; Fat 14.15g; Sodium 284mg; Carbs 42.08g; Fiber 8.1g; Sugar 13.18g; Protein 12.59g

Chickpeas Swiss Chard with Black Pepper

Prep time: 20 minutes | Cook time: 15 minutes | Serves: 4

1 bunch Swiss chard
2 tablespoons extra-virgin olive oil
1 onion, thinly sliced
2 garlic cloves, minced
1 teaspoon ground cumin
½ teaspoon red pepper flakes
1 (14-ounce) can diced tomatoes seasoned with basil
and garlic
1 (15-ounce) can no-salt-added chickpeas, rinsed and drained
Zest and juice of 1 lemon (about 3 tablespoons juice)
½ cup chopped walnuts
Freshly ground black pepper

1. Trim the chard, separate the stems and leaves. 2. Cook the oil to heat over medium heat in a big skillet. Add the onion and garlic when the pan is hot, stirring it for 3-4 minutes from time to time. 3. At same time, add the chard stems and cook it for 3-4 minutes till the onion becomes soft. 4. Add and cook the cumin and red pepper flakes, for 1 minute. And add the tomatoes with their juice and the chickpeas, cook to warm for 3-4 minutes. 5. Cover a lid after add the chard leaves, cook till wilted for 2 minutes. 6. Turn off the heat. Add the lemon zest and juice, walnuts, and pepper.
Per Serving: Calories 248; Fat 11.97g; Sodium 207mg; Carbs 29.01g; Fiber 9g; Sugar 7.33g; Protein 9.79g

Cream Soup with Almond

Prep time: 30 minutes | Cook time: 15-20 minutes | Serves: 4

1 tablespoon canola or sunflower oil
1 onion, chopped
2 cups stir-fry vegetables, fresh or frozen
1 tablespoon grated fresh ginger
2 teaspoons red or green curry paste
1 teaspoon ground turmeric
1 (14-ounce) can diced no-salt-added tomatoes
1 (15-ounce) can no-salt-added-chickpeas, rinsed and drained
¼ cup smooth almond butter
2 cups reduced-sodium vegetable broth

1. Cook the oil to heat over medium-high heat in a big skillet. As it is hot, cook the onion for 4-5 minutes, till it becomes translucent. 2. Add and cook stir-fry vegetables, for 3- 4 minutes. Then add and cook the ginger, curry paste, and turmeric, and cook for 1 more minute. 3. Stir and boil to the tomatoes with their juice, chickpeas, almond butter, and broth. Lower the heat and simmer, stirring occasionally, for 5- 10 minutes, till warmed completely.
Per Serving: Calories 348; Fat 15.57g; Sodium 319mg; Carbs 42.08g; Fiber 13.1g; Sugar 10.89g; Protein 14.35g

Crispy Quesadillas with Black Bean

Prep time: 25 minutes | Cook time: 4 minutes | Serves: 4

1 (15-ounce) can no-salt-added black beans, rinsed and drained
¼ cup lower-sodium store-bought salsa
¾ cup shredded Cheddar cheese, divided

1 red bell pepper, seeded and chopped, divided
2 tablespoons canola or sunflower oil, divided
4 large, whole-grain tortillas

1. Mix the beans and salsa together in a food processor. Or by using a fork and a potato masher to mash them in a large bowl. 2. ¼ of the bean mixture (about ½ cup) need to spreading over each tortilla. Drizzle each with 3 tablespoons of cheese and ¼ of the bell pepper. And then fold in half. 3. Heat a large, heavy skillet over medium heat in advance. Brush 1 tablespoon of oil to the skillet. Put the first two quesadillas in the skillet. Cover and cook for 2 minutes till their bottom become crispy. Flip to cook for over 2 minutes until the other side is done. 4. Cook the remaining two quesadillas by using the rest of 1 tablespoon oil, let the first two warm in the oven if you want.
Per Serving: Calories 342; Fat 19.72g; Sodium 496mg; Carbs 28.73g; Fiber 2.7g; Sugar 2.9g; Protein 12.96g

Pinto Beans and Rice with Cheese Pinto Beans

Prep time: 25 minutes | Cook time: 8 minutes | Serves: 3

¾ cup uncooked parboiled brown rice
2 teaspoons extra-virgin olive oil
1 cup fresh or frozen chopped onion
1 (15-ounce) can no-salt-added pinto beans, rinsed and drained
1 (14-ounce) can no-salt-added diced tomatoes

⅔ cup spicy salsa
1 cup frozen broccoli florets
1 tablespoon freshly squeezed lime juice
⅔ cup shredded aged Cheddar cheese
½ teaspoon red pepper flakes (optional)

1. Base on the package to cook the rice. 2. Heat the oil over medium-high heat in a big skillet. Add and cook the onion till soft, for 4-5 minutes. Then add and boil the beans, tomatoes with their juice, and salsa. 3. When the water boiled, add the broccoli, lower the heat and simmer for 2-3 minutes. Transfer the broccoli when it is crisp-tender but keeps bright green. 4. Add the rice when it is cooked, whisk the lime juice, decorate the dish with shredded Cheddar and red pepper flakes (if needed).
Per Serving: Calories 395; Fat 13.69g; Sodium 658mg; Carbs 55.95g; Fiber 9.3g; Sugar 9.68g; Protein 15.83g

Tomatoes & Spinach Polenta

Prep time: 25 minutes | Cook time: 15 minutes | Serves: 3

1 tablespoon extra-virgin olive oil
1 small yellow onion, chopped
2 garlic cloves, minced
1 teaspoon dried thyme
1 (15-ounce) can no-salt-added black beans, rinsed and drained
1 (14-ounce) can no-salt-added

diced tomatoes
⅔ cup cornmeal (also called corn grits)
2⅔ cups water, divided
1 bunch spinach, large stems removed
½ cup grated Parmesan cheese

1. Set the medium heat to heat the oil in a large sauté pan. Add and sauté the onion, garlic, and thyme for 3-5 minutes till the onion is soft. Add the beans and the tomatoes with their juice, and simmer over a low heat. Cook the polenta. 2. Mix and combine the cornmeal with ⅔ cup of water in a small bowl. Set aside. 3. Boil the rest 2 cups of water over high heat in a small saucepan, lower the heat and stir the cornmeal-water mixture. Stir occasionally till the polenta becomes smooth and creamy-liked for 10 minutes, add more water if needed. 4. Stir the spinach into the beans and tomatoes, cover a lid and cook till the spinach is wilted for 2 minutes. Mix to corporate. 5. Scoop the polenta into bowls, decorate the beans, tomatoes, and spinach on the top. Drizzle with the parmesan.
Per Serving: Calories 288; Fat 8.33g; Sodium 446mg; Carbs 43.53g; Fiber 7.4g; Sugar 4.42g; Protein 12.46g

Tasty Fried Rice with Peanut

Prep time: 20 minutes | Cook time: 8 minutes | Serves: 4

2 tablespoons reduced-sodium soy sauce
3 tablespoons rice vinegar
1 tablespoon sugar
5 large eggs
2 tablespoons peanut oil
3 cups cooked brown rice

½ cup frozen peas
1 (14-ounce) bag coleslaw mix
1 teaspoon minced fresh ginger
3 garlic cloves, chopped
½ cup roughly chopped lightly salted peanuts

1. Add and combine the soy sauce, vinegar, and sugar in a small bowl. Set aside. 2. Crack and whisk the eggs into a bowl. 3. Set the high heat to heat the oil in a skillet. As it is hot, add and fry the rice for 2 minutes. Cook the peas and coleslaw mix for 3 minutes, and then mix the ginger and garlic and cook for 1 more minute. 4. Lower the heat to medium, make the vegetables and rice to the side, add the eggs. Stir to cook till slightly scrambled. 5. Pour sauce over the rice and eggs and mix to combine well. Top the food with peanuts.
Per Serving: Calories 678; Fat 44.42g; Sodium 248mg; Carbs 50.76g; Fiber 7.8g; Sugar 6.59g; Protein 23.73g

Rich-Vitamin Bowl with Farro

Prep time: 30 minutes | Cook time: 40 minutes | Serves: 4

1 (12-ounce) package fresh or frozen cubed butternut squash
1 tablespoon canola or sunflower oil
⅛ teaspoon salt
½ cup uncooked farro
4 cups mixed greens, torn into bite-size pieces

1 red, yellow, or orange bell pepper, seeded and chopped
¾ cup hummus
1 (15-ounce) can no-salt-added chickpeas, rinsed and drained
½ cup sunflower seeds
½ cup pickled beets, chopped

1. Set the oven heat to 420°F in advance. Cover a piece of parchment paper over a rimmed baking sheet. Chill a large salad bowl in the freezer. 2. Add and combine the squash with oil in a big bowl, drizzle with the salt. Plate and spread out the squash on the baking sheet. Bake for 18-25 minutes till the squash becomes soft, kneading every 10 minutes to prevent it from burning. (Fresh ones needs longer time to frozen.) 3. Base on the package to cook the farro. 4. Plate the cooked farro to the chilled bowl, put it aside to cool for 5 minutes. Add and mix the greens, bell pepper, hummus, chickpeas, and sunflower seeds. 5. Decorate the dish with the beets and baked squash.
Per Serving: Calories 508; Fat 19.38g; Sodium 363mg; Carbs 71.78g; Fiber 16g; Sugar 21.41g; Protein 18.64g

Parmesan Orzo with Sweet Leek

Prep time: 25 minutes | Cook time: 10-12 minutes | Serves: 4

2 tablespoons extra-virgin olive oil	Zest and juice of 1 lemon (about 3 tablespoons juice)
1 garlic clove, minced	1 (15-ounce) can butter beans, rinsed and drained
1-pound leeks (white and very light green parts only), thinly sliced	2 tablespoons fresh thyme leaves or 1 teaspoon dried
½ red bell pepper	½ cup grated Parmesan cheese
¾ cup uncooked orzo	¼ cup pine nuts

1. Adjust the heat to medium and heat the olive oil in a large, nonstick skillet. Once it becomes hot, add and stir the garlic for 30 seconds or so. And then add sliced leeks. Cover and cook for 8-10 minutes, stirring frequently. Add a bit of water if it shows dry. 2. When the leeks are cooked, add the diced bell pepper to the skillet. 3. By using another pot to cook the orzo till al dente. Spoon out ¼ cup of the pasta cooking water before draining. 4. As the leeks are soft, add and stir in the cooked orzo, reserved ¼ cup of cooking water, and the lemon zest and juice. Add and cook the beans, cover a lid to warm about 2 minutes. 5. Turn off the heat, slowly stir in the cheese. Top the dish with pine nuts.
Per Serving: Calories 294; Fat 13.26g; Sodium 314mg; Carbs 40.46g; Fiber 6.3g; Sugar 19.19g; Protein 8.68g

Fried Egg Sandwich with Wholesome Spinach

Prep time: 10 minutes | Cook time: 10 minutes | Serves: 2

2 slices whole-wheat or multigrain bread	1 teaspoon olive oil
Nonstick cooking spray	2 eggs
1 cup spinach	¼ cup fat-free cottage cheese
1 teaspoon freshly squeezed lemon juice	Freshly ground black pepper
	2 tablespoons grated Parmesan

1. Set the oven to broil in advance. 2. Using cooking spray to gently spray both sides of the bread, broil bread until gently toasted for 1 minute per side. 3. Mix and combine the spinach and lemon juice in a small bowl, set aside. 4. Set medium-high heat to cook olive oil in a small skillet, fry the eggs for 2- 3 minutes till the whites are set. 5. Spread the cottage cheese on the toast. Top the dish with dressed spinach. Put the sliced egg onto the spinach. Dress with pepper and drizzle each egg with half of the Parmesan. An open-faced sandwich could be served.
Per Serving: Calories 222; Fat 7.99g; Sodium 509mg; Carbs 21.96g; Fiber 2.7g; Sugar 2.57g; Protein 16.48g

Sweet Quiche with Greens

Prep time: 5 minutes | Cook time: 25 minutes | Serves: 2

3 eggs	3 button mushrooms, chopped
2 egg whites	1 scallion, white and green parts, chopped
¼ cup skim milk	
¼ cup shredded reduced-fat mozzarella, divided	½ cup shredded spinach
1 teaspoon butter, divided	6 cherry tomatoes, quartered
	Freshly ground black pepper

1. Beat the eggs and stir with egg whites, milk, and half of the cheese in a small bowl. Set aside. 2. Heat the oven to 350°F in advance, and then grease 2 (8-ounce) ramekins with ¼ teaspoon of butter. Set aside. 3. Heat to melt the rest of ¾ teaspoon of butter in a small skillet, add and sauté the mushrooms and scallion for 2 minutes, till become soft. Add the spinach and sauté for 1 minute, till wilted. 4. Evenly plate the vegetables and the tomatoes into the ramekins. Add into egg mixture evenly, top with the remaining cheese for each quiche. Roast the quiches for 15-20 minutes, to be puffed and gently browned. It is proper to serve the food with pepper.
Per Serving: Calories 357; Fat 20.78g; Sodium 382mg; Carbs 21.95g; Fiber 3.4g; Sugar 9.83g; Protein 23.95g

Quesadillas with Portobello Mushroom

Prep time: 10 minutes | Cook time: 15 minutes | Serves: 2

1 teaspoon olive oil	pesto
2 medium portobello mushroom caps (about 3 inches in diameter), thinly sliced	4 sun-dried tomatoes, chopped
	1 scallion, white and green parts, cut into ⅛-inch-thick slices
2 (8-inch) whole-wheat tortillas	¼ cup shredded low-fat Monterey Jack
2 tablespoons prepared basil	

1. Set the medium-high heat to cook the olive oil in a skillet. Cook to sauté the mushroom for 4 minutes. Remove from the heat, set aside. 2. Heat the grill to medium heat in advance. 3. Each tortilla need spreading 1 tablespoon of pesto. After dividing the mushrooms, sun-dried tomatoes, and scallion evenly between the tortillas, spread the out. Drizzle each tortilla with 2 tablespoons of cheese. Fold the tortillas in half, and then flat them softly. 4. Transfer the tortillas on the grill and cook for 2 minutes per side till slightly fried. Serve the dish with quesadilla.
Per Serving: Calories 269; Fat 11.01g; Sodium 439mg; Carbs 32.77g; Fiber 7.4g; Sugar 1.63g; Protein 13.59g

Tasty Falafel with Pinto Bean

Prep time: 15 minutes | Cook time: 10 minutes | Serves: 2

1 cup canned pinto beans, rinsed and drained	1 egg white
	1 teaspoon olive oil
¼ cup shredded low-fat Cheddar	1 (6-inch) pita, cut into two pockets
2 tablespoons whole-wheat bread crumbs	
	¼ avocado, diced
1 tablespoon finely chopped scallion	1 plum tomato, diced
	2 tablespoons fat-free sour cream
¼ teaspoon ground cumin	
Pinch ground coriander	Juice from ½ lime

1. Roughly mash the beans with a fork in an average bowl. Add and mix the cheese, bread crumbs, scallion, cumin, and coriander. Stir in the egg white till nearly combined, add and mix the bean mixture. Shape the bean mixture into 2 ½-inch-thick patties. 2. Adjust the heat to medium-high to cook the olive oil in a big skillet. Cook it till browned. Flip the food for another side and cook for about 3 minutes. 3. Cook to stuff each pita half with one patty. Cut the avocado and tomato evenly between them. 4. Decorate the top of each pita with 1 tablespoon sour cream and a squeeze of lime juice. Serve the dish!
Per Serving: Calories 317; Fat 8.49g; Sodium 308mg; Carbs 46.04g; Fiber 11.1g; Sugar 6.63g; Protein 16.9g

Sauced Pizza with Tomato

Prep time: 10minutes | Cook time: 5 minutes | Serves: 2

1 (8-inch) prepared pizza crust
Nonstick cooking spray
2 tablespoons homemade or prepared basil pesto
1 tomato, thinly sliced
2 tablespoons chopped fresh

basil, or 1 tablespoon dried basil
Pinch red pepper flakes
¼ cup shredded reduced-fat mozzarella

1. In the middle of the oven, put a rack. And heat the oven in advance for broiling. 2. While baking the crust, lightly spray some oil to the edge of crust. Spread the pesto on the cover the crust, except a ½-inch border around the edges. Order the tomato slices in overlapping concentric circles on the pizza. Cast the basil and red pepper flakes over the tomatoes evenly, do in the same way for basil by using cheese. 3. Roast the pizza and broil for 5 minutes till the crust becomes crispy and the cheese is done. Divide the pizza into 4 slices. Serve it.
Per Serving: Calories 396; Fat 21.42g; Sodium 523mg; Carbs 36.61g; Fiber 4g; Sugar 7.31g; Protein 17.57g

Linguine with Lemon Asparagus

Prep time: 5 minutes | Cook time: 20 minutes | Serves: 2

16 asparagus spears, trimmed of woody ends and cut into 2-inch pieces
1 teaspoon olive oil
2 teaspoons minced garlic
2 teaspoons all-purpose flour
1 cup skim milk
1 tablespoon chopped fresh

thyme or 1 teaspoon dried thyme
1 tablespoon freshly squeezed lemon juice
½ teaspoon lemon zest
2 cups cooked whole-wheat linguine
¼ cup grated Parmesan, divide

1. Boil the water to pickle the asparagus, blanch till crisp-softened. For 2 minutes. Cool it quickly and set aside. 2. Adjust the medium-high heat to cook the olive oil in a big skillet. Cook to sauté the garlic for 2 minutes. By adding the flour and whisk it to made a paste for 1 minute, add the milk, thyme, lemon juice, and zest. Lower the heat to sauce, and stir frequently till cream- liked for 3 minutes. Add the linguine, asparagus, and 2 tablespoons of the Parmesan. 3. Plate the food in two dishes and topped each one with 1 tablespoon of the remaining Parmesan.
Per Serving: Calories 331; Fat 3.72g; Sodium 173 mg; Carbs 61.76g; Fiber 4.7g; Sugar 17.73 g; Protein 16.45g

Yummy Macaroni with Cheese

Prep time: 10 minutes | Cook time: 55 minutes | Serves: 2

⅓ cup skim milk
½ cup (3 ounces) diced butternut squash
½ cup shredded low-fat Cheddar
Pinch dry mustard

8 ounces (4 cups) cooked whole-wheat penne
1 tablespoon freshly grated Parmesan

1. Set the 350°F to heat the oven in advance. 2. Put the large saucepan over medium-high heat and cook milk and squash in the pan. Boil the milk and lower the heat. Simmer the squash till it is softened for 25 minutes. 3. Blend the squash mixture in a food processor. Purée and then pour it back into the saucepan. Add and mix the Cheddar, mustard, and penne. 4. Prepare a 6-by-6-inch

baking dish, and then transfer the pasta mixture on to the dish, drizzle the top with the Parmesan. Roast it till bubbly and gently browned for 20 minutes.
Per Serving: Calories 251; Fat 3.25g; Sodium 382mg; Carbs 41.29g; Fiber 4g; Sugar 7.09g; Protein 16.85g

Roasted Ziti & Summer Squash

Prep time: 10 minutes | Cook time: 20 minutes | Serves: 2

Nonstick cooking spray
1 teaspoon olive oil
2 cups chopped zucchini (about 1 large)
1 scallion, white and green parts, sliced
1 teaspoon minced garlic
1 tomato, chopped
½ cup fat-free shredded Cheddar
2 tablespoons fat-free cottage

cheese
1 egg, beaten
1 tablespoon chopped fresh basil, or 1½ teaspoons dried basil
1 tablespoon chopped fresh oregano, or 1 teaspoon dried oregano
Pinch sea salt
Pinch red pepper flakes
4 cups cooked whole-wheat ziti

1. Set the 400°F to heat the oven in advance. Spray a 6-by-6-inch baking dish with the cooking spray. 2. Place a skillet over high heat to cook the olive oil. Sauté the zucchini, scallion, and garlic for 2 minutes till tender. And then add the tomatoes, cook to sauté for another 3 minutes. Turn off the heat, add and mix in the rest of the ingredients. 3. Scoop out the pasta mixture into the baking dish. Roast till bubbly and gently browned for 15 minutes.
Per Serving: Calories 492; Fat 6.42g; Sodium 476mg; Carbs 84.16g; Fiber 14.3g; Sugar 6.29g; Protein 31.23g

Parmesan Stacks with Eggplant Basil

Prep time: 10 minutes | Cook time: 15 minutes | Serves: 4

1½ cups whole-wheat bread crumbs
1 eggplant, cut into ¼-inch-thick slices
2 eggs, beaten
2 tablespoons extra-virgin olive oil
½ onion, finely chopped
4 garlic cloves, minced

1 (28-ounce) can crushed tomatoes
1 tablespoon dried Italian seasoning
½ teaspoon sea salt
¼ teaspoon red pepper flakes
4 ounces grated Parmesan cheese
¼ cup chopped fresh basil

1. Set the 400°F to heat the oven in advance. 2. Make the bread crumb spread on a plate. 3. Let eggplant slices dip in the beaten egg and then the bread crumb fully. 4. Place the coated eggplant in a single layer on one or more rimmed baking sheets if needed. 5. Roast for 12 minutes and flip half through. 6. Meanwhile, place a large saucepan over the medium-high heat to cook the olive oil. 7. Add and cook the onion, stir frequently till tender for 3 minutes. 8. Cook and add the garlic, stirring from time to time for 30 seconds. 9. Add and simmer the tomatoes with their juices, Italian seasoning, salt, and red pepper flakes. Lower the heat to medium-heat, stirring frequently for 10 minutes. 10. Layer the eggplant slices and sauce in four stacks equally, spread the remaining sauce over the top of them. Garnish with the Parmesan cheese and basil. Serve the dish.
Per Serving: Calories 282; Fat 14.44g; Sodium 532mg; Carbs 21.23g; Fiber 6g; Sugar 8.11g; Protein 18.01g

Spicy Eggplant Tagine

Prep time: 15 minutes | Cook time: 120 minutes | Serves: 2

1 eggplant, cut into ½-inch cubes	¼ teaspoon ground turmeric
1 tomato, chopped	Pinch allspice
1 red bell pepper, seeded, deribbed, and julienned	Pinch cayenne
½ onion, chopped	½ cup low-sodium vegetable stock
1 teaspoon minced garlic	1 teaspoon harissa
1 tablespoon olive oil	¼ cup coarsely chopped fresh parsley
½ teaspoon ground cumin	2 lemon wedges
½ teaspoon ground coriander	

1. At 300°F, heat the oven in advance. 2. Add and mix the eggplant, tomato, bell pepper, onion, and garlic in a large lidded casserole dish. Pour a little bit olive oil into the vegetable. Add and mix with the cumin, coriander, turmeric, allspice, and cayenne. Add the stock. 3. Roast for 2 hours with a lid till the vegetables are softened. Add and stir in harissa. Topped with the parsley and lemon wedges. Serve the dish.
Per Serving: Calories 197; Fat 8.33g; Sodium 92mg; Carbs 31.54g; Fiber 11.4g; Sugar 16.89g; Protein 5.41g

Nourishing Curry with Root Vegetable

Prep time: 10 minutes | Cook time: 20 minutes | Serves: 2

1 teaspoon olive oil	diced
2 shallots, peeled and diced	1 carrot, peeled and cut into 1-inch chunks
½ teaspoon minced garlic	1 cup canned lentils, rinsed and drained
1 tablespoon curry powder or paste	1 tomato, chopped
1 parsnip, peeled and cut into 1-inch chunks	½ cup low-sodium vegetable stock
1 sweet potato, peeled and	

1. Place a large saucepan over medium-high heat to cook the olive oil. Cook to sauté the shallots and garlic till tender for 2 minutes. Add and sauté the curry powder for another 1 minute. 2. After adding the rest of the ingredients, boil the stew. Lower the heat and simmer till the vegetable becomes softened for 15 minutes.
Per Serving: Calories 223; Fat 3.56g; Sodium 102mg; Carbs 45.59g; Fiber 9.1g; Sugar 11.63g; Protein 7.56g

Zest Stew with Tomato

Prep time: 10 minutes | Cook time: 15 minutes | Serves: 2

1 teaspoon olive oil	canned chickpeas, rinsed and drained
1 sweet onion, finely chopped	1 tomato, diced
1 teaspoon minced garlic	½ cup low-sodium vegetable stock
1 teaspoon peeled, grated fresh ginger	2 tablespoons low-fat plain Greek yogurt
1 teaspoon ground cumin	2 tablespoons chopped fresh cilantro
½ teaspoon ground coriander	
1 (15-ounce) can low-sodium crushed tomatoes	
1 (15-ounce) can sodium-free	

1. Place a large saucepan over medium-high heat to cook the

olive oil. Add and sauté the onion and garlic for 4 minutes till the vegetable are tender. Add and cook the ginger, cumin, and coriander for 1 minutes. 2. Add and boil the crush tomatoes, chickpeas, tomato, and stock. Lower the heat and simmer for 10 minutes till the sauce thicken. Serve the dish with the yogurt and cilantro.
Per Serving: Calories 361; Fat 7.81g; Sodium 520mg; Carbs 60.29g; Fiber 14.4g; Sugar 27.29g; Protein 15.99g

Tasty Stew with Curried Chickpea

Prep time: 15minutes | Cook time: 10 minutes | Serves: 2

1 teaspoon olive oil	1 (15-ounce) can chickpeas, rinsed and drained
1 onion, chopped	2 tomatoes, chopped
½ teaspoon minced garlic	½ cup spinach, shredded
1 teaspoon curry powder	2 tablespoons fat-free plain Greek yogurt
½ teaspoon ground cumin	
½ teaspoon ground coriander	

1. Place a large saucepan over medium-high heat to cook the olive oil. Cook and sauté the curry powder, cumin, and coriander for another 2 minutes. 2. Cook to stir the chickpeas and tomatoes till the chickpeas are heated completely, for nearly 5 minutes. Add and sauté the spinach for 1 minute till it becomes wilted. Remove from the heat and pour some yogurt to stir.
Per Serving: Calories 256; Fat 6.41g; Sodium 332mg; Carbs 40.24g; Fiber 11.3g; Sugar 11.18g; Protein 12.55g

Appetizing Cake with Sweet Potato

Prep time: 15 minutes | Cook time: 15 minutes | Serves: 2

1 tablespoon olive oil, divided	crumbs
¼ sweet onion, finely chopped	1 teaspoon freshly squeezed lime juice
2 teaspoons minced garlic	1 egg white
1 peeled, grated sweet potato (about 1 cup)	Pinch sea salt
1 cup sodium-free chickpeas, rinsed and drained	Pinch freshly ground black pepper
¼ cup whole-wheat bread	

1. Set the 400°F to heat the oven in advance. 2. Place a big skillet over medium-high heat to cook 1 teaspoon of olive oil, cook to sauté the onion and garlic till tender for 2 minutes. Add and stir in the sweet potato. Sauté for 2 minutes. Turn off the heat. 3. Put the chickpeas, bread crumbs, lime juice, and egg white to the processor. And then pulse gradually till the chickpeas are ground and the mixture can be held together. Distribute the sweet potato mixture into two equal 4-inch patties, and then flatten them to about ¾ inch. 4. In a skillet to heat the rest of 2 teaspoons of olive oil, cook the patties for 3 minutes till it each side becomes browned. Bake for another 5 minutes.
Per Serving: Calories 253; Fat 9.97g; Sodium 309mg; Carbs 31.86g; Fiber 7.3g; Sugar 6.21g; Protein 10.47g

Quinoa Stew with Red Lentil

Prep time: 5 minutes | Cook time: 25 minutes | Serves: 2

1 teaspoon olive oil
½ onion, chopped
1 celery stalk, diced
1 teaspoon minced garlic
2 cups low-sodium vegetable stock
1 carrot, peeled and diced
1 tomato, diced
½ cup red lentils, rinsed

¼ cup quinoa, rinsed
1 tablespoon chopped fresh thyme, or 1 teaspoon dried thyme
Pinch hot pepper flakes
Sea salt
Freshly ground black pepper
1 tablespoon chopped fresh parsley

1. Place a large saucepan over the medium-high heat to cook the olive oil. Cook to sauté the onion, celery, and garlic for 3 minutes, till softened. 2. Add and boil the vegetable stock, carrot, tomato, lentils, and quinoa. Lower the heat to simmer the stew for 15-20 minutes. 3. Mix and whisk the thyme and chili flakes after removing from the heat. Drizzle some salt and pepper, and then top them with the parsley. Serve the dish.
Per Serving: Calories 365; Fat 5.71g; Sodium 210mg; Carbs 64.3g; Fiber 10.7g; Sugar 12.01g; Protein 18.6g

Full-Bodied Zucchini

Prep time: 10 minutes | Cook time: 40 minutes | Serves: 4

4 medium zucchini, halved lengthwise and a small amount of the flesh scooped out
2 tablespoons extra-virgin olive oil
1 red onion, chopped
1 red bell pepper, stemmed and chopped
1 fennel bulb, chopped
8 ounces' shiitake mushrooms,

sliced
4 garlic cloves, minced
1 (15-ounce) can crushed tomatoes
1 (15-ounce) can lentils, drained and rinsed
1 tablespoon dried Italian seasoning
½ teaspoon sea salt
¼ teaspoon red pepper flakes

1. Set the 400°F to heat the oven in advance. Line a baking sheet with parchment paper. 2. Slice the zucchini halves, place them on the prepared baking sheet. 3. Set the medium-high heat to cook the olive oil in a large pot. 4. Mix and cook the onion, bell pepper, fennel, and mushrooms, for 5 minutes, whisk frequently till the vegetable shows browned. 5. Cook and mix the garlic, stir them frequently for 30 seconds. 6. Add and simmer the tomatoes with their juices, lentils, Italian seasoning, salt, and red pepper flakes. Cook to stir occasionally for 5 minutes. 7. Scoop the mixture into the zucchini boats. Roast it till the zucchini becomes tender for 25 minutes. Serve the dish.
Per Serving: Calories 249; Fat 4.07g; Sodium 673mg; Carbs 44.14g; Fiber 14.7g; Sugar 11.43g; Protein 13.27g

Italian Pasta with Tomatoes

Prep time: 10 minutes | Cook time: 0 | Serves: 4

1 (12-ounce) jar roasted red peppers, drained
¼ cup extra-virgin olive oil
1 garlic clove, minced
½ cup almonds, chopped
2 medium tomatoes, seeded and chopped
¼ cup fresh Italian parsley

2 tablespoons red wine vinegar
1 teaspoon paprika
½ teaspoon red pepper flakes
½ teaspoon sea salt
8 ounces' whole-wheat angel-hair pasta, cooked according to package instructions and drained

1. Add and mix the red peppers, olive oil, garlic, almonds, tomatoes, parsley, red wine vinegar, paprika, red pepper flakes, and salt in a blender or food processor. Pulse for 20 one-second till the texture is similar to pesto. 2. Add the hot pasta and toss well. Serve.
Per Serving: Calories 161; Fat 6.57g; Sodium 586mg; Carbs 23.22g; Fiber 3.6g; Sugar 5.62g; Protein 4.67g

Vegetable Broth with Spiced Lentil

Prep time: 10 minutes | Cook time: 20 minutes | Serves: 6

2 tablespoons extra-virgin olive oil
1 onion, finely chopped
3 carrots, peeled and chopped
2 red bell peppers, seeded and roughly chopped
3 garlic cloves, minced
2 tablespoons whole-wheat flour
3 cups low-sodium vegetable broth

1 (15-ounce) can crushed tomatoes, drained
2 (15-ounce) cans lentils, drained and rinsed
1 teaspoon ground cumin
1 teaspoon ground coriander
1 teaspoon ground cinnamon
½ teaspoon sea salt
1 cup whole-wheat orzo, cooked according to package instructions

1. Place a large pot over medium-high heat to cook the olive oil. 2. Add and cook the onion, carrots, and bell peppers, stirring frequently for 4 minutes till the vegetable shows browned. 3. Add and cook the garlic, stirring frequently for 30 seconds. 4. Add and cook the flour, stirring for 1minute. 5. Add the broth to boil, during the cooking, scrape any browned bits from the bottom of the pan. Add and cook the tomatoes, lentils, cumin, coriander, cinnamon, and salt. 6. Lower the heat to medium. Stir frequently for 10 minutes till the vegetable becomes softened. 7. Add and stir the cooked orzo. Cook to stir for over 2 minutes. Serve the dish.
Per Serving: Calories 215; Fat 3.33g; Sodium 420mg; Carbs 39.14g; Fiber 10.5g; Sugar 12g; Protein 10.92g

Mediterranean Stew with White Bean

Prep time: 10 minutes | Cook time: 15 minutes | Serves: 6

2 tablespoons extra-virgin olive oil
1 red onion, finely chopped
1 red bell pepper, seeded and roughly chopped
4 garlic cloves, minced
3 tablespoons whole-wheat flour
6 cups low-sodium vegetable broth

2 (15-ounce) cans white beans, drained and rinsed
1 teaspoon ground cumin
1 teaspoon dried ground oregano
½ teaspoon ground allspice
½ teaspoon sea salt
¼ teaspoon freshly ground black pepper
2 tablespoons chopped fresh cilantro

1. Place a large pot over the medium-high heat to cook the olive oil. 2. Add and cook the onion and bell pepper. Stir frequently for 5 minutes. 3. Add and cook the garlic. Stir frequently for 30 seconds. 4. Add and cook the flour. Stir frequently for 1 minute. 5. Add the broth to boil, during the cooking, scrape any browned bits from the bottom of the pan. 6. Add and boil the beans, cumin, oregano, allspice, salt, and black pepper. Stir frequently. Lower the heat to medium and cook for over 5 minutes. Stir frequently. 7. Decorate with the cilantro. Serve the dish.
Per Serving: Calories 111; Fat 3.4g; Sodium 378mg; Carbs 19g; Fiber 3.7g; Sugar 8.92g; Protein 4.19g

Tasty Veggies Stew

Prep time: 10minutes | Cook time: 20 minutes | Serves: 6

2 tablespoons extra-virgin olive oil	cut into ½-inch cubes
1 onion, finely chopped	2 (15-ounce) cans chickpeas,
2 carrots, peeled and chopped	drained and rinsed
3 garlic cloves, minced	1 (15-ounce) can chopped
3 tablespoons whole-wheat flour	tomatoes, drained
4 cups low-sodium vegetable broth	½ teaspoon ground cinnamon
	1 teaspoon ground cumin
2 sweet potatoes, peeled and	½ teaspoon sea salt

1. Place a large pot over the medium-high heat to cook the olive oil. 2. Add and cook the onion and carrots, stirring frequently for 5 minutes. 3. Add and cook the garlic, stirring frequently for 30 seconds. 4. Add and cook flour, stirring frequently for 1 minute. 5. Add the broth to boil, during the cooking, scrape any browned bits from the bottom of the pan. 6. Add and boil the sweet potatoes, chickpeas, tomatoes, cinnamon, cumin, and salt. 7. Lower the heat to medium. Stir frequently for 10 minutes. Serve the dish.
Per Serving: Calories 256; Fat 5.1g; Sodium 631mg; Carbs 46.12g; Fiber 10.4g; Sugar 15.21g; Protein 10.01g

Mushroom & Pepper Ragout Spaghetti

Prep time: 10 minutes | Cook time: 15 minutes | Serves: 4

3 tablespoons extra-virgin olive oil	½ teaspoon sea salt
2 shallots, minced	¼ teaspoon freshly ground black pepper
1 pound cremini mushrooms, chopped	3 garlic cloves, minced
1 red bell pepper, seeded and chopped	½ cup dry red wine
1 teaspoon dried thyme	8 ounces' whole-wheat spaghetti, cooked according to package instructions and drained
¼ teaspoon red pepper flakes	

1. Place a large pot over the medium-high heat to cook the olive oil. 2. Add and cook the shallots for 3 minutes, and then cook the mushrooms, bell pepper, thyme, red pepper flakes, salt, and black pepper. Stir them frequently till the mushrooms shows browned for 5- 7 minutes. 3. Add and cook the garlic, stirring frequently for 30 seconds. 4. Pour the wine into the pot, add the broth to boil, during the cooking, scrape any browned bits from the bottom of the pan. Simmer and stir for over 2-3 minutes till the wine is decreased by half. 5. Mix the hot pasta. Serve the dish.
Per Serving: Calories 154; Fat 5.27g; Sodium 524mg; Carbs 21.74g; Fiber 4.2g; Sugar 3.86g; Protein 7.13g

Fiber-Rich Couscous

Prep time: 10 minutes | Cook time: 40 minutes | Serves: 4

6 shallots, quartered	3 tablespoons extra-virgin olive oil
3 large carrots, peeled and sliced	1 tablespoon chopped fresh rosemary
2 fennel bulbs, cut into 1-inch cubes	½ teaspoon sea salt
1 butternut squash, seeded and chopped into 1-inch cubes	¼ teaspoon freshly ground black pepper
2 medium zucchini, cut into 1-inch cubes	1 cup whole-wheat couscous, cooked according to package instructions
2 red bell peppers, seeded and cut into large pieces	

1. Set the 475°F to heat the oven in advance. 2. Add and mix the shallots, carrots, fennel, squash, zucchini, and bell peppers. And then season with the olive oil, rosemary, salt, and black pepper. 3. On two large rimmed baking sheets, spread the mixture in its single layer. 4. Roast for 40 minutes till the vegetables show browned. 5. Scoop the cooked couscous. Serve.
Per Serving: Calories 159; Fat 5.13 g; Sodium 450mg; Carbs 27.01g; Fiber 6.4g; Sugar 8.13g; Protein 4.71g

Stuffed Eggplant with Quinoa

Prep time: 10 minutes | Cook time: 60 minutes | Serves: 4

2 medium eggplants, all but about ½ inch of the flesh scooped out	drained and rinsed
	1 (15-ounce) can crushed tomatoes, drained
2 tablespoons extra-virgin olive oil	Zest and juice of 1 lemon, divided
1 onion, chopped	1 teaspoon dried oregano
2 garlic cloves, minced	½ teaspoon sea salt
1 (15-ounce) can white beans,	2 cups cooked quinoa

1. Set the 350°F to heat the oven in advance. Line a rimmed baking sheet with parchment paper. 2. Cut the eggplant halves and spread them out the baking sheet. 3. Set the medium-high heat to cook the olive oil in a large skillet. Add and cook the onion for 3 minutes. 4. Add and cook the garlic, stir frequently for 30 seconds. 5. Add and cook the white beans, tomatoes, lemon zest, oregano, and salt, stir frequently for 5 minutes. 6. Add and stir the quinoa and lemon juice. 7. Scoop the mixture into the eggplant halves. 8. Roast the food for 50 minutes. Serve the dish.
Per Serving: Calories 256; Fat 5.93g; Sodium 495mg; Carbs 46.61g; Fiber 14.8g; Sugar 15.35g; Protein 8.87g

Greens Couscous with White Beans

Prep time: 10 minutes | Cook time: 15 minutes | Serves: 4

¾ cup freshly squeezed orange juice, divided	chopped
	1 garlic clove, minced
½ cup water	1 (15-ounce) can white beans, drained and rinsed
1 cup whole-wheat instant couscous	1-pint grape tomatoes, halved
2 tablespoons extra-virgin olive oil	1 teaspoon dried oregano
1 red onion, chopped	½ teaspoon sea salt
1 red bell pepper, seeded and	2 cups baby spinach

1. Place a medium saucepan over the medium-high heat to cook ½ cup of orange juice and the water. Bring to a boil. 2. Add and whisk the couscous. Cover to rest and continue to stir for 10 minutes. 3. Place a big skillet over the medium-high heat to cook the olive oil when the couscous sets. 4. Add and cook the onion and bell pepper, stirring frequently for 4 minutes. 5. Add and cook the garlic, stirring for 30 seconds. 6. Add and stir the beans, tomatoes, oregano, and salt for 4 minutes, and then gradually add the spinach, cook for 1 minute. Besides, add and cook over for 1 minute the remaining ¼ cup of orange juice. 7. By using a fork to fluff the couscous and scoop the sauce over it. Serve the dish.
Per Serving: Calories 129; Fat 3.7g; Sodium 369 mg; Carbs 22.25g; Fiber 3.5g; Sugar 6.7g; Protein 3.97g

Brussels Sprout & Balsamic Glaze

Prep time: 10 minutes | Cook time: 30 minutes | Serves: 2

½ pound Brussels sprouts, trimmed and halved
Fresh cracked black pepper
1 tablespoon olive oil

Sunflower seeds to taste
2 teaspoons balsamic glaze
2 wooden skewers

1. Place the wooden skewers on a largely sized foil. 2. Put the sprouts on the skewers and drizzle oil, sprinkle sunflower seeds and pepper. 3. Cover skewers with foil. 4. Heat the grill in advance and transfer skewers covered foil in the grill. 5. Cook to grill for 30 minutes, turning over the side every 5-6 minutes. 6. Uncover the food and drizzle balsamic glaze on top. 7. Serve the dish.
Per Serving: Calories 147; Fat 8.09g; Sodium 36mg; Carbs 17.16g; Fiber 8.2g; Sugar 3.68g; Protein 5.82g

Greek Spinach Dip

Prep time: 4 minutes | Cook time: 0 minute | Serves: 2

5 ounces' spinach, raw
1 cup Greek yogurt
½ tablespoon onion powder
¼ teaspoon garlic sunflower

seeds
Black pepper to taste
¼ teaspoon Greek Seasoning

1. Put the listed in a blender. 2. Emulsify. 3. Cook the dressing. Serve the dish.
Per Serving: Calories 101; Fat 0.96g; Sodium 125mg; Carbs 10.44g; Fiber 2.2g; Sugar 5.28g; Protein 14.3g

Sticky-Nice Rice with Cauliflower

Prep time: 5 minutes | Cook time: 6 minutes | Serves: 2

1 head grated cauliflower head
1 tablespoon coconut aminos
1 pinch of sunflower seeds

1 pinch of black pepper
1 tablespoon garlic powder
1 tablespoon sesame oil

1. Place and grate the cauliflower in a food processor 2. Place a pan over medium heat and add the sesame oil. 3. Add grated cauliflower and pour coconut aminos. 4. Cook the food, for 4-6 minutes. 5. Serve the dish.
Per Serving: Calories 137; Fat 9.49g; Sodium 51mg; Carbs 11.3g; Fiber 3.6g; Sugar 2.96g; Protein 4.32g

Homemade Mushroom Over Rice

Prep time: 5 minutes | Cook time: 15 minutes | Serves: 4

4 ½ cups cauliflower, riced
3 tablespoons coconut oil
1 pound Portobello mushrooms, thinly sliced
1-pound white mushrooms, thinly sliced
2 shallots, diced

¼ cup organic vegetable broth
Sunflower seeds and pepper to taste
3 tablespoons chives, chopped
4 tablespoons almond butter
½ cup kite ricotta/cashew cheese, grated

1. Place a large skillet over the medium-high heat and add 2 tablespoons of coconut oil. 2. Add and sauté the mushrooms for 3 minutes till they become tender. 3. After clearing skillet of mushrooms and liquid, put them aside. 4. Add the remaining 1 tablespoon oil to the skillet. 5. Toss and cook the shallots for 1 minute. 6. Add and stir the cauliflower rice for 2 minutes, till coated with oil. 7. Add and boil the broth and riced cauliflower for 5 minutes. 8. Turn off the heat and remove the pot, whisk the mushrooms and liquid. 9. Add the Parmesan cheese, chives, and almond butter. 10. Sprinkle with sunflower seeds and pepper to season. 11. Serve the dish!
Per Serving: Calories 335; Fat 24.21g; Sodium 306mg; Carbs 21.7g; Fiber 8g; Sugar 8.49g; Protein 15.53g

Creamy Cabbage with Sunflower Seeds

Prep time: 10 minutes | Cook time: 10 minutes | Serves: 4

2 ounces' almond butter
1 ½ pounds green cabbage, shredded
1 ¼ cups coconut cream

Sunflower seeds and pepper to taste
8 tablespoons fresh parsley, chopped

1. Place a skillet over medium heat and add the almond butter. Heat until it has melted. 2. Add and sauté the cabbage till it becomes browned. 3. Lower the heat to stir the cream. 4. Cook to simmer the food. 5. Sprinkle with sunflower seeds and pepper. 6. Decorate the food with parsley. Serve the dish! 7. Serve the dish!
Per Serving: Calories 408; Fat 37.54g; Sodium 509mg; Carbs 17.35g; Fiber 6.5g; Sugar 5.55g; Protein 8.16g

Parmesan Cheese with Roasted Green Beans

Prep time: 10 minutes | Cook time: 20 minutes | Serves: 4

1 whole egg
2 tablespoons olive oil
Sunflower seeds and pepper to taste

1-pound fresh green beans
5 ½ tablespoons grated parmesan cheese

1. Set the 400°F to heat the oven in advance. 2. Beat the eggs and whisk them in a bowl with oil and spices. 3. Add and mix the beans. 4. Line a parchment paper in a baking pan, pour parmesan cheese and mixture. 5. Bake in the preheated oven for 15-20 minutes. 6. Serve the dish.
Per Serving: Calories 133; Fat 10.6g; Sodium 142mg; Carbs 6.08g; Fiber 2.2g; Sugar 0.95g; Protein 4.76g

Blistered Beans with Almond

Prep time: 10 minutes | Cook time: 20 minutes | Serves: 4

1-pound fresh green beans, ends trimmed
1 ½ tablespoon olive oil
¼ teaspoon sunflower seeds
1 ½ tablespoons fresh dill,

minced
Juice of 1 lemon
¼ cup crushed almonds
Sunflower seeds as needed

1. Set the 400°F to heat the oven in advance. 2. Add the green beans, olive oil, and the sunflower seeds. 3. Prepare a large sized sheet pan, spread the food in one single layer. 4. Roast it in the preheated oven for 10 minutes, stirring from time to time. Then continue roasting for another 8-10 minutes. 5. Turn off the heat, and keep whisking in the lemon juice alongside the dill. 6. Put the almonds and some flaked sunflower seeds over the dish. Serve.
Per Serving: Calories 86; Fat 6.49g; Sodium 3mg; Carbs 7.29g; Fiber 2.8g; Sugar 1.21g; Protein 1.91g

Fast-Homemade Tomato Platter

Prep time: 10 Minutes + 2-3 hours chilling time | Cook time: 0 | Serves: 8

⅓ cup olive oil
1 teaspoon sunflower seeds
2 tablespoons onion, chopped
¼ teaspoon pepper
½ garlic, minced

1 tablespoon fresh parsley, minced
3 large fresh tomatoes, sliced
1 teaspoon dried basil
¼ cup red wine vinegar

1. Place the tomatoes in a shallow dish. 2. Add the remaining ingredients in a mason jar, cover and shake it completely. 3. Pour the mix over tomato slices. 4. Chill the dish for 2-3 minutes. 5. Serve the dish!
Per Serving: Calories 86; Fat 9.12g; Sodium 2mg; Carbs 0.81g; Fiber 0.2g; Sugar 0.34g; Protein 0.23g

Brussels Sprouts with Lemon Juice

Prep time: 10 minutes | Cook time: 0 minute | Serves: 4

1 pound Brussels sprouts, trimmed and shredded
8 tablespoons olive oil
1 lemon, juice and zested

Sunflower seeds and pepper to taste
¾ cup spicy almond and seed mix

1. Add and mix lemon juice, sunflower seeds, pepper, and olive oil in a bowl. 2. Mix them completely. 3. Stir and toss the shredded Brussels sprouts. 4. Cook to stir for 10 minutes. 5. Add nuts and toss for a while. 6. Serve the dish.
Per Serving: Calories 296; Fat 27.85g; Sodium 29mg; Carbs 11.17g; Fiber 4.4g; Sugar 2.83g; Protein 4.07g

Fried Zucchini with Red Pepper Sauce

Prep time:10 minutes | Cook time: 20 minutes | Serves: 6

2 medium zucchini, grated on a box grater
½ red onion, grated
1 red bell pepper, seeded and very finely chopped or grated
1 garlic clove, minced
1 egg, beaten
½ cup almond flour

¼ cup chopped fresh dill
¾ teaspoon sea salt, divided
¼ teaspoon freshly ground black pepper
1 (12-ounce) jar roasted red peppers, drained
½ cup nonfat plain Greek yogurt

1. Set the 400°F to heat the oven in advance. Line two large baking sheets with parchment paper and set aside. 2. By using a tea towel or paper towel to wrap the grated zucchini. Squeeze out the water, after that, put into a large bowl. 3. Add and mix the bell pepper, garlic, egg, almond flour, dill, ½ teaspoon of salt, and the black pepper. 4. Roll the mixture into 12 balls, plate them on the prepared baking sheets. Make them into fritters. 5. Bake for 20 minutes, and flip halfway. 6. At the same time, mix and combine the roasted red peppers, Greek yogurt, and the remaining ¼ teaspoon of salt. 7. Scoop the sauce over the fritters. Serve the dish.
Per Serving: Calories 44; Fat 0.98g; Sodium 310mg; Carbs 5.76g; Fiber 0.9g; Sugar 3.47g; Protein 3.69g

Garbanzo Beans with Spinach

Prep time: 5-10 minutes | Cook time: 0 | Serves: 4

1 tablespoon olive oil
½ onion, diced
10 ounces' spinach, chopped

12 ounces' garbanzo beans
½ teaspoon cumin

1. Place a skillet over medium-high heat and add olive oil. Heat it. 2. Add and cook the onions and garbanzo for 5 minutes. 3. Add and stir spinach, cumin, and garbanzo beans, and then season with sunflower seeds. 4. Smash the food softly. 5. Heat the food, serve it.
Per Serving: Calories 192; Fat 5.93g; Sodium 63mg; Carbs 27.3g; Fiber 8.3g; Sugar 4.97g; Protein 9.76g

Sweet Garlic Tomatoes

Prep time: 10 minutes | Cook time: 50 minutes | Serves: 4

4 garlic cloves, crushed
1-pound mixed cherry tomatoes
3 thyme sprigs, chopped

Pinch of sunflower seeds
Black pepper as needed
¼ cup olive oil

1. Set the 325°F to heat the oven in advance. 2. Add the tomatoes, olive oil, and thyme in a baking dish. 3. Sprinkle with sunflower seeds and pepper and mix. 4. Bake in the preheated oven for 50 minutes. 5. Distribute tomatoes and pan juices. Serve the dish. 6. Enjoy the food!
Per Serving: Calories 201; Fat 14.15g; Sodium 1mg; Carbs 19.75g; Fiber 2.8g; Sugar 14.59g; Protein 1.65g

Honey Celeriac

Prep time: 10 minutes | Cook time: 20 minutes | Serves: 4

2 celeriac, washed, peeled and diced
2 teaspoons extra-virgin olive oil

1 tablespoon honey
½ teaspoon ground nutmeg
Sunflower seeds and pepper as needed

1. Set the 400°F to heat the oven in advance. 2. Line a baking sheet with aluminum foil, let it close the side. 3. Add and toss celeriac and olive oil in a large bowl. 4. Spread celeriac on a baking sheet evenly. 5. Roast for 20 minutes. 6. Place to a large bowl. 7. Pour honey and nutmeg. 8. By using a potato masher to mash the mixture. 9. Sprinkle the dressing with sunflower seeds and pepper 10. Serve the dish.
Per Serving: Calories 34; Fat 1.47g; Sodium 29mg; Carbs 5.5g; Fiber 6.3g; Sugar 4.49g; Protein 0.34g

Unique Dish with Kale

Prep time: 15 minutes | Cook time: 10 minutes | Serves: 6

12 cups kale, chopped
2 tablespoons lemon juice
1 tablespoon olive oil

1 teaspoon coconut aminos
Sunflower seeds and pepper as needed

1. Place a steamer insert the saucepan. 2. Pour the water to the saucepan up to its bottom. 3. Set the medium-heat to boil the water with a lid. 4. Add the kale and steam for 7-8 minutes. 5. Add the lemon juice, olive oil, sunflower seeds, coconut aminos, and pepper in a large bowl. 6. Add the steamed kale and mix well. 7. Toss and serve. 8. Enjoy the dish.
Per Serving: Calories 40; Fat 2.81g; Sodium 13mg; Carbs 3.28g; Fiber 1.2g; Sugar 0.89g; Protein 1.49g

Spicy Chips with Kale

Prep time: 10 minutes | Cook time: 25 minutes | Serves: 4

3 cups kale, stemmed and thoroughly washed, torn in 2-inch pieces
1 tablespoon extra-virgin olive
oil
½ teaspoon chili powder
¼ teaspoon sea sunflower seeds

1. Set the 300°F to heat the oven in advance. 2. Line 2 baking sheets with parchment paper, and keep it aside. 3. Pat dry the kale, place it to a large bowl. 4. Add olive oil and toss. 5. Cook carefully to coat each leaf with olive oil. 6. Sprinkle the kale with chili powder and sunflower seeds. Toss it completely. 7. Put the kale to baking sheets and spread into a single layer. 8. Bake in the preheated oven for 25 minutes till crispy. 9. Cool the chips for 5 minutes. Serve the dish. 10. Enjoy!
Per Serving: Calories 21; Fat 1.75g; Sodium 45mg; Carbs 1.26g; Fiber 0.6g; Sugar 0.3g; Protein 0.61g

Tantalizing Portobello Mushrooms

Prep time: 15 minutes | Cook time: 60 minutes | Serves: 4

4 Portobello mushrooms
2 tablespoons extra-virgin olive oil, divided
1 red onion, chopped
1 tablespoon dried Italian seasoning
6 cups baby spinach
½ (12-ounce) jar roasted red peppers, drained and chopped
½ teaspoon sea salt
3 garlic cloves, minced
¼ cup pine nuts
1 cup cooked brown rice
½ cup crumbled feta cheese

1. Set the 375°F to heat the oven in advance. Line a baking sheet with parchment paper. 2. After scooping out the stems and black gills, place the mushrooms to be cavity-side up, and put them on the prepared baking sheet. 3. Place a large skillet over the medium-high heat to cook the olive oil. Add and cook the onion and Italian seasoning for 4 minutes. 4. Add and cook the spinach, roasted red peppers, and salt for 2 minutes or more, until the spinach is just wilted. Add and cook the garlic for 30 seconds, stir frequently. 5. Turn off the heat, add and whisk the pine nuts and rice. 6. Scoop out the mixture into the mushroom cups, drizzle the feta cheese on their top. 7 Bake till the mushrooms become softened for 50 minutes. Serve the dish.
Per Serving: Calories 257; Fat 13.65g; Sodium 724mg; Carbs 27.89g; Fiber 4.4g; Sugar 7.55g; Protein 9.19g

Scrambled Tofu with Green Bean and Carrot

Prep time: 15 minutes | Cook time: 20 minutes | Serves: 4

1 (14-ounce) package extra-firm tofu
2 tablespoons canola oil
1-pound green beans, chopped
2 carrots, peeled and thinly sliced
½ cup store-bought lower-sodium stir-fry sauce
2 cups Fluffy Brown Rice
2 scallions, thinly sliced
2 tablespoons sesame seeds

1. Line a kitchen towel on the plate, place the tofu on the towel and then cover the tofu with another kitchen towel; place a heavy pot on top, changing towels every time they become soaked. 2. Let the tofu sit within 15 minutes to remove the moisture; when done, cut the tofu into 1-inch cubes. 3. In the skillet, heat the canola oil over medium-high heat; add the tofu cubes and cook them for 10 minutes or until all sides become browned, flipping every 1 to 2 minutes; transfer the tofu cubes to a plate. 4. Still in the skillet, add the green beans and carrots in the hot oil, sauté them for 4 to 5 minutes until crisp and slightly tender. 5. Put the tofu cubes back to the skillet, drizzle the sauce over the tofu cubes and vegetables and let them simmer for 2 to 3 minutes longer. 6. Serve over rice, then top with scallions and sesame seeds.
Per Serving: Calories 317; Fat 16.69g; Sodium 21mg; Carbs 30.98g; Fiber 5.3g; Sugar 1.99g; Protein 15.05g

Baked Flatbreads with Spinach, Tomatoes & Feta

Prep time: 15 minutes | Cook time: 10 minutes | Serves: 2

2 cups fresh baby spinach, coarsely chopped
2 teaspoons olive oil
2 slices naan, or another flatbread
¼ cup sliced black olives
2 plum tomatoes, thinly sliced
1 teaspoon salt-free Italian seasoning blend
¼ cup crumbled feta

1. Preheat the oven to 400 degrees F. 2. In the skillet, heat 3 tablespoons of water over medium heat; add the spinach, cover the skillet and steam the spinach for 2 minutes until wilted. Drain off any excess water and set aside. 3. Evenly drizzle the oil onto both flatbreads, top each flatbread with the olives, tomatoes, spinach, seasoning and feta, then bake them in the oven for 5 to 7 minutes or light browned. 4. Cut each flatbread into 4 pieces and serve.
Per Serving: Calories 139; Fat 10.3g; Sodium 404mg; Carbs 5.74g; Fiber 1.6g; Sugar 2.99g; Protein 6.62g

Brown Rice Noodles with Veggie Stir-Fry

Prep time: 15 minutes | Cook time: 20 minutes | Serves: 6

8 ounces brown rice noodles
⅓ cup natural peanut butter
3 tablespoons unsalted vegetable broth
1 tablespoon low-sodium soy sauce
2 tablespoons of rice wine vinegar
1 tablespoon honey
2 teaspoons sesame oil
1 teaspoon sriracha (optional)
1 tablespoon canola oil
1 red bell pepper, thinly sliced
1 zucchini, cut into matchsticks
2 large carrots, cut into matchsticks
3 large eggs, beaten
¾ teaspoon kosher or sea salt
½ cup unsalted peanuts, chopped
½ cup cilantro leaves, chopped

1. Boil a large pot of water and then cook the rice noodles according to the package directions. 2. While cooking the noodles, mix up the peanut butter, vegetable broth, soy sauce, rice wine vinegar, honey, sesame oil and sriracha in a bowl. Set aside for later use. 3. In the skillet, heat the canola oil over medium heat; add the red bell pepper, zucchini, carrots and sauté them for 2 to 3 minutes until slightly soft. 4. Stir in the eggs and fold with a spatula until scrambled; add the cooked rice noodles, sauce and salt. Toss to combine. 5. When cooked, apportion the food between serving plates and evenly top each serving with the peanuts and cilantro.
Per Serving: Calories 437; Fat 24.11g; Sodium 441mg; Carbs 47.92g; Fiber 4.1g; Sugar 8.64g; Protein 11.05g

Tasty Tofu Burrito Bowls with Cilantro Avocado Sauce

Prep time: 15 minutes | Cook time: 15 minutes | Serves: 4

For the sauce:
¼ cup plain nonfat Greek yogurt
½ cup fresh cilantro leaves
½ ripe avocado, peeled
Zest and juice of 1 lime
2 garlic cloves, peeled
¼ teaspoon kosher or sea salt
2 tablespoons water
For the burrito bowls:
1 (14-ounce) package extra-firm tofu
1 tablespoon canola oil
1 yellow or orange bell pepper, diced
2 tablespoons taco seasoning
¼ teaspoon kosher or sea salt
2 cups fluffy brown rice
1 (15-ounce) can black beans, drained

1. In the blender, add all the sauce ingredients and then purée them until smooth. Store the sauce in the refrigerator and use until ready for use. 2. Line a kitchen towel on the plate and place the tofu on the towel; cover the tofu with another kitchen towel and then place a heavy pot on top, changing towels if they become soaked. 3. Let the tofu stand within 15 minutes to remove the moisture. Cut the tofu into 1-inch cubes. 4. In the skillet, heat the canola oil over medium heat; add the tofu, bell pepper and sauté them for 4 to 5 minutes, breaking up the tofu into smaller pieces; stir in the taco seasoning, salt and ¼ cup of water. 5. Evenly divide the rice and black beans among 4 bowls, top each bowl of rice with the tofu mixture and the cilantro avocado sauce.
Per Serving: Calories 326; Fat 14.33g; Sodium 627mg; Carbs 35.66g; Fiber 6.1g; Sugar 3.73g; Protein 17.09g

Sweet Potato Patties with Guacamole

Prep time: 15 minutes | Cook time: 10 minutes | Serves: 4

For the guacamole:
2 ripe avocados, peeled and pitted
½ jalapeño, seeded and finely minced
¼ red onion, peeled and finely diced
¼ cup fresh cilantro leaves, chopped
Zest and juice of 1 lime
¼ teaspoon kosher or sea salt
For the cakes:
3 sweet potatoes, cooked and peeled
½ cup cooked black beans
1 large egg
½ cup panko bread crumbs
1 teaspoon ground cumin
1 teaspoon chili powder
½ teaspoon kosher or sea salt
¼ teaspoon ground black pepper
2 tablespoons canola oil

To make the guacamole: Mash the avocado and put them in a bowl, then stir in the jalapeño, red onion, cilantro, salt, lime zest and juice.
To make the cakes: 1. In another suitable bowl, add the cooked sweet potatoes and black beans, mash them until a paste form; stir in the egg, bread crumbs, cumin, chili powder, salt and black pepper until combined. Form the mixture into 4 patties. 2. In the skillet, heat the canola oil over medium heat; add the patties and cook them for 3 to 4 minutes on each side until browned and crispy. 3. Transfer the patties to the serving plate and top them with the guacamole, enjoy.
Per Serving: Calories 378; Fat 25.59g; Sodium 534mg; Carbs 38.54g; Fiber 12.1g; Sugar 8.22g; Protein 7.82g

Lentil Avocado Tacos in Stock

Prep time: 15 minutes | Cook time: 35 minutes | Serves: 6

1 tablespoon canola oil
½ yellow onion, peeled and diced
2-3 garlic cloves, minced
1½ cups dried lentils
½ teaspoon kosher or sea salt
3 to 3½ cups unsalted vegetable
or chicken stock
2½ tablespoons store-bought low-sodium taco seasoning
16 (6-inch) corn tortillas, toasted
2 ripe avocados, peeled and sliced

1. In the skillet, heat the canola oil over medium heat; add the onion and sauté for 4 to 5 minutes until soft; add the garlic and sauté for 30 seconds until fragrant; add the lentils, salt and stock, bring to a simmer and keep simmering them for 25 to 35 minutes. 2. When there's only a small amount of liquid left in the pan, and the lentils are al dente, stir in the taco seasoning and let simmer for 1 to 2 minutes longer. 3. Spoon the lentil mixture into tortillas and serve with the avocado slices.
Per Serving: Calories 403; Fat 16.44g; Sodium 254mg; Carbs 57.28g; Fiber 9.2g; Sugar 5.67g; Protein 13.54g

Roasted Vegetable Enchiladas with Cilantro

Prep time: 15 minutes | Cook time: 45 minutes | Serves: 8

2 zucchinis, diced
1 red bell pepper, seeded and sliced
1 red onion, peeled and sliced
2 ears corn
2 tablespoons canola oil
1 can no-salt-added black beans, drained
1½ tablespoons chili powder
2 teaspoons ground cumin
⅛ teaspoon kosher or sea salt
½ teaspoon ground black pepper
8 (8-inch) whole-wheat tortillas
1 cup Enchilada Sauce or store-bought enchilada sauce
½ cup shredded Mexican-style cheese
½ cup plain nonfat Greek yogurt
½ cup cilantro leaves, chopped

1. Preheat oven to 400 degrees F. 2. In the baking pan, place the zucchini, red bell pepper and red onion; place the ears of corn separately on the same baking sheet. Drizzle all with the canola oil and toss to coat. 3. Roast the food for 10 to 12 minutes, until the vegetables are tender. 4. Cut the corn from the cob, transfer the corn kernels, zucchini, red bell pepper and onion to a bowl, stir in the black beans, chili powder, cumin, salt and black pepper until combined. 5. Clean the baking pan and oil it with the cooking spray. Arrange the tortillas to the greased baking dish. 6. Evenly distribute the vegetable bean filling into each tortilla. Pour half of the enchilada sauce and sprinkle half of the shredded cheese on top of the filling. 7. Roll each tortilla into enchilada shape and place them seam-side down. Pour the remaining enchilada sauce and sprinkle the remaining cheese over the enchiladas. 8. Bake the food in the oven for 25 minutes at 375 degrees until the cheese is melted and bubbly. 9. Serve the enchiladas with Greek yogurt and chopped cilantro.
Per Serving: Calories 227; Fat 8.62g; Sodium 576mg; Carbs 31.6g; Fiber 6.6g; Sugar 5.09g; Protein 8.37g

Chickpea Cauliflower Tikka Masala

Prep time: 15 minutes | Cook time: 40 minutes | Serves: 6

2 tablespoons olive oil
1 yellow onion, peeled and diced
4 garlic cloves, peeled and minced
1-inch piece fresh ginger, peeled and minced
2 tablespoons Garam Masala
1 teaspoon kosher or sea salt
½ teaspoon ground black pepper
¼ teaspoon ground cayenne pepper
½ small head cauliflower, small florets

2 (15-ounce) cans no-salt-added chickpeas, rinsed and drained
1 (15-ounce) can no-salt-added petite diced tomatoes, drained
1½ cups unsalted vegetable broth
½ (15-ounce) can coconut milk
Zest and juice of 1 lime
½ cup fresh cilantro leaves, chopped, divided
1½ cups cooked fluffy brown rice, divided

1. In the stockpot, heat the olive oil over medium heat; add the onion and sauté for 4 to 5 minutes; add the garlic, ginger, garam masala, cayenne pepper, salt and black pepper, sauté them for 30 to 60 seconds or until fragrant. 2. Add the cauliflower florets, chickpeas, diced tomatoes and vegetable broth, increase to medium-high and let the food simmer for 15 minutes, until the cauliflower is fork-tender. Transfer them to a bowl or plate. 3. Still in the stockpot, add the coconut milk, lime juice, lime zest and half of the cilantro. 4. Serve the dish with the rice and the remaining chopped cilantro.
Per Serving: Calories 405; Fat 22.37g; Sodium 441mg; Carbs 44.28g; Fiber 10.3g; Sugar 8.45g; Protein 11.44g

Parmesan Eggplant Stacks

Prep time: 15 minutes | Cook time: 20 minutes | Serves: 4

1 large eggplant, cut into thick slices
2 tablespoons olive oil, divided
¼ teaspoon kosher or sea salt
¼ teaspoon ground black pepper
1 cup panko bread crumbs

¼ cup freshly grated Parmesan cheese
5 to 6 garlic cloves, minced
½ pound fresh mozzarella, sliced
1½ cups lower-sodium marinara
½ cup fresh basil leaves, torn

1. Preheat the oven to 425 degrees F. 2. Coat the eggplant slices with 1 tablespoon of olive oil and sprinkle with the salt and black pepper, arrange them to the baking sheet and then roast them in the oven for 10 to 12 minutes, until soft with crispy edges. 3. Remove the eggplant and set the oven to a low broil. 4. In a bowl, add the bread crumbs, Parmesan cheese, garlic and the remaining olive oil. 5. Remove the cooled eggplant from the baking sheet and clean it. Create layers on the same baking sheet by stacking a roasted eggplant slice with a slice of mozzarella, a tablespoon of marinara, and a tablespoon of the bread crumb mixture, repeating with 2 layers of each ingredient. 6. Cook the food under the broiler for 3 to 4 minutes until the cheese is melted and bubbly. 7. With the basil leaves, serve and enjoy.
Per Serving: Calories 361; Fat 16.03g; Sodium 679mg; Carbs 19.41g; Fiber 5.5g; Sugar 7.04g; Protein 36g

Mayonnaise with Spicy Wasabi

Prep time: 15 minutes | Cook time: 0 | Serves: 4

1 cup mayonnaise   ½ tablespoon wasabi paste

1. Add and mix wasabi paste and mayonnaise in a bowl. 2. Mix to combine. 3. Cool to chill if you need.
Per Serving: Calories 131; Fat 10.76g; Sodium 63mg; Carbs 9.34g; Fiber 0.1g; Sugar 2.6g; Protein 0.25g

Tomato and Olive Orecchiette Pasta

Prep time: 15 minutes | Cook time: 25 minutes | Serves: 6

12 ounces orecchiette pasta
2 tablespoons olive oil
1-pint cherry tomatoes, quartered
½ cup Basil Pesto or store-bought pesto
¼ cup Kalamata olives, sliced
1 tablespoon dried oregano leaves

¼ teaspoon kosher or sea salt
½ teaspoon freshly cracked black pepper
¼ teaspoon crushed red pepper flakes
2 tablespoons freshly grated Parmesan cheese

1. Boil a large pot of water and then cook the orecchiette; when cooked, drain and transfer the pasta to the nonstick skillet. 2. Put the skillet over medium-low heat, then heat the olive oil; add the cherry tomatoes, pesto, olives, oregano, salt, black pepper, and crushed red pepper flakes, cook them with the orecchiette for 8 to 10 minutes until heated throughout. 3. Serve the pasta with the freshly grated Parmesan cheese.
Per Serving: Calories 152; Fat 6.89g; Sodium 231mg; Carbs 20.34g; Fiber 3.7g; Sugar 0.8g; Protein 3.05g

Stuffed Portobello Mushroom Burgers

Prep time: 15 minutes | Cook time: 25 minutes | Serves: 4

1 tablespoon olive oil
4 large portobello mushrooms, washed and dried
½ yellow onion, peeled and diced
4 garlic cloves, peeled and minced
1 can cannellini beans, drained
½ cup fresh basil leaves, torn
½ cup panko bread crumbs

⅛ teaspoon kosher or sea salt
¼ teaspoon ground black pepper
1 cup lower-sodium marinara, divided
½ cup shredded mozzarella cheese
4 whole-wheat buns, toasted
1 cup fresh arugula

1. Preheat the oven to low broil. 2. In the skillet, heat the olive oil over medium-high heat; add the mushroom and sear the mushrooms for 4 to 5 minutes on each side, until slightly soft. Arrange them to the baking sheet. 3. Still in the skillet, sauté the onion for 4 to 5 minutes until slightly soft; add the garlic and sauté for 30 to 60 seconds. 4. Transfer them to a bowl, add the cannellini beans and smash with the back of a fork to form a chunky paste; stir in the basil, bread crumbs, salt, and black pepper and half of the marinara. 5. Cook the mixture in the skillet for 5 minutes longer. 6. Remove the bean mixture from the stove and divide among the mushroom caps. Spoon the remaining marinara over the stuffed mushrooms and top each with the mozzarella cheese. 7. Broil them in the oven for 3 to 4 minutes, until the cheese is melted and bubbly. 8. Transfer the burgers to the toasted whole-wheat buns and top with the arugula, enjoy.
Per Serving: Calories 252; Fat 10g; Sodium 337mg; Carbs 24.59g; Fiber 3.3g; Sugar 2.04g; Protein 17.58g

Gnocchi with Tomato Basil Sauce and Parmesan

Prep time: 15 minutes | Cook time: 25 minutes | Serves: 6

2 tablespoons olive oil
½ yellow onion, peeled and diced
3 cloves garlic, peeled and minced
1 (32-ounce) can no-salt-added crushed San Marzano tomatoes
¼ cup fresh basil leaves
2 teaspoons Italian seasoning
½ teaspoon kosher or sea salt
1 teaspoon granulated sugar

½ teaspoon ground black pepper
⅛ teaspoon crushed red pepper flakes
1 tablespoon heavy cream (optional)
12 ounces gnocchi
¼ cup freshly grated Parmesan cheese

1. In the stockpot, heat the olive oil over medium heat; add the onion and sauté for 5 to 6 minutes until soft; add the garlic and sauté for 30 to 60 seconds until fragrant. 2. Add the tomatoes, red pepper flakes, basil, Italian seasoning, sugar, salt and black pepper, then bring to simmer and keep simmering them for 15 minutes. (You can add the heavy cream.) 3. Transfer the tomato mixture to a blender and purée them until smooth. 4. Cook the gnocchi according to the package instructions; when cooked, apportion them between 6 bowls. 5. Pour the sauce over the gnocchi and top with the Parmesan cheese, enjoy.
Per Serving: Calories 178; Fat 9.54g; Sodium 483mg; Carbs 20.32g; Fiber 3.9g; Sugar 6.67g; Protein 4.37g

Tomatoes

Prep time: 10 minutes | Cook time: 30 minutes | Serves: 6

1 cup carrot, diced
½ cup bell pepper, diced
1 cup spinach, chopped
1 tablespoon olive oil
1 teaspoon chili powder

1 cup tomatoes, chopped
4 ounces low-fat cottage cheese
1 eggplant, sliced
1 cup low-sodium chicken broth

1. In the saucepan, sauté the carrot, bell pepper, spinach with the olive oil and chili powder for 5 minutes. 2. Make the layer of sliced eggplants in the casserole mold and top it with vegetable mixture; add the tomatoes and cottage cheese. 3. Bake the lasagna in the oven for 30 minutes at 375 degrees F. 4. When done, serve and enjoy.
Per Serving: Calories 124; Fat 6.92g; Sodium 192mg; Carbs 9.46g; Fiber 3.9g; Sugar 5.15g; Protein 7.69g

Pumpkin Linguine Pasta with Parmesan

Prep time: 15 minutes | Cook time: 30 minutes | Serves: 6

1-pound whole-grain linguine
1 tablespoon olive oil
3 garlic cloves, peeled and minced
2 tablespoons chopped fresh sage
1½ cups pumpkin purée
1 cup unsalted vegetable stock
½ cup low-fat evaporated milk

¾ teaspoon kosher or sea salt
½ teaspoon ground black pepper
½ teaspoon ground nutmeg
¼ teaspoon ground cayenne pepper
½ cup freshly grated Parmesan cheese, divided

1. Boil a large pot of water and then cook the whole-grain linguine. Reserve ½ cup of pasta water and drain the rest. Set the pasta aside. 2. In the skillet, heat the olive oil over medium heat; add the garlic, sage and sauté them for 1 to 2 minutes until soft and fragrant; add the pumpkin purée, stock, milk, and reserved pasta water, let them simmer for 4 to 5 minutes until thickened. 3. Whisk in the salt, black pepper, nutmeg, cayenne pepper, half of the Parmesan cheese and the cooked whole-grain linguine. 4. Evenly divide the pasta among 6 bowls, top them with the remaining Parmesan cheese and enjoy.
Per Serving: Calories 344; Fat 4.66g; Sodium 472mg; Carbs 65.61g; Fiber 6.8g; Sugar 2.96g; Protein 15.28g

Quinoa & Mushroom-Stuffed Peppers

Prep time: 15 minutes | Cook time: 35 minutes | Serves: 2

2 large green bell peppers, halved
1½ teaspoons olive oil, divided
½ cup quinoa
½ cup minced onion
1 garlic clove, pressed or minced

1 cup chopped portobello mushrooms
3 tablespoons grated Parmesan cheese, divided
4 ounces tomato sauce

1. Preheat the oven to 400 degrees F. 2. Put the pepper halves on your prepared baking sheet, brush the insides of peppers with ½ teaspoon of olive oil and then bake them in the oven for 10 minutes. 3. In the saucepan over medium heat, cook the quinoa according to the package directions. Set aside. 4. In the skillet, heat the remaining olive oil over medium heat; add the onion and sauté them for 3 minutes until translucent; add the garlic and sauté for 1 minute; add the mushrooms and reduce the heat to medium-low, cover the skillet and then cook the food for 5 to 6 minutes until the liquid evaporates. 5. Add tomato sauce, mushroom mixture and 1 tablespoon of Parmesan to the quinoa, stir them well. Spoon the quinoa mixture into each pepper half and sprinkle with the remaining Parmesan. 6. Return the peppers to the oven and bake then for 10 to 15 more minutes until tender. 7. Serve and enjoy.
Per Serving: Calories 269; Fat 8.5g; Sodium 157mg; Carbs 39g; Fiber 5g; Sugar 4.48g; Protein 11.48g

Mushroom Risotto

Prep time: 15 minutes | Cook time: 20 minutes | Serves: 2

2 cups low-sodium vegetable or chicken broth
1 teaspoon olive oil
8 ounces baby portobello mushrooms, thinly sliced

½ cup frozen peas
1 teaspoon butter
1 cup Arborio rice
1 tablespoon grated Parmesan cheese

1. Pour the broth into a microwave-proof glass measuring cup. Microwave on high for 1½ minutes or until hot. 2. In the saucepan, heat the oil over medium heat; add the mushrooms and sauté them for 1 minute, then cover the pan and cook the mushrooms for 3 minutes or until soft. Stir in the peas and reduce the heat to low. 3. Put the mushroom batter to the saucepan's sides and melt the butter in the middle; add the rice and stir for 1 to 2 minutes to lightly toast; add the hot broth, ½ cup at a time, and stir gently. 4. As the broth is cooked into the rice, continue adding more broth, ½ cup at a time, stirring after each addition, until all broth is added. Once all of the liquid is absorbed (this should take 15 minutes), remove from the heat. 5. Serve with Parmesan cheese on the top.
Per Serving: Calories 322; Fat 18.46g; Sodium 210mg; Carbs 45.68g; Fiber 15.9g; Sugar 9.92g; Protein 15.43g

Loaded Tofu Burrito with Greek Yogurt

Prep time: 15 minutes | Cook time: 20 minutes | Serves: 2

4 ounces extra-firm tofu, pressed and cut into 2-inch cubes
2 teaspoons mesquite salt-free seasoning, divided
2 teaspoons canola oil
1 cup thinly sliced bell peppers

½ cup diced onions
⅔ cup of black beans, drained
2 (10-inch) whole-wheat tortillas
1 tablespoon sriracha
Nonfat Greek yogurt, for serving

1. Put the tofu and 1 teaspoon of seasoning in a medium zip-top plastic freezer bag, toss until the tofu is well coated. 2. In the skillet, heat the oil over medium-high heat; add the coated, allow the tofu to brown for 6 minutes, turning halfway through. When lightly browned, transfer the tofu to a small bowl and set aside. 3. Still in the skillet, sauté the peppers and onions for 5 minutes until tender; lower the heat to medium-low, then put the beans and the remaining seasoning, cook them for 5 minutes. 4. For the burritos, lay each tortilla flat on a work surface. Place half of the tofu in the center of each tortilla, top with half of the pepper-bean mixture, and drizzle with the sriracha. 5. Fold the bottom portion of each tortilla up and over the tofu mixture. Then fold each side into the middle, tuck in, and tightly roll it up toward the open end. 6. Serve with a dollop of yogurt.
Per Serving: Calories 489; Fat 13.11g; Sodium 546mg; Carbs 72.36g; Fiber 17.2g; Sugar 8.23g; Protein 25.19g

Simple Tofu Scramble

Prep time: 15 minutes | Cook time: 15 minutes | Serves: 1

½ tablespoon olive oil
½ red onion, chopped
2 cups chopped spinach
8 ounces firm tofu, drained well

1 teaspoon ground cumin
½ teaspoon garlic powder
Optional for serving: sliced avocado or sliced tomatoes

1. In the skillet, heat the olive oil over medium heat; add the onion and sauté for 5 minutes; add the spinach and then cover the skillet, let the food steam for 2 minutes. 2. Move the veggies to one side of the pan. 3. Crumble the tofu into the open area in the pan, breaking it up with a fork; add the cumin and garlic to the crumbled tofu, mix well and sauté them for 5 to 7 minutes until the tofu is slightly browned. 4. Serve immediately with whole-grain bread, fruit, or beans. You can also serve sliced avocado and tomatoes.
Per Serving: Calories 315; Fat 20.79g; Sodium 72mg; Carbs 13.94g; Fiber 3.5g; Sugar 3.8g; Protein 25.39g

Black-Bean and Vegetable Burrito with Cherry Tomatoes

Prep time: 15 minutes | Cook time: 15 minutes | Serves: 4

½ tablespoon olive oil
2 red or green bell peppers, chopped
1 zucchini or summer squash, diced
½ teaspoon chili powder
1 teaspoon cumin
Freshly ground black pepper

2 cans black beans drained and rinsed
1 cup cherry tomatoes, halved
4 (8-inch) whole-wheat tortillas
Optional for serving: spinach, sliced avocado, chopped scallions, or hot sauce

1. In the skillet, heat the oil over medium heat; add the bell peppers and

sauté for 4 minutes until crisp-tender; add the zucchini, chili powder, cumin and black pepper, sauté them for 5 minutes until the vegetables are tender. 2. Add the black beans, cherry tomatoes and cook them for 5 minutes. 3. Divide between 4 burritos and serve topped with optional ingredients as desired.
Per Serving: Calories 171; Fat 6.18g; Sodium 228mg; Carbs 24.82g; Fiber 5.7g; Sugar 4.42g; Protein 5.61g

Baked Eggs in Avocado with Tortillas

Prep time: 15 minutes | Cook time: 15 minutes | Serves: 2

2 avocados
Juice of 2 limes
Freshly ground black pepper
4 eggs
2 (8-inch) whole-wheat or corn

tortillas, warmed
Optional for serving: halved cherry tomatoes and chopped cilantro

1. Preheat the oven to 450 degrees F. 2. Scrape out the center of halved avocado using a spoon about 1½ tablespoons. 3. Drizzle lime juice over the avocados and season with black pepper, then place it on the baking sheet. 4. Crack an egg into the avocado. 5. Bake the food in the oven for 10 to 15 minutes. 6. Garnish with optional cilantro and cherry tomatoes and serve with warm tortillas.
Per Serving: Calories 587; Fat 41.89g; Sodium 350mg; Carbs 40.68g; Fiber 17.8g; Sugar 3.4g; Protein 19.32g

Lentil and Carrot Quiche

Prep time: 15 minutes | Cook time: 35 minutes | Serves: 2

1 cup green lentils, boiled
½ cup carrot, grated
1 onion, diced
1 tablespoon olive oil

¼ cup flax seeds meal
1 teaspoon ground black pepper
¼ cup of soy milk

1. Sauté the onion with olive oil in the skillet until light brown. 2. In a suitable bowl, add the cooked onion, lentils, carrot, flax seeds meal, black pepper and soy milk, stir them until homogenous. 3. Transfer the mixture to the baking pan and flatten well. 4. Bake the mixture in the oven for 35 minutes at 375 degrees F. 5. When done, serve and enjoy.
Per Serving: Calories 280; Fat 8.64g; Sodium 44mg; Carbs 37.11g; Fiber 2.6g; Sugar 5.26g; Protein 18.31g

Easy-to-Make Corn Patties

Prep time: 15 minutes | Cook time: 10 minutes | Serves: 1

½ cup chickpeas, cooked
1 cup corn kernels, cooked
1 tablespoon fresh parsley, chopped
1 teaspoon chili powder

½ teaspoon ground coriander
1 tablespoon tomato paste
1 tablespoon almond meal
1 tablespoon olive oil

1. Add the cooked chickpeas to a bowl, mash them and then combine them with corn kernels, parsley, chili powder, ground coriander, tomato paste and almond meal. 2. Stir the mixture until homogenous and form small patties from them. 3. In the skillet, heat the olive oil; add the patties and cook them for 3 minutes on each side, until they are golden brown. 4. Dry the cooked patties with the paper towel if needed. Serve and enjoy.
Per Serving: Calories 468; Fat 18.72g; Sodium 101mg; Carbs 63.84g; Fiber 11.8g; Sugar 10.9g; Protein 13.79g

Carrot Eggplant Lasagna with Tofu Spinach Stir Fry

Prep time: 15 minutes | Cook time: 10 minutes | Serves: 2

9-ounce firm tofu, cubed
3 tablespoons low-sodium soy sauce
1 teaspoon sesame seeds
1 tablespoon sesame oil
1 cup spinach, chopped
¼ cup of water

1. In the mixing bowl, mix up the soy sauce and sesame oil; add the tofu cubes and marinate them for 10 minutes. 2. Roast the marinated tofu cubes in the heated skillet for 1½ minutes on each side. 3. Add the remaining soy sauce mixture, water and chopped spinach, cover the skillet and wait for 5 minutes longer. 4. When done, serve and enjoy.
Per Serving: Calories 269 Fat 18.88g; Sodium 797mg; Carbs 7.34g; Fiber 3.6g; Sugar 0.18g; Protein 22.77g

Veggie Pasta Stuffed Sweet Potatoes

Prep time: 20 minutes | Cook time: 30 minutes | Serves: 2

1 sweet potato
¼ cup whole-grain penne pasta
1 teaspoon tomato paste
1 teaspoon olive oil
¼ teaspoon minced garlic
1 tablespoon soy milk

1. Preheat the oven to 375 degrees F. 2. Cut the sweet potato in half and use the fork to pierce them 3-4 times. Transfer them to the baking pan. 3. Sprinkle the sweet potato halves with the olive oil and bake them in the oven for 25-30 minutes or until the vegetables are tender. 4. While baking the sweet potato, in a bowl, mix up the penne pasta, tomato paste, minced garlic and soy milk. 5. When the sweet potatoes are cooked, scoop out the vegetable meat and mix it up with a penne pasta mixture. 6. Fill the sweet potatoes with the pasta mixture. 7. Serve and enjoy.
Per Serving: Calories 134; Fat 2.92g; Sodium 41mg; Carbs 24.87g; Fiber 3.7g; Sugar 3.5g; Protein 3.38g

Tofu Tomato Masala

Prep time: 10 minutes | Cook time: 25 minutes | Serves: 2

8-ounce tofu, chopped
½ cup of soy milk
1 teaspoon garam masala
1 teaspoon olive oil
1 teaspoon ground paprika
½ cup tomatoes, chopped
½ onion, diced

1. In the saucepan, heat the olive oil; add the diced onion and sauté them until light brown. 2. Add the ground paprika, garam masala, tomatoes and then bring to boil; stir in the soy milk and let the food simmer for 5 minutes. 3. Add the chopped tofu and let the meal cook for 3 minutes longer. 4. When done, turn off the heat and let the meal rest for 10 minutes before serving.
Per Serving: Calories 237; Fat 13.8g; Sodium 92mg; Carbs 13.38g; Fiber 4.4g; Sugar 5.59g; Protein 19.85g

Easy Tofu Parmigiana

Prep time: 15 minutes | Cook time: 8 minutes | Serves: 2

6-ounce firm tofu, roughly sliced
1 teaspoon coconut oil
1 teaspoon tomato sauce
½ teaspoon Italian seasonings

1. In the mixing bowl, mix up the tomato sauce and Italian seasonings. 2. Brush the sliced tofu with the tomato mixture and wait for 10 minutes to marinate them. 3. In the skillet, heat the coconut oil; roast the sliced tofu in the hot oil for 3 minutes on each side or until the tofu are golden brown. 4. When done, serve and enjoy.
Per Serving: Calories 148; Fat 9.67g; Sodium 100mg; Carbs 4.6g; Fiber 2.2g; Sugar 0.38g; Protein 13.52g

Mushroom Onion Scramble

Prep time: 10 minutes | Cook time: 20 minutes | Serves: 2

2 cups mushrooms, sliced
1 teaspoon whole-grain wheat flour
1 tablespoon coconut oil
1 onion, chopped
1 teaspoon dried thyme
1 garlic clove, diced
1 teaspoon ground black pepper
½ cup of soy milk

1. In the saucepan, heat the coconut oil; add the mushrooms, onion and sauté them for 10 minutes. 2. Sprinkle the vegetables with ground black pepper, thyme and garlic; add the soy milk and then bring the mixture to boil. 3. Add the flour and stir them well until homogenous. 4. Cook the mushroom stroganoff until it thickens. 5. When done, serve and enjoy.
Per Serving: Calories 121; Fat 8.19g; Sodium 37mg; Carbs 10.99g; Fiber 1.6g; Sugar 5.71g; Protein 2.2g

Eggplant Potato Croquettes

Prep time: 15 minutes | Cook time: 5 minutes | Serves: 2

1 eggplant, peeled, boiled
2 potatoes, mashed
2 tablespoons almond meal
1 teaspoon chili pepper
1 tablespoon coconut oil
1 tablespoon olive oil
¼ teaspoon ground nutmeg

1. Blend the eggplant in the blender or food processor until smooth. 2. Mix the blended eggplant with the mashed potato, chili pepper, coconut oil and ground nutmeg. 3. Make the croquettes from the eggplant mixture. 4. In the skillet, heat the olive oil; roast the croquettes in the hot oil for 2 minutes on each side or until they are light brown. 5. When done, serve and enjoy.
Per Serving: Calories 335; Fat 14.95g; Sodium 17mg; Carbs 48.35g; Fiber 12.5g; Sugar 12.21g; Protein 6.84g

Vegetable-Stuffed Portobello

Prep time: 10 minutes | Cook time: 20 minutes | Serves: 2

4 Portobello mushroom caps
½ zucchini, grated
1 tomato, diced
1 teaspoon olive oil
½ teaspoon dried parsley
¼ teaspoon minced garlic

1. Preheat the oven to 400 degrees F. Line the baking tray with a piece of baking paper. 2. In the mixing bowl, mix up the diced tomato, grated zucchini with the dried parsley and minced garlic. 3. Fill the mushroom caps with zucchini mixture and transfer them to the baking tray. 4. Bake the vegetables in the oven for 20 minutes or until they are soft. 5. When done, serve and enjoy.
Per Serving: Calories 40; Fat 2.51g; Sodium 5mg; Carbs 3.79g; Fiber 1.1g; Sugar 2.34g; Protein 1.76g

Chile Rellenos with Potato Mixture

Prep time: 10 minutes | Cook time: 30 minutes | Serves: 2

2 chili peppers
2 ounces vegan Mozzarella cheese, shredded
2 ounces tomato puree
1 tablespoon coconut oil

2 tablespoons whole-grain wheat flour
1 tablespoon potato starch
¼ cup water
½ teaspoon chili flakes

1. Preheat the oven to 375 degrees F. 2. Bake the chili peppers in the oven for 15 minutes. 3. While baking the chili peppers, pour the tomato puree in the saucepan and add the chili flakes, bring the mixture to boil and then remove the pan from the heat. 4. In a suitable bowl, mix up the potato starch, flour and water. 5. When the chili peppers are cooked, make the cuts in them and remove the seeds; fill them with the shredded cheese and use the toothpicks to secure the cutes. 6. In the skillet, heat the coconut oil; dip the chili peppers in the flour mixture and then roast them in the hot oil until they are golden brown. 7. Sprinkle the cooked chilies with potato puree mixture. Serve hot.
Per Serving: Calories 166; Fat 7.25g; Sodium 249mg; Carbs 16.05g; Fiber 2.8g; Sugar 2.97g; Protein 11.65g

Homemade Carrot Cakes

Prep time: 10 minutes | Cook time: 10 minutes | Serves: 4

1 cup carrot, grated
1 tablespoon semolina
1 egg, beaten

1 teaspoon Italian seasonings
1 tablespoon sesame oil

1. Mix up the grated carrot, semolina, egg and Italian seasonings in the mixing bowl; form the carrot cakes from the mixture. 2. Heat up sesame oil in the skillet; roast the carrot cakes in the hot oil for 4 minutes on each side. 3. When done, serve and enjoy.
Per Serving: Calories 69; Fat 4.54g; Sodium 87mg; Carbs 5.03g; Fiber 1g; Sugar 1.42g; Protein 2g

Tofu Turkey with Mushroom Mixture

Prep time: 15 minutes | Cook time: 75 minutes | Serves: 6

1 onion, diced
1 cup mushrooms, chopped
1 bell pepper, chopped
12 ounces firm tofu, crumbled

1 teaspoon dried rosemary
1 tablespoon avocado oil
½ cup marinara sauce
1 teaspoon miso paste

1. Sauté onion, mushrooms, bell pepper, rosemary, miso paste and avocado oil in the saucepan for 10 to 15 minutes or until the ingredients are cooked. 2. Put ½ part of tofu in the round baking pan. Press well and make the medium hole in the center. 3. Put the mushroom mixture in the tofu hole and top it with marinara sauce. 4. Add remaining tofu and press it well. Cover the meal with foil. 5. Bake the tofu turkey in the oven for 60 minutes at 395 degrees F. 6. When done, serve and enjoy.
Per Serving: Calories 130; Fat 7.75g; Sodium 52mg; Carbs 7.37g; Fiber 2.3g; Sugar 2.71g; Protein 10.21g

Baked Cauliflower Tots

Prep time: 15 minutes | Cook time: 20 minutes | Serves: 4

1 cup cauliflower, shredded
3 ounces vegan Parmesan, grated
⅓ cup flax seeds meal

1 egg, beaten
1 teaspoon Italian seasonings
1 teaspoon olive oil

1. Preheat the oven to 375 degrees F. Line the baking tray with baking paper. 2. Mix up the shredded cauliflower, vegan Parmesan, flax seeds meal, egg and Italian seasonings in a bowl. 3. Knead the cauliflower mixture. Add water if needed. 4. Make the cauliflower tots from the mixture and then arrange the cauliflower tots to the baking tray. 5. Sprinkle them with the olive oil and bake them in the oven for 15 to 20 minutes or until golden brown. 6. When done, serve and enjoy.
Per Serving: Calories 156; Fat 3.61g; Sodium 321mg; Carbs 16.43g; Fiber 0.6g; Sugar 0.95g; Protein 14.89g

Whole Grain Spaghetti

Prep time: 5 minutes | Cook time: 10 minutes | Serves: 2

1 teaspoon dried basil
¼ cup soy milk
6 ounces whole-grain spaghetti

2 cups water
1 teaspoon ground nutmeg

1. In the pot, boil the water and then cook the spaghetti in the hot water for 8-10 minutes. 2. In the saucepan, bring the soy milk to boil. 3. Drain the cooked spaghetti and mix them up with soy milk, ground nutmeg and dried basil. 4. Stir the meal well before serving.
Per Serving: Calories 126; Fat 1.48g; Sodium 25mg; Carbs 24.9g; Fiber 4.2g; Sugar 2.34g; Protein 5.17g

Sautéed Tomatoes with Onion

Prep time: 5 minutes | Cook time: 15 minutes | Serves: 3

2 cups plum tomatoes, roughly chopped
½ cup onion, diced
½ teaspoon garlic, diced

1 teaspoon Italian seasonings
1 teaspoon canola oil
1 chili pepper, chopped

1. Heat the canola oil in the saucepan; add the onion, chili pepper and sauté them for 5 minutes. 2. Add tomatoes, garlic and Italian seasonings, stir well and then cover the pan. 3. Let the meal cook for 10 minutes longer. 4. When done, serve and enjoy.
Per Serving: Calories 49; Fat 1.75g; Sodium 76mg; Carbs 7.79g; Fiber 1.9g; Sugar 4.3g; Protein 1.46g

Simple Vegan Simmering

Prep time: 10 minutes | Cook time: 25 minutes | Serves: 4

½ cup bulgur
1 cup tomatoes, chopped
1 chili pepper, chopped
1 cup red kidney beans, cooked

2 cups low-sodium chicken broth
1 teaspoon tomato paste
½ cup celery stalk, chopped

1. In the saucepan, add all ingredients and stir them well. 2. Cover the pan and simmer the food for 25 minutes over medium-low heat. 3. When done, serve and enjoy.
Per Serving: Calories 82; Fat 2.84g; Sodium 52mg; Carbs 10.8g; Fiber 2.1g; Sugar 2.27g; Protein 4.95g

Spinach and Artichoke Heart Casserole

Prep time: 5 minutes | Cook time: 30 minutes | Serves: 3

2 cups spinach, chopped
4-ounce artichoke hearts, chopped
¼ cup low-fat yogurt

1 teaspoon Italian seasonings
2 ounces vegan mozzarella, shredded

1. Preheat the oven to 365 degrees F. 2. Mix up all ingredients in the casserole mold and then cover the mold with foil. 3. Bake the food in the oven for 30 minutes. 4. When done, serve and enjoy.
Per Serving: Calories 65; Fat 0.45g; Sodium 276mg; Carbs 7.36g; Fiber 2.9g; Sugar 2.28g; Protein 8.92g

Homemade Falafel

Prep time: 10 minutes | Cook time: 25 minutes | Serves: 6

2 cups chickpeas, cooked
1 yellow onion, diced
3 tablespoons olive oil
1 cup fresh parsley, chopped

1 teaspoon ground cumin
½ teaspoon coriander
2 garlic cloves, diced

1. Preheat the oven to 375 degrees F. Line the baking tray with a piece of baking paper. 2. In the blender or food processor, add all the ingredients and then blend them until smooth. 3. Make the balls from the chickpeas mixture and press them gently in the shape of the falafel. 4. Put the falafel in the baking tray and bake them in the oven for 25 minutes. 5. When done, serve and enjoy.
Per Serving: Calories 163; Fat 8.35g; Sodium 11mg; Carbs 17.82g; Fiber 4.9g; Sugar 3.5g; Protein 5.47g

Tasty Vegan Risotto

Prep time: 10 minutes | Cook time: 25 minutes | Serves: 6

1 teaspoon dried saffron
1 cup short-grain rice
1 tablespoon olive oil
2 cups water
1 teaspoon chili flakes

6 ounces artichoke hearts, chopped
½ cup green peas
1 onion, sliced
1 cup bell pepper, sliced

1. In the saucepan, add the water and rice and then cook the rice for 15 minutes. 2. While cooking the rice, heat the olive oil in the skillet; add the onion, bell pepper, chili flakes and dried saffron, sauté them for 5 minutes. 3. Add the onion mixture, artichoke hearts and green peas to the cooked rice, stir them well and cook them for 10 minutes over low heat. 4. When done, serve and enjoy.
Per Serving: Calories 162; Fat 3.4g; Sodium 84mg; Carbs 29.6g; Fiber 3.6g; Sugar 1.46g; Protein 4.27g

Garlicky Mushroom Cakes

Prep time: 15 minutes | Cook time: 10 minutes | Serves: 4

2 cups mushrooms, chopped
3 garlic cloves, chopped
1 tablespoon dried dill
1 egg, beaten

¼ cup rice, cooked
1 tablespoon sesame oil
1 teaspoon chili powder

1. Grind the mushrooms in the food processor; add the garlic, dill,

chili powder, egg and rice, blend the mixture for 10 seconds. 2. Form the medium-size mushroom cakes from the mixture. 3. Heat the sesame oil for 1 minute in the skillet; cook the mushroom cakes in the hot oil for 5 minutes on each side over medium heat. 4. When done, serve and enjoy.
Per Serving: Calories 90; Fat 6.49g; Sodium 38mg; Carbs 7.3g; Fiber 2.7g; Sugar 1.13g; Protein 4.35g

Glazed Eggplant Rings

Prep time: 10 minutes | Cook time: 10 minutes | Serves: 4

3 eggplants, sliced
1 tablespoon liquid honey
1 teaspoon minced ginger
2 tablespoons lemon juice

3 tablespoons avocado oil
½ teaspoon ground coriander
3 tablespoons water

1. Rub the eggplants with ground coriander. 2. Heat the avocado oil in the skillet for 1 minute; add the eggplant slices to the hot oil and arrange them in one layer, cook them for 1 minute on each side. 3. Transfer the eggplant in the bowl. 4. Still in the skillet, add the minced ginger, liquid honey, lemon juice, water and then bring them to boil. 5. Put the cooked eggplant slices back to the skillet, coat them with the mixture and cook them for 2 minutes longer. 6. When done, serve and enjoy.
Per Serving: Calories 214; Fat 4.69g; Sodium 11.26mg; Carbs 29.11g; Fiber 12.4g; Sugar 19.02g; Protein 4.08g

Golden Sweet Potato Balls

Prep time: 15 minutes | Cook time: 10 minutes | Serves: 4

1 cup sweet potato, mashed, cooked
1 tablespoon fresh cilantro, chopped
1 egg, beaten

3 tablespoons ground oatmeal
1 teaspoon ground paprika
½ teaspoon ground turmeric
2 tablespoons coconut oil

1. Mix the mashed sweet potato, fresh cilantro, egg, ground oatmeal, paprika and turmeric in a mixing bowl well until smooth. 2. Form the small balls from the mixture. 3. Heat the coconut oil in the saucepan; cook the balls in the hot oil for 10 minutes on all sides or until golden brown. 4. When done, serve and enjoy.
Per Serving: Calories 174; Fat 10.52g; Sodium 103mg; Carbs 16.96g; Fiber 2.6g; Sugar 3.64g; Protein 4.76g

Easy Chickpea Curry

Prep time: 10 minutes | Cook time: 10 minutes | Serves: 4

1 ½ cup chickpeas, boiled
1 teaspoon curry powder
½ teaspoon garam masala
1 cup spinach, chopped

1 teaspoon coconut oil
¼ cup soy milk
1 tablespoon tomato paste
½ cup water

1. Heat the coconut oil in the saucepan; add the curry powder, garam masala, tomato paste and soy milk, stir them until smooth and then bring them to boil. 2. Add water, spinach and chickpeas, stir them well and then cover the pan. 3. Let the food cook for 5 minutes over the medium heat.
Per Serving: Calories 125; Fat 3.19g; Sodium 32mg; Carbs 19.15g; Fiber 5.4g; Sugar 4.32g; Protein 6.2g

Carrot Lentil Soup

Prep time: 15 minutes | Cook time: 30 minutes | Serves: 4

1 tablespoon olive oil
2 carrots, peeled and chopped
2 celery stalks, diced
1 onion, chopped
1 teaspoon dried thyme
½ teaspoon garlic powder

freshly ground black pepper
1 (28-ounce) can no-salt diced tomatoes, drained
1 cup dry lentils
5 cups water
low-sodium salt

1. Heat the oil in a pot over medium heat; sauté the carrot, celery and onion in the hot oil for 5 minutes; add the thyme, garlic powder, black pepper and sauté them for 30 seconds. 2. Pour in the drained diced tomatoes and cook for a few more minutes, often stirring to enhance their flavor. 3. Add the lentils, water and a pinch of salt; raise the heat and bring to a boil, then partially cover the pot and reduce heat to maintain a gentle simmer. 4. Simmer the food for 30 minutes, or until lentils are tender but still hold their shape. 5. Ladle the food into serving bowls and serve with a fresh green salad and whole-grain bread.
Per Serving: Calories 107; Fat 4.11g; Sodium 89mg; Carbs 16.97g; Fiber 5.8g; Sugar 7.44g; Protein 4.06g

Quinoa Tomato Bowl

Prep time: 15 minutes | Cook time: 15 minutes | Serves: 4

1 cup quinoa
2 cups water
1 cup tomatoes, diced
1 cup sweet pepper, diced

½ cup rice, cooked
1 tablespoon lemon juice
½ teaspoon lemon zest, grated
1 tablespoon olive oil

1. In the pot, add the water and quinoa, cook them for 15 minutes. Let the quinoa rest for 10 minutes. 2. Transfer the cooked quinoa in the serving bowl, stir in the olive oil, rice, sweet pepper, tomatoes, lemon zest and lemon juice. 3. Enjoy.
Per Serving: Calories 248; Fat 9.18g; Sodium 8mg; Carbs 37.74g; Fiber 7g; Sugar 2.19g; Protein 8.54g

Vegan Chickpeas Meatloaf

Prep time: 10 minutes | Cook time: 30 minutes | Serves: 6

1 cup chickpeas, cooked
1 onion, diced
1 tablespoon ground flax seeds
½ teaspoon chili flakes

1 tablespoon coconut oil
½ cup carrot, diced
½ cup celery stalk, chopped
1 tablespoon tomato paste

1. Preheat the oven to 365 degrees F. Line the loaf mold with baking paper. 2. Heat up coconut oil in the saucepan; add the onion, carrot, celery stalk and sauté them for 8 minutes until they are soft. 3. Add chickpeas, chili flakes and ground flax seeds. 4. Transfer the mixture to a blender and blend the mixture until smooth. 5. Transfer the blended mixture to the prepared load mold. 6. Flatten it well and spread with tomato paste. 7. Bake the meatloaf in the oven for 20 minutes. 8. When done, serve and enjoy.
Per Serving: Calories 85; Fat 3.46g; Sodium 24mg; Carbs 11.25g; Fiber 3.1g; Sugar 3.05g; Protein 3.19g

Red Beans and Rice with Spinach

Prep time: 15 minutes | Cook time: 45 minutes | Serves: 2

½ cup dry brown rice
1 cup water, plus ¼ cup
1 can red beans, drained
1 tablespoon ground cumin
Juice of 1 lime

4 handfuls of fresh spinach
Optional toppings: avocado, chopped tomatoes, Greek yogurt, onions

1. Mix rice plus water in a pot and bring to a boil; when boiled, cover the pot and reduce heat to low. Cook the rice for 30 to 40 minutes. 2. While cooking the rice, add the beans, ¼ cup of water, cumin and lime juice to a medium skillet, then simmer them for 5 to 7 minutes. 3. Once the liquid is mostly gone, remove from the heat and add the spinach. Cover and let spinach wilt for 2 to 3 minutes. Mix in with the beans. 4. Serve beans with rice and the toppings you like.
Per Serving: Calories 357; Fat 3.51g; Sodium 334mg; Carbs 68.21g; Fiber 9.8g; Sugar 5.97g; Protein 15.48g

Black-Bean and Onion Soup

Prep time: 15 minutes | Cook time: 20 minutes | Serves: 4

1 yellow onion
1 tablespoon olive oil
2 cans black beans, drained
1 cup diced fresh tomatoes
5 cups low-sodium vegetable

broth
¼ teaspoon freshly ground black pepper
¼ cup chopped fresh cilantro

1. Sauté the onion with the olive oil for 4 to 5 minutes in a large saucepan over medium heat. 2. Add the black beans, tomatoes, vegetable broth, black pepper and bring them to boil; when boiled, adjust heat to simmer and simmer them for 15 minutes. 3. Ladle the soup into a blender and process until somewhat smooth. Blend them in batches. 4. Put them back to the pot, add the cilantro, and heat until warmed through. 5. Serve immediately.
Per Serving: Calories 109; Fat 4.52g; Sodium 178mg; Carbs 16.46g; Fiber 2.6g; Sugar 11.1g; Protein 3.59g

Baked Sweet Potatoes with Greek Yogurt

Prep time: 15 minutes | Cook time: 20 minutes | Serves: 4

4 sweet potatoes
½ cup nonfat or low-fat plain Greek yogurt
Freshly ground black pepper
1 teaspoon olive oil

1 red bell pepper, cored and diced
½ red onion, diced
1 teaspoon ground cumin
1 (15-ounce) can chickpeas, drained and rinsed

1. Use a fork to prick the potatoes and then bake them in the oven at 400 degrees F for 45 minutes. 2. In the bowl, mix up the yogurt and black pepper. Set aside for later use. 3. In the pot, heat the oil over medium heat; add the bell pepper, cumin, onion, black pepper, chickpeas and sauté them for 5 minutes. 4. When the potatoes are cooked, slice them lengthwise down the middle and then top each half with a portion of the bean mixture and 1 to 2 tablespoons of yogurt mixture. 5. Serve and enjoy.
Per Serving: Calories 242; Fat 3.43g; Sodium 230mg; Carbs 45.71g; Fiber 8.5g; Sugar 11.32g; Protein 8.63g

White Beans with Spinach

Prep time: 15 minutes | Cook time: 10 minutes | Serves: 2

1 tablespoon olive oil
4 small plum tomatoes, halved lengthwise
10 ounces frozen spinach, defrosted and squeezed of excess water
2 garlic cloves, thinly sliced

2 tablespoons water
¼ teaspoon freshly ground black pepper
1 can white beans, drained
Juice of 1 lemon

1. Heat the oil in the skillet over medium-high heat; add the tomatoes, cut-side down, and sauté them for 3 to 5 minutes; turn and cook within 1 minute more. Transfer to a plate. 2. Reduce heat to medium and add the spinach, garlic, water, and pepper to the skillet, sauté them for 2 to 3 minutes until the spinach is heated through. 3. Return the tomatoes to the skillet, add the white beans and lemon juice, sauté them for 1 to 2 minutes until heated through.
Per Serving: Calories 146; Fat 8.31g; Sodium 110mg; Carbs 15.82g; Fiber 7.2g; Sugar 3.47g; Protein 7.22g

Black-Eyed Peas and Greens Power Salad

Prep time: 15 minutes | Cook time: 10 minutes | Serves: 2

1 tablespoon olive oil
3 cups purple cabbage, chopped
5 cups baby spinach
1 cup shredded carrots

1 can black-eyed peas, drained
Juice of ½ lemon
Low-sodium salt
Freshly ground black pepper

1. In a medium pan, sauté the oil and cabbage for 1 to 2 minutes over medium heat. 2. Add the spinach and cover the pan, cook the spinach for 3 to 4 minutes on medium heat, until greens are wilted. 3. Transfer the cooked spinach to a bowl, add the carrots, black-eyed peas, salt, pepper and a splash of lemon juice, toss well before serving.
Per Serving: Calories 254; Fat 8g; Sodium 214mg; Carbs 39.08g; Fiber 12.7g; Sugar 14.86g; Protein 11.64g

Portobello Mushroom Cheeseburgers with Avocado

Prep time: 15 minutes | Cook time: 10 minutes | Serves: 4

4 portobello mushrooms, caps removed and brushed clean
1 tablespoon olive oil
½ teaspoon freshly ground black pepper
1 tablespoon red wine vinegar

4 slices reduced-fat Swiss cheese, sliced thin
4 whole-wheat 100-calorie sandwich thins
½ avocado, sliced thin

1. Heat-up a skillet or grill pan over medium-high heat. 2. Clean the mushrooms and remove the stems. Brush each cap with olive oil and sprinkle with black pepper. 3. In the skillet over medium-high heat, place the mushrooms in skillet cap-side up and cook for about 8 minutes, flipping halfway through. 4. Sprinkle with the red wine vinegar and flip; add the cheese and cook for 2 more minutes. For optimal melting, place a lid loosely over the pan. 5. Toast the sandwich thins. Top each thin with sliced avocado. Enjoy immediately.
Per Serving: Calories 206; Fat 9.68g; Sodium 204mg; Carbs 17.6g; Fiber 3.9g; Sugar 2.29g; Protein 13.04g

Butternut Squash and Macaroni

Prep time: 15 minutes | Cook time: 20 minutes | Serves: 2

1 cup whole-wheat ziti macaroni
2 cups peeled and cubed butternut squash
1 cup nonfat or low-fat milk, divided

Freshly ground black pepper
1 teaspoon Dijon mustard
1 tablespoon olive oil
¼ cup shredded low-fat cheddar cheese

1. Cook the pasta until al dente. 2. In the saucepan over medium-high heat, add the butternut squash, ½ cup of milk and black pepper; bring them to simmer and then lower the heat, cook them for 8 to 10 minutes until fork-tender. 3. Add squash and Dijon mustard in the blender, then purée them until smooth. 4. In the skillet, heat the olive oil over medium heat; add the squash purée and the remaining milk, simmer them for 5 minutes. 5. Add the cheese and pasta, stir them to combine. 6. Serve immediately.
Per Serving: Calories 309; Fat 11.18g; Sodium 229mg; Carbs 41.93g; Fiber 5.2g; Sugar 9.75g; Protein 14.2g

Tomato-Pea Pasta

Prep time: 15 minutes | Cook time: 15 minutes | Serves: 2

½ cup whole-grain pasta of choice
8 cups water, plus ¼ for finishing
1 cup frozen peas
1 tablespoon olive oil
1 cup cherry tomatoes, halved

¼ teaspoon freshly ground black pepper
1 teaspoon dried basil
¼ cup grated Parmesan cheese (low-sodium)

1. Cook the pasta al dente; add the water to the same pot you used to cook the pasta, and when it's boiling, add the peas and cook them for 5 minutes. Drain and set aside. 2. Heat the oil in the large skillet over medium heat; add the cherry tomatoes and cover the skillet, then let the tomatoes soften for 5 minutes, stirring a few times. 3. Add the black pepper, basil, pasta, peas and ¼ cup of water, stir and remove from the heat. 4. Top with the Parmesan and serve.
Per Serving: Calories 216; Fat 11.37g; Sodium 141mg; Carbs 19.58g; Fiber 4.2g; Sugar 9.58g; Protein 10.61g

Vegetable Scrambled with Brown Rice

Prep time: 15 minutes | Cook time: 10 minutes | Serves: 4

For the sauce:
⅓ cup garlic vinegar
1½ tablespoons dark molasses
1 teaspoon onion powder
For the fried rice:
1 teaspoon olive oil

2 lightly beaten whole eggs + 4 egg whites
1 cup frozen mixed vegetables
1 cup frozen edamame
2 cups cooked brown rice

To make the sauce: In a glass jar, add all the sauce ingredients and combine them well.
To make the fried rice: 1. Heat the oil in the skillet over medium-high heat; add eggs and egg whites, cook them for 1 minute until the eggs set. 2. Break up eggs with the spatula into small pieces; add the frozen mixed vegetables, frozen edamame and sauté for 4 minutes. 3. Add the brown rice and sauce to the vegetable-and-egg mixture, cook them for 5 minutes or until heated through. 4. Serve immediately.
Per Serving: Calories 232; Fat 4.13g; Sodium 55mg; Carbs 38.58g; Fiber 5.9g; Sugar 8.45g; Protein 9.89g

Chickpeas-Rosemary Omelet

Prep time: 15 minutes | Cook time: 15 minutes | Serves: 2

½ tablespoon olive oil
4 eggs
¼ cup grated Parmesan cheese
1 (15-ounce) can chickpeas, drained and rinsed
2 cups packed baby spinach
1 cup button mushrooms, chopped
2 sprigs rosemary, leaves picked (or 2 teaspoons dried rosemary)
Low-sodium salt
Freshly ground black pepper

1. Preheat the oven to 400 degrees F. Line the spring form pan with baking paper and grease generously with olive oil. 2. Lightly whisk the eggs and Parmesan in a bowl. 3. In the pan, place the chickpeas, layer the spinach and mushrooms on the top, then pour the egg mixture on top and scatter the rosemary; season with the salt and pepper. 4. Bake the food in the oven for 15 minutes until golden and puffy and the center feels firm and springy. 5. Slice before serving.
Per Serving: Calories 402; Fat 18.71g; Sodium 724mg; Carbs 34.25g; Fiber 9.3g; Sugar 6.49g; Protein 25.92g

Chilled Cucumber-Avocado Soup

Prep time: 15 minutes | Cook time: 0 | Serves: 4

2 English cucumbers, peeled and diced, plus ¼ cup reserved for garnish
1 avocado, peeled, pitted, and chopped, plus ¼ cup reserved for garnish
1½ cups nonfat or low-fat plain Greek yogurt
½ cup cold water
⅓ cup loosely packed dill, plus sprigs for garnish
1 tablespoon freshly squeezed lemon juice
¼ teaspoon freshly ground black pepper
¼ teaspoon salt
1 clove garlic

1. Add the yogurt, cold water, garlic, lemon juice, salt and black pepper to the blender, then purée them until smooth. 2. Divide soup among 4 bowls. Cover each bowl with plastic wrap and refrigerate the food for 30 minutes. 3. You can serve the dish with the cucumber, avocado and dill sprigs.
Per Serving: Calories 127; Fat 7.04g; Sodium 214mg; Carbs 11.58g; Fiber 3g; Sugar 7.64g; Protein 6g

Blended Cauliflower Mix

Prep time: 10 minutes | Cook time: 10 minutes | Serves: 4

16 cups water (enough to cover cauliflower)
1 head cauliflower (about 3 pounds), trimmed and cut into florets
4 garlic cloves
1 tablespoon olive oil
¼ teaspoon salt
⅛ teaspoon freshly ground black pepper
2 teaspoons dried parsley

1. Boil a large pot of water, cook the cauliflower and garlic in the hot water for 10 minutes, then strain. 2. Move them back to the hot pan, and let them stand within 2 to 3 minutes with the lid on. 3. Transfer the cauliflower mixture to the blender, add the olive oil, salt, pepper and then purée them until smooth. 4. Add the parsley and mix until combined. 5. You can garnish this meal with additional olive oil. Serve immediately.
Per Serving: Calories 51; Fat 3.58g; Sodium 185mg; Carbs 4.39g; Fiber 1.4g; Sugar 1.3g; Protein 1.49g

Simple Roasted Brussels Sprouts

Prep time: 5 minutes | Cook time: 20 minutes | Serves: 4

1½ pounds Brussels sprouts, trimmed and halved
2 tablespoons olive oil
¼ teaspoon salt
½ teaspoon freshly ground black pepper

1. Preheat the oven to 400 degrees F. 2. Toss the Brussels sprouts and olive oil in a large mixing bowl until evenly coated. 3. Transfer the Brussels sprouts to a large baking sheet, cut-side down with the flat part touching the baking sheet. Sprinkle with salt and pepper. 4. Bake the Brussels sprouts in the oven for 20 to 30 minutes or until the Brussels sprouts are lightly charred and crisp on the outside and toasted on the bottom. The outer leaves will be extra dark, too. 5. Serve immediately.
Per Serving: Calories 134; Fat 7.27g; Sodium 188mg; Carbs 15.46g; Fiber 6.6g; Sugar 3.74g; Protein 5.79g

Chapter 4 Seafood Recipes

Salmon-Peaches Mix

Prep time: 10 minutes | Cook time: 10 minutes | Serves: 4

1 tablespoon balsamic vinegar
1 teaspoon thyme, chopped
1 tablespoon ginger, grated
4 tablespoons olive oil

Black pepper to the taste
2 red onions, cut into wedges
3 peaches cut into wedges
4 salmon steaks

1. Add and whisk the vinegar with ginger, thyme, 3 tablespoons olive oil, and black pepper in a small bowl. 2. Mix and combine the onion with peaches, 1 tablespoon oil, and pepper in another bowl. 3. Sprinkle the black pepper into the salmon. 4. Cook the food in a grill with medium heat. Plate the food. 5. Add and cook the peaches and onions on the same grill for 4 minutes on each side, divide next to the salmon, sprinkle the vinegar mix. Serve the dish.
Per Serving: Calories 397; Fat 20.87g; Sodium 124mg; Carbs 17.93g; Fiber 2.8g; Sugar 12.97g; Protein 34.51g

Savory Salmon-Beans Mix

Prep time: 10 minutes | Cook time: 20 minutes | Serves: 4

2 tablespoons coconut aminos
½ cup olive oil
1½ cups low-sodium chicken stock
6 ounces' salmon fillets
2 garlic cloves, minced
1 tablespoon ginger, grated

1 cup canned black beans, no-salt-added, drained and rinsed
2 teaspoons balsamic vinegar
¼ cup radishes, grated
¼ cup carrots, grated
¼ cup scallions, chopped

1. Mix and whisk the aminos with half of the oil in a bowl. 2. Plate the salmon in a baking dish, pour coconut aminos and the stock. Toss and chill for 10 minutes, add the preheated broiler. Set the medium-high heat to cook for 4 minutes on each side. 3. Place a pan over medium-high heat and cook the rest of olive oil. 4. Add and cook the garlic, ginger and black beans for 3 minutes, stirring from time to time. 5. Add and cook vinegar, radishes, carrots and scallions for 5 minutes. Toss well. 6. Plate fish and the black beans. Serve the dish.
Per Serving: Calories 388; Fat 30.89g; Sodium 230mg; Carbs 14.13g; Fiber 4.4g; Sugar 1.36g; Protein 14.8g

Lemony Salmon with Pomegranate

Prep time: 20 minutes | Cook time: 10 minutes | Serves: 4

1 tablespoon olive oil
4 salmon fillets, skinless and boneless
4 tablespoons sesame paste
Juice of 1 lemon

1 lemon, cut into wedges
½ cucumber, chopped
Seeds from 1 pomegranate
A bunch of parsley, chopped

1. Place a pan over medium-high heat and cook the olive oil. Add and cook the salmon for 5 minutes on each side. 2. Mix sesame paste with lemon juice in a bowl. 3. Add and toss cucumber, parsley and pomegranate seeds. 4. Divide the food over the salmon. Serve the dish!
Per Serving: Calories 320; Fat 18.21g; Sodium 82mg; Carbs 7.44g; Fiber 1.8g; Sugar 1.14g; Protein 32.58g

Veggie Mix & Salmon

Prep time: 10 minutes | Cook time: 30 minutes | Serves: 6

3 red onions, cut into wedges
¾ cup green olives, pitted
3 red bell peppers, cut into strips
½ teaspoon smoked paprika

Black pepper to the taste
5 tablespoons olive oil
6 salmon fillets, skinless and boneless
2 tablespoons parsley, chopped

1. Line a baking sheet in an oven, spread bell peppers, onions and olives. 2. Add smoked paprika, black pepper, and 3 tablespoons olive oil. Mix to coat. Bake the food at 375°F for 15 minutes, plate them. 3. Place a pan over medium-high heat to cook the olive oil. 4. Add and cook the salmon. Add black pepper, and then cook and stir for 10 minutes, each side of salmon needs to be cooked. 5. Put it beside the bell peppers and olives mix, drizzle parsley on the top. 6. Serve the dish!
Per Serving: Calories 248; Fat 15.07g; Sodium 58mg; Carbs 8.03g; Fiber 1.5g; Sugar 3.94g; Protein 20.28g

Asparagus Mix & Creamy Salmon

Prep time: 10 minutes | Cook time: 10 minutes | Serves: 6

1 tablespoon lemon zest, grated
1 tablespoon lemon juice
Black pepper to the taste
1 cup coconut cream

1-pound asparagus, trimmed
20 ounces' salmon, skinless and boneless
1-ounce parmesan cheese, grated

1. Bring together some water in a pot over medium heat, and then add a pinch of salt. 2. Add and cook asparagus for 1 minute, and then transfer to a bowl filled with ice water, drain and put in a bowl. 3. Then boil some water over medium heat and add salmon to cook for 5 minutes, and then drain it. 4. Mix lemon peel with cream and lemon juice in a bowl. 5. Place a pan over medium-high heat. Add and cook asparagus, cream, and pepper for over 1 minute, plate them into two plates, add the salmon and decorate with grated parmesan. 6. Serve the dish.
Per Serving: Calories 285; Fat 18.87g; Sodium 136mg; Carbs 7.31g; Fiber 2.6g; Sugar 1.94g; Protein 23.66g

Yogurt Dip & Greek Salmon

Prep time: 10 minutes | Cook time: 15 minutes | Serves: 4

4 medium salmon fillets, skinless and boneless
1 fennel bulb, chopped
Black pepper to the taste
¼ cup low-sodium veggie stock
1 cup non-fat yogurt

¼ cup green olives pitted and chopped
¼ cup chives, chopped
1 tablespoon olive oil
1 tablespoon lemon juice

1. Add the fennel, salmon fillets, black pepper, and stock in a baking dish. 2. Set the 390°F to heat the oven for 10 minutes. Distribute them into two plates. 3. Mix and whisk yogurt with chives, olives, lemon juice, olive oil, and black pepper in a bowl. 4. Pour the mixture over the salmon. Serve the dish!
Per Serving: Calories 280; Fat 9.04g; Sodium 128mg; Carbs 14.43g; Fiber 2.3g; Sugar 10.48g; Protein 34.86g

Fresh Sprouts Salmon

Prep time: 10 minutes | Cook time: 20 minutes | Serves: 6

2 tablespoons brown sugar
1 teaspoon onion powder
1 teaspoon garlic powder
1 teaspoon smoked paprika

3 tablespoons olive oil
1¼ pounds Brussels sprouts, halved
6 medium salmon fillets, boneless

1. Add and mix sugar with onion powder, garlic powder, smoked paprika and 2 tablespoons olive oil in a bowl. 2. Put and spread Brussels sprouts on a lined baking sheet. 3. Sprinkle with the remaining of the olive oil, mix to coat. And then set the oven to 450°F to heat the oven, put and bake the food for 5 minutes. 4. Add salmon fillets brush with prepared sugar, and then bake the food for over 15 minutes. 5. Plate the food into two plates. Serve the dish.
Per Serving: Calories 228; Fat 10.65g; Sodium 72mg; Carbs 12.02g; Fiber 3.8g; Sugar 4.77g; Protein 22.41g

Beets Mix & Salmon

Prep time: 10 minutes | Cook time: 35 minutes | Serves: 4

1-pound medium beets, sliced
6 tablespoons olive oil
1 and ½ pounds salmon fillets, skinless and boneless
Black pepper to the taste

1 tablespoon chives, chopped
1 tablespoon parsley, chopped
3 tablespoon shallots, chopped
1 tablespoon lemon zest, grated
¼ cup lemon juice

1. Add and mix beets with ½ tablespoon oil in a bowl, toss to coat. Sprinkle the dressing with black pepper, spread on a lined baking sheet. Set the oven to 450°F to bake the food for 20 minutes. 2. Brush the remaining olive oil over the salmon, bake it for over 15 minutes or more. 3. Add and combine the chives with the parsley, shallots, lemon zest, and lemon juice in a bowl. 4. Sprinkle the chives mix on the top of salmon, plate the food. Serve the dish.
Per Serving: Calories 458; Fat 28.02g; Sodium 219mg; Carbs 14.57g; Fiber 3.7g; Sugar 9.33g; Protein 37.23g

Appetizing Mix with Garlic Shrimp

Prep time: 10 minutes | Cook time: 10 minutes | Serves: 4

1-pound shrimp, deveined and peeled
2 teaspoons olive oil
6 tablespoons lemon juice
3 tablespoons dill, chopped

1 tablespoon oregano, chopped
2 garlic cloves, chopped
Black pepper to the taste
¾ cup non-fat yogurt
½ pound cherry tomatoes, halved

1. Place a pan over medium-high heat to cook the olive oil. 2. Add and cook the shrimp for 3 minutes. 3. Add and mix lemon juice, dill, oregano, garlic, black pepper, yogurt, and tomatoes. Cook for 5 minutes or more. Serve the food.
Per Serving: Calories 198; Fat 3.18g; Sodium 152mg; Carbs 16.59g; Fiber 2.2g; Sugar 11.73g; Protein 27.78g

Potatoes Mix Salmon

Prep time: 10 minutes | Cook time: 10 minutes | Serves: 4

1½ pounds potatoes, chopped
1 tablespoon olive oil
4 ounces smoked salmon, chopped
1 tablespoon chives, chopped

2 teaspoons prepared horseradish
¼ cup coconut cream
Black pepper to the taste

1. Set the medium-high heat to cook the olive oil in a pan. Add and cook the potatoes for 10 minutes. 2. Add and mix the salmon chives, horseradish, cream and black pepper. Cook for over 1 minutes. Plate the food and serve it!
Per Serving: Calories 260; Fat 10.81g; Sodium 145mg; Carbs 32.09g; Fiber 4.3g; Sugar 2.11g; Protein 10.11g

Cod Mash with Broccoli

Prep time: 10 minutes | Cook time: 20 minutes | Serves: 4

2 cups broccoli, chopped
4 cod fillets, boneless, chopped
1 white onion, chopped
2 tablespoons olive oil

1 cup of water
1 tablespoon low-fat cream cheese
½ teaspoon ground black pepper

1. Brush the olive oil over the cod and place in a saucepan, and then roast it for 1 minutes per side. 2. Select out the cream cheese, add the remaining ingredients and cook to boil for 18 minutes. 3. Drain the water, add creamy cheese. Whisk the meal completely.
Per Serving: Calories 165; Fat 7.94g; Sodium 374mg; Carbs 3.98g; Fiber 1.1g; Sugar 1.75g; Protein 19.06g

Enticing Lemony Salmon

Prep time: 10 minutes | Cook time: 10 minutes | Serves: 2

4 medium salmon fillets, skinless and boneless
1 tablespoon lemon juice
1 tablespoon dried oregano

1 teaspoon dried thyme
¼ teaspoon onion powder
1 tablespoon olive oil

1. Cook to heat the olive oil in a skillet. 2. Drizzle the season with dried oregano, thyme, onion powder, and lemon juice. 3. Plate the fish in the skillet, cook for each side of fish for 4 minutes.
Per Serving: Calories 240; Fat 12.24g; Sodium 72mg; Carbs 2.72g; Fiber 1.3g; Sugar 0.32g; Protein 28.87g

Zesty Seabass with Ginger

Prep time: 5 minutes | Cook time: 10 minutes | Serves: 2

1 tablespoon ginger, grated
2 tablespoons sesame oil
¼ teaspoon chili powder

4 sea bass fillets, boneless
1 tablespoon margarine

1. Cook to heat the sesame oil and margarine in a skillet. 2. Add chili powder and ginger. 3. Add and cook the sea-bass for 3 minutes on each side. 4. Cover and simmer the fish over low heat for 3 minutes.
Per Serving: Calories 424; Fat 24.52g; Sodium 188mg; Carbs 0.76g; Fiber 0.2g; Sugar 0.08g; Protein 47.67g

Bean-Pepper Salad

Prep time: 6 minutes | Cook time: 0 | Serves: 4

1 can pinto beans, drained	Freshly ground black pepper
2 bell peppers, cored and chopped	Juice of 2 limes
1 cup corn kernels	1 tablespoon olive oil
Low-sodium salt	1 avocado, chopped

1. In a large bowl, mix up the beans, corn, peppers, olive oil, lemon juice, salt and black pepper. Let the salad stand in the refrigerator for 30 minutes. 2. Add the chopped avocado and serve.
Per Serving: Calories 234; Fat 12.01g; Sodium 247mg; Carbs 28.81g; Fiber 8.7g; Sugar 3.22g; Protein 7.4g

Appetizing Yogurt with Shrimp

Prep time: 5 minutes | Cook time: 10 minutes | Serves: 2

1-pound shrimp, peeled	1 teaspoon lemon zest, grated
1 tablespoon margarine	1 chili pepper, chopped
¼ cup low-fat yogurt	

1. Heat to melt the margarine in a skillet, add the chili pepper, roast it for 1 minute. 2. Add the shrimps and lemon zest. 3. Roast each side of the shrimp for 4 minutes, flipping once halfway through cooking. 4. Add the yogurt and mix with shrimps. Cook for 5 minutes.
Per Serving: Calories 272; Fat 7.37g; Sodium 295mg; Carbs 4.52g; Fiber 0.3g; Sugar 3.37g; Protein 47.67g

Fennel Seeds Aromatic Salmon

Prep time: 8 minutes | Cook time: 10 minutes | Serves: 2

4 medium salmon fillets, skinless and boneless	2 tablespoons olive oil
1 tablespoon fennel seeds	1 tablespoon lemon juice
	1 tablespoon water

1. In a skillet, add the olive oil and heat well. 2. Add and bake fennel seeds for 1 minute. 3. Add salmon fillets, mix with lemon juice 4. Add some water, adjust to medium heat to roast each side of the fish for 8 minutes, turning once halfway through cooking. 5. Serve and enjoy!
Per Serving: Calories 301; Fat 19.29g; Sodium 74mg; Carbs 2.04g; Fiber 1.2g; Sugar 0.19g; Protein 29.03g

Wasabi Cod Salad

Prep time: 12 minutes | Cook time: 12 minutes | Serves: 4

4 medium cod fillets, skinless and boneless	teaspoon
	Black pepper to the taste
2 tablespoons mustard	2 cups baby arugula
1 tablespoon tarragon, chopped	1 small red onion, sliced
1 tablespoon capers, drained	1 small cucumber, sliced
4 tablespoons olive oil+ 1	2 tablespoons lemon juice

1. Add and mix mustard with 2 tablespoons olive oil, tarragon, and capers in a bowl. 2. Place a pan over medium-high heat to cook 1 teaspoon oil. Add the fish, sprinkle black pepper, cook for 6 minutes on each side. After that, cut the food into 6 cubes. 3. Mix and combine the arugula with onion, cucumber, lemon juice, cod, and mustard in a salad bowl. Toss them fully. Serve the dish.
Per Serving: Calories 142; Fat 5.41g; Sodium 492mg; Carbs 4.41g; Fiber 1.1g; Sugar 1.82g; Protein 18.87g

Shrimp Quesadillas with Tortillas

Prep time: 16 minutes | Cook time: 5 minutes | Serves: 2

2 whole wheat tortillas	1 de-seeded plump tomato
½ teaspoon ground cumin	¾ cup grated non-fat mozzarella cheese
4 cilantro leaves	
3 ounces diced cooked shrimp	¼ cup diced red onion

1. Add and combine the grated mozzarella cheese and the warm, cooked shrimp in a bowl, 2. Add and mix the ground cumin, red onion, and tomato. Spread the mixture on the tortillas evenly. 3. Cook to heat the tortillas till crispy in a non-stick pan. 4. Add the cilantro leaves and fold over the tortillas. After pressing the food, slice the tortillas. 5. Serve the dish!
Per Serving: Calories 254; Fat 5g; Sodium 922mg; Carbs 25.12g; Fiber 5.9g; Sugar 2.27g; Protein 27.47g

Spiced Salmon with Peas & Parsley Dressing

Prep time: 15 minutes | Cook time: 15 minutes | Serves: 4

16 ounces' salmon fillets, boneless and skin-on	2 cups water
	½ teaspoon oregano, dried
1 tablespoon parsley, chopped	½ teaspoon sweet paprika
10 ounces' peas	2 garlic cloves, minced
9 ounces' vegetable stock, low sodium	A pinch of black pepper

1. Add and mix the garlic, parsley, paprika, oregano and stock. 2. Add some water to the Instant pot. 3. Add steam basket. 4. Make fish fillets inside the steamer basket. 5. Drizzle with pepper. 6. Cook on high pressure with its lid for 10 minutes. 7. Release the pressure naturally over 10 minutes. 8. Plate the fish. 9. Add the peas, cook on high pressure with its lid for another 5 minutes. Quick release the pressure. 10. Distribute the peas next to the fillets. Sprinkle the dressing and parsley on the top. 11. Serve the dish!
Per Serving: Calories 235; Fat 9.69g; Sodium 115mg; Carbs 10.15g; Fiber 2.7g; Sugar 5.89g; Protein 27.29g

Tuna Sandwich

Prep time: 15 minutes | Cook time: 5 minutes | Serves: 2

2¼ tablespoons olive oil	½ cup diced onion
1 peeled and diced medium cucumber	½ teaspoon salt
	1 can flavored tuna
¼ tablespoon pepper	½ cup shredded spinach
4 whole wheat bread slices	

1. Add the spinach, tuna, onion, oil, salt, and pepper in a blender, pulse for 10-20 seconds. 2. Toast the bread and mix the diced cucumber with tuna mixture. When the bread is already done, add the mixture to it. 3. Cut the bread half. Serve the dish. It is proper to store in the fridge.
Per Serving: Calories 382; Fat 17.68g; Sodium 501mg; Carbs 36.46g; Fiber 5.6g; Sugar 3.38g; Protein 22.76g

Easy-to-Cook Mussels

Prep time: 10 minutes | Cook time: 10 minutes | Serves: 2

2-pound cleaned mussels
4 minced garlic cloves
2 chopped shallots
lemon and parsley

2 tablespoons butter
½ cup broth
½ cup white wine

1. Clean the mussels and remove the beard. Select out the closed ones. 2. Sauté the chopped onion and butter. 3. Add and sauté the onion and garlic, for 1 minute. 4. After adding the broth and wine, cover a lip and cook for 5 minutes on high pressure. 5. Release the pressure naturally over 10 minutes. 6. Decorate with parsley. Serve the dish!
Per Serving: Calories 546; Fat 22.9g; Sodium 1624mg; Carbs 23.52g; Fiber 0.6g; Sugar 2.23g; Protein 28.92g

Mozzarella Shrimp Mix

Prep time: 10 minutes | Cook time: 30 minutes | Serves: 10

½ pound shrimp, already peeled and deveined
1 cup avocado mayonnaise
½ cup low-fat mozzarella cheese, shredded
3 garlic cloves, minced

¼ teaspoon hot sauce
1 tablespoon lemon juice
A drizzle of olive oil
½ cup scallions, sliced

1. Mix mozzarella, hot sauce, mayo, garlic and lemon juice in a bowl. Stir them fully. 2. Set the 350°F to heat the oven in advance. Add and toss scallions and shrimp, and then pour them into a baking dish greased with olive oil. 3. Plate the food. Serve the dish!
Per Serving: Calories 73; Fat 4.36g; Sodium 96mg; Carbs 2.1g; Fiber 1.2g; Sugar 0.3g; Protein 6.88g

Tasty Vegetable with Smoked Salmon

Prep time: 10 minutes | Cook time: 0 | Serves: 8

3 tablespoons beet horseradish, prepared
1-pound smoked salmon, skinless, boneless and flaked
2 teaspoons lemon zest, grated
4 radishes, chopped

½ cup capers, drained and chopped
⅓ cup red onion, roughly chopped
3 tablespoons chives, chopped

1. Add and mix the salmon with the beet horseradish, lemon zest, radish, capers, onions, and chive in a bowl. Toss the food fully. 2. Serve cold and enjoy!
Per Serving: Calories 123; Fat 3.23g; Sodium 124mg; Carbs 8.3g; Fiber 3.1g; Sugar 4.98g; Protein 15.14g

Mango Shrimp

Prep time: 10 minutes | Cook time: 0 minute | Serves: 4

3 tablespoons balsamic vinegar
3 tablespoons coconut sugar
6 tablespoons avocado mayonnaise
3 mangos, peeled and cubed

3 tablespoons parsley, finely chopped
1-pound shrimp, peeled, deveined and cooked

1. Add and mix vinegar with sugar, and then toss with mayo in a bowl. 2. Add and combine the mango with the parsley and shrimp, add the mayo in another bowl. Toss them well. Serve the dish!
Per Serving: Calories 331; Fat 5.59g; Sodium 165mg; Carbs 49.32g; Fiber 4.1g; Sugar 42.99g; Protein 25.07g

Yogurt Trout

Prep time: 10 minutes | Cook time: 0 minutes | Serves: 8

4 ounces smoked trout, skinless, boneless and flaked
¼ cup coconut cream
1 tablespoon lemon juice
⅓ cup non-fat yogurt

1½ tablespoons parsley, chopped
3 tablespoons chives, chopped
Black pepper to the taste
A drizzle of olive oil

1. Add and mix trout with yogurt, cream, black pepper, chives, lemon juice in a bowl. Drain and whisk. 2. Drizzle the olive oil. Serve the dish!
Per Serving: Calories 65; Fat 4.45g; Sodium 28mg; Carbs 1.97g; Fiber 0.3g; Sugar 1.04g; Protein 4.63g

Swordfish with Roasted Lemon

Prep time: 10 minutes | Cook time: 70-80 minutes | Serves: 4

¼ cup parsley, chopped
½ teaspoon garlic, chopped
½ teaspoon canola oil
4 swordfish fillets, 6 ounces each
¼ teaspoon sunflower seeds

1 tablespoon sugar
2 lemons, quartered and seeds removed

1. Set the 375°F to heat the oven in advance. 2. Add and mix sugar, sunflower seeds, and lemon wedges in a small bowl. Toss to coat. 3. Add the lemons in a shallow baking dish with aluminum foil. 4. Roast for 1 hour till lemons slightly shows tender and browned. 5. Cook to heat the grill, put the rack 4 inches away from heat. 6. Use cooking spray to cover a baking pan. 7. Put the fish into the pan and spread garlic on the top of fish, brush some olive oil over the fish. 8. Grill per side for 5 minutes till fillet shows opaque. 9. Plate the fish, add roasted lemon on its top. 10. Add the parsley. Decorate the lemon wedge. Serve the dish!
Per Serving: Calories 266; Fat 12.07g; Sodium 140mg; Carbs 4.04g; Fiber 0.2g; Sugar 2.6g; Protein 33.7g

Spring Salmon Mix with Cherry Tomatoes

Prep time: 10 minutes | Cook time: 0 minute | Serves: 4

2 tablespoons scallions, chopped
2 tablespoons sweet onion, chopped
1½ teaspoons lime juice
1 tablespoon chives, minced
1 tablespoon olive oil

1-pound smoked salmon, flaked
1 cup cherry tomatoes, halved
Black pepper to the taste
1 tablespoon parsley, chopped

1. Add and mix the scallions with sweet onion, lime juice, chives, oil, salmon, tomatoes, black pepper and parsley in a bowl. 2. Toss the food fully. 3. Serve the dish!
Per Serving: Calories 285; Fat 11.74g; Sodium 510mg; Carbs 19.49g; Fiber 2.5g; Sugar 13.64g; Protein 25.53g

Veggie-Salmon Salad

Prep time: 10 minutes | Cook time: 0 | Serves: 4

3 tablespoons balsamic vinegar
2 tablespoons olive oil
⅓ cup Kalamata olives, pitted and minced
1 garlic clove, minced
Black pepper to the taste
½ teaspoon lemon zest, grated
1-pound green beans, blanched and halved
½ pound cherry tomatoes, halved
½ fennel bulb, sliced
½ red onion, sliced
2 cups baby arugula
¾ pound smoked salmon, flaked

1. Add and mix the green beans with cherry tomatoes, fennel, onion, arugula, and salmon in a bowl. 2. Add the mix vinegar, oil, olives, garlic, black pepper and lemon zest. 3. Serve the dish!
Per Serving: Calories 302; Fat 14.55g; Sodium 478mg; Carbs 23.68g; Fiber 5.9g; Sugar 14.76g; Protein 21.28g

Fennel and Yellow Onion Shrimp

Prep time: 10 minutes | Cook time: 30 minutes | Serves: 4

1 teaspoon lemon juice
Black pepper to the taste
½ cup avocado mayo
½ teaspoon sweet paprika
3 tablespoons olive oil
1 fennel bulb, chopped
1 yellow onion, chopped
2 garlic cloves, minced
1 cup canned tomatoes, no-salt-added and chopped
1½ pounds big shrimp, peeled and deveined
¼ teaspoon saffron powder

1. Add and mix the garlic with lemon juice, black pepper, mayo, and paprika in a bowl. 2. Add and toss the shrimp. 3. Place a pan over medium-high heat to cook the olive oil. Toss and cook the shrimp, fennel, onion and garlic mix, toss and cook for 4 minutes. 4. Add and toss tomatoes and saffron, distribute them into bowls. 5. Serve the dish!
Per Serving: Calories 326; Fat 16.36g; Sodium 240mg; Carbs 10.87g; Fiber 4.2g; Sugar 5.01g; Protein 36.2g

Shrimp and Orzo in Chicken Stock

Prep time: 10 minutes | Cook time: 30 minutes | Serves: 4

1-pound shrimp, peeled and deveined
Black pepper to the taste
3 garlic cloves, minced
1 tablespoon olive oil
½ teaspoon oregano, dried
1 yellow onion, chopped
2 cups low-sodium chicken stock
2 ounces' orzo
½ cup water
4 ounces canned tomatoes, no-salt-added and chopped
Juice of 1 lemon

1. Place a pan over medium-high heat to cook the olive oil. Add and cook the onion, garlic, and oregano for 4 minutes. Stir it well. 2. Add and cook to stir orzo for over 2 minutes. 3. Boil the stock and the water with a lid. Lower the heat to cook for 12 minutes. 4. Set the 400°F to heat the oven. And lemon juice, tomatoes, black pepper, and shrimp to bake for 15 minutes. 5. Plate them. Serve the dish!
Per Serving: Calories 189; Fat 4.92g; Sodium 240mg; Carbs 11.45g; Fiber 1.7g; Sugar 3.06g; Protein 26.89g

Scallops with Lemon and Garlic

Prep time: 10 minutes | Cook time: 5 minutes | Serves: 4

1 tablespoon olive oil
1¼ pounds dried scallops
2 tablespoons all-purpose flour
¼ teaspoon sunflower seeds
4-5 garlic cloves, minced
1 scallion, chopped
1 pinch of ground sage
1 lemon juice
2 tablespoons parsley, chopped

1. Place a non-stick skillet over medium-high heat to cook the olive oil. 2. Heat the skillet with olive oil. 3. Add the scallops alongside sunflower seeds and flour in a medium bowl. 4. Transfer the scallops to the skillet, add the scallions, garlic, and sage. 5. Cook to sauté the food for 3-4 minutes till they become opaque. 6. Add and mix the lemon juice and parsley. 7. Serve hot!
Per Serving: Calories 153; Fat 4.29g; Sodium 558mg; Carbs 9.96g; Fiber 0.5g; Sugar 0.46g; Protein 17.93g

Savory Salmon with Walnut

Prep time: 10 minutes | Cook time: 14 minutes | Serves: 3 to 4

½ cup walnuts
2 tablespoons stevia
½ tablespoon Dijon mustard
¼ teaspoon dill
2 salmon fillets (3 ounces each)
1 tablespoon olive oil
Sunflower seeds and pepper to taste

1. Set the 350°F to heat the oven in advance. 2. Add and process walnuts, mustard, stevia. 3. Place a skillet over medium-high heat to cook the olive oil. 4. Heat the pan with olive oil. 5. Add salmon and sear for 3 minutes. 6. Add the walnut mixture to coat. 7. Bake the coated salmon in the preheated oven for 8 minutes. 8. Serve the dish.
Per Serving: Calories 152; Fat 11.96g; Sodium 43mg; Carbs 15.87g; Fiber 0.8g; Sugar 0.3g; Protein 10.33g

Glazed Salmon with Coconut Aminos

Prep time: 45 minutes | Cook time: 10 minutes | Serves: 4

4 pieces' salmon fillets, 5 ounces each
4 tablespoons coconut aminos
4 teaspoons olive oil
2 teaspoons ginger, minced
4 teaspoons garlic, minced
2 tablespoons sugar-free ketchup
4 tablespoons dry white wine
2 tablespoons red boat fish sauce, low-sodium

1. Add and mix coconut aminos, garlic, ginger, and fish sauce in a bowl. 2. After adding salmon, marinate the food for 15 to 20 minutes. 3. Set the medium-heat to plate the prepared food. 4. Heat the skillet with olive oil, add and cook the salmon fillet for 3-4 minutes per side. 5. Remove dish once crispy. 6. Add sauce and wine, set the low degree to simmer. 7. Return salmon to the glaze and flip till both sides show glazed. 8. Serve the dish!
Per Serving: Calories 238; Fat 10.91g; Sodium 131mg; Carbs 3.65g; Fiber 0.7g; Sugar 1.41g; Protein 29.74g

Stuffed Salmon with Avocado

Prep time: 10 minutes | Cook time: 30 minutes | Serves: 2

1 ripe organic avocado
2 ounces wild caught smoked salmon
1-ounce cashew cheese

2 tablespoons extra virgin olive oil
Sunflower seeds as needed

1. Slice avocado in half and deseed. 2. Add the remaining ingredients to a food processor till roughly chopped. 3. Add the avocado. 4. Serve the dish!
Per Serving: Calories 358; Fat 30.57g; Sodium 187mg; Carbs 13.15g; Fiber 7.3g; Sugar 1.41g; Protein 11.97g

Garlic Tomato Mussels

Prep time: 10 minutes | Cook time: 23 minutes | Serves: 4

3 tablespoons olive oil
2 pounds' mussels, scrubbed
Pepper to taste
3 cups canned tomatoes, crushed
1 shallot, chopped

2 garlic cloves, minced
2 cups low sodium vegetable stock
⅓ cup cilantro, chopped

1. Place a pan over medium-high heat to cook the olive oil. Add shallot, and then stir-cook for 3 minutes. 2. Add garlic, stock, tomatoes, pepper, lower the heat to stir and simmer for 10 minutes. 3. Add and toss mussels and cilantro together. 4. Simmer for over 10 minutes with a lid. 5. Serve the dish!
Per Serving: Calories 341; Fat 16.22g; Sodium 726mg; Carbs 19.62g; Fiber 2.3g; Sugar 7.31g; Protein 29.54g

Zesty Platter with Broccoli

Prep time: 4 minutes | Cook time: 14 minutes | Serves: 2

6-ounce tilapia, frozen
1 tablespoon almond butter
1 tablespoon garlic, minced

1 teaspoon lemon pepper seasoning
1 cup broccoli florets, fresh

1. Set the 350°F to heat the oven in advance. 2. Put the fish in aluminum foil packets. 3. Make the broccoli around fish. 4. Sprinkle lemon pepper on its top. 5. Close and seal the packets. 6. Bake for 14 minutes. 7. Add and mix garlic and almond butter in a bowl, and after the stirring, keep the mixture on the side. 8. Transfer the packet to platter. 9. Add the almond butter on the top of fish and broccoli. Serve the dish!
Per Serving: Calories 146; Fat 7.48g; Sodium 53mg; Carbs 2.49g; Fiber 0.9g; Sugar 0.22g; Protein 18.15g

Mackerel with Orange

Prep time: 10 minutes | Cook time: 10 minutes | Serves: 4

4 mackerel fillets, skinless and boneless
4 spring onion, chopped
1 teaspoon olive oil
1-inch ginger piece, grated

Black pepper as needed
Juice and zest of 1 whole orange
1 cup low sodium fish stock

1. Sprinkle the black pepper and rub olive oil to the skillet. 2. Add stock, orange juice, ginger, orange zest, and onion to Instant Pot. 3. Put a steamer basket and add the fillets. 4. Cook on high pressure

with its lid for 10 minutes. 5. Release the pressure naturally over 10 minutes. 6. Plate the fillets, drizzle the orange sauce on the top of fish.
Per Serving: Calories 236; Fat 4.12g; Sodium 239mg; Carbs 20.34g; Fiber 0.8g; Sugar 14.93g; Protein 29.88g

Savory Salmon with Hot Pepper

Prep time: 10 minutes | Cook time: 7 minutes | Serves: 4

4 salmon fillets, boneless and skin-on
2 tablespoons assorted chili peppers, chopped

Juice of 1 lemon
1 lemon, sliced
1 cup water
Black pepper

1. Pour the water to the Instant Pot. 2. Add and cook steamer basket and add salmon fillets. Sprinkle the fillet with salt and pepper. 3. Add the lemon juice on its top. 4. Put the lemon slices on the top. 5. Cook on high pressure with its lid closed for 7minutes. 6. Release the pressure naturally over 10 minutes. 7. Plate the salmon and lemon slices. Serve the dish!
Per Serving: Calories 186; Fat 5.47g; Sodium 74mg; Carbs 4.15g; Fiber 0.6g; Sugar 1.76g; Protein 29.14g

Homemade Mussels

Prep time: 10 minutes | Cook time: 5 minutes | Serves: 4

2 tablespoons butter
2 chopped shallots
4 minced garlic cloves
½ cup broth

½ cup white wine
2 pounds cleaned mussels
Lemon and parsley for serving

1. Clean the mussels and remove the beard. 2. Select out the fine ones. 3. Add and sauté the chopped onion and butter. 4. Whisk and cook to sauté the onions. 5. Add and cook the garlic for 1 minute. 6. Add broth and wine. 7. Cook on high pressure with its lid for 5minutes. 8. Release the pressure naturally over 10 minutes. 9. Sprinkle the parsley. Serve the dish!
Per Serving: Calories 263; Fat 11.07g; Sodium 750mg; Carbs 11.47g; Fiber 0.3g; Sugar 1.08g; Protein 28.16g

Salmon with Lemon Pepper

Prep time: 5 minutes | Cook time: 6 minutes | Serves: 3

¾ cup water
Few sprigs of parsley, basil, tarragon, basil
1 pound of salmon, skin on
3 teaspoons ghee

¼ teaspoon salt
½ teaspoon pepper
½ lemon, thinly sliced
1 whole carrot, julienned

1. Cook and sauté the water and herbs. 2. Put a steamer rack inside the pot and place the salmon. 3. Sprinkle the ghee, salt, and pepper. Cover the salmon with the lemon slices. 4. Cook on high pressure with its lid for 3 minutes. 5. Release the pressure naturally over 10 minutes. 6. Plate the salmon to a serving platter. 7. Sauté the vegetable in the pot, for 12 minutes. 8. Serve the dish!
Per Serving: Calories 239; Fat 10.58g; Sodium 324mg; Carbs 3.23g; Fiber 0.7g; Sugar 1.55g; Protein 31.41g

Sautéed Scallops with Garlic and Parsley

Prep time: 5 minutes | Cook time: 25 minutes | Serves: 4

8 tablespoons almond butter
2 garlic cloves, minced
16 large sea scallops

Sunflower seeds and pepper to taste
1½ tablespoons olive oil

1. Drizzle the sunflower seeds and pepper to the scallops. 2. Place a skillet over medium-high heat to cook the olive oil. 3. Cook to sauté the scallops for 2 minutes per side, repeat till the food is done. 4. Add and melt the almond butter. 5. Stir and cook the garlic for 15 minutes. 6. Place the scallops to the skillet and whisk to coat. 7. Serve the dish!
Per Serving: Calories 338; Fat 29.08g; Sodium 474mg; Carbs 4.74g; Fiber 0.1g; Sugar 0.05g; Protein 14.96g

Rainbow Trout Fillets with Lemon

Prep time: 20 minutes | Cook time: 40 minutes | Serves: 4

2 rainbow trout fillets
1 tablespoon olive oil
2 teaspoon garlic salt

1 teaspoon ground black pepper
1 fresh jalapeno pepper, sliced
1 lemon, sliced

1. Set the 400°F to heat the oven in advance. 2. Rinse the fillets and then pat them dry. 3. Spread the fillet with olive oil, add some garlic salt and black pepper. 4. Put every seasoned fillets on a large sized sheet of aluminum foil. 5. Add some jalapeno slices on top, and squeeze the lemon juice over the fish. 6. Make the lemon slices on the top pf the fillets. 7. Seal up the foil carefully so that keep a fine, enclosed packet. 8. Put the packets on the baking sheet. 9. Bake them for 20 minutes. 10. As the flakes shows flake off with a fork, you can serve the dish!
Per Serving: Calories 132; Fat 6.2g; Sodium 25mg; Carbs 1.98g; Fiber 0.3g; Sugar 0.47g; Protein g

Tasty Salmon with Cucumber Platter

Prep time: 10 minutes | Cook time: 0 | Serves: 4

2 cucumbers, cubed
2 teaspoons fresh squeezed lemon juice
4 ounces' non-fat yogurt

1 teaspoon lemon zest, grated
Pepper to taste
2 teaspoons dill, chopped
8 ounces smoked salmon, flaked

1. Add and mix cucumbers, lemon juice, lemon zest, pepper, dill, salmon, yogurt in a bowl. 2. Serve the dish!
Per Serving: Calories 127; Fat 4.67g; Sodium 259mg; Carbs 5.81g; Fiber 1g; Sugar 4.22g; Protein 15.11g

Turn with Cream Cheese

Prep time: 10 minutes | Cook time: 0 | Serves: 4

6 ounces canned tuna, drained and flaked
3 teaspoons fresh lemon juice

1 teaspoon onion, minced
8 ounces' low-fat cream cheese
¼ cup parsley, chopped

1. Add and mix the tuna, cream cheese, lemon juice, parsley, and onion in a bowl. 2. Serve the dish!
Per Serving: Calories 164; Fat 9.14g; Sodium 312mg; Carbs 7.68g; Fiber 0.6g; Sugar 4.59g; Protein 13.14g

Wholesome Salmon with Cinnamon

Prep time: 10 minutes | Cook time: 10 minutes | Serves: 4

2 salmon fillets, boneless and skin on
Pepper to taste

1 tablespoon cinnamon powder
1 tablespoon organic olive oil

1. Place a pan over medium-high heat to cook the olive oil. 2. Stir in pepper and cinnamon. 3. Skin side up the fish, cook salmon in the skillet for 5 minutes on each side. 4. Plate the food. Serve the dish!
Per Serving: Calories 280; Fat 11.23g; Sodium 100mg; Carbs 2.65g; Fiber 1.2g; Sugar 0.62g; Protein 40.18g

Scallop & Strawberry Mix

Prep time: 10 minutes | Cook time: 6 minutes | Serves: 4

4 ounces' scallops
½ cup Pico De Gallo
½ cup strawberries, chopped

1 tablespoon lime juice
Pepper to taste

1. Place a pan over medium-high heat to cook the olive oil. Add and cook each side of scallops for 3 minutes. 2. Remove heat. 3. Add and mix the strawberries, lime juice, Pico De Gallo, scallops, and pepper in a bowl. 4. Serve the dish!
Per Serving: Calories 44; Fat 0.56g; Sodium 262mg; Carbs 6.68g; Fiber 0.5g; Sugar 3.52g; Protein 3.78g

Salmon with Orange Dish

Prep time: 10 minutes | Cook time: 15 minutes | Serves: 4

4 salmon fillets
1 cup orange juice
2 tablespoons arrowroot and

water mixture
1 teaspoon orange peel, grated
1 teaspoon black pepper

1. Add the listed ingredients to the pot. 2. Cook the high pressure for 12 minutes with a lid. 3. Release the pressure naturally. 4. Serve the dish!
Per Serving: Calories 203; Fat 5.44g; Sodium 72mg; Carbs 7.77g; Fiber 0.4g; Sugar 5.18g; Protein 29.05g

Creamy Shrimp

Prep time: 10 minutes | Cook time: 0 | Serves: 4

1 pound shrimp, cooked, peeled and deveined
1 tablespoon coconut cream
¼ teaspoon jalapeno, chopped

½ teaspoon lime juice
1 tablespoon parsley, chopped
Pinch of pepper

1. Add shrimp, cream, jalapeno, lime juice, parsley, and pepper in a bowl. 2. Toss fully and divide into small bowl. 3. Serve the dish!
Per Serving: Calories 114; Fat 1.91g; Sodium 136mg; Carbs 1.48g; Fiber 0.3g; Sugar 0.63g; Protein 23.19g

Attractive Coconut Haddock with Haddock Fillet

Prep time: 10 minutes | Cook time: 12 minutes | Serves: 3

4 haddock fillets, 5 ounces each, boneless
2 tablespoons coconut oil, melted
1 cup coconut, shredded and

unsweetened
¼ cup hazelnuts, ground
Sunflower seeds to taste

1. Set the 400°F to heat the oven in advance. Line a baking sheet with parchment paper. 2. Rub the fish fillet, drizzle the dressing with sunflower seeds. 3. Add and stir hazelnuts and shredded coconut in a bowl. 4. Spread the fish fillet the coconut mix for both sides. Mix to coat. 5. Plate the baking fish, brush with coconut oil and then bake for 12 minutes till they become flaky. 6. Serve the dish!
Per Serving: Calories 144; Fat 12.18g; Sodium 123mg; Carbs 3.64g; Fiber 1.5g; Sugar 1.93g; Protein 6.32g

Mouthwatering Lemon Salmon Dish

Prep time: 5 minutes | Cook time: 15 minutes | Serves: 3

2 salmon fillets, 6 ounces each, skin on
Sunflower seeds to taste
1-pound asparagus, trimmed

2 cloves garlic, minced
3 tablespoons almond butter
¼ cup cashew cheese

1. Set the 400°F to heat the oven in advance. 2. Line a baking sheet with oil. 3. Dry the salmon by using a kitchen towel (seasons as needed). 4. Put salmon onto the baking sheet, make asparagus around it. 5. Place a pan over medium-high heat to cook the olive oil and melt almond butter. 6. Add and cook the garlic for 3 minutes. 7. Pour the sauce over the salmon. 8. After drizzling the cheese to salmon, bake for 12 minutes till the food is cooked. 9. Serve the dish!
Per Serving: Calories 200; Fat 15.98g; Sodium 163mg; Carbs 7.03g; Fiber 3.3g; Sugar 3.13g; Protein 9.51g

Palatable Stew with Brazilian Shrimp

Prep time: 20 minutes | Cook time: 25 minutes | Serves: 4

4 tablespoons lime juice
1 ½ tablespoons cumin, ground
1 ½ tablespoons paprika
2 ½ teaspoons garlic, minced
1 ½ teaspoons pepper
2 pounds' tilapia fillets, cut into

bits
1 large onion, chopped
3 large bell peppers, cut into strips
1 can (14 ounces) tomato, drained
1 can (14 ounces) coconut milk
Handful of cilantro, chopped

1. Add and mix lime juice, cumin, paprika, garlic, and pepper in a large bowl. 2. Add tilapia and stir to coat. 3. Marinate for 20 minutes with the lid covered. 4. Cook on high pressure with its lid for 10 minutes, add olive oil. 5. Add and cook onions for 3 minutes until softened. 6. Put the pepper strips, tilapia, and tomatoes to a skillet 7. Add and simmer coconut milk for 20 minutes. 8. At the last few minutes, add the cilantro. 9. Serve the food!
Per Serving: Calories 292; Fat 5.07g; Sodium 188mg; Carbs 16.08g; Fiber 4.1g; Sugar 7.32g; Protein 48.65g

Mouthwatering Cajun Snow Crab

Prep time: 10 minutes | Cook time: 10 minutes | Serves: 2

1 lemon, fresh and quartered
3 tablespoons Cajun seasoning
2 bay leaves

4 snow crab legs, precooked and defrosted
Golden ghee

1. Fill a large pot almost halfway with sunflower seeds and water. 2. Boil the water. 3. Squeeze the lemon juice into the pot, stir the rest of the lemon. 4. Add bay leaves and Cajun seasoning 5. Cook for 1 minute. 6. And the crab legs and boil for 8 minutes. 7. To make dipping sauce, melt the ghee. 8. Serve the dish!
Per Serving: Calories 81; Fat 2.96g; Sodium 125mg; Carbs 6.45g; Fiber 1g; Sugar 0.73g; Protein 8.37g

Grilled Shrimp with Cajun Seasoning

Prep time: 25 minutes | Cook time: 5 minutes | Serves: 8

1-pound medium shrimp, peeled and deveined
1 lime, juiced

½ cup olive oil
3 tablespoons Cajun seasoning

1. Add and mix lime juice, Cajun seasoning, and olive oil in a re-sealable zip bag. 2. Add and shake shrimp, and marinate for 20 minutes. 3. To prepare, heat your outdoor grill to medium heat in advance. 4. Gently grease the grate. 5. Fish out the shrimp, and cook for 2 minutes per side. 6. Serve the dish!
Per Serving: Calories 166; Fat 14.2g; Sodium 322mg; Carbs 2.06g; Fiber 0.2g; Sugar 0.12g; Protein 7.9g

Flavorful Salmon over Lentils

Prep time: 15 minutes | Cook time: 50 minutes | Serves: 4

1 cup dried brown lentils
4 (4-ounce) salmon fillets
½ teaspoon salt, divided
¼ teaspoon freshly ground black pepper

2 tablespoons extra-virgin olive oil
1 onion, chopped
1 carrot, finely chopped
1 teaspoon dried thyme

1. Preheat the oven to 400°F. Line a baking sheet with parchment paper. 2. Add the lentils to the large saucepan and cover them with water by 2-inch; bring to a boil. 3. When boiled, reduce the heat to low and simmer the lentils for 20 minutes; remove the lentils from the heat and drain. 4. While cooking the lentils, place the salmon on the baking sheet; season the salmon with ¼ teaspoon of salt and the pepper. 5. Bake the salmon in the preheat oven for 15 to 20 minutes until it flakes easily with a fork, and then remove the baking sheet from the oven. 6. Heat the oil in the skillet over medium-high heat; add onion and carrot, and sauté them for 3 to 5 minutes; add the remaining salt, thyme, and lentils, mix them well and turn off the heat. 7. Serve the salmon fillets on a bed of lentils.
Per Serving: Calories 269; Fat 15g; Sodium 792mg; Carbs 7.9g; Fiber 1.2g; Sugar 1.6g; Protein 25.5g

Calamari Citrus with Cilantro

Prep time: 10 minutes | Cook time: 5 minutes | Serves: 4

1 lime, sliced
1 lemon, sliced
2 pounds' calamari tubes and tentacles, sliced
Pepper to taste
¼ cup olive oil
2 garlic cloves, minced
3 tablespoons lemon juice
1 orange, peeled and cut into segments
2 tablespoons cilantro, chopped

1. Add and mix calamari, pepper, lime slices, lemon slices, orange slices, garlic, oil, cilantro, and lemon juice in a bowl. Toss completely. 2. Place a pan over medium-high heat to cook the olive oil. 3. Add and cook the calamari for 5 minutes. 4. Divide into bowls. Serve the dish!
Per Serving: Calories 569; Fat 20.23g; Sodium 973mg; Carbs 22.43g; Fiber 1.1g; Sugar 4.35g; Protein 71.13g

Spicy Salmon

Prep time: 10 minutes | Cook time: 10 minutes | Serves: 4

4 salmon fillets
2 tablespoons olive oil
1 teaspoon cumin, ground
1 teaspoon sweet paprika
1 teaspoon chili powder
½ teaspoon garlic powder
Pinch of pepper

1. Add and mix the cumin, paprika, onion, chili powder, garlic powder, and pepper in a bowl. Add and toss the salmon into the mixture. 2. Place a pan over medium-high heat to cook the olive oil. 3. Add and cook the salmon for 5 minutes, turning once halfway through cooking. 4. Plate the food. Serve the dish!
Per Serving: Calories 241; Fat 12.41g; Sodium 93mg; Carbs 2.23g; Fiber 0.7g; Sugar 0.7g; Protein 29.11g

Seafood Salad

Prep time: 10 minutes | Cook time: 20 minutes | Serves: 6

12 ounces' sea scallops
4 tablespoons olive oil+ 2 teaspoons
4 teaspoons coconut aminos
1 ½ cup quinoa, already cooked
2 teaspoons garlic, minced
1 cup snow peas, sliced
⅓ cup balsamic vinegar
1 cup scallions, sliced
⅓ cup red bell pepper, chopped
¼ cup cilantro, chopped

1. Mix scallops with half of the coconut aminos in a bowl. 2. Place a pan over medium-high heat to cook the 1 tablespoon olive oil. Add quinoa and cook to stir for 8 minutes. 3. Add and cook the garlic and snow peas for 5 minutes or more. Turn off the heat. 4. Mix 3 tablespoons olive oil with the rest of the coconut aminos and vinegar, stir fully, add the quinoa mix, scallions, and bell pepper. 5. Place another pan over medium-high heat to cook the 2 teaspoons olive oil. Add the scallops and cook for 1 minute on each side. 6. Add the quinoa mix. Toss slightly. Drizzle cilantro. Serve the dish!
Per Serving: Calories 333; Fat 13.61g; Sodium 391mg; Carbs 34.68g; Fiber 3.5g; Sugar 2.74g; Protein 18.18g

Mussels Mix with Spanish

Prep time: 10 minutes | Cook time: 23 minutes | Serves: 4

3 tablespoons olive oil
2 pounds' mussels, scrubbed
Black pepper to the taste
3 cups canned tomatoes, crushed
1 shallot, chopped
2 garlic cloves, minced
2 cups low-sodium veggie stock
⅓ cup cilantro, chopped

1. Place a pan over medium-high heat to cook the olive oil. Add shallot and cook to stir for 3 minutes. 2. Add and cook to stir garlic, stock, tomatoes, and black pepper, simmer for 10 minutes. 3. Add and mussels and cilantro, simmer with a lid for 10 minutes. Plate the food. 4. Serve the dish!
Per Serving: Calories 338; Fat 15.87g; Sodium 726mg; Carbs 19.61g; Fiber 2.3g; Sugar 7.3g; Protein 29.54g

Assorted Soup with Salmon and Veggies

Prep time: 10 minutes | Cook time: 22 minutes | Serves: 6

2 tablespoons olive oil
1 leek, chopped
1 red onion, chopped
Black pepper to the taste
2 carrots, chopped
4 cups low-sodium veggie stock
4 ounces' salmon, skinless, boneless and cubed
½ cup coconut cream
1 tablespoon dill, chopped

1. Place a pan over medium-high heat to cook the olive oil. 2. Add and mix the leek and onion, cook for 7 minutes. 3. Add and boil the black pepper, carrots, and stock, whisk and cook for 10 minutes. 4. Add and boil salmon, cream and dill for over 5-6 minutes. Plate the food. Serve the dish!
Per Serving: Calories 195; Fat 13.46g; Sodium 194mg; Carbs 14.29g; Fiber 2.5g; Sugar 7.46g; Protein 6.93g

Salad with Cooked Salmon

Prep time: 10 minutes | Cook time: 0 | Serves: 12

3 yellow tomatoes, seedless and chopped
1-pound smoked salmon, boneless, skinless and flaked
1 red tomato, seedless and chopped
Black pepper to the taste
1 cup watermelon, seedless and
chopped
1 red onion, chopped
1 mango, peeled, seedless and chopped
2 jalapeno peppers, chopped
¼ cup parsley, chopped
3 tablespoons lime juice

Add and mix the tomatoes with mango, watermelon, onion, salmon, black pepper, jalapeno, parsley, and lime juice in a bowl. Serve the dish!
Per Serving: Calories 82; Fat 1.95g; Sodium 269mg; Carbs 8.9g; Fiber 1.3g; Sugar 5.64g; Protein 8.08g

Crispy Salad with Salmon and Cucumber

Prep time: 10 minutes | Cook time: 0 minute | Serves: 4

2 cucumbers, cubed
2 teaspoons lemon juice
4 ounces' non-fat yogurt
1 teaspoon lemon zest, grated
Black pepper to the taste
2 teaspoons dill, chopped
8 ounces smoked salmon, flaked

1. Add and mix the cucumbers with the lemon juice, lemon zest, black pepper, dill, salmon, and yogurt in a bowl. 2. Serve the dish!
Per Serving: Calories 104; Fat 2.71g; Sodium 394mg; Carbs 5.8g; Fiber 1g; Sugar 4.21g; Protein 13.77g

Tasty Tuna with Chickpea Salad

Prep time: 10 minutes | Cook time: 0 minute | Serves: 4

1 English cucumber, chopped	tuna, drained
1 (15-ounce) can chickpeas, drained and rinsed	½ red onion, sliced
	¼ cup lemon vinaigrette
2 (5-ounce) cans water-packed	

1. Mix together the cucumber, chickpeas, tuna, and onion in a large bowl. 2. Drizzle the mixture with the vinaigrette, and toss them to combine. 3. Serve the tuna with the cucumber-chickpeas salad at room temperature or cold.
Per Serving: Calories 157; Fat 3g; Sodium 228mg; Carbs 26.6g; Fiber 7g; Sugar 5g; Protein 8g

Avocado-Tuna Sandwich

Prep time: 10 minutes | Cook time: 0 minute | Serves: 2

1 (5-ounce) can of water-packed tuna, drained	2 tablespoons extra-virgin olive oil
1 ripe avocado, pitted, peeled, and chopped	¼ teaspoon salt
2 scallions, green and white parts, minced	¼ teaspoon freshly ground black pepper
Juice of ½ lemon	4 whole-wheat bread slices

1. Mix all the ingredients except the bread slices in a bowl. 2. Place two bread slices on the serving plate, divide the tuna mixture onto them and then top them with the remaining bread slices. Enjoy.
Per Serving: Calories 450; Fat 30.5g; Sodium 593mg; Carbs 38g; Fiber 11g; Sugar 4g; Protein 10.3g

Salmon Cakes

Prep time: 5 minutes | Cook time: 35 minutes | Serves: 4

1-pound salmon fillets	1 large egg
½ teaspoon salt, divided	2 garlic cloves, minced
¼ teaspoon freshly ground black pepper	½ teaspoon dried dill
½ cup bread crumbs	2 tablespoons extra-virgin olive oil

1. Preheat the oven to 400°F. Line a baking sheet with parchment paper. 2. Place the salmon on the baking sheet, and season the salmon with ¼ teaspoon of salt and the pepper. 3. Bake the salmon in the preheated oven for 15 to 20 minutes. 4. When the time is up, remove the salmon flesh from the skin; transfer the flesh to a mixing bowl, removing any bones. 5. Add the bread crumbs, egg, garlic, dill, and the remaining salt to the bowl, and mix them well; form the mixture into 4 patties. 6. Heat the oil in the skillet over medium heat; add the patties and cook them for 6 minutes on each side. 7. Serve and enjoy.
Per Serving: Calories 308; Fat 17g; Sodium 899mg; Carbs 10.5g; Fiber 0.7g; Sugar 0.9g; Protein 27g

Herbed Whole Branzino

Prep time: 5 minutes | Cook time: 25 minutes | Serves: 2

4 garlic cloves, peeled	2 lemons, sliced, divided
2 thyme sprigs	¼ teaspoon salt
1 oregano sprig	¼ teaspoon freshly ground black pepper
1 whole branzino, dressed and rinsed	

1. Preheat it to 450°F. 2. Place the garlic, thyme, oregano, and half of the lemon slices inside the branzino; season the outside with salt and black pepper. 3. Place the branzino on the baking pan and. 4. Roast the branzino in the preheated oven for 18 to 22 minutes. 5. When the time is up, remove the branzino from the oven, fillet it and serve with the remaining lemon slices.
Per Serving: Calories 218; Fat 5g; Sodium 430mg; Carbs 0g; Fiber 0g; Sugar 1.2g; Protein 46.7g

Easy Baked Halibut Steaks

Prep time: 5 minutes | Cook time: 15 minutes | Serves: 4

4 (4-ounce) halibut steaks	¼ teaspoon freshly ground black pepper
2 tablespoons extra-virgin olive oil	1 lemon, cut into wedges
1 teaspoon za'atar	2 tablespoons chopped fresh parsley
½ teaspoon salt	

1. Turn on the oven and preheat it to 400°F. Line a baking sheet with parchment paper. 2. Place the halibut steaks on the baking sheet, drizzle the steaks with oil and season them with za'atar, salt, and pepper on both sides. 3. Bake the halibut steaks in the preheated oven for 6 to 8 minutes. 4. When the time is up, flip the halibut steaks and cook for 5 minutes longer until the halibut steaks flake easily with a fork. 5. Serve the halibut topped with the lemon wedges and parsley.
Per Serving: Calories 164; Fat 8g; Sodium 369mg; Carbs 0g; Fiber 0g; Sugar 0g; Protein 21g

Walnut-Crusted Fillets

Prep time: 5 minutes | Cook time: 20 minutes | Serves: 4

¼ cup chopped walnuts	1-pound sole or tilapia fillets
¼ cup shredded Parmesan cheese	2 tablespoons extra-virgin olive oil
2 tablespoons chopped fresh parsley	¼ teaspoon salt
1 tablespoon chopped fresh basil leaves	¼ teaspoon freshly ground black pepper

1. Heat the oven to 400°F ahead of time. 2. Add the walnuts and cheese to the food processor, and process them until they form crumbs; add the parsley and basil, and beat until combined. 3. Coat the fillets with oil, season them with salt and pepper, and then place on the baking sheet. 4. Rub the fillets with the walnut and cheese mixture. 5. Bake the fillets in the preheated oven for 15 to 20 minutes until the fillets flake easily with a fork and the breading has browned. 6. Serve and enjoy.
Per Serving: Calories 166; Fat 10.2g; Sodium 655mg; Carbs 1.8g; Fiber 0.4g; Sugar 0.2g; Protein 16.7g

Poached Fillets in Tomato-Caper Sauce

Prep time: 5 minutes | Cook time: 30 minutes | Serves: 4

1 (28-ounce) can low-sodium diced tomatoes
¼ cup capers, drained, rinsed, and finely chopped
3 garlic cloves, minced
1 teaspoon paprika
½ teaspoon salt
¼ teaspoon freshly ground black pepper
1 pound cod or halibut fillets

1. Add the tomatoes with their juices, capers, garlic, paprika, salt, and pepper to a large saucepan over medium heat, mix them and bring to a simmer; simmer them for 15 minutes, stirring occasionally. 2. Slide the fillets into the saucepan and cook for 10 to 15 minutes. 3. When done, serve and enjoy.
Per Serving: Calories 263; Fat 16g; Sodium 543mg; Carbs 11g; Fiber 2g; Sugar 8g; Protein 17.8g

Herb Shrimp in White Wine

Prep time: 5 minutes | Cook time: 10 minutes | Serves: 4

2 tablespoons extra-virgin olive oil
6 garlic cloves, minced
½ cup dry white wine
1 pound shrimp, peeled and deveined
¼ teaspoon salt
Juice of 1 lemon
2 tablespoons chopped fresh parsley

1. Heat the oil in the skillet over medium-high heat; add the garlic and sauté for 30 seconds. 2. Pour the white wine in the skillet, and simmer for 2 to 3 minutes. 3. Add the shrimp and cook for 3 to 5 minutes. 4. Turn off the heat and sprinkle the salt and lemon juice over the shrimp. 5. Garnish this dish parsley and enjoy.
Per Serving: Calories 205; Fat 10.4g; Sodium 502mg; Carbs 2.7g; Fiber 0.2g; Sugar 0.4g; Protein 26g

Salmon over Chickpeas-Arugula Salad

Prep time: 5 minutes | Cook time: 25 minutes | Serves: 4

4 (4-ounce) salmon fillets
2 tablespoons extra-virgin olive oil, divided
¼ teaspoon salt
¼ teaspoon freshly ground black pepper
1 (15-ounce) can chickpeas, drained and rinsed
½ teaspoon ground cumin
4 cups arugula
¼ cup Lemon Vinaigrette

1. Preheat the oven to 400°F. Line the baking sheet with parchment paper. 2. Arrange the salmon fillets on the baking sheet. 3. Drizzle the salmon with 1 tablespoon of oil, season it with the salt and pepper. 4. Bake the salmon in the preheated oven for 16 to 20 minutes until the salmon has cooked through and flakes easily with a fork; when the time is up, remove the baking sheet from the oven. 5. Heat the remaining oil in the skillet over medium-high heat; add the chickpeas and cumin, and sauté them for 2 to 3minutes. 6. Turn off the heat and mix in the arugula until wilted. 7. Transfer the chickpeas and arugula to the serving plate, place the salmon on them and drizzle with vinaigrette. 8. Enjoy.
Per Serving: Calories 390; Fat 17.7g; Sodium 868mg; Carbs 26g; Fiber 7g; Sugar 5g; Protein 31.5g

Delicious Cod Parcels

Prep time: 15 minutes | Cook time: 15 minutes | Serves: 4

4 cups baby spinach
2 cups sliced shiitake mushrooms
4 (4-ounce) cod fillets
½ teaspoon Old Bay seasoning
½ teaspoon salt
¼ teaspoon freshly ground black
pepper
¼ cup chopped scallions, green and white parts
2 tablespoons extra-virgin olive oil

1. Preheat the oven to 425°F. 2. Tear 4 (12-inch) square pieces of aluminum foil. 3. Place 1 cup of spinach and ½ cup of mushrooms on each piece of foil, and then place one cod piece on top. 4. Add the Old Bay, salt, and pepper, sprinkle with the scallions, and drizzle with the oil. 5. Crease up the packets to seal and enclose the cod. 6. Place the packets on the baking sheet in the oven. 7. Bake the food for 15 minutes. 8. When done, carefully uncrease the packets and serve.
Per Serving: Calories 189; Fat 7.5g; Sodium 371mg; Carbs 12.3g; Fiber 2.4g; Sugar 3g; Protein 19.5g

Pan-Fried Fillets with Veggies

Prep time: 10 minutes | Cook time: 20 minutes | Serves: 4

1 pound cod, halibut, or Mahi Mahi fillets
½ teaspoon salt
¼ teaspoon freshly ground black pepper
1 tablespoon extra-virgin olive oil
1 red bell pepper, cored and chopped
1 red onion, chopped
2 cups cherry tomatoes
¼ cup of chopped pitted green olives

1. Season the fillets with the salt and pepper. 2. Heat the oil in the pan or skillet over medium-high heat; add the bell pepper and onion, and sauté them for 3 to 5 minutes, or until softened; add the tomatoes and olives, and sauté for 1 to 2 minutes. 3. Nestle the fillets on top of the vegetables, cover the skillet, and then cook the food for 5 to 10 minutes, or until the fillets flake easily with a fork. 4. When done, serve and enjoy.
Per Serving: Calories 138; Fat 4g; Sodium 643mg; Carbs 6.6g; Fiber 1.6g; Sugar 3.7g; Protein 18.5g

Shrimp Tomato Paella

Prep time: 5 minutes | Cook time: 40 minutes | Serves: 4

2 tablespoons extra-virgin olive oil, divided
1-pound large shrimp, peeled and deveined
1 onion, chopped
2 cups medium-grain white rice
3½ cups water
1 (14½-ounce) can low-sodium diced tomatoes, drained
½ teaspoon paprika
¼ teaspoon salt
¼ teaspoon freshly ground black pepper

1. Heat 1 tablespoon of oil in the skillet over medium-high heat. 2. Add the shrimp and cook them for 2 to 3 minutes per side; transfer them to a plate. 3. In the same skillet, heat the remaining oil over medium heat; add the onion and sauté for 3 to 5 minutes; add the rice and mix them to coat the rice with the oil. 4. Add the water, tomatoes, paprika, salt, and pepper, and bring to a boil. 5. When boiled, reduce the heat to a simmer, and cover the skillet, and then cook the food for 20 to 25 minutes until the water has been absorbed. 6. Serve the shrimp with the tomato mixture.
Per Serving: Calories 534; Fat 8.6g; Sodium 870mg; Carbs 88g; Fiber 4.3g; Sugar 5.4g; Protein 23g

Mussels with White Wine Sauce

Prep time: 15 minutes | Cook time: 15 minutes | Serves: 4

2 pounds mussels
½ cup dry white wine
2 tablespoons extra-virgin olive
oil
3 garlic cloves, minced
¼ cup chopped fresh parsley

1. Pour the dry white wine in a large pot, add the mussels, and then bring to a boil. 2. Cover the pot and reduce the heat to low; cook the mussels for 5 to 7 minutes until they release juices and have opened. 3. Remove the mussels from the pot but leave the liquid in the pot. Discard any mussels that have not opened. 4. Set the liquid aside for a couple of minutes, and then pour the liquid off the top into a small bowl, leaving behind the grit and sediment. 5. Heat the oil in the saucepan over medium heat; add the garlic and sauté for 30 seconds. 6. Add the cooking liquid and simmer for 2 to 3 minutes, or until slightly reduced. 7. Pour the sauce over the mussels, garnish them with some parsley and enjoy.
Per Serving: Calories 299; Fat 15g; Sodium 870mg; Carbs 9.6g; Fiber 0.2g; Sugar 0.1g; Protein 30g

Baked Salmon Fillets

Prep time: 5 minutes | Cook time: 20 minutes | Serves: 4

Zest and juice of ½ lemon
1 tablespoon extra-virgin olive oil
2 teaspoons whole-grain mustard
½ teaspoon dried rosemary
¼ teaspoon salt
¼ teaspoon freshly ground black pepper
1 pound salmon fillets

1. Preheat the oven to 400°F. Line the baking sheet with parchment paper. 2. Mix the lemon zest and juice, oil, mustard, rosemary, salt, and pepper in a bowl. 3. Place the salmon fillets on the baking sheet and spread the lemon mixture on them. 4. Bake the salmon fillets for 16 to 20 minutes or until they flake easily with a fork. 5. Serve and enjoy.
Per Serving: Calories 190; Fat 9.7g; Sodium 667mg; Carbs 0.7g; Fiber 0.2g; Sugar 0.2g; Protein 23.5g

Pan-Seared Cod Fillets with Chard

Prep time: 5 minutes | Cook time: 15 minutes | Serves: 4

3 tablespoons extra-virgin olive oil, divided
2 garlic cloves, minced
1-pound Swiss chard, both leaves and stems, thick stems removed, thinly sliced
4 (4-ounce) cod fillets
¼ teaspoon salt
¼ teaspoon freshly ground black pepper
1 lemon, cut into wedges

1. Heat 1½ tablespoons of oil in the pan over medium heat; add the garlic and sauté for 30 seconds; add the chard and sauté for 6 to 8 minutes; remove the pan from the heat. 2. Season the cod with salt and pepper according to personal preference. 3. Heat the remaining oil in a large skillet over medium-high heat; add the cod and sear for 3 to 5 minutes per side. 4. Serve the cod atop the chard with the lemon wedges on the side.
Per Serving: Calories 396; Fat 25g; Sodium 1033mg; Carbs 16g; Fiber 8.8g; Sugar 2.5g; Protein 28g

Baked Mussels in Red Curry

Prep time: 10 minutes | Cook time: 20 minutes | Serves: 4

3 pounds mussels, scrubbed and debearded
2 cups low-sodium fish broth or chicken broth
1 tablespoon olive oil
1 garlic clove, minced
1 tablespoon red curry paste

1. Turn on the oven and preheat it to 500°F. 2. In a large baking dish, spread the mussels. 3. Pour the broth over the mussels, and cover with aluminum foil. 4. Bake the mussels for 10 minutes; remove the foil and transfer the mussels to a large bowl, reserving the juices and removing any that didn't open. 5. Heat the olive oil in the saucepan over medium heat; add the garlic and sauté for 1 minute. 6. Add the prepared cooking juices and the curry paste to the saucepan, increase the heat, and bring the mixture to a boil. 7. When boiled, reduce heat and simmer the food for 5 minutes. 8. Divide the mussels evenly between 4 large bowls, and pour ½ cup of broth into each bowl. 9. Enjoy.
Per Serving: Calories 348; Fat 12g; Sodium 844mg; Carbs 14g; Fiber 0g; Sugar 0g; Protein 42g

Shrimp with Broccoli

Prep time: 15 minutes | Cook time: 20 minutes | Serves: 4

Cooking spray
4 tablespoons olive oil, divided
2 garlic cloves, minced
1 teaspoon Italian seasoning
½ teaspoon salt, divided
¼ teaspoon freshly ground black
pepper, divided
1 pound broccoli, cut into bite-size florets
⅛ teaspoon red pepper flakes
1½ pounds large shrimp, peeled, deveined, and tails removed

1. Preheat the oven to 400°F. Grease the large baking sheet with cooking spray. 2. Mix garlic, the Italian seasoning, 2 tablespoons of olive oil, ¼ teaspoon of salt, and ⅛ teaspoon of pepper in the bowl. 3. Add the broccoli to the Italian seasoning mixture, and mix to coat. 4. Spread the broccoli in a single layer on the baking sheet, and roast them in the preheated oven for 8 minutes. 5. In the same medium bowl used for the broccoli, stir well the red pepper flakes, the remaining olive oil, and the remaining ¼ teaspoon of salt, remaining ⅛ teaspoon of pepper. 6. Coat the shrimp with the spice mixture. 7. Take the pan out of the oven, and spread the shrimp in a single layer on the broccoli; cook the food for another 10 minutes. 8. Serve immediately.
Per Serving: Calories 274; Fat 15g; Sodium 494mg; Carbs 7g; Fiber 0g; Sugar 3g; Protein 32g

Miso-Glazed Tuna Steaks

Prep time: 10 minutes | Cook time: 15 minutes | Serves: 4

Cooking spray
⅓ cup white miso
⅓ cup sake
⅓ cup mirin
2 tablespoons brown sugar
4 (5-ounce) tuna steaks

1. Turn on the oven and preheat it to 400°F. Coat the baking dish with cooking spray. 2. Add the miso, sake, mirin, and brown sugar to the saucepan over low heat, stir constantly for about 2 minutes. 3. Pour the glaze into a medium bowl and coat the tuna with the glaze; cover the bowl and store in the refrigerator for at least 30 minutes. 4. Remove the tuna from the glaze and place in the baking dish. Discard any remaining glaze. 5. Bake the tuna for 12 minutes. 6. Serve the fish warm.
Per Serving: Calories 271; Fat 1g; Sodium 959mg; Carbs 23g; Fiber 2g; Sugar 6.2g; Protein 37.7g

Creole-Style Shrimp and Grits

Prep time: 10 minutes | Cook time: 20 minutes | Serves: 4

2¼ cups water, divided
½ cup quick-cooking grits or polenta
¼ teaspoon salt, divided
1 tablespoon olive oil
1½ pounds large shrimp, peeled and deveined
3 garlic cloves, minced
2 cups low-sodium chicken broth
1 teaspoon Creole seasoning
2 tablespoons cornstarch
⅛ teaspoon freshly ground black pepper
1 lemon, sliced

1. Add 2 cups of water to a small saucepan and bring to a boil; when boiled, add the grits and ⅛ teaspoon of salt, and then reduce the heat to low, cover the pan and simmer the grits for about 7 minutes. 2. Heat the olive oil in a big frying pan over medium heat; add the shrimp and sauté for 2 minutes; transfer the shrimp to the plate. 3. Mix the cornstarch with the remaining ¼ cup of water in a small bowl. 4. Add the garlic to the frying pan and sauté for 1 minute until fragrant; add the broth and Creole seasoning, and bring to a boil. 5. Add the cornstarch mixture to the skillet and sauté for 2 minutes until the sauce thickens. 6. Put the shrimp back to the skillet and stir fry them for 4 minutes; sprinkle with the pepper and the remaining salt. 7. Distribute the grits among 4 bowls, top each with ¼ of the shrimp and several lemon slices.
Per Serving: Calories 119; Fat 5.5g; Sodium 301mg; Carbs 14g; Fiber 1.6g; Sugar 3g; Protein 4g

Veggie Crab Soba Noodles

Prep time: 15 minutes | Cook time: 10 minutes | Serves: 4

8 ounces soba (buckwheat) noodles
1 large cucumber, diced
1 ripe avocado, pitted, peeled, and diced
1-pound canned crabmeat, drained and gently rinsed
¼ cup Thai dressing

1. Pour some water into a large pot over high heat and bring to a boil. 2. Add the soba noodles to the boiled water and cook for about 8 minutes. 3. Drain the noodles in a colander and rinse under cold water; transfer the noodles in a large bowl and set aside. 4. After the noodles are cooled, mix the noodles with the cucumber, avocado, and crabmeat. 5. Drizzle the Thai Dressing over the noodles, and gently mix to evenly coat; enjoy.
Per Serving: Calories 476; Fat 22g; Sodium 658mg; Carbs 51g; Fiber 7g; Sugar 4g; Protein 24g

Tomato Fish Stew

Prep time: 5 minutes | Cook time: 25 minutes | Serves: 4

2 (14-ounce) cans no-added-sodium diced tomatoes, divided
2 tablespoons olive oil
1 onion, diced
3 garlic cloves, minced
2 tablespoons herbes de Provence
1 (8-ounce) bottle clam juice
1¼ pounds cod, cut into 2-inch chunks
¼ teaspoon salt
⅛ teaspoon freshly ground black pepper

1. Add 1 can of diced tomatoes to a blender and blend until the mixture is smooth. 2. Heat the olive oil in the saucepan over medium heat; add the onion and sauté for 3 minutes; add the garlic and herbes de Provence, and sauté them for 1 minute until fragrant. 3. Add the blended tomatoes, the remaining can of diced tomatoes, and the clam juice to the pan, lightly stir well; bring the mixture to a boil, reduce heat and simmer the mixture for 10 minutes. 4. Add the cod, cover the pan, and poach for about 10 minutes. 5. Add the

salt and pepper, and mix well to combine. 6. Serve and enjoy.
Per Serving: Calories 233; Fat 8g; Sodium 815mg; Carbs 16.9g; Fiber 4.5g; Sugar 8g; Protein 24g

Braised Cod over Tomatoes

Prep time: 10 minutes | Cook time: 15 minutes | Serves: 4

1¼ pounds cod, cut into 4 equal pieces
¼ teaspoon salt
⅛ teaspoon freshly ground black pepper
2 tablespoons olive oil
2 pounds (about 8) Roma or plum tomatoes, cut into ¼-inch-thick slices
1 garlic clove, sliced
1 tablespoon dried oregano
⅛ teaspoon red pepper flakes
Juice of ½ lemon

1. Sprinkle the cod with salt and pepper on both sides. 2. Heat the olive oil in the frying pan over medium heat; when the oil is shimmering, layer the tomatoes evenly on the bottom of the skillet, and then sprinkle with the garlic, oregano, and red pepper flakes. 3. Arrange the cod evenly over the tomatoes; cover the pan and cook for 15 minutes. 4. Transfer the fish to a plate and put the tomatoes in the frying pan. Break up the tomatoes and drizzle them with the lemon juice. 5. Spoon the tomatoes over the fish before serving.
Per Serving: Calories 366; Fat 7.6g; Sodium 619mg; Carbs 54.4g; Fiber 2.7g; Sugar 51g; Protein 22.7g

Spiced Tilapia Fillets

Prep time: 10 minutes | Cook time: 10 minutes | Serves: 4

Cooking spray
1¼ pounds tilapia, cut into 4 fillets
2 tablespoons olive oil
½ teaspoon garlic powder
½ teaspoon paprika
½ teaspoon Italian seasoning
¼ teaspoon salt
⅛ teaspoon freshly ground black pepper
½ cup easy mango chutney

1. Preheat the broiler. Spray a baking tray with cooking spray. 2. Coat the tilapia with the olive oil on both sides. 3. Mix the garlic powder, paprika, Italian seasoning, salt, and pepper in the bowl. 4. Sprinkle both sides of the tilapia with the spice mixture. 5. Arrange the tilapia in a single layer on the baking sheet. 6. Broil the tilapia for 5 minutes on each side. 7. Place one tilapia fillet on each of 4 plates, and top each with 2 tablespoons of chutney.
Per Serving: Calories 212; Fat 9.3g; Sodium 245mg; Carbs 3.8g; Fiber 0.5g; Sugar 3g; Protein 28.8g

Tuna Wrap

Prep time: 10 minutes | Cook time: 30 minutes | Serves: 2

7 ounces no-salt-added canned tuna, in water
1 cucumber, diced
1 orange bell pepper, diced
1 tablespoon stone-ground mustard
2 low-sodium whole wheat wraps
4 tablespoons Tzatziki

1. Mix well the tuna, cucumber, bell pepper, and mustard in a medium mixing bowl. 2. Add 2 tablespoons of the dip and 1 cup of the tuna mixture on a whole wheat wrap. Wrap tightly and dig in!
Per Serving: Calories 322; Fat 11g; Sodium 578mg; Carbs 22g; Fiber 2.7g; Sugar 11.5g; Protein 32g

Mediterranean Trout with Cherry Tomatoes

Prep time: 15 minutes | Cook time: 10 minutes | Serves: 4

4 (5-ounce) skin-on trout or grouper fillets
½ teaspoon salt, divided
¼ teaspoon freshly ground black pepper, divided
2 tablespoons olive oil
2 tablespoons white cooking wine

1 garlic clove, minced
1 cup cherry tomatoes, halved lengthwise
1 red onion, thinly sliced
¼ cup Kalamata olives, halved lengthwise
1 lemon, sliced

1. Preheat the oven to 400°F. 2. Sprinkle the flesh side of the fish with ¼ teaspoon of salt and ⅛ teaspoon of pepper. 3. Mix the olive oil, wine, garlic, the remaining salt, and the remaining pepper in the bowl. 4. Place a piece of parchment paper flat on the counter. 5. Arrange 1 trout fillet on the parchment paper and top it with ¼ each of the cherry tomatoes, onion, olives, and lemon slices on the lower half. 6. Crease the parchment paper in half over the fish. Gently roll the edges of the open sides of the paper, tucking the ends under the packet. 7. Repeat this step for the remaining 3 fillets. 8. Work in batches, arrange two packets on the baking sheets, and bake the food for 10 minutes. 9. Cut several 3-inch slits in the packets to let steam escape with a sharp knife.
Per Serving: Calories 212; Fat 9g; Sodium 430mg; Carbs 3g; Fiber 0.8g; Sugar 1.5g; Protein 28g

Honey Sesame Shrimp

Prep time: 5 minutes | Cook time: 10 minutes | Serves: 4

¼ cup honey
2 teaspoons minced garlic
2 teaspoons grated fresh ginger
1 teaspoon sesame oil
Sea salt, for seasoning
Freshly ground black pepper, for

seasoning
1 pound shrimp, peeled and deveined
1 scallion, thinly sliced on the bias

1. Turn on the oven and preheat it to 450°F. Line the baking dish with parchment paper. 2. Mix the honey, garlic, ginger, sesame oil, salt, and pepper in a bowl. 3. Add the shrimp to the bowl and mix to coat. 4. Evenly spread the shrimp in the baking dish. 5. Bake the shrimp for about 10 minutes. 6. Top the shrimp with the scallion and serve.
Per Serving: Calories 175; Fat 1.7g; Sodium 137mg; Carbs 18g; Fiber 0.2g; Sugar 17.5g; Protein 23g

Coconut Salmon

Prep time: 5 minutes | Cook time: 15 minutes | Serves: 4

½ cup unsweetened coconut flakes
2 tablespoons olive oil
1¼ pounds skin-on salmon
Zest and juice of 2 limes

¼ cup water
½ cup coconut milk
¼ teaspoon curry powder
½ teaspoon salt

1. Toast the coconut in a medium sauté pan for 3 minutes, and then set aside to cool. 2. Wipe out the pan with a clean paper towel, then heat the olive oil over medium heat. 3. After the oil shimmers, add the salmon, skin-side down, and sprinkle with the lime zest. 4. Pour in some water, cover, and steam the food for 8

to 10 minutes. 5. Transfer the salmon to a platter. 6. Replace the pan to medium heat, and cook off any extra liquid in the pan. 7. Add the lime juice, coconut milk, toasted coconut flakes, curry powder, and salt, and bring to a boil. 8. Reduce heat to a simmer and cook for 2 minutes, stirring occasionally. 9. Cut the fish into 4 equal pieces, spoon the sauce over the fish before serving warm.
Per Serving: Calories 407; Fat 25g; Sodium 874mg; Carbs 9g; Fiber 2g; Sugar 5g; Protein 38g

Delicious Salmon with Leeks and Asparagus

Prep time: 15 minutes | Cook time: 120-150 minutes | Serves: 4

1¼ pounds skin-on salmon
¼ teaspoon salt
⅛ teaspoon freshly ground black pepper
1 leek, cleaned and chopped

¾ pound asparagus, trimmed and halved crosswise
¾ cup water
¾ cup white cooking wine

1. Cut a large piece of aluminum foil and line the bottom of the slow cooker. 2. Sprinkle the flesh side of the salmon with the salt and pepper. 3. Place the salmon on the bottom of the slow cooker, skin side down. 4. Top the salmon with the leek, asparagus, water, and wine and then cook on low for 2 to 2½ hours. 5. Take out the foil and gently slide the salmon and vegetables onto a serving plate.
Per Serving: Calories 263; Fat 8.6g; Sodium 700mg; Carbs 8g; Fiber 3g; Sugar 3g; Protein 40g

Sea Bass with Tomato-Fennel Sauce

Prep time: 15 minutes | Cook time: 20 minutes | Serves: 4

Cooking spray
1 medium fennel bulb
1 red onion, thinly sliced
4 plum tomatoes, diced
2 lemons
4 (5-ounce) sea bass fillets

¼ teaspoon salt
⅛ teaspoon freshly ground black pepper
2 tablespoons olive oil
1 teaspoon mustard
1 garlic clove, minced

1. Turn on the oven and preheat it to 450°F. Grease the baking tray with cooking spray. 2. Remove the fronds from the fennel bulb and set aside; chop the fennel bulb and the fronds separately. 3. Evenly scatter the fennel bulb, onion, and tomatoes on the baking sheet; bake them in the preheated oven for 5 minutes. 4. Cut 1 lemon into thin slices. 5. Sprinkle the sea bass with the salt and pepper. 6. Take out the baking sheet from the oven, top the vegetables with the sea bass and then place the lemon slices over the sea bass. 7. Return the sheet to the oven and bake for 15 minutes longer. 8. Juice the second lemon. 9. To make a dressing, mix the lemon juice, olive oil, mustard, garlic, and chopped fennel fronds in the bowl. 10. Put 1 sea bass fillet on each of 4 plates, and top each with ¾ cup of vegetables and 1 tablespoon of dressing. 11. Enjoy.
Per Serving: Calories 271; Fat 9.9g; Sodium 296mg; Carbs 18.6g; Fiber 2.7g; Sugar 14g; Protein 27g

Catfish and Shrimp Boil

Prep time: 15 minutes | Cook time: 25 minutes | Serves: 4

4 (4-ounce) catfish fillets, cut into 2 pieces each
½ pound shrimp, peeled and deveined
1 tablespoon Cajun seasoning
4 russet potatoes, cut into eighths
2 ears of corn, cut into 4 pieces on the cob
½ cup water
Sea salt, for seasoning
Freshly ground black pepper, for seasoning

1. Turn on the oven and preheat it to 400°F. Cut 4 pieces of aluminum foil, each 12 inches square with the edges turned up to form a rough bowl. 2. Mix the catfish, shrimp, and Cajun seasoning together in a bowl. 3. Divide the potatoes and corn between the foil pieces and top with the catfish and shrimp. 4. Drizzle the fish and vegetables with water and lightly season then with some salt and pepper according to personal preference. 5. Crease the foil up to form tightly sealed packets and put them on a baking sheet. 6. Bake the food in the preheated oven for 20 to 25 minutes.
Per Serving: Calories 524; Fat 5g; Sodium 727mg; Carbs 81.5g; Fiber 7g; Sugar 4.8g; Protein 40g

Crab Cakes

Prep time: 15 minutes, plus 1 hour chilling | Cook time: 10 minutes | Serves: 4

1-pound canned lump crabmeat, drained and picked over
¼ cup coconut flour
1 scallion, finely chopped
1 egg, beaten
½ teaspoon minced garlic
Juice and zest of ½ lemon
Sea salt, for seasoning
Freshly ground black pepper, for seasoning
2 tablespoons olive oil

1. Add some salt and pepper to season the crab mixture according to personal preference. 2. Divide the crab mixture into 8 cakes. 3. Chill the crab cakes, covered, in the refrigerator for 1 hour to firm them up. 4. Heat the olive oil in the frying pan over medium-high heat. 5. Pan sear the crab cakes for 5 minutes per side until they are golden. 6. Serve warm.
Per Serving: Calories 197; Fat 10.4g; Sodium 374mg; Carbs 1.7g; Fiber 0.3g; Sugar 0.8g; Protein 23g

Flavorful Crab-Shrimp–Stuffed Avocados

Prep time: 20 minutes | Cook time: 0 minute | Serves: 4

4 avocados, pitted
½ pound crabmeat
½ pound cooked shrimp, peeled, deveined and roughly chopped
1 red bell pepper, seeded and finely chopped
1 scallion, sliced on the bias
Sea salt, for seasoning
Freshly ground black pepper, for seasoning

1. Scoop out the center of the avocados, leaving a ½-inch layer of fruit in each half. 2. Rearrange the scooped-out portion to a large bowl and put the avocado halves aside. 3. Add the crabmeat, shrimp, bell pepper, and scallion to the bowl and stir properly. 4. Add some salt and pepper according to personal preference. 5. Spoon the seafood filling into the avocado halves before serving.
Per Serving: Calories 433; Fat 31g; Sodium 675mg; Carbs 18g; Fiber 14g; Sugar 2g; Protein 26g

Delicious Salmon and Summer Squash

Prep time: 15 minutes | Cook time: 20 minutes | Serves: 4

2 tablespoons freshly squeezed lemon juice
1 cup sliced yellow summer squash
2 tablespoons sliced shallot
1 tablespoon chopped fresh oregano leaves
½ tablespoon olive oil
⅛ teaspoon salt
⅛ teaspoon freshly ground black pepper
1 cup sliced medium zucchini
2 (6-ounce) skinless salmon fillets
1 teaspoon grated lemon zest, divided

1. Turn on the oven and preheat it to 400°F. 2. Combine the lemon juice, yellow squash, shallot, oregano, olive oil, salt, and pepper in a medium bowl. 3. Put 2 large parchment rectangles on the work surface and let the short side of the parchment closest to you. 4. Place half the zucchini slices lengthwise on half of one parchment rectangle, overlapping them. 5. Arrange a salmon fillet on the zucchini, sprinkle with half the lemon zest, and then put half the yellow squash mixture on the top. 6. Crease the parchment over the ingredients. Repeat with the other piece of parchment and the remaining ingredients. To seal the packets, begin at one corner and tightly Crease over the edges about ½ inch all around, overlapping the creases. Place the packets on a baking sheet and bake for about 17 minutes. 7. Cut the packets open, being careful to avoid escaping steam, and with a spatula gently transfer the salmon and vegetables to two plates. Spoon any liquid remaining in the parchment over the salmon and vegetables.
Per Serving: Calories 152; Fat 7.8g; Sodium 447mg; Carbs 1.8g; Fiber 0.4g; Sugar 0.6g; Protein 17.8g

Mustard Salmon with Asparagus

Prep time: 10 minutes | Cook time: 15 minutes | Serves: 2

10 asparagus spears, trimmed 1 inch from bottom
¼ teaspoon freshly ground black pepper
1 lemon, divided
2 (4-ounce) salmon fillets, skin removed
2 tablespoons stone-ground mustard
¼ cup chopped fresh dill

1. Turn on the oven and preheat it to 375°F. Line a baking sheet with parchment paper. 2. Put the asparagus on the baking sheet and sprinkle with pepper. Divide the asparagus into sections, five for each fish. 3. Cut the lemon in half. Reserve half for squeezing after the fish is cooked, and slice the other half into ¼-inch thick slices. 4. Place the lemon slices in the middle of the asparagus and then place the fish on top of the lemons. 5. Combine the mustard and dill. Divide and evenly spread half the mixture on top of each fish in a small mixing bowl. 6. Cook the food in the preheated oven for 15 minutes. 7. Squeeze the lemon juice from the prepared lemon half on both fillets and enjoy.
Per Serving: Calories 221; Fat 9g; Sodium 440mg; Carbs 4g; Fiber 1g; Sugar 1g; Protein 32g

Roasted Salmon Fillets

Prep time: 5 minutes | Cook time: 15 minutes | Serves: 4

1 (6-ounce) salmon fillet, cut into 2 pieces	1 lemon, cut into wedges, for garnish
Salt	Parsley, for garnish
Freshly ground black pepper	

1. Turn on the oven and preheat it to 450°F. 2. Add some salt and pepper according to personal preference. 3. Place the salmon skin-side down on a nonstick baking sheet or in a nonstick pan. 4. Bake the salmon for 12 to 15 minutes. 5. Serve the salmon with the lemon wedges and fresh parsley.
Per Serving: Calories 54; Fat 2g; Sodium 21mg; Carbs 1g; Fiber 0g; Sugar 0.3g; Protein 8.6g

Rainbow Trout B aked in Foil

Prep time: 10 minutes | Cook time: 15 minutes | Serves: 4

1½ teaspoons olive oil, divided, plus more for greasing the foil	4 fresh thyme sprigs
2 small rainbow trout, deboned	Freshly chopped parsley, for garnish
Salt	Freshly chopped thyme, for garnish
Freshly ground black pepper	Lemon wedges, for serving
1 cup peeled, seeded, and chopped tomato	
2 garlic cloves, minced	

1. Turn on the oven and preheat it to 450°F. 2. Cut two pieces of heavy-duty aluminum foil 3 inches longer than your fish. Grease the back of foil with olive oil and place a trout in each square. 3. Season both sides with salt and pepper, then open flat. 4. Combine the tomato, garlic, salt, pepper, and 1 teaspoon of olive oil in a bowl. 5. Spoon equal amounts of the tomato mixture over the middle of each trout. Place 2 thyme sprigs on top of each, and crease the two sides of the trout together. Drizzle ¼ teaspoon of olive oil over each fish. 6. Making sure the trout are in the middle of each square, crease the foil up loosely, grab it at the edges, and crimp together tightly to make a packet. 7. Put them on a baking sheet and bake them in the preheated oven for 10 to 15 minutes, then check one pack after 10 minutes. Meat should be opaque and easily separated when tested with a fork. 8. Place each packet on a plate. Carefully cut across the top to open the packets, taking care not to let the steam burn you. Gently remove the fish from the packets and pour the juices over. Sprinkle with parsley and thyme before serving with lemon wedges.
Per Serving: Calories 320; Fat 16g; Sodium 177mg; Carbs 105g; Fiber 1g; Sugar 1.4g; Protein 39g

Flavorful Sesame-Crusted Tuna Steaks

Prep time: 5 minutes | Cook time: 12 minutes | Serves: 4

Olive oil nonstick cooking spray	6 tablespoons sesame seeds
½ tablespoon olive oil	Salt
1 teaspoon sesame oil	Freshly ground black pepper
2 (6-ounce) ahi tuna steaks	

1. Turn on the oven and preheat it to 450°F and lightly spray a baking sheet with cooking spray. 2. Mix the olive oil and sesame oil in a bowl; coat the tuna steaks with the oil mixture. 3. Add the sesame seeds to a bowl. Press the steaks into the seeds and cover all sides. 4. Place the tuna steaks on the baking sheet, and add some salt and pepper according to personal preference. 5. Bake the tuna steaks for 4 to 6 minutes per side. 6. Serve warm.
Per Serving: Calories 194; Fat 11g; Sodium 44mg; Carbs 1.4g; Fiber 1.4g; Sugar 0g; Protein 23g

Salmon Scallop Skewers

Prep time: 30 minutes | Cook time: 12 minutes | Serves: 4

1 (8-ounce) can pineapple chunks in 100% pineapple juice, drained, reserving 2 tablespoons juice	4 ounces skinless, boneless wild salmon fillets, cut into 1-inch cubes
1 tablespoon freshly squeezed lemon juice	4 ounces scallops
1 tablespoon snipped fresh tarragon or 1 teaspoon dried tarragon	1 zucchini, cut into ½-inch-thick slices
¼ teaspoon dry mustard	1 red bell pepper, cut into 1-inch squares
⅛ teaspoon salt	1 red onion, cut into 1-inch pieces
	8 button mushrooms

1. Preheat an outdoor grill. 2. Combine the 2 tablespoons of prepared pineapple juice, the lemon juice, tarragon, mustard, and salt in the bowl. 3. Place the salmon and scallops in a resealable bag, add the marinade and seal the bag. Turn the fish and scallops to coat well. Put into the refrigerator and marinate for 1 to 2 hours, turning once. 4. Bring just enough water to cover the zucchini (1 to 2 inches) to a boil in the pot. Add the zucchini, cover the pot and cook for 3 to 4 minutes. Drain and cool. 5. Remove the seafood from the bag, reserving the marinade. Alternately thread the salmon, scallops, zucchini, bell pepper, onion, mushrooms, and pineapple on 4 metal skewers. Coat with the prepared marinade. 6. Grill, uncovered, directly over medium coals for 8 to 12 minutes, turning once, until the scallops turn opaque and the salmon flakes easily when tested with a fork. 7. Put two skewers of meat on each plate.
Per Serving: Calories 124; Fat 2g; Sodium 307mg; Carbs 15g; Fiber 1.5g; Sugar 11g; Protein 12.8g

Salmon Burgers with Yogurt Mustard Sauce

Prep time: 10 minutes | Cook time: 20 minutes | Serves: 4

2 tablespoons ground flaxseed	1 teaspoon dried dill weed
5 tablespoons water	¼ teaspoon freshly ground black pepper
2 (6-ounce) cans no-salt-added salmon, in water	½ cup fat-free plain Greek yogurt
2 medium shallots, finely diced (about ½ cup)	2 heaping teaspoons stone-ground mustard

1. Turn on the oven and preheat it to 400°F. Line a baking sheet with parchment paper. 2. Combine the flaxseed with the water and let the mixture stand for 5 minutes until it congeals. 3. Put the salmon and separate with a fork; add the shallots, dill, pepper, and flaxseed mixture, and then mix them well until you can easily form a patty. 4. Divide the mixture into fourths and create four roughly equal-size patties. Place the patties on the baking sheet. 5. Bake the patties for 15 minutes; when the time is up, flip them and bake for another 5 minutes. 6. Mix the yogurt and mustard in a small mixing bowl. 7. Top each salmon burger with 2 tablespoons of the yogurt dressing. 8. Serve and enjoy.
Per Serving: Calories 184; Fat 8g; Sodium 80mg; Carbs 6g; Fiber 2g; Sugar 3g; Protein 22g

Salmon Fillets and Tomato Cucumber Medley

Prep time: 15 minutes | Cook time: 15 minutes | Serves: 4

1 tablespoon olive oil, divided, plus more for oiling
2 (6-ounce) salmon fillets
¼ teaspoon salt, divided
¼ teaspoon freshly ground black pepper, divided
1 tablespoon freshly squeezed lemon juice, plus 1 teaspoon
¼ cup minced shallots
1 tablespoon coarsely chopped fresh tarragon, plus 1 tablespoon fresh tarragon leaves
¼ cup red wine vinegar
4 ounces thin-skinned cucumber, such as English or Persian, sliced
2 medium tomatoes, sliced
2 tablespoons chopped flat-leaf parsley
¼ cup plain nonfat Greek yogurt
1 small garlic clove, grated
1 teaspoon freshly grated lemon zest
¼ cup toasted whole-grain breadcrumbs

1. Turn on the oven and preheat it to 375°F. Line a baking sheet with aluminum foil and grease it. 2. Sprinkle the salmon with ⅛ teaspoon salt, ⅛ teaspoon of pepper, ½ tablespoon of olive oil, and 1 tablespoon of lemon juice. Place it skin-side down on the baking sheet. 3. Bake the salmon for 10 to 13 minutes, then remove it from the oven and keep it warm. 4. Add the shallots, chopped tarragon, and vinegar to a frying pan, and then boil them over high heat for 4 to 5 minutes, stirring often until the vinegar evaporates but the shallots still look wet. 5. Add ½ tablespoon of olive oil, the remaining ⅛ teaspoon of salt, the remaining ⅛ teaspoon of pepper, the cucumber and tomatoes, and cook them for 1 to 2 minutes until softened. 6. Remove from the heat and mix in the parsley. 7. Combine the yogurt, garlic, lemon zest, and remaining 1 teaspoon of lemon juice in a bowl. Put aside. 8. Divide the tomato-cucumber mixture between two serving plates. Top each plate with a piece of salmon, half of the yogurt dressing, and half of the toasted bread crumbs. Garnish with the fresh tarragon leaves. 9. Enjoy.
Per Serving: Calories 212; Fat 10g; Sodium 575mg; Carbs 8.5g; Fiber 1g; Sugar 2g; Protein 21g

Salmon en Papillote with Sugar Snap Peas

Prep time: 5 minutes | Cook time: 15 minutes | Serves: 2

2 (4-ounce) salmon fillets, scaled
¼ teaspoon freshly ground black pepper
8 chopped thyme sprigs, divided
3 tablespoons lemon juice
½ cup sugar snap peas
½ cup cherry tomatoes, halved

1. Turn on the oven and preheat it to 400°F. Line a baking sheet with parchment paper. 2. Create two envelopes from parchment paper. To make one, take a medium-size piece of parchment paper (about 6 inches), crease it in half and make a sharp crease. Cut it into a half-moon shape with the closed section facing you. 3. Place 1 fish fillet in each envelope and top it with 4 chopped thyme sprigs, ⅛ teaspoon of pepper, and 1½ tablespoons of lemon juice. Divide the sugar snap peas and cherry tomatoes between the envelopes. 4. Pinch together the edges of the parchment paper to close the envelopes. 5. Cook the food for 10 to 15 minutes, then open the envelopes and ensure the fish is flaky. 6. Serve and enjoy.
Per Serving: Calories 166; Fat 4.5g; Sodium 60mg; Carbs 6g; Fiber 2g; Sugar 1.6g; Protein 24g

Tacos with Cabbage Slaw

Prep time: 10 minutes | Cook time: 6 minutes | Serves: 4

8 ounces skinless flounder fillets, cut into 1-inch chunks
1 teaspoon ground cumin
⅛ teaspoon salt
⅛ teaspoon freshly ground black pepper
1 cup thinly sliced red cabbage
½ avocado, chopped
2 tablespoons freshly squeezed lime juice
3 teaspoons olive oil, divided
4 corn tortillas, warmed
Fresh cilantro, for garnish

1. Mix together the flounder, cumin, salt, and pepper in a small bowl. 2. Mix together the cabbage, avocado, lime juice, and 1 teaspoon of olive oil in another small bowl. Heat the remaining olive oil in the skillet over medium-high heat; add the flounder and cook for 2 minutes on each side. 3. Place 2 hot tortillas on each plate. 4. Divide the fish into tacos and top with cabbage-avocado salad. Garnish with fresh coriander and serve.
Per Serving: Calories 173; Fat 9g; Sodium 265mg; Carbs 15g; Fiber 4g; Sugar 1g; Protein 9g

Garlic Mackerel Fillets

Prep time: 10 minutes | Cook time: 5 minutes | Serves: 4

2 (4-ounce) mackerel fillets
Salt
2 garlic cloves, minced
Juice of ½ lemon
Freshly ground black pepper

1. Line a baking sheet with aluminum foil and lay the fillets on it. Sprinkle with salt and let stand for 5 minutes. 2. Preheat the broiler. 3. Mix the garlic, lemon juice, and some pepper in a bowl. 4. Pour the mixture over the mackerel. 5. Broil the fillets for 5 minutes and then serve immediately.
Per Serving: Calories 63; Fat 1g; Sodium 90mg; Carbs 1g; Fiber 0g; Sugar 0.2g; Protein 12g

Fish and Chips

Prep time: 10 minutes | Cook time: 15 minutes | Serves: 2

1 large zucchini
2 egg whites
½ cup almond meal
1 large garlic clove, minced
1¼ teaspoon dried thyme, divided
1¼ teaspoon dried basil, divided
2 (4-ounce) cod fillets, skinned and cut into 1-inch strips
1 teaspoon avocado oil
¼ teaspoon freshly ground black pepper
4 tablespoons tartar sauce

1. Turn on the oven and preheat it to 425°F. Line the baking sheet with parchment paper. 2. Thinly cut the zucchini into small coins. Press the coins with paper towels to draw out excess moisture. The drier you get the coins, the crispier they'll get. 3. Beat the egg whites in a medium bowl. 4. Combine the almond meal, garlic, 1 teaspoon of thyme, and 1 teaspoon of basil in a medium shallow plate. 5. Coat the fish strips on both sides with the egg whites. Dredge the fish strips in the almond meal mixture and coat well. 6. Place each strip separately on the arranged baking sheet. 7. Combine the oil, pepper, and the remaining ¼ teaspoon of thyme and ¼ teaspoon of basil in a medium mixing bowl. Add the zucchini coins and mix to coat evenly. Place separately on the baking sheet. 8. Bake the food for 12 minutes, flipping the fish halfway through, until lightly golden on each side.
Per Serving: Calories 328; Fat 17g; Sodium 239mg; Carbs 13g; Fiber 5g; Sugar 7g; Protein 32g

Peppercorn-Crusted Tuna Steaks

Prep time: 5 minutes | Cook time: 8 minutes | Serves: 4

Olive oil nonstick cooking spray
2 (6-ounce) tuna steaks
1 teaspoon freshly grated lime zest
⅛ teaspoon salt

½ teaspoon freshly ground black pepper
1 garlic clove, minced
Lemon wedges, for serving

1. Preheat the broiler, and coat the baking pan with cooking spray. 2. Place the fish in the baking pan. 3. Combine the lime zest, salt, pepper, and garlic in the bowl, and then sprinkle the mixture over the fish. 4. Broil the fish for 7 to 8 minutes. 5. Transfer each steak to a serving plate before serving with lemon wedges.
Per Serving: Calories 317; Fat 11g; Sodium 233mg; Carbs 1g; Fiber 0g; Sugar 0g; Protein 51g

Cabbage Salmon Tacos

Prep time: 10 minutes | Cook time: 15 minutes | Serves: 2

2 (4-ounce) salmon fillets
2 tablespoons lemon juice
¼ teaspoon paprika
¼ teaspoon garlic powder
4 low-sodium whole wheat mini taco shells

1 tablespoon and 1 teaspoon Arugula-Basil Pesto, divided
1 cup cabbage slaw with carrots (or ¾ cup cabbage, cut into matchsticks, and ½ cup carrots, cut into matchsticks), divided

1. Preheat the grill to high. Line the baking sheet with parchment paper. 2. Place the fish skin-side down on the arranged baking sheet. Add the lemon juice, paprika, and garlic powder evenly to the fillets. 3. Bake the fish for 8 minutes, then flip and bake for another 5 minutes. 4. To each taco shell, add 1 teaspoon of pesto, ¼ cup of cabbage slaw, and about 2 ounces of fish. Use a fork to separate the fish and flake onto the taco.
Per Serving: Calories 409; Fat 23g; Sodium 749mg; Carbs 24g; Fiber 4g; Sugar 4g; Protein 28g

Avocado Fish Florentine

Prep time: 5 minutes | Cook time: 10 minutes | Serves: 2

2 teaspoons avocado oil, divided
2 garlic cloves, minced
1 red bell pepper, diced
1 (6-ounce) bag fresh spinach (about 4 cups)
¼ cup cashew cream dressing

2 (4-ounce) rainbow trout fillets, skinned and thoroughly patted dry
¼ teaspoon freshly ground black pepper

1. Heat 1 teaspoon of oil over medium heat in a medium skillet. Add the garlic and bell pepper and simmer for about 2 minutes. 2. Add the spinach and mix well now and then for about 2 minutes. 3. Remove from the heat and add the dressing. 4. Heat the remaining oil over medium heat in another medium skillet for 2 minutes. 5. Add the fillets and add pepper, cook them for 2 minutes on each side, until the middle puffs up and the spatula can easily lift the fish. 6. Divide the spinach mixture evenly on two plates so that it encompasses the fish fillets on top and bottom, then serve.
Per Serving: Calories 400; Fat 25g; Sodium 90mg; Carbs 16g; Fiber 3g; Sugar 3g; Protein 31g

Simple Skillet-Seared Salmon with Chimichurri Sauce

Prep time: 5 minutes | Cook time: 10 minutes | Serves: 2

2 teaspoons avocado oil
2 (4-ounce) salmon fillets, skin intact but scaled

½ teaspoon Mediterranean seasoning rub blend
1 tablespoon Chimichurri sauce

1. Heat the oil in the skillet over medium heat for 3 minutes. 2. Add the fish to the pan, skin-side down. 3. Season each flesh side of the fish with ¼ teaspoon of the seasoning blend. 4. Cook for another 3 minutes and the fish is easily flipped with a spatula. 5. Flip and cook the flesh side for 2 to 3 minutes. 6. Plate the salmon, add ½ tablespoon of the sauce to each piece before serving.
Per Serving: Calories 189; Fat 9.5g; Sodium 199mg; Carbs 1g; Fiber 0.3g; Sugar 0.4g; Protein 23.4g

Mahi Mahi with Greens

Prep time: 10 minutes | Cook time: 15 minutes | Serves: 2

2 teaspoons toasted sesame oil
1 whole leek (including green top), diced (about 2 cups)
1 packed tablespoon grated ginger
3 bunches baby bok choy,

separated
2 (4-ounce) mahi mahi fillets, skinned
¼ teaspoon freshly ground black pepper
¼ teaspoon garlic powder

1. Heat the sesame oil in the pot over medium heat, add the leek, and then sauté for 1 to 2 minutes. 2. Add the ginger and bok choy, mix well to combine, cover the pot and cook for 5 minutes. 3. Move the bok choy to the side and add the mahi mahi fillets in the pot so that they touch the surface of the pot. 4. Season the fillets with the pepper and garlic powder and cook for 3 minutes. Flip the mahi mahi and add the leek, ginger, and bok choy mixture on top and then cook for another 2 to 3 minutes. 5. Serve and enjoy.
Per Serving: Calories 193; Fat 6g; Sodium 192mg; Carbs 8g; Fiber 5g; Sugar 3g; Protein 24g

Baked Rainbow Trout Fillets

Prep time: 5 minutes | Cook time: 15 minutes | Serves: 2

½ cup chopped fresh parsley (about ¼ bunch)
¼ cup unsalted pecans
¼ teaspoon ground cumin
¼ teaspoon freshly ground black

pepper
2 teaspoons avocado oil
1 large navel orange, divided
2 (4-ounce) rainbow trout fillets, skin removed

1. Turn on the oven and preheat it to 375°F. Line a baking sheet with parchment paper. 2. Pulse the parsley, pecans, cumin, pepper, and oil in the blender. 3. Zest the outside of the orange then slice the orange in half, and then add the zest to the parsley-pecan mixture. 4. Place half the parsley-pecan mixture on top of each fillet (about 1½ tablespoons each). Squeeze the other half of the orange on top. 5. Bake the food for 10 to 12 minutes. 6. Serve warm.
Per Serving: Calories 3226; Fat 19g; Sodium 45mg; Carbs 15g; Fiber 4g; Sugar 8.6g; Protein 26g

Pistachio Halibut

Prep time: 5 minutes | Cook time: 15 minutes | Serves: 2

1 tablespoon Dijon mustard	pepper
1 teaspoon pure maple syrup	2 (4-ounce) halibut fillets, skin on,
1 teaspoon avocado oil	scaled
2 garlic cloves, minced	2 tablespoons unsalted pistachios
½ teaspoon freshly ground black	

1. Turn on the oven and preheat it to 425°F. Line a baking sheet with parchment paper. 2. Combine the mustard, maple syrup, oil, garlic, and pepper in a medium mixing bowl. 3. Coat the halibut fillets evenly with the mustard mixture, and then place them on the arranged baking sheet. 4. Top each fillet with 1 tablespoon of pistachios, and cook for 12 to 15 minutes. 5. Serve warm.
Per Serving: Calories 294; Fat 22g; Sodium 178mg; Carbs 6g; Fiber 1g; Sugar 3g; Protein 18.4g

Easy Sardines Puttanesca

Prep time: 10 minutes | Cook time: 15 minutes | Serves: 2

2 teaspoons avocado oil	¼ cup low-sodium Kalamata
1 medium yellow onion, diced	olives, quartered
2 large garlic cloves, minced	½ teaspoon dried oregano
1-pound medium Roma	½ cup fresh chopped fresh parsley
tomatoes, cut into ½-inch pieces	¼ teaspoon red pepper flakes
7½ ounces no-salt-added canned	½ teaspoon freshly ground black
sardines, in water	pepper

1. Heat the oil over medium-high heat in a medium skillet. Add the onions and garlic and sauté for 2 minutes. 2. Add the tomatoes, cover the skillet and cook for 5 minutes. 3. Drain the sardines and mash well with a fork in a small bowl. 4. Add the sardines, olives, oregano, parsley, red pepper flakes, and black pepper to the tomato, onion, and garlic mixture. Stir well, cover the skillet again and cook over medium-low heat for another 5 minutes. 5. Serve on top of ½ cup of whole wheat pasta or bean pasta.
Per Serving: Calories 160; Fat 4.5g; Sodium 149mg; Carbs 23g; Fiber 7g; Sugar 9.6g; Protein 4.8g

Delicious Pork and Couscous

Prep time: 10 minutes | Cook time: 25 minutes | Serves: 4

2 tablespoons extra-virgin olive	2½ cups water
oil	½ cup chopped sun-dried
4 thick-cut pork chops, trimmed	tomatoes
½ onion, chopped	3 cups chopped spinach
1½ cups Israeli couscous	

1. Heat the oil in the skillet over medium-high heat. 2. Add the pork chops, and brown on both sides for about 1½ minutes per side; transfer the pork chops to a plate. 3. Reduce the heat to medium; add the onion into the skillet, and cook for 3 to 5 minutes. 4. Put in the couscous, and brown for 1 to 2 minutes. 5. Add the water, and deglaze the skillet by scraping up any browned bits on the bottom. 6. Add the sun-dried tomatoes, bring to a simmer, and then cook for 5 minutes. 7. Return the pork chops to the skillet. 8. Cover the skillet, and reduce the heat to medium-low, and then cook the food for 6 to 8 minutes. If the couscous dries out during cooking, add a splash or two more water to keep it moist. 9. Stir in the spinach until wilted. 10. Serve warm.
Per Serving: Calories 248; Fat 6.68g; Sodium 502mg; Carbs 19.54g; Fiber 2.4g; Sugar 3.27g; Protein 27.24g

Delicious Pistachio-Crusted Flounder

Prep time: 15 minutes | Cook time: 15 minutes | Serves: 4

Cooking spray	½ cup raw shelled pistachios,
¼ cup gluten-free Dijon mustard	finely chopped
½ teaspoon salt, divided	2 tablespoons cornmeal
⅛ teaspoon freshly ground black	¼ cup chopped fresh parsley
pepper	4 (5-ounce) flounder fillets

1. Turn on the oven and preheat it to 400°F. Spray a baking tray with cooking spray. 2. Mix the Dijon mustard, pepper, and ¼ teaspoon of salt in a small bowl. 3. Mix the pistachios, cornmeal, parsley, and the remaining salt in another small bowl. 4. Coat both sides of 1 flounder fillet with the mustard mixture, and then dredge both sides in the pistachio mixture 5. Place the flounder on the baking sheet. 6. Do the same with the remaining 3 fillets, leaving ½ inch between pieces. 7. Bake the flounder pieces for about 15 minutes. 8. When the time is up, serve and enjoy.
Per Serving: Calories 240; Fat 11g; Sodium 1397mg; Carbs 9.3g; Fiber 2.5g; Sugar 1.4g; Protein 26g

Flank Steak Hummus Salad

Prep time: 15 minutes | Cook time: 15 minutes | Serves: 4

1 pound flank steak	½ English cucumber, chopped
Salt	½ cup yogurt-herb dressing,
Freshly ground black pepper	divided
8 cups chopped romaine lettuce	½ cup garlic hummus

1. Preheat the broiler to high. 2. Season the steak with salt and pepper, and then place the steak on the baking sheet. 3. Broil the steak in the preheated broiler for 5 to 6 minutes. 4. Flip the steak, and broil for 4 to 7 more minutes. 5. When done, set the steak aside for 10 minutes, then thinly slice against the grain. 6. Toss the lettuce and cucumber in a bowl. 7. Drizzle with half of the dressing, and toss again. 8. Serve the salad topped with the steak and hummus. 9. Drizzle with the remaining dressing if desired.
Per Serving: Calories 249; Fat 9.65g; Sodium 157mg; Carbs 11.62g; Fiber 3.5g; Sugar 2.98g; Protein 28.22g

Chicken Breasts with Orzo Salad

Prep time: 10 minutes | Cook time: 15 minutes | Serves: 4

1-pound boneless, skinless chicken breasts, diced	½ cup chopped sun-dried tomatoes
½ cup lemon vinaigrette, divided	¼ cup chopped Kalamata olives
1 cup whole-wheat orzo	Salt
	Freshly ground black pepper

1. Add the chicken and ¼ cup of vinaigrette to the bowl, and then let the chicken marinate for 10 minutes. 2. Fill a large saucepan with water and bring to a boil. 3. Add the orzo, and cook the orzo according to the package directions; when cooked, drain the orzo. 4. Add the chicken and marinade to the large skillet over medium-high heat, and sauté them for 5 to 7 minutes. 5. Toss together the chicken, orzo, sun-dried tomatoes, olives, and remaining ¼ cup of vinaigrette. Add some salt and pepper consistent with personal preference. 6. Enjoy.
Per Serving: Calories 265; Fat 3.8g; Sodium 302mg; Carbs 28.08g; Fiber 4.4g; Sugar 3.43g; Protein 31.42g

Chicken and Tomato Stew with Tahini

Prep time: 5 minutes | Cook time: 30 minutes | Serves: 4

1 tablespoon extra-virgin olive oil	diced tomatoes
½ onion, finely chopped	½ cup quinoa
8 ounces boneless, skinless chicken breast	½ teaspoon salt
2 cups water	¼ teaspoon freshly ground black pepper
1 (15-ounce) can low-sodium	½ cup tahini

1. Heat the oil in the pot over medium heat. 2. Add the onion, and cook for 3 to 5 minutes. 3. Add the chicken, and cook, stirring now and then, for 5 minutes. 4. Add the water, tomatoes with their juices, quinoa, salt, and pepper, and then simmer for 20 minutes or until the quinoa is tender. 5. Stir in the tahini, and combine well to heat through. 6. Serve warm.
Per Serving: Calories 366; Fat 19.99g; Sodium 477mg; Carbs 26.59g; Fiber 5.5g; Sugar 5.03g; Protein 22.12g

Baked Chicken and Tomatoes with Mozzarella

Prep time: 5 minutes | Cook time: 25 minutes | Serves: 4

1 pound chicken breasts (about 2 breasts), halved lengthwise into 4 pieces	¼ teaspoon freshly ground black pepper
½ teaspoon garlic powder	½ cup fresh basil leaves
½ teaspoon salt	4 mozzarella cheese slices
	2 large tomatoes, finely chopped

1. Turn on the oven and preheat it to 400°F. 2. Season the chicken with the garlic powder, salt, and pepper. 3. Place the chicken on a baking sheet. 4. Bake the chicken for 18 to 22 minutes. 5. Remove the baking sheet from the oven, evenly distribute the basil on top of the chicken. 6. Place 1 cheese slice on each breast. 7. Put on the top the tomatoes. 8. Return the baking sheet to the oven, set the oven to broil on high, and then broil for 2 to 3 minutes. 9. Serve warm.
Per Serving: Calories 226; Fat 6.85g; Sodium 377mg; Carbs 4.81g; Fiber 1.2g; Sugar 2.75g; Protein 34.9g

Chicken Breasts with Mushroom Sauce

Prep time: 5 minutes | Cook time: 15 minutes | Serves: 4

1 tablespoon olive oil, divided	sliced
2 (6-ounce) skinless, boneless chicken breasts	1 portobello mushroom, sliced
¼ teaspoon salt, divided	2 garlic cloves, minced
⅛ teaspoon freshly ground black pepper	¼ cup dry white wine, cooking wine, or low-sodium broth
¼ cup chopped shallots	1 teaspoon flour
4 ounces button mushrooms,	½ cup water
	2 teaspoons minced fresh thyme

1. Sprinkle the chicken with ⅛ teaspoon salt and the pepper. 2. Heat 1 teaspoon of olive oil in a large nonstick skillet over medium-high heat, swirling to coat. 3. Add the chicken to the skillet and cook for about 3 minutes on each side. Transfer to a plate and keep warm. 4. Add the shallots and mushrooms to the skillet and sauté for about 4 minutes. 5. Add the garlic and sauté for 1 minute. 6. Add the wine and stir, scraping the pan to loosen any browned bits from the bottom. Heat until boils and cook until the liquid almost evaporates. 7. Sprinkle the mushroom mixture with the remaining salt and the flour, and sauté them for 30 seconds. 8. Add the water to the skillet and heat it until it is boiling; cook the food for 2 minutes more. 9. Remove the skillet from the heat, add the remaining 2 teaspoons of olive oil and the thyme, and stir until fully mixed. 10. Pour the sauce over the chicken, serve and enjoy.
Per Serving: Calories 191; Fat 5.87g; Sodium 289mg; Carbs 23.42g; Fiber 3.5g; Sugar 1.05; Protein 14.42g

Chicken Cauliflower Bowls

Prep time: 10 minutes | Cook time: 20 minutes | Serves: 4

1-pound boneless, skinless chicken breasts, halved lengthwise
½ teaspoon Italian seasoning
¼ cup freshly ground black pepper
2 tablespoons extra-virgin olive

oil, divided
4 cups cauliflower rice
1 (15-ounce) can artichoke hearts, drained
¼ cup chopped Kalamata olives

1. Season the chicken with the Italian seasoning, salt, and pepper. 2. Heat in a skillet 1 tablespoon of oil over medium-high heat. 3. Add the chicken, and cook for 3 to 5 minutes. 4. Flip the chicken, and cook on the other side for 3 to 5 minutes. 5. Transfer the chicken to a chopping block. Thinly slice the chicken across the grain. 6. Heat the remaining oil in the same skillet over medium-high heat. 7. Add the cauliflower rice, and cook for 5 to 8 minutes. 8. Add the artichoke hearts and olives, combine well to heat through. 9. Serve the cauliflower and vegetables topped with the chicken.
Per Serving: Calories 213; Fat 6.13g; Sodium 294mg; Carbs 10.4g; Fiber 4.7g; Sugar 2.48g; Protein 29.82g

Tahini Beef Pita Sandwiches

Prep time: 5 minutes | Cook time: 15 minutes | Serves: 4

12 ounces flank steak
½ teaspoon garlic powder
½ teaspoon salt
¼ teaspoon freshly ground black pepper

2 tablespoons extra-virgin olive oil
4 whole-wheat pita rounds, halved
½ cup Tahini Dressing

1. Season the steak with the garlic powder, salt, and pepper. 2. Heat the oil in the frying pan over medium-high heat. 3. Add the steak, and sear for 5 to 7 minutes per side. 4. Set the steak aside for 5 minutes, then thinly slice against the grain. 5. Stuff several slices of steak into the pita halves. 6. Drizzle with the dressing. Enjoy.
Per Serving: Calories 398; Fat 24.12g; Sodium 410mg; Carbs 22.16g; Fiber 4.9g; Sugar 0.39g; Protein 26.18g

Shredded Chicken Soup

Prep time: 10 minutes | Cook time: 40 minutes | Serves: 6

8 cups store-bought low-sodium broth
8 ounces boneless, skinless chicken breast
1 cup long-grain white rice
2 large eggs

⅓ cup freshly squeezed lemon juice
1 teaspoon grated lemon zest
½ teaspoon salt
¼ teaspoon freshly ground black pepper

1. Add the stock to the saucepan and bring the stock to a simmer over medium heat. 2. Add the chicken and cook for 15 to 20 minutes. 3. Turn off the heat, transfer the chicken to a bowl, and set aside to cool; once cooled, use 2 forks to shred the chicken. 4. Return the chicken to the stock, and add the rice. 5. Cover the pot and cook the food over medium heat for 15 minutes, and then reduce the heat to medium-low. 6. Mix the eggs, lemon juice, and lemon zest in a bowl; ladle a cup of the stock into the mixture to temper the sauce. 7. Whisk the egg mixture into the saucepan continuously for 1 minute, and then remove the pan from the heat. 8. Season the soup with salt and pepper.
Per Serving: Calories 261; Fat 4.24g; Sodium 576mg; Carbs 38.8g; Fiber 2.2g; Sugar 9.98g; Protein 18.08g

Veggie Chicken Bowls

Prep time: 5 minutes | Cook time: 15 minutes | Serves: 4

2 cups water
1 cup quinoa
1 pound chicken breast tenders
1 teaspoon za'atar
¼ teaspoon salt
¼ teaspoon freshly ground black

pepper
2 tablespoons extra-virgin olive oil
1 (15-ounce) can chickpeas, drained and rinsed
4 cups baby spinach

1. Add the water and quinoa to the saucepan, and bring to a boil; when boiled, reduce the heat to a simmer. 2. Cover the saucepan, and cook the quinoa over low heat for 15 minutes. 3. Season the chicken with the za'atar, salt, and pepper. 4. Heat the oil in the skillet over medium-high heat. 5. Add the chicken, and sauté for 2 to 3 minutes; flip, and cook for 3 to 5 minutes. 6. Serve the quinoa topped with the chicken, chickpeas, and spinach.
Per Serving: Calories 417; Fat 10.25g; Sodium 434mg; Carbs 43.58g; Fiber 7.7g; Sugar 3.15g; Protein 36.9g

Baked Chicken with Artichoke

Prep time: 10 minutes | Cook time: 30 minutes | Serves: 4

2 tablespoons extra-virgin olive oil
4 bone-in chicken thighs, skin removed
¾ teaspoon low-sodium salt, divided
½ teaspoon freshly ground black pepper, divided

1 (15-ounce) can low-sodium diced tomatoes, drained
¼ cup water
1 (15-ounce) can quartered artichoke hearts, drained
¼ cup pitted Kalamata olives
¼ cup chopped fresh parsley

1. Turn on the oven and preheat it to 350°F. 2. Season the chicken with ¼ teaspoon of salt and ¼ teaspoon of pepper. 3. Heat the oil in the oven-safe skillet over medium-high heat; add the chicken, and cook for 2 to 3 minutes per side. Transfer the chicken to a plate. 4. Stir the tomatoes and water into the skillet, and deglaze by scraping up any browned bits from the bottom. 5. Add the artichoke hearts, olives, remaining ½ teaspoon of salt, and ¼ teaspoon of pepper. Mix to combine. 6. Nestle the chicken into the skillet. Remove from the heat. 7. Transfer the skillet to the oven, and bake the food for 20 minutes. 8. Top the food with parsley before serving.
Per Serving: Calories 293; Fat 11.16g; Sodium 377mg; Carbs 4.81g; Fiber 1.2g; Sugar 2.75g; Protein 34.9g

Herbed Chicken Kebabs

Prep time: 10 minutes + 30 minutes to rest | Cook time: 15 minutes | Serves: 4

1-pound boneless, skinless chicken breasts, cut into 1-inch dice
Juice of 1 lemon
2 tablespoons extra-virgin olive oil

5 garlic cloves, minced
1 teaspoon dried rosemary
1 teaspoon dried oregano
½ teaspoon salt
¼ teaspoon freshly ground black pepper

1. Mix the chicken pieces with the remaining ingredients and marinate them for 30 minutes. 2. Thread the chicken pieces onto 8 skewers. 3. Preheat a grill on medium-high heat. 4. Place the skewers on the grill, and cook for 5 to 7 minutes. Flip, and cook for 5 to 8 minutes. 5. Serve warm.
Per Serving: Calories 166; Fat 4.95g; Sodium 429mg; Carbs 2.39g; Fiber 0.3g; Sugar 0.35g; Protein 26.66g

Lemony Chicken Thighs and Brussels Sprouts

Prep time: 5 minutes | Cook time: 25 minutes | Serves: 4

4 bone-in chicken thighs, skin removed	oil
½ teaspoon low-sodium salt, divided	1 onion, cut into half-moons
¼ teaspoon freshly ground black pepper	1 pound Brussels sprouts, trimmed and halved
2 tablespoons extra-virgin olive	1 cup store-bought low-sodium vegetable broth
	Juice of 1 lemon

1. Turn on the oven and preheat it to 350°F. 2. Season the chicken with ½ teaspoon of salt and the pepper. 3. Heat the oil over medium-high heat. 4. Place the chicken in the skillet so that the side that had skin faces the bottom, and sear for 3 to 5 minutes, then flip. 5. Scatter the onion and Brussels sprouts around the chicken. 6. Pour in the stock, and bring to a simmer. Remove from the heat. 7. Transfer the skillet to the oven, and bake for 20 minutes. Stop heating. 8. Sprinkle the lemon juice over the top of the chicken and Brussels sprouts.
Per Serving: Calories 363; Fat 14.81g; Sodium 421mg; Carbs 19.77g; Fiber 5.5g; Sugar 8.74g; Protein 39.08g

Lime Chicken with Tomato-Avocado Salsa

Prep time: 10 minutes | Cook time: 12 minutes | Serves: 4

For the chicken	1 tablespoon finely chopped onion
2 tablespoons minced fresh cilantro	2 tablespoons minced fresh cilantro
1½ tablespoons freshly squeezed lime juice	2 tablespoons freshly squeezed lime juice
2 teaspoons olive oil	1 small peach, peeled and finely chopped
⅛ teaspoon salt	
½ teaspoon ground cumin	⅛ teaspoon salt
2 (6-ounce) skinless, boneless chicken breasts	⅛ teaspoon freshly ground black pepper
Olive oil nonstick cooking spray	½ avocado, peeled and finely chopped
For the salsa	
½ cup chopped plum tomato	
¼ cup chopped red bell pepper	

To make the chicken: 1. Combine the cilantro, lime juice, olive oil, salt, and cumin. Add the chicken to the marinade and toss to coat. Refrigerate for 30 minutes. Remove the chicken from the marinade. 2. Heat a large non-stick skillet over medium-high heat. Once the pan is hot, spray the frying pan with cooking spray. Add the chicken to the pan and cook for 6 minutes on each side.
To make the salsa: 1. Combine the tomato, bell pepper, onion, cilantro, lime juice, peach, salt, and pepper. 2. Add the avocado and stir gently to combine. Serve the chicken topped with the salsa.
Per Serving: Calories 182; Fat 10.13g; Sodium 191mg; Carbs 14.59g; Fiber 2.7g; Sugar 10.58g; Protein 10g

Chicken Breast with Penne and Pesto

Prep time: 5 minutes | Cook time: 15 minutes | Serves: 4

8 ounces penne	2 tablespoons extra-virgin olive oil, divided
8 ounces boneless, skinless chicken breast, thinly sliced	2 cups chopped asparagus
Salt	½ cup store-bought pesto
Freshly ground black pepper	¼ cup shredded Parmesan cheese

1. Add some water to a large saucepan and bring to a boil. 2. Cook the penne consistent with the package directions, until al dente. Stop heating. Drain. 3. At the same time, season the chicken with salt and pepper. 4. Heat 1 tablespoon of oil in the skillet over medium-high heat; add the chicken, and sauté for 5 to 7 minutes. 5. Transfer the chicken to a plate. 6. Heat the remaining oil in the same skillet over medium-high heat; add the asparagus, and sauté for 3 to 5 minutes. 7. Add the chicken, penne, and pesto to the skillet. Mix to combine 8. Turn off the heat, add some salt and pepper consistent with personal preference. 9. Serve topped with the cheese.
Per Serving: Calories 239; Fat 12.37g; Sodium 497mg; Carbs 13.83g; Fiber 3.3g; Sugar 2.34g; Protein 18.5g

Pesto Chicken Pizza

Prep time: 10 minutes | Cook time: 20 minutes | Serves: 4

1 premade pizza dough	½ cup chopped artichoke hearts
1 tablespoon extra-virgin olive oil	4 ounces fresh mozzarella cheese, thinly sliced and nonfat
⅓ cup Basil-Walnut Pesto	
1 cup shredded cooked chicken	

1. Turn on the oven and preheat it to 425°F. 2. Spread the dough into a thin crust on a large baking sheet, then poke it several times with a fork. 3. Spread the dough with the oil. 4. Bake the dough in the preheated oven for 7 minutes. 5. Remove the baking sheet from the oven, spread the pesto on the dough in an even layer to within about ½ inch of the edges. 6. Spread the chicken and artichokes out evenly over the pizza, and top them with cheese. 7. Return the baking sheet to the oven, and bake for 7 to 10 minutes longer. 8. Serve warm.
Per Serving: Calories 240; Fat 14.47g; Sodium 485mg; Carbs 6.44g; Fiber 1.9g; Sugar 0.8g; Protein 14.47g

Slow Roasted Beef Roast

Prep time: 15 minutes | Cook time: 75 minutes | Serves: 6

1 tablespoon olive oil	1 (28-ounce) can whole tomatoes with their juices
1 medium yellow onion, sliced	¼ teaspoon fine sea salt
1 tablespoon garlic, minced	½ teaspoon ground black pepper
1½ pound beef roast, cut into pieces	¼ cup cilantro, finely chopped

1. Turn on the oven and preheat it to 350°F, gas mark 4. 2. Heat the olive oil in a cast iron over high heat. 3. Add the sliced onion, and cook for 3 to 5 minutes. 4. Add the minced garlic, and cook for 30 seconds. 5. Add the beef pieces, and fry for 5 to 6 minutes. 6. Add the whole tomatoes with their juices, fine sea salt, and ground black pepper. heat until it boils, and remove from the heat. 7. Cover the pot with a lid, and place it in the oven. Cook for 1 hour, or until the meat is tender, stirring now and then, and scraping the bottom. Remove from the oven, and put it aside for 10 minutes. 8. Skim any fat from the top of the mixture with a spoon. 9. Serve the roast with your choice of vegetables, and sprinkle with chopped cilantro.
Per Serving: Calories 199; Fat 9.16g; Sodium 553mg; Carbs 5.98g; Fiber 0.7g; Sugar 3.93g; Protein 24.67g

Worcestershire Turkey Burgers

Prep time: 10 minutes | Cook time: 10 minutes | Serves: 4

1 pound ground turkey
¼ cup crumbled feta cheese
2 tablespoons chopped fresh basil leaves

1 large egg
1 teaspoon Worcestershire sauce
¼ teaspoon freshly ground black pepper

1. Combine the turkey, cheese, basil, egg, Worcestershire sauce, and pepper. 2. Form the mixture into 4 patties. 3. Add the patties to a large nonstick skillet over medium-high heat, and cook for 3 to 4 minutes per side. 4. Serve with your favorite burger toppings.
Per Serving: Calories 208; Fat 11.82g; Sodium 168mg; Carbs 0.93g; Fiber 0g; Sugar 0.55g; Protein 24.33g

Chicken Thighs with Onion and Bell Pepper

Prep time: 10 minutes | Cook time: 35 minutes | Serves: 4

2 tablespoons extra-virgin olive oil
4 bone-in chicken thighs, skin removed
¼ teaspoon salt

¼ teaspoon freshly ground black pepper
1 large onion, sliced
1 red bell pepper, cored and sliced
1 recipe Marinara Sauce

1. Season the chicken with the salt and pepper. 2. Heat the oil in the skillet over medium-high heat; add the chicken thighs, and brown them for 2 to 3 minutes per side. 3. Transfer the chicken to a plate. 4. Add the onion and bell pepper to the skillet, and sauté for 3 to 5 minutes. 5. Add the marinara sauce, combine well and bring to a simmer. 6. Return the chicken to the skillet, and simmer for 20 minutes. 7. Serve warm.
Per Serving: Calories 379; Fat 27.85g; Sodium 343mg; Carbs 5.57g; Fiber 0.9g; Sugar 2.67g; Protein 25.3g

Braised Beef with Parsley

Prep time: 10 minutes | Cook time: 15 minutes | Serves: 6

1 tablespoon extra-virgin olive oil
1 onion, sliced
3 garlic cloves, minced
1½ pounds beef chuck roast, cut into 1-inch pieces

1 (28-ounce) can whole tomatoes
½ teaspoon freshly ground black pepper
¼ cup chopped fresh parsley

1. Turn on the oven and preheat it to 350°F. 2. Heat the oil in a large oven-safe pot over medium-high heat; add the onion and sauté for 3 to 5 minutes; add garlic and sauté for 30 seconds. 3. Add the roast, and cook for 5 to 6 minutes, browning it on all sides. 4. Add the tomatoes with their juices, salt, and pepper, and bring to a boil. Remove the pot from the heat. 5. Cover the pot with a lid, and transfer to the oven. Cook, stirring now and then and scraping up the browned bits off the bottom of the pot, for 1 hour. 6. When the time is up, let the food sit for 10 minutes. 7. Skim any fat from the top of the mixture with a large spoon. 8. Serve the roast topped with the parsley.
Per Serving: Calories 187; Fat 7.86g; Sodium 280mg; Carbs 5.81g; Fiber 2.9g; Sugar 3.67g; Protein 24.6g

Garlicky Pork Tenderloin

Prep time: 5 minutes | Cook time: 30 minutes | Serves: 6

1 teaspoon dried thyme
½ teaspoon ground cumin
½ teaspoon onion powder
¼ teaspoon salt
¼ teaspoon freshly ground black

pepper
1½ pounds pork tenderloin
1 tablespoon extra-virgin olive oil
3 garlic cloves, minced

1. Turn on the oven and preheat it to 400°F. 2. Combine the thyme, cumin, onion powder, salt, and pepper. Combine well. 3. Press the mixture into the pork tenderloin on all sides. 4. Heat the oil over medium-high heat in an oven-safe skillet; add the garlic, and sauté for 30 seconds. 5. Add the pork tenderloin and brown on all sides for 2 to 3 minutes per side. 6. When done, transfer the skillet to the oven, and cook in the preheated oven for 15 to 20 minutes. 7. Serve warm.
Per Serving: Calories 137; Fat 3.52g; Sodium 178mg; Carbs 0.84g; Fiber 0.1g; Sugar 0.03g; Protein 23.93g

Lamb Onion Skewers

Prep time: 15 minutes | Cook time: 15 minutes | Serves: 8

1 pound ground lamb
1 small onion, chopped
2 tablespoons chopped fresh mint leaves
1 teaspoon ground cumin

1 teaspoon ground coriander
½ teaspoon salt
¼ teaspoon freshly ground black pepper

1. Mix the lamb with onion, mint, cumin, coriander, salt, and pepper in a bowl. 2. Divide the mixture into 4 pieces, shape around 8 skewers with your wet hands. 3. Preheat a grill on medium-high heat. 4. Place the kebabs on the grill, and cook on all sides for 2 to 3 minutes per side. 5. When the time is up, cook the kebabs for 3 to 5 more minutes. 6. Serve and enjoy.
Per Serving: Calories 114; Fat 7.11g; Sodium 179mg; Carbs 1.03g; Fiber 0.2g; Sugar 0.39g; Protein 11.69g

Lamb Stew with Chickpea

Prep time: 5 minutes | Cook time: 55 minutes | Serves: 4

2 tablespoons extra-virgin olive oil
1-pound boneless lamb shoulder (stew meat), diced
1 large onion, chopped
2 carrots, chopped
1 (15-ounce) can chickpeas,

drained and rinsed
2 teaspoons ras el hanout
4 cups water
½ teaspoon salt
¼ teaspoon freshly ground black pepper

1. Heat the oil in a large pot over medium-high heat. 2. Add the lamb, and brown on all sides for 3 to 5 minutes per side. Leaving the juices in the pot, transfer the lamb to a plate. 3. Add the onion and carrots to the pot, and cook for 3 to 5 minutes. 4. Add the chickpeas and ras el hanout, combine well. 5. Add the lamb back to the pot, along with any juices that have collected on the plate. Add the water, and heat it until it is boiling. 6. Reduce the heat to low. Cover the pot, and simmer for 30 to 40 minutes. 7. Add some salt and pepper before serving.
Per Serving: Calories 296; Fat 10.8g; Sodium 609mg; Carbs 21.33g; Fiber 5.6g; Sugar 5.61g; Protein 27.95g

Easy Beef Skewers

Prep time: 10 minutes | Cook time: 15 minutes | Serves: 8

Aluminum foil	1 teaspoon paprika
1 pound ground beef	1 teaspoon ground coriander
1 shallot, finely chopped	½ teaspoon fine sea salt
2 tablespoons mint leaves, finely chopped	¼ teaspoon ground black pepper

1. Turn on the oven and preheat it to 400°F. Line a baking sheet with aluminum foil. 2. Mix the ground beef, chopped shallot, chopped mint, paprika, ground coriander, fine sea salt, and ground black pepper in a medium-sized mixing bowl. 3. Divide the mixture into 8 portions. Mold and shape the meat around 8 skewers with your wet hands. 4. Over medium-high heat, heat a nonstick frying pan. 5. Place the skewers in the pan, and fry for 2 to 3 minutes per side. Remove from the heat. 6. Place the skewers on the baking sheet, and bake in the oven for 3 to 5 minutes. 7. Serve immediately.

Per Serving: Calories 111; Fat 7.26g; Sodium 184mg; Carbs 0.54g; Fiber 0.42g; Sugar 0.21g; Protein 11.12g

Dijon Chicken Breasts

Prep time: 10 minutes | Cook time: 20 minutes | Serves: 4

¼ cup freshly squeezed lime juice	⅛ teaspoon salt
¼ cup chopped fresh cilantro	¼ teaspoon freshly ground black pepper
2 garlic cloves, minced	
2 tablespoons Dijon mustard	2 (4-ounce) skinless, boneless chicken breasts
½ tablespoon olive oil	
½ tablespoon chili powder	

1. Add the lime juice, cilantro, garlic, mustard, olive oil, chili powder, salt, and pepper to a food processor and pulse until they are fully mixed. 2. Put the chicken breasts in a baking dish. Pour the marinade over the chicken, cover, and put into the refrigerator to store for more than 15 minutes or up to 6 hours. 3. Uncover and bake the food in the oven for 18 to 20 minutes at 350°F. 4. Serve warm.

Per Serving: Calories 62; Fat 2.6g; Sodium 212mg; Carbs 2.87g; Fiber 0.8g; Sugar 0.42; Protein 7.2g

Balsamic Chicken Breasts

Prep time: 10 minutes | Cook time: 35 minutes | Serves: 4

½ cup balsamic vinegar, plus 2 tablespoons	⅛ teaspoon salt
	Freshly ground black pepper
1 teaspoon olive oil	Olive oil cooking spray
1 tablespoon chopped fresh rosemary	2 (6-ounce) boneless, skinless chicken breasts
1 garlic clove, minced	Fresh rosemary sprigs, for garnish

1. Stir together ½ cup of balsamic vinegar, olive oil, rosemary, garlic, salt, and pepper in a small saucepan over medium-high heat; bring to a boil, lower the heat to medium, and simmer the sauce for about 3 minutes. 2. Let the sauce rest in the refrigerator for about 15 minutes. 3. Coat a 9-by-9-inch baking dish with cooking spray. Put the chicken in the dish and pour the cooled marinade over the chicken. Refrigerate the chicken for 30 minutes. 4. Turn on the oven and preheat it to 400°F. Take the dish out from the refrigerator, cover it with aluminum foil and bake for 35 minutes. 5. Transfer the chicken to serving plates. Pour the cooked marinade into a small saucepan. Add the remaining 2 tablespoons of balsamic vinegar and cook for 3 to 5 minutes. 6. Pour the sauce

over the chicken and serve garnished with fresh rosemary.

Per Serving: Calories 113; Fat 5.15g; Sodium 112mg; Carbs 5.8g; Fiber 0.1g; Sugar 4.77g; Protein 9.09g

Chicken Lettuce Wraps

Prep time: 5 minutes | Cook time: 20 minutes | Serves: 4

½ tablespoon olive oil	1 garlic clove, minced
½ tablespoon dark sesame oil	2 (6-ounce) skinless, boneless chicken breasts
½ tablespoon rice vinegar	
½ tablespoon low-sodium soy sauce	Olive oil nonstick cooking spray
	4 Boston lettuce leaves
1 teaspoon chili sauce (such as sriracha)	½ cup fresh mint leaves
	½ cup bean sprouts
1 teaspoon peeled and grated fresh ginger	½ cup sliced red bell pepper
	2 tablespoons chopped peanuts
½ teaspoon freshly grated lime zest	1 lime, cut into 4 wedges

1. Whisk together the olive oil and sesame oil, vinegar, soy sauce, chili sauce, ginger, lime zest, and garlic in a bowl. Reserve 1 tablespoon of the mixture. 2. Add the remaining mixture to a large resealable bag, add the chicken breasts, seal the bag, and marinate in the refrigerator for 1 hour, turning now and then. 3. Remove the chicken from the bag and remove the marinade. 4. Coat a large nonstick grill pan with cooking spray, add the chicken and sauté for 12 minutes over medium-high heat, turning once halfway through. 5. When cooked, let the chicken cool for 5 minutes and then slice it thinly. Divide the chicken among the lettuce leaves. 6. Top each lettuce leaf with mint, sprouts, bell pepper, and ½ teaspoon of the reserved dressing. 7. Garnish with the chopped peanuts, wrap like a burrito, and serve with the lime wedges.

Per Serving: Calories 223; Fat 10.25g; Sodium 339mg; Carbs 6.69g; Fiber 1.1g; Sugar 1.51g; Protein 27.97g

Spiced Chicken Breasts with Yellow Onions

Prep time: 10 minutes | Cook time: 30 minutes | Serves: 4

1 teaspoon ground cinnamon	1 tablespoon olive oil, divided
1 teaspoon paprika	2 (6-ounce) skinless, boneless chicken breasts
¾ teaspoon ground cumin	
½ teaspoon ground cardamom	⅛ teaspoon salt
½ teaspoon ground coriander	Olive oil nonstick cooking spray
½ teaspoon ground ginger	1 cup sliced yellow onion
½ teaspoon ground turmeric	1 teaspoon honey

1. Combine together the cinnamon, paprika, cumin, cardamom, coriander, ginger, and turmeric in a bowl. Heat ½ tablespoon of olive oil in a large ovenproof skillet over medium-low heat, swirling to coat. 2. Add the spice mixture to the skillet and cook, stirring frequently, for about 3 minutes. 3. Combine the spice mixture and chicken breasts in a large resealable bag, seal, and shake well to coat the chicken. Marinate the chicken in the refrigerator for 10 minutes. 4. Turn on the oven and preheat it to 350°F. Take the chicken from the bag and sprinkle with the salt. 5. Heat the skillet over medium-high heat and lightly coat it with cooking spray. Add the chicken and cook for about 4 minutes. Turn the chicken over and cook for 1 minute more. 6. Remove the chicken from the pan. Add the remaining ½ tablespoon of olive oil to the pan, swirling to coat. 7. Add the onion and sauté for 2 minutes. Return the chicken to the pan and drizzle the honey over all. 8. Bake for 10 minutes.

Per Serving: Calories 145; Fat 9.93g; Sodium 108mg; Carbs 4.78g; Fiber 1.1g; Sugar 2.52g; Protein 9.34g

Chicken Breasts with Plum Salsa

Prep time: 10 minutes | Cook time: 30 minutes | Serves: 4

For the chicken
1 teaspoon brown sugar
¼ teaspoon ground cumin
¼ teaspoon garlic powder
⅛ teaspoon salt
1 teaspoon olive oil
2 (6-ounce) skinless, boneless chicken breasts
For the plum salsa

1 cup chopped ripe plum
2 tablespoons chopped fresh cilantro
2 tablespoons chopped red onion
2 tablespoons chopped red bell pepper
2 teaspoons cider vinegar
¼ teaspoon hot sauce
⅛ teaspoon salt

To make the chicken 1. Combine the brown sugar, cumin, garlic powder, and salt in a bowl. Rub the chicken all over with the mixture. 2. Heat the olive oil in a nonstick skillet over medium heat. Add the chicken and cook for 6 minutes per side.
To make the plum salsa 1. Combine all the salsa in a medium-size bowl. 2. Serve the salsa over the chicken.
Per Serving: Calories 148; Fat 5.18g; Sodium 203mg; Carbs 16.61g; Fiber 0.8g; Sugar 15.43g; Protein 9.27g

Lentil, Onion and Beef Bolognese

Prep time: 10 minutes | Cook time: 30 minutes | Serves: 6

1-pound lean ground beef
½ teaspoon fine sea salt, divided
Ground black pepper
1 small red onion, chopped
1 tablespoon garlic, minced
½ cup uncooked red lentils, rinsed

1 (28-ounce) can whole, no-salt-added tomatoes with their juices
1-pound white mushrooms, sliced
⅔ cup water
2 tablespoons tomato paste
1 tablespoon Italian seasoning

1. Heat a large, heavy bottom pan over high heat. 2. Once hot, add the ground beef, use a fork to break it up, and season with ¼ teaspoon salt and some ground black pepper, and then cook for 2 to 3 minutes. 3. Add the chopped onion and minced garlic, and sauté for 5 to 7 minutes. 4. Add the red lentils, whole tomatoes with their juice, sliced mushrooms, water, tomato paste, and Italian seasoning. When it boils, reduce the heat to low, and allow to simmer for 15 minutes, stirring now and then. Season properly. 5. Serve over zucchini noodles or spaghetti squash.
Per Serving: Calories 275; Fat 8.84g; Sodium 411mg; Carbs 24.09g; Fiber 4.1g; Sugar 9.77g; Protein 26.37g

Delicious Lamb Chop Couscous

Prep time: 10 minutes | Cook time: 25 minutes | Serves: 4

2 tablespoons avocado oil
4 lamb loin chops
½ red onion, finely chopped
1½ cups couscous

2½ cups water
½ cup Roma tomatoes, chopped
3 cups spinach, chopped

1. In a large frying pan over high heat, heat the avocado oil. 2. Add the lamb chops, and fry for 1½ minutes per side. Transfer the lamb chops to a plate, and cover. 3. Reduce the heat to low, add the chopped onion and fry them for 3 to 5 minutes. 4. Add the couscous, and brown for 1 to 2 minutes. 5. Add the water, and scrape the bottom to deglaze the pan. 6. Add the chopped tomatoes, and chopped spinach, combine and allow to simmer for 5 minutes. 7. Put the lamb chops into the pan, and cover with a lid. 8. Cook the food for 6 to 8 minutes, or until the couscous is tender. 9. Serve immediately.
Per Serving: Calories 321; Fat 22.31g; Sodium 64mg; Carbs 18.46g; Fiber 1.9g; Sugar 2.72g; Protein 12.22g

Stir-Fried Pork Tenderloin with Sweet Peas

Prep time: 10 minutes | Cook time: 30 minutes | Serves: 4

1 (1-pound) boneless pork tenderloin
¼ teaspoon fine sea salt
Ground black pepper
3 tablespoons olive oil, divided
2 teaspoons ginger, grated
1 tablespoon garlic, crushed
1 medium red bell pepper, seeded and chopped

1 medium green bell pepper, seeded and chopped
2 medium granny smith apples, cored and cut into chunks
2 tablespoons apple cider vinegar
1½ tablespoon reduced-sodium tamari
1 cup sweet peas

1. Cut the pork tenderloin in half, lengthwise, and thinly slice each half. Add some salt and pepper consistent with personal preference. 2. Heat 1 tablespoon olive oil in a large, heavy bottom pan over high heat. Add the pork slices after hot and dry them on both sides for 3 to 5 minutes. 3. Add the grated ginger and crushed garlic, and cook for 1 minute. Transfer the food to a plate. 4. Add the chopped red bell pepper, chopped green bell pepper, and apple chunks to the pan, and cook for 3 to 4 minutes. 5. Combine the apple cider vinegar, tamari, and the remaining 2 tablespoons of olive oil in a small mixing bowl, and whisk until mixed. 6. Add the vinegar mixture to the apple mixture and cook them for about 2 minutes. 7. Add the sweet peas and pork slices, and cook until warmed through. 8. Serve warm.
Per Serving: Calories 330; Fat 17.43g; Sodium 221mg; Carbs 16.91g; Fiber 3.8g; Sugar 10.49g; Protein 25.98g

Pork Medallions with Baby Carrots

Prep time: 10 minutes | Cook time: 30 minutes | Serves: 4

1 (1-pound) boneless pork tenderloin roast, sliced into thick medallions
¼ teaspoon fine sea salt
Ground black pepper
1 tablespoon avocado oil
1 large brown onion, cut into wedges
1 cup reduced-sodium chicken

stock
1-pound baby carrots
2 tablespoons organic honey
¼ teaspoon ground cinnamon
¼ teaspoon ground cumin
¼ teaspoon ground turmeric
1 cup uncooked couscous
1 teaspoon lime juice

1. Season the pork medallions with fine sea salt and ground black pepper. 2. In a large, heavy bottom pan, heat the avocado oil over high heat until hot, add the pork and cook for 3 minutes per side. 3. Transfer the pork to a plate, and cover the plate. 4. Lower the heat down to medium, and fry the onion wedges for 3 to 4 minutes. 5. Turn the heat up to high, and add the chicken stock, baby carrots, organic honey, ground cinnamon, ground cumin, and ground turmeric. Mix to combine. 6. After boiling, turn the heat down to low, and cook for 7 to 8 minutes. 7. Cook the couscous consistent with the instructions on the package. 8. Return the pork medallions to the pan, along with the lime juice, and cook until heated through. 9. Serve the pork and vegetables over the couscous.
Per Serving: Calories 343; Fat 10.94g; Sodium 424mg; Carbs 32.8g; Fiber 5.3g; Sugar 15g; Protein 28.8g

Flavorful Spicy Beef Roast

Prep time: 10 minutes | Cook time: 30 minutes | Serves: 6

1 teaspoon dried rosemary	¼ teaspoon fine sea salt
½ teaspoon paprika	¼ teaspoon ground black pepper
½ teaspoon red chili flakes	1½ pounds beef tenderloin
½ teaspoon cayenne pepper	1 tablespoon avocado oil
½ teaspoon ground coriander	3 bay leaves
½ teaspoon onion powder	3 thyme sprigs
½ teaspoon garlic powder	

1. Turn on the oven and preheat it to 400°F. 2. Mix the dried rosemary, paprika, red chili flakes, cayenne pepper, ground coriander, onion powder, garlic powder, fine sea salt, and ground black pepper in a small mixing bowl. 3. Rub the spice mixture all over the beef tenderloin. 4. Heat the avocado oil over high heat in the oven-safe frying pan; add the bay leaves and thyme sprigs, and cook for 30 seconds. 5. Add the tenderloin, and fry for 2 to 3 minutes on all sides. Turn off the heat. 6. Place the oven safe frying pan in the oven, and cook for 15 to 20 minutes. 7. Remove the pan from the oven, discard the bay leaves and thyme sprigs. 8. Serve immediately.
Per Serving: Calories 205; Fat 10.48g; Sodium 169mg; Carbs 1.19g; Fiber 0.4g; Sugar 0.17g; Protein 25.37g

Pork Chops with Parmesan Cheese

Prep time: 10 minutes | Cook time: 25 minutes | Serves: 4

2 tablespoons avocado oil	½ cup sun-dried tomatoes, chopped
4 thick pork chops, fat trimmed	3 cups kale, finely chopped
½ red onion, chopped	¼ cup parmesan cheese, grated
1½ cups couscous	
2½ cups water	

1. In a heavy bottom pan, heat the avocado oil over high heat. 2. Add the pork chops, and fry for 1½ minutes on each side. Transfer the pork chops to a plate. 3. Reduce the heat to medium; add the chopped onion, and cook for 3 to 5 minutes. 4. Add the couscous, and cook for 1 to 2 minutes. 5. Pour in the water, scrape the bottom to deglaze the pan. 6. Add the chopped sun-dried tomatoes, and allow to simmer for 5 minutes. 7. Return the pork chops to the pan, cover, and reduce the heat to low; cook the pork chops for 6 to 8 minutes. 8. Turn off the heat, and combine in the grated parmesan cheese and chopped kale, stirring until the kale is wilted. Serve.
Per Serving: Calories 324; Fat 14.88g; Sodium 183mg; Carbs 22.48g; Fiber 2.5g; Sugar 4.95g; Protein 24.99g

Tahini Chicken Salad

Prep time: 10 minutes | Cook time: 10 minutes | Serves: 2

2 teaspoons avocado oil	pepper
2 large garlic cloves, minced	1 tablespoon lemon juice
1 (8-ounce) chicken breast, cubed	2 tablespoons water
3 tablespoons unsalted tahini	2 celery stalks, diced
½ teaspoon ground turmeric	1 Honeycrisp apple, cut into
¼ teaspoon freshly ground black	½-inch pieces

1. Heat the oil and garlic in the skillet over medium heat for 2 minutes. 2. Add the chicken breast and cook for 4 minutes on one side; flip the chicken breast and cook for another 2 minutes. 3. Add the tahini, turmeric, pepper, lemon juice, and water in a large

mixing bowl and combine thoroughly. 4. Add in the browned chicken breast, celery, and apples and combine well. 5. Enjoy over a lettuce wrap, salad, or on one or two slices of whole wheat bread. 6. If kept in an airtight container in the refrigerator, it will keep for up to 3 days.
Per Serving: Calories 381; Fat 23.9g; Sodium 95mg; Carbs 15.33g; Fiber 2.8g; Sugar 9.94g; Protein 27.17g

Chicken Lettuce Wrap

Prep time: 10 minutes | Cook time: 5 minutes | Serves: 2

2 teaspoons avocado oil	1 teaspoon grated ginger
2 garlic cloves, minced, divided	3 tablespoons unsalted peanut butter
½ cup diced shallots	4 tablespoons water
8 ounces lean ground chicken or turkey breast	6 large butter lettuce leaves

1. Combine the ginger, remaining garlic clove, peanut butter, and water in a mixing bowl. 2. Heat the oil in a medium skillet over medium heat; add 1 minced garlic clove and the shallots, and sauté for 1 to 2 minutes. 3. Add the ground chicken and break into pieces, sauté the ground meat for 5 minutes until lightly golden and cooked through. 4. Add the ginger mixture to the skillet and cook for about 1 minute. 5. Divide the chicken mixture into the lettuce cups and serve. 6. If kept in an airtight container in the refrigerator, it will keep for up to 3 days.
Per Serving: Calories 377; Fat 26.39g; Sodium 90mg; Carbs 10.77g; Fiber 2.4g; Sugar 4.82g; Protein 27.63g

Strip Steak Quinoa with Dressing

Prep time: 10 minutes | Cook time: 30 minutes | Serves: 4

For the quinoa:	2 spring onions, finely chopped
1 cup uncooked quinoa	⅓ cup pine nuts
12 ounces strip steak, any fat trimmed	For the dressing:
	¼ cup olive oil
⅛ teaspoon fine sea salt	3 tablespoon apple cider vinegar
Ground black pepper	2 tablespoon reduced-sodium tamari
1 tablespoon olive oil	
1 large iceberg lettuce head, finely chopped	2 tablespoons organic honey

For the quinoa: 1. Cook the quinoa consistent with the instructions on the package. 2. When it's cooking, place a medium-sized mixing bowl in the freezer. 3. Once the quinoa is done cooking, take the mixing bowl out, and transfer the cooked quinoa to the bowl. Let it sit to cool for a few minutes. 4. Pat the strip steak dry with a paper towel, and add some salt and pepper consistent with personal preference. 5. Heat the olive oil in a large, heavy bottom pan over high heat. 6. When hot, add the strip steak, and brown for 5 to 6 minutes on each side. 7. Place the strip steak on a chopping block, and put aside for 5 minutes, then slice thinly. **For the dressing:** 1. Combine the olive oil, apple cider vinegar, tamari, and organic honey in large mixing bowl, and whisk to incorporate. 2. Add the chopped iceberg lettuce, chopped spring onion, and cooled quinoa, and mix them well. 3. Divide the dressing onto serving plates, and top them with the strip steak slices and pine nuts. 4. Enjoy.
Per Serving: Calories 550; Fat 29.67g; Sodium 651mg; Carbs 44.51g; Fiber 6.1g; Sugar 13.12g; Protein 30.02g

Lamb, Beans and Veggie Stew

Prep time: 10 minutes | Cook time: 50 minutes | Serves: 4

2 tablespoons olive oil	drained and rinsed
1-pound boneless lamb shoulder, diced	1 teaspoon paprika
1 large brown onion, finely chopped	1 teaspoon ground coriander
2 large carrots, peeled and chopped	½ teaspoon ground ginger
1 (15-ounce) can garbanzo beans,	4 cups water
	Fine sea salt
	Ground black pepper

1. In a large stockpot over high heat, heat the olive oil. 2. Add the diced lamb, and brown for 3 to 5 minutes per side. Leave the juices in the pot, and transfer the lamb onto a plate. 3. Add the chopped onion and chopped carrots to the pot, and cook for 3 to 5 minutes. 4. Add the garbanzo beans, paprika, ground coriander and ground ginger, and mix to combine. 5. Transfer the lamb back into the pot, along with the juices that collected on the plate. Add the water, and heat until it boils. 6. Reduce the heat to low, cover the pot, and allow to simmer for 30 to 40 minutes. 7. Season the dish with fine sea salt and ground black pepper before serving.
Per Serving: Calories 284; Fat 16.72g; Sodium 155mg; Carbs 10.89g; Fiber 3.4g; Sugar 3.93g; Protein 24.08g

Chicken, Pasta, and Asparagus Salad with Pesto

Prep time: 15 minutes | Cook time: 15 minutes | Serves: 4

8 ounces uncooked bowtie pasta	pieces
1 pound asparagus	½ cup walnut pesto
1 tablespoon extra-virgin olive oil	2 medium ripe tomatoes, chopped
12 ounces boneless, skinless chicken breasts, cut into bite-size	¼ cup grated Parmesan cheese (optional)

1. In a cooking pot, pour water and bring to boil. Add the pasta and cook according to the package instruction until al dente, about 4 minutes. 2. Cut off the woody ends from the asparagus and cut its spears into 1-inch pieces. 3. Then scoop out ½ cup of cooking water. Add asparagus to the pasta pot and bring together to a boil. Let it boil for about 4 minutes. 4. In a large skillet, add oil and heat over medium-high heat. Add chicken to sauté until cooked through, about 5 to 10 minutes. Add tomatoes and stir. 5. Turn off the heat. Drain the asparagus and pasta. Add in the pasta pot again and add pesto and the ¼ cup of reserved cooking water. 6. Add tomatoes, and chicken in the pot. More cooking water can be added if it seems dry. 7. Add parmesan cheese on the top, as desired. 8. Serve and enjoy!
Per Serving: Calories 393; Fat 19g; Sodium 453mg; Carbs 25g; Fiber 6.5g; Sugar 4g; Protein 33g

Shredded Chicken Breasts

Prep time: 10 minutes | Cook time: 15 minutes | Serves: 2

2 (4-ounce) chicken breasts	1 cup cannellini beans drained and rinsed
2 cups low-sodium veggie broth or homemade vegetable broth	1 teaspoon Barbeque seasoning rub blend
2 tablespoons lime juice	
2 garlic cloves, minced	

1. Cook the chicken breasts and veggie broth in a medium pot over medium heat for 10 minutes. 2. Shred the chicken with two forks carefully in a pot and then add the lime juice, garlic, beans, and barbeque seasoning. Stir them well, cover the pot, and cook for another 5 minutes, until the beans and onions have softened. 3. Serve on top of a salad, lettuce cup, or whole wheat soft taco shell. 4. If kept in an airtight container in the refrigerator, it will keep for up to 3 days.
Per Serving: Calories 143; Fat 2.13g; Sodium 285mg; Carbs 16.14g; Fiber 3g; Sugar 8.18g; Protein 16.64g

Chili Chicken and Vegetables

Prep time: 15 minutes | Cook time: 15 minutes | Serves: 4

¾ cup uncooked parboiled brown rice	pieces
2 tablespoons canola or sunflower oil, divided	1½ cups reduced-sodium chicken broth
5 cups frozen sliced bell peppers and onions	⅓ cup natural peanut butter (smooth or crunchy)
¼ teaspoon kosher salt (optional)	2 tablespoons chili powder
Freshly ground black pepper (optional)	1 teaspoon dried tarragon
12 ounces boneless, skinless chicken breasts, cut into bite-size	1 cup frozen corn kernels
	Juice of 1 lime (about 2 tablespoons)
	½ cup chopped fresh cilantro

1. Cook the rice as the package directed. 2. In a large skillet, heat 1 tablespoon of oil over medium-high heat. When heated, add onions and peppers in the skillet and season with salt and pepper, as you like. 3. Cook and stir for about 3 to 4 minutes, or until soften. Then add in a plate and set aside. 4. In the skillet, add the remaining oil and sauté the chicken for about 5 to 10 minutes, or until the chicken is fully cooked with its opaque juices. Add the cooked chicken to the plate with sliced onions and bell peppers. 5. Then pour in chicken broth, and add chili powder, tarragon, and peanut butter in the skillet. Cook and stir. 6. Once the sauce thickens, add the corn. Then add the plated vegetables and chicken in the skillet and mix well. 7. Turn off heat and drizzle with lime juice. Sprinkle with cilantro and mix well. 8. Serve over rice. Enjoy!
Per Serving: Calories 454; Fat 20g; Sodium 839mg; Carbs 35g; Fiber 5g; Sugar 8g; Protein 36g

Chicken Cacciatore with Sun-Dried Tomatoes

Prep time: 5minutes | Cook time: 10 minutes | Serves: 2

spoons avocado oil	dried tomatoes, thinly sliced
½ cup diced yellow onion	2 (4-ounce) chicken breasts
1 cup baby portabella mushrooms, thinly sliced	½ teaspoon freshly ground black pepper
2 tablespoons low-sodium Kalamata olives, chopped	1 cup no-salt-added tomato sauce
4 tablespoons low-sodium sun-	

1. Heat the oil and onions in a medium skillet over medium heat for 2 minutes. 2. Add the mushrooms, olives, and sun-dried tomatoes, and cook them for 1 minute. 3. Add the chicken and season with pepper. Cook on one side for 4 minutes until ¼-inch of the bottom of the chicken turns white and the bottom is lightly browned. 4. Flip the chicken, add the tomato sauce, and combine well. Cook for 2 to 3 minutes. 5. Portion, plate, and serve. 6. If kept in an airtight container in the refrigerator, it will keep for up to 3 days.
Per Serving: Calories 231; Fat 12.68g; Sodium 80mg; Carbs 16.4g; Fiber 3.2g; Sugar 11.16g; Protein 14.84g

Zucchini-Chicken Kabobs

Prep time: 10 minutes | Cook time: 15 minutes | Serves: 4

1-pound lean ground chicken or turkey breast
1 cup shredded zucchini
½ cup yellow finely diced
onion
1 tablespoon Mediterranean Seasoning Rub Blend
1 cup cherry tomatoes

1. Set an oven rack 6 inches from the broiler and turn on the oven and preheat it to broil. Line a baking sheet with parchment paper. 2. Combine the chicken, zucchini, onion, and seasoning blend in a medium mixing bowl. Let marinate for more than 10 minutes. 3. Scoop 1 heaping tablespoon of the chicken mixture and form the mixture into 1-inch meatballs, making about 8 balls. Add the cherry tomatoes to the parchment paper. 4. Broil for 5 to 7 minutes on one side. Flip the rectangles and cook for an additional 4 to 5 minutes until golden brown and juicy. The tomatoes should be blistered. 5. Serve with a whole grain side of your choice. If kept in an airtight container in the refrigerator, it will keep for up to 3 days.
Per Serving: Calories 197; Fat 9.27g; Sodium 228mg; Carbs 8.17g; Fiber 1.2g; Sugar 5.48g; Protein 20.58g

Barbeque Chicken Breasts

Prep time: 5 minutes | Cook time: 20 minutes | Serves: 2

2 (4-ounce) chicken breasts, flattened 1-inch thick
2 teaspoons sesame seeds
1 cup diced pineapple
1 cup diced green bell peppers
1 cup Barbeque Sauce

1. Turn on the oven and preheat it to 400°F. Line a baking sheet with parchment paper. 2. Place the chicken on the prepared baking sheet and put on the top sesame seeds. 3. Surround the chicken with the pineapple and green peppers. Coat the chicken with barbeque sauce and cook for 10 to 15 minutes. 4. Serve with a side of your choice, or if kept in an airtight container in the refrigerator, it will keep for up to 3 days.
Per Serving: Calories 132; Fat 2.73g; Sodium 285mg; Carbs 16.14g; Fiber 3g; Sugar 8.18g; Protein 16.64g

Lime Chicken Breasts

Prep time: 5 minutes | Cook time: 10 minutes | Serves: 2

2 (4-ounce) chicken breasts
2 tablespoons Chile-Lime Glaze
¼ teaspoon garlic powder
¼ teaspoon freshly ground black
pepper
2 tablespoons chopped fresh cilantro
2 tablespoons lime juice

1. Marinate the chicken with the glaze, garlic powder, pepper in a large mixing bowl, and cilantro for more than 10 minutes. 2. In a medium skillet over medium-low heat, cook the chicken for 5 to 7 minutes on each side, until lightly browned and cooked through. 3. Add the lime juice over the chicken. 4. Serve on salad or paired with a side dish of your choice. 5. If kept in an airtight container in the refrigerator, it will keep for up to 3 days.
Per Serving: Calories 108; Fat 5.29g; Sodium 37mg; Carbs 3.1g; Fiber 0.3g; Sugar 0.53g; Protein 12.07g

Baked Chicken Cubes

Prep time: 5 minutes | Cook time: 15 minutes | Serves: 2

2 tablespoons Mediterranean Seasoning Rub Blend
4 teaspoons avocado oil
2 tablespoons lemon juice
8 ounces chicken, cut into 1-inch cubes
1 large red onion, cut into rings

1. Turn on the oven and preheat it to 450°F. Line a baking sheet with parchment paper. 2. Combine the seasoning blend, oil, and lemon juice in a large mixing bowl. Add the chicken and coat well with the mixture. Marinate the chicken for more than 5 minutes. 3. Place the onions on the prepared baking sheet, add the chicken on top, and bake for 12 to 15 minutes. 4. Serve with your desired toppings and enjoy. 5. If kept in an airtight container in the refrigerator, it will keep for up to 3 days.
Per Serving: Calories 238; Fat 12.1g; Sodium 87mg; Carbs 4.22g; Fiber 0.6g; Sugar 0.59g; Protein 23.59g

Chicken Breast with Arugula-Basil Pesto

Prep time: 10 minutes | Cook time: 20 minutes | Serves: 2

2 (4-ounce) chicken breasts
1 cup fresh spinach
1 tablespoon Arugula-Basil
Pesto
2 teaspoons paprika

1. Turn on the oven and preheat it to 375°F. Line a baking sheet with parchment paper. 2. Pound each chicken breast flat with a meat tenderizer until the breast is even and thin. 3. Combine the spinach and pesto. 4. Place the chicken breasts on the prepared baking sheet and divide the spinach mixture to evenly place half inside the middle of each tender. 5. Fold the chicken breasts in half and rub 1 teaspoon of paprika on the outside of each chicken breast. 6. Cook the food in the oven for 20 minutes until the chicken is cooked through. 7. Serve on a plate with a side dish of your choice. 8. If kept in an airtight container in the refrigerator, it will keep for up to 3 days.
Per Serving: Calories 108; Fat 5.6g; Sodium 49mg; Carbs 1.81g; Fiber 1.1g; Sugar 0.31g; Protein 12.59g

Baked Parmesan Chicken

Prep time: 15 minutes | Cook time: 20 minutes | Serves: 4

3 to 4 medium tomatoes, cut into wedges
3 tablespoons extra-virgin olive oil, divided
¼ teaspoon kosher salt (optional)
1 pound chicken breast cutlets or tenders
½ cup whole-wheat panko breadcrumbs
½ cup grated Parmesan cheese, divided
2 tablespoons ground flaxseed
½ teaspoon paprika
½ teaspoon garlic powder
½ teaspoon ground mustard
¼ teaspoon freshly ground black pepper

1. Before cooking, heat your oven to 400 degrees F. 2. On a rimmed baking sheet, arrange the tomato wedges and drizzle over with 1 tablespoon of oil. 3. Add salt to season and place into the preheated oven. Roast. 4. At the same time, prepare a second baking sheet and line with parchment paper. Place the chicken pieces on the baking sheet and brush with 1 tablespoon of oil. 5. Mix together the flaxseed, half the Parmesan cheese, panko, garlic powder, black pepper, ground mustard, and paprika in a medium bowl. 6. Drizzle the mixture over the chicken and top with 1 tablespoon of oil. 7. Bake in the oven about 20 minutes, or until fully cooked. Check after 15 minutes' cooking. 8. Then add the browned tomatoes and the rest Parmesan cheese over the baked chicken. 9. Serve and enjoy!
Per Serving: Calories 456; Fat 25g; Sodium 899mg; Carbs 17g; Fiber 4g; Sugar 3g; Protein 41g

Lemon-Basil Chicken

Prep time: 10 minutes | Cook time: 20 minutes | Serves: 2

8 ounces chicken breast, cubed
4 cups baby bell peppers
¾ teaspoon Mediterranean Seasoning Rub Blend

2 heaping tablespoons chopped fresh basil
2 tablespoons lemon juice
1 teaspoon avocado oil

1. Turn on the oven and preheat it to 375°F. Line a baking sheet with parchment paper and place the chicken and bell peppers on top. 2. Combine the seasoning blend, basil, lemon juice, and oil in a small bowl. 3. Coat all the pieces evenly with the seasoning mixture on the baking sheet. 4. Bake the chicken for 20 minutes. 5. Divide the chicken into even portions and serve. 6. If kept in an airtight container in the refrigerator, it will keep for up to 3 days.
Per Serving: Calories 257; Fat 13.01g; Sodium 78mg; Carbs 10g; Fiber 1.5g; Sugar 4.99g; Protein 25.63g

Fried Chicken Strips

Prep time: 15 minutes | Cook time: 15 minutes | Serves: 2

2½ tablespoons unsalted raw pumpkin seeds, crushed
2 tablespoons unsalted raw sesame seeds
½ teaspoon freshly ground black pepper

1 teaspoon dried oregano
2 egg whites
8 ounces chicken breast, cut into 1-inch-thick, 2-inch-long strips

1. Turn on the oven and preheat it to 400°F. Line a baking sheet with parchment paper. 2. Combine the pumpkin seeds, sesame seeds, pepper, and oregano in a medium mixing bowl. 3. Pour the egg whites in a shallow medium bowl. 4. Dip both sides of the chicken strips into the egg mixture, and then fully coat each strip with the seed mixture. 5. Place the chicken strips on the baking sheet and cook them in the oven for 10 minutes. 6. Divide and serve with a side of your choice. 7. If kept in an airtight container in the refrigerator, it will keep for up to 3 days.
Per Serving: Calories 314; Fat 18.97g; Sodium 131mg; Carbs 4.51g; Fiber 2.4g; Sugar 0.42g; Protein 31.48g

Chicken Fajitas with Bell Peppers

Prep time: 10 minutes | Cook time: 10 minutes | Serves: 2

8 ounces chicken breast, cut into 1-inch strips
1 small onion, diced (about ⅓ cup)
1 teaspoon Barbeque Seasoning Rub Blend
1 teaspoon avocado oil

2 bell peppers (any color), cut into ½-inch strips
¼ teaspoon freshly ground black pepper
Juice of 1 lime (about 2 tablespoons)

1. In a freezer bag, combine the chicken, onion, and barbeque seasoning. Let the chicken marinate when prepping the other 2. Heat the oil in a medium skillet over medium heat; add the bell peppers and black pepper and cook for about 5 minutes. 3. Add the chicken mixture and stir now and then for another 5 minutes. 4. Add the lime juice and serve. 5. If kept in an airtight container in the refrigerator, it will keep for up to 3 days.
Per Serving: Calories 258; Fat 12.89g; Sodium 181mg; Carbs 10.44g; Fiber 1.6g; Sugar 4.31g; Protein 25.12g

Chicken with Green Beans and Pine Nuts

Prep time: 5 minutes | Cook time: 15 minutes | Serves: 2

2 teaspoons avocado oil
3 garlic cloves, minced
1½ cups green beans, cut into 2-inch pieces
1 tablespoon unsalted raw pine nuts

8 ounces chicken breast, cut into 6 even strips
¼ teaspoon freshly ground black pepper
1 tablespoon finely chopped fresh basil

1. Heat the oil and garlic in a medium skillet over medium heat for 1 to 2 minutes. 2. Add the green beans and pine nuts and cook for about 3 minutes. 3. Add the chicken and season with the pepper and basil, cook for 3 minutes on one side. 4. Flip the chicken, stir and cook for an additional 3 to 5 minutes. 5. Divide between two serving plates and serve. 6. If kept in an airtight container in the refrigerator, it will keep for up to 3 days.
Per Serving: Calories 293; Fat 17.55g; Sodium 75mg; Carbs 8.11g; Fiber 2.5g; Sugar 1.16g; Protein 25.95g

Pistachio Chicken Pieces

Prep time: 5 minutes | Cook time: 25 minutes | Serves: 2

½ cup blueberries
2 tablespoons shelled unsalted raw pistachios
¼ cup chopped fresh parsley

2 tablespoons balsamic vinegar
¼ teaspoon freshly ground black pepper
2 (4-ounce) pieces of chicken

1. Turn on the oven and preheat it to 375°F. Line a baking dish with parchment paper. 2. In a medium mixing bowl, combine the blueberries, pistachios, parsley, vinegar, and pepper until fully mixed. 3. Place the chicken in the baking dish and pour the blueberry mixture on top. 4. Bake the food for 20 to 25 minutes. 5. Serve on a plate with a side dish of your choice. 6. If kept in an airtight container in the refrigerator, it will keep for up to 3 days.
Per Serving: Calories 145; Fat 5.17g; Sodium 51mg; Carbs 11.05g; Fiber 2g; Sugar 6.74g; Protein 13.75g

Juicy Turkey Cauliflower Burgers

Prep time: 10 minutes | Cook time: 15 minutes | Serves: 4

2 cups cauliflower florets (about ½ medium cauliflower head)
1 small yellow onion, quartered
8 ounces frozen spinach,

thawed
1-pound lean ground turkey
1½ teaspoons Mediterranean Seasoning Rub Blend

1. Set an oven rack 6 inches from the broiler and turn on the oven and preheat it to broil. Line a baking sheet with parchment paper. 2. Pulse the cauliflower and onion for 1 to 2 minutes in a blender. 3. Combine the spinach, cauliflower and onion mixture, turkey, and the spice blend. Combine well and form into 8 medium patties and place them on the baking sheet. 4. Broil the food for 10 minutes on one side, flip when lightly golden and juicy, and then broil for 3 minutes on the other side. 5. Serve on a whole wheat bun with lettuce and tomato, on top of a salad, or in a collard green wrap. If kept in an airtight container in the refrigerator, it will keep for up to 3 days.
Per Serving: Calories 210; Fat 9.95g; Sodium 214mg; Carbs 7.3g; Fiber 3.2g; Sugar 2.25g; Protein 24.57g

Crispy Seared Chicken

Prep time: 15 minutes | Cook time: 10 minutes | Serves: 4

1-pound boneless, skinless chicken breasts	Freshly ground black pepper
¼ teaspoon kosher salt	2 tablespoons canola or sunflower oil

1. Use paper towels to pat the chicken breasts dry. Add salt and pepper to season. 2. In a large skillet, heat oil over medium-high heat. When the oil is heated, add the chicken breasts in the pan. Cover the lid and sear for 5 minutes, or until the undersides are golden and crispy. An internal meat thermometer should read 165 degrees F. 3. Then flip to the other side and sear for 5 minutes or more. 4. Remove the seared chicken to a flat cutting board. Allow it to cool and then slice into your desired size. 5. Serve and enjoy!
Per Serving: Calories 242; Fat 11g; Sodium 704mg; Carbs 0g; Fiber 0g; Sugar 0g; Protein 34g

Chicken and Pasta Salad

Prep time: 15 minutes | Cook time: 15 minutes | Serves: 4

8 ounces uncooked whole-wheat penne	2 tablespoons extra-virgin olive oil
2 cups chopped cooked chicken	Zest and juice of 1 lemon (about 3 tablespoons juice)
1 (5-ounce) package arugula, trimmed of large stems and torn into bite-size pieces if necessary	⅓ cup grated Parmesan cheese
½ cup sliced jarred roasted red peppers	Freshly ground black pepper (optional)

1. In a cooking pot, pour in water and bring to boil. Then cook the pasta to just firm according to the package guidance. Drain and rinse under cool water. 2. In a large salad bowl, add the chopped chicken, roasted peppers, oil, lemon juice, lemon zest, and arugula and mix well. 3. Then toss together the mixture with the cooked pasta. Add black pepper and cheese, as you desired. 4. Serve and enjoy!
Per Serving: Calories 496; Fat 21g; Sodium 215mg; Carbs 50.6g; Fiber 7.7g; Sugar 1.5g; Protein 31g

Chicken and Artichoke over Quinoa

Prep time: 15 minutes | Cook time: 20 minutes | Serves: 4

1 cup uncooked quinoa	marinated artichoke hearts, drained
2 teaspoons unsalted butter	
1-pound boneless, skinless chicken thighs, cut into bite-size pieces	1 tablespoon freshly squeezed lemon juice
2 medium zucchini, cut into bite-size pieces	¼ cup grated Parmesan cheese (optional)
1 garlic clove, minced (optional)	¼ cup minced fresh flat-leaf parsley (optional)
1 (12-ounce) jar quartered	

1. Prepare the quinoa as the package directed. 2. In a large skillet, add butter and heat over medium-high heat. 3. When the butter is heated, add the chicken and cook about 2 minutes per side, or until brown. 4. Then add garlic and zucchini and cook for 5 to 10 minutes, or until fully cooked. 5. Add the artichoke hearts and cook until warmed. 6. Turn off heat and add cheese, parsley, and lemon juice. 7. Serve over the quinoa. Enjoy!
Per Serving: Calories 411; Fat 14.7g; Sodium 645mg; Carbs 33g; Fiber 6g; Sugar 0.4g; Protein 37g

Roasted Chicken with Tomatoes and Pasta

Prep time: 15 minutes | Cook time: 20 minutes | Serves: 4

1-pound boneless, skinless chicken thighs, cut into bite-size pieces	1 teaspoon dried basil
⅛ teaspoon kosher salt (optional)	8 ounces uncooked whole-wheat rotini
¼ teaspoon freshly ground black pepper (optional)	10 Kalamata olives, pitted and sliced
4 cups cherry tomatoes, halved	¼ teaspoon red pepper flakes (optional)
4 garlic cloves, minced	¼ cup grated Parmesan cheese (optional)
1 tablespoon canola or sunflower oil	

1. Before cooking, heat your oven to 450 degrees F. 2. Toss salt and pepper over the chicken to season, as you like. 3. In a large bowl, add the tomatoes, oil, basil, chicken, and garlic and combine well. Spread the mixture evenly over a rimmed baking sheet. 4. Then roast in the preheated oven about 15 to 20 minutes, or until cooked through, tossing. The internal temperature of the meat should be 165 degrees F. 5. In a cooking pot, pour water and bring to a boil. Then add the pasta and cook until just al dente according to the package instruction. Ged rid of excess water from the pasta. 6. Add chicken, tomatoes, and pasta in a suitable bowl. Add olives and pepper flakes and toss well. 7. Drizzle over with Parmesan cheese, as you like. 8. Serve and enjoy!
Per Serving: Calories 545; Fat 16.5g; Sodium 824mg; Carbs 67g; Fiber 10.5g; Sugar 19g; Protein 37g

Chicken & Gnocchi with Cheeses

Prep time: 15 minutes | Cook time: 40 minutes | Serves: 4

1 ½ pounds boneless skinless chicken breasts	¾ cup shredded mozzarella
Kosher salt	½ cup freshly grated Parmesan
Freshly ground black pepper	3 cup packed baby spinach
2 tablespoons extra-virgin olive oil, divided	8 ounces baby Bella mushrooms, sliced
1 small shallot, diced	2 cloves garlic, minced
1 ¼ cups half and half	2 teaspoons fresh thyme leaves
Pinch crushed red pepper flakes	1 teaspoon dried oregano
1 (17-ounce) package gnocchi	1 cup low-sodium chicken broth

1. Toss evenly the chicken with salt and pepper to season. 2. In a large pan, add 1 tablespoon of oil and heat over medium-high heat. When heated, add the chicken and cook about 8 minutes, flipping once halfway through cooking, or until brown. Remove from the pan. 3. Add the rest oil in the pan and heat over medium heat. When heated, add the shallots and mushrooms about 5 minutes, or until golden. 4. Add thyme, garlic, and oregano and cook about 1 minute or more, or until fragrant. 5. Pour in broth and scrape down any brown bits off the pot. 6. Add the half and half, salt, pepper, and a sprinkle of red pepper flakes. Bring to a boil and then add the chicken to cook again about 8 to 10 minutes. The internal thermometer should read 165 degrees F. 7. Then turn off the heat and transfer the chicken to a plate. 8. Add the cheeses in the pan. Cover until melted. Then add the spinach and stir to let it wilt. 9. Add more salt and pepper as you like.
Per Serving: Calories 725; Fat 21g; Sodium 814mg; Carbs 78g; Fiber 9g; Sugar 7g; Protein 61g

Chicken Cooked in Wine

Prep time: 15 minutes | Cook time: 30 minutes | Serves: 4

1 tablespoon unsalted butter plus
1 tablespoon extra-virgin olive oil
1-pound boneless, skinless chicken thighs, pounded to ½-inch thickness
¼ teaspoon kosher salt
Freshly ground black pepper
3 large carrots, peeled and thinly
sliced on the diagonal
8 ounces sliced mushrooms
1 yellow onion, sliced
1 cup dry red wine
1 cup reduced-sodium chicken broth
1 tablespoon tomato paste
3 fresh thyme sprigs

1. Season the chicken with salt and pepper. 2. In a heavy skillet, melt the Better Butter over medium-high heat. When the butter bubbles, add the seasoned chicken, and cook until both sides are brown, about 2 to 4 minutes in total. Then set it aside on a plate. 3. Add mushrooms, onion, and carrots in the skillet and cook for 3 to 4 minutes, or until the onion starts to soften. 4. Add in wine, tomato paste, thyme, and broth and cook about 7 to 8 minutes, or until the vegetables are just crisp. 5. Cook the chicken again in the pan and simmer about 5 to 10 minutes, or until fully cooked. 6. When cooked, discard the thyme and transfer to a serving bowl. 7. Serve and enjoy!
Per Serving: Calories 326; Fat 15g; Sodium 771mg; Carbs 14g; Fiber 2.7g; Sugar 6g; Protein 31.5g

Air-Fried Chicken Breast

Prep time: 15 minutes | Cook time: 20 minutes | Serves: 2

1 large egg, beaten
¼ cup all-purpose flour
¾ cup panko breadcrumbs
Kosher salt
Freshly ground black pepper
2 boneless skinless chicken
breasts
⅓ cup freshly grated Parmesan
2 teaspoons lemon zest
1 teaspoon dried oregano
½ teaspoon cayenne pepper

1. In a small basin, beat the eggs. In a second basin, add the flour. 2. In a plate, add Parmesan, panko, oregano, cayenne, and lemon zest and mix well. Then add salt and pepper to season, as you desired. 3. Dip the chicken in flour, then the beaten eggs, and then the panko mixture until well coated. 4. Arrange into an air fryer basket. Cook at 375 degrees F for 10 minutes and check the doneness. 5. Then cook again for 5 minutes or more to golden brown.
Per Serving: Calories 589; Fat 12g; Sodium 591mg; Carbs 48g; Fiber 2.6g; Sugar 3g; Protein 69g

Buttery Tuscan Chicken with Spinach

Prep time: 15 minutes | Cook time: 20 minutes | Serves: 4

1 tablespoon extra-virgin olive oil
4 boneless skinless chicken breasts
Kosher salt
1 ½ cups cherry tomatoes, halved
3 cups baby spinach
½ cup heavy cream
¼ cup freshly grated Parmesan
Lemon wedges, for serving
Freshly ground black pepper
1 teaspoon dried oregano
3 tablespoons butter
3 cloves' garlic, minced

1. Toss salt, oregano, and pepper over the chicken to season. 2. In a pan, add oil and heat over medium heat. When heated, add the seasoned chicken and cook until golden, about 16 minutes, flipping once halfway through cooking. Transfer to a plate and allow it to sit. 3. In the skillet, add butter and heat over medium heat to melt. Add garlic and cook about 1 minute, or until fragrant. 4. Add salt and pepper to season. Then add the cherry tomatoes and cook until the tomatoes begin to burst. 5. Add spinach and cook until wilt. 6. In a saucepan, add Parmesan and heavy cream and bring together to a boil. Cook over low heat about 3 minutes, or until the sauce thickens. 7. Add the cooked chicken in the skillet and cook until fully cooked, about 5 to 7 minutes. 8. Add lemon slices to serve. Enjoy!
Per Serving: Calories 489; Fat 29g; Sodium 566mg; Carbs 8g; Fiber 1g; Sugar 3g; Protein 52g

Homemade Turkey Hamburgers

Prep time: 15 minutes | Cook time: 30 minutes | Serves: 6

1 pound ground turkey
½ cup rolled oats
¼ cup sun-dried tomatoes in oil, drained and chopped
¼ cup finely chopped red onion
¼ cup chopped fresh cilantro
2 garlic cloves, minced
6 whole-wheat hamburger buns
1 avocado, peeled, pitted, and sliced
6 lettuce leaves (optional)
6 tomato slices (optional)

1. Set up an oven rack and place it about 3 inches from the broiler. 2. Heat the broiler ahead. 3. Prepare a rimmed baking sheet and line with aluminum foil. 4. Combine together the oats, sun-dried tomatoes, cilantro, garlic, and onion in a large bowl. Make the mixture into 6 ½-inch-thick patties. 5. Arrange the patties onto the prepared baking sheet and broil for 6 to 8 minutes, flipping once halfway cooking through. The internal meat thermometer should read 165 degrees F. 6. To prepare the burger, arrange avocado, tomato, lettuce, and buns on a serving plate. 7. Start assemble your own burgers! 8. Serve and enjoy!
Per Serving: Calories 326; Fat 16g; Sodium 814mg; Carbs 12g; Fiber 2.6g; Sugar 4g; Protein 31g

Mediterranean Grilled Chicken with Summer Squash and Farro

Prep time: 30 minutes | Cook time: 30 minutes | Serves: 4

3 tablespoons extra-virgin olive oil, plus more for oiling the baking sheet
1¼ cups uncooked farro
1 large sweet onion, cut into 3 or 4 thick slices
2 pounds (about 8 small) assorted summer squash, cut lengthwise into ½-inch-thick slices
1½ cups bite-size cooked chicken
pieces
¼ cup crumbled goat cheese
¼ cup chopped walnuts
¼ cup chopped fresh flat-leaf parsley (optional)
2 tablespoons freshly squeezed lemon juice
½ teaspoon kosher salt, divided
Freshly ground black pepper

1. Heat your grill to medium high beforehand. For an oven, heat to 425 degrees F before cooking and grease a rimmed baking sheet. 2. Toss the squash slices and onion with oil on both sides. Then arrange the greased squash slices and onion on the preheated grill or the greased baking sheet. 3. Then cook each side for 6 to 8 minutes, or until both sides of the vegetables are golden brown. 4. Combine together the walnuts, goat cheese, parsley, lemon juice, the rest olive oil, and chicken in a large bowl. Then add salt and pepper to season. Mix in the cooked farro. 5. When the vegetables are cooked, remove them from heat and transfer to a cutting board. 6. Then cut into your desired-size pieces. Mix together the pieces with salad. 7. Serve and enjoy!
Per Serving: Calories 403; Fat 18g; Sodium 382mg; Carbs 41g; Fiber 7g; Sugar 31g; Protein 25g

Chicken and Oat Risotto with Veggies

Prep time: 15 minutes | Cook time: 20 minutes | Serves: 4

4 cups reduced-sodium chicken broth

1 tablespoon extra-virgin olive oil

1 small onion, finely chopped

1-pound sliced mushrooms

1-pound boneless, skinless chicken thighs, cut into bite-size pieces

1¼ cups quick-cooking steel-cut oats

1 (10-ounce) package frozen chopped kale (about 4 cups)

½ cup grated Parmesan cheese (optional)

Freshly ground black pepper (optional)

1. Pour the broth in a suitable saucepan, and then simmer over medium-low heat. 2. In a large, non-stick skillet, add the olive oil and heat over medium-high heat. Add mushrooms and onion and cook about 5 minutes, or until the onion is just fragrant. 3. Then move the vegetables to the side and add the chicken thighs. Allow it to sit about 2 minutes, or until the vegetables are browned. 4. Stir in the oats and cook about 1 minute. Then pour in ½ cup of the hot broth and stir to absorb. 5. Pour and stir in ½ cup of the hot broth or hot water, in case you run out of broth, once at a time until the oats absorb well. 6. After 10 minutes, the oats and chicken are almost cooked through. 7. Add the frozen kale. Cook and stir until warm. Then add black pepper and Parmesan cheese on the top. 8. Serve and enjoy!
Per Serving: Calories 604; Fat 23g; Sodium 1180mg; Carbs 56g; Fiber 8g; Sugar 3g; Protein 46g

Beef Chili with Onion

Prep time: 10 minutes | Cook time: 30 minutes | Serves: 2

1 cup lean ground beef

1 onion, diced

1 tablespoon olive oil

1 cup crushed tomatoes

½ cup red kidney beans, cooked

½ cup water

1 teaspoon chili seasonings

1. In a suitable saucepan, add olive oil. When the olive oil is heated, add lean ground beef. 2. Cook the ground beef for 7 minutes over medium heat. 3. Then add the diced onion and chili seasonings. Stir them together and then cook them for 10 minutes. 4. Add water, red kidney tomatoes, and crushed tomatoes, and stir the chili well. 5. Close the lid and simmer it for 13 minutes.
Per Serving: Calories 295; Fat 13g; Sodium 193mg; Carbs 18g; Fiber 6g; Sugar 6g; Protein 28g

Stuffed Chicken with Cheeses

Prep time: 15 minutes | Cook time: 40 minutes | Serves: 4

1-pound boneless skinless chicken breasts

1 cup panko breadcrumbs

1 teaspoon dried oregano

½ teaspoon garlic powder

½ cup freshly grated Parmesan, divided

Olive oil, for frying

2 cups marinara

¼ cup thinly sliced basil

8 ounces fresh mozzarella

Kosher salt

Freshly ground black pepper

1 cup all-purpose flour

3 eggs, beaten

2 tablespoons chopped parsley

1. Butterfly each chicken breasts. Add mozzarella in the pocket and seal by pressing their edges. Toss the chicken breasts with salt and pepper, as you desired. 2. Heat your oven to 425 degrees

F beforehand. 3. In a bowl, beat the eggs. In a second bowl, add the flour. In a third bowl, add the panko breadcrumbs. 4. Add the dried oregano, half the parmesan, garlic powder, and half teaspoon salt in the breadcrumbs and whisk well. 5. Add the stuffed chicken in the flour. Get rid of any excess flour from the chicken. Coat with the beaten egg mixture. Then dredge into the breadcrumb bowl to coat. 6. In a large pan, add a thin coating of olive oil and heat over medium heat. 7. Then add the chicken and cook about 8 minutes, flipping once halfway through cooking, or until both sides of the chicken are brown. 8. Pour the marinara around the chicken and add basil on the top. 9. Remove from heat and sprinkle over the chicken with the rest half Parmesan. 10. Bake in your preheated oven until the chicken is fully cooked, about 20 minutes. 11. When cooked, add parsley to garnish, as you desired. 12. Serve and enjoy!
Per Serving: Calories 639; Fat 14g; Sodium 902mg; Carbs 61g; Fiber 6g; Sugar 10g; Protein 63g

Chicken, Bell Pepper, and Onion Fajitas

Prep time: 15 minutes | Cook time: 15 minutes | Serves: 2

½ cup plus 1 tablespoon extra-virgin olive oil

¼ cup lime juice, from about three limes

2 teaspoons cumin

Freshly ground black pepper

2 bell peppers, thinly sliced

1 large onion, thinly sliced

Tortillas, for serving

½ teaspoon crushed red pepper flakes

1-pound boneless skinless chicken breasts

Kosher salt

1. Toss the chicken with salt and pepper to season until well coated. 2. In a large mixing bowl, add lime juice, red pepper flakes, ½ cup of oil, and cumin. Then add the chicken and mix together. Put in the refrigerator to marinate for about half an hour or up to 2 hours. 3. In a big pan, add the rest oil and heat over medium heat. Then add the marinated chicken and cook about 16 minutes, or until both sides are brown and fully cooked. Then set it aside to cool, about 10 minutes. Transfer to a cutting board and slice into strips. 4. Cook the bell peppers and onion in the skillet, about 5 minutes, or until tender. 5. Mix with the chicken strips. 6. Serve alongside tortillas.
Per Serving: Calories 738; Fat 39g; Sodium 909mg; Carbs 37g; Fiber 3.5g; Sugar 7g; Protein 57g

Pork and Veggie Chili

Prep time: 10 minutes | Cook time: 1 hour 10 minutes | Serves: 6

1 green bell pepper, chopped

1 pound pork, cubed

1 yellow onion, chopped

4 carrots, chopped

Black pepper to the taste

26 ounces canned tomatoes, no-

salt-added and chopped

1 teaspoon onion powder

1 tablespoon parsley, chopped

4 teaspoons chili powder

1 teaspoon garlic powder

1 teaspoon sweet paprika

1. Heat up a pot over medium-high heat, and add the meat and brown for 5 minutes. 2. Add bell pepper, carrots, onions, tomatoes, black pepper, onion powder, chili powder, paprika, and garlic powder, toss, bring to a simmer, and then simmer over medium heat, cover the pot and cook for 1 hour and 5 minutes. 3. Toss in parsley and divide them into bowls and serve. 4. Enjoy!
Per Serving: Calories 229; Fat 11g; Sodium 267mg; Carbs 12.5g; Fiber 5g; Sugar 6.7g; Protein 21.6g

Creamy Chicken with Fettuccine

Prep time: 15 minutes | Cook time: 20 minutes | Serves: 4

2 tablespoons extra-virgin olive oil
2 boneless skinless chicken breasts
Kosher salt
½ cup heavy cream
1 cup freshly grated Parmesan
Freshly chopped parsley for garnish
Freshly ground black pepper
1 ½ cups whole milk
1 ½ cups low-sodium chicken broth
2 cloves garlic, minced
8 ounces fettuccine

1. Toss salt and pepper over chicken to season. 2. In a large skillet, add the oil and heat over medium-high heat. When heated, add the seasoned chicken and cook until both sides are fully cooked and golden, about 16 minutes, flipping once halfway through cooking. Then let it set aside for 10 minutes to cool. 3. Meanwhile, mix together the milk, garlic, and broth together in a pan until well incorporated. Then simmer about 3 minutes and add salt and pepper, as you like. 4. Stir in the fettuccine and cook until al dente, about 8 minutes. 5. Add Parmesan and the heavy cream and mix well. Bring to a simmer to thicken the sauce. 6. Turn off the heat and add the chicken slices. Add parsley to garnish, as you like. 7. Serve and enjoy!
Per Serving: Calories 616; Fat 17g; Sodium 434mg; Carbs 66g; Fiber 2g; Sugar 15g; Protein 48g

Thai-style Pork Meatballs

Prep time: 10 minutes | Cook time: 10 minutes | Serves: 4

1 pound pork, ground
⅓ cup cilantro, chopped
1 cup red onion, chopped
4 garlic cloves, minced
1 tablespoon ginger, grated
1 Thai chili, chopped
2 tablespoons olive oil

1. In a bowl, combine the meat with cilantro, onion, garlic, ginger, and chili, stir well and shape the mixture into medium meatballs. 2. Heat up a pan over medium-high heat and add the oil. When it is heated, add the meatballs, cook them for 5 minutes on each side, divide them between plates and serve with a side salad. 3. Enjoy!
Per Serving: Calories 329; Fat 19.5g; Sodium 68mg; Carbs 7g; Fiber 1g; Sugar 3g; Protein 30g

Enticing Sesame Chicken Thighs

Prep time: 15 minutes | Cook time: 40 minutes | Serves: 4

⅓ cup low-sodium soy sauce
¼ cup extra-virgin olive oil
2 tablespoons honey
4 bone-in, skin-on chicken thighs (about 2 pound)
Thinly sliced green onions for garnish
Toasted sesame seeds for garnish
2 tablespoons chili garlic sauce
Juice of 1 lime
2 cloves garlic, minced
2 teaspoons freshly grated ginger

1. In a large mixing bowl, add oil, honey, chili garlic sauce, ginger, soy sauce, and garlic and mix well. Reserve half cup of the marinade sauce. 2. Use the remaining half the sauce to coat the chicken in a basin. Cover and place in a refrigerator to marinade for at least half an hour. 3. Then transfer two thighs to an air fryer basket and cook at 400 degrees F until the internal thermometer reads about 165 degrees F, about 15 to 20 minutes. 4. When cooked, transfer the chicken thighs into an aluminum foil tent. Repeat with the remaining chicken thighs. 5. In a small saucepan, pour in the reserved marinade sauce and bring to a boil over medium heat. Then cook over low heat until the sauce slightly thickens, about 4 to 5 minutes. 6. Drizzle the thickened sauce over the chicken thighs to serve. Add toasted sesame seeds and green onions to garnish. 7. Serve and enjoy!
Per Serving: Calories 1176; Fat 114g; Sodium 998mg; Carbs 15g; Fiber 1g; Sugar 10g; Protein 24g

Braised Chicken Pozole

Prep time: 15 minutes | Cook time: 6 to 8 hours | Serves: 6

4 cups low-sodium chicken broth
3 boneless skinless chicken breasts
2 Poblano peppers, chopped
Freshly ground black pepper
2 (15-ounce) cans hominy, drained, and rinsed
Thinly sliced radishes for garnish
Sliced green cabbage for garnish
Fresh cilantro, for garnish
1 white onion, chopped
2 cloves garlic, minced
1 tablespoon cumin
1 tablespoon oregano
2 teaspoons chili powder
2 teaspoons kosher salt

1. Combine all ingredients except the hominy and garnishes in a slow cooker—Cook the chicken on low until soft and cooked through, for about 6 to 8 hours on low. 2. Carefully remove the chicken from the slow cooker and shred using two forks. Return the hominy to the slow cooker and simmer for another 30 minutes. 3. To serve, ladle soup into bowls and top with radish, cabbage, and cilantro.
Per Serving: Calories 261; Fat 5g; Sodium 1212mg; Carbs 22g; Fiber 4.5g; Sugar 4.5g; Protein 31g

Creamy Chicken Chili

Prep time: 15 minutes | Cook time: 30 minutes | Serves: 3

1 tablespoon extra-virgin olive oil
1 small yellow onion, diced
1 jalapeño, seeded and minced
2 cloves garlic, minced
1 teaspoon dried oregano
1 teaspoon ground cumin
2 (4.5-ounce) cans green chilies
1 ½ cups frozen corn
½ cup sour cream
Freshly chopped cilantro for garnish
¼ cup shredded Monterey Jack
¼ cup crushed tortilla chips
3 boneless skinless chicken breasts, cut into thirds
5 cups low-sodium chicken broth
Freshly ground black pepper
Kosher salt
2 (15-ounce) cans of white beans

1. In a large saucepan, add the oil and heat over medium heat. When heated, add jalapeno and onion and cook about 5 minutes, or until tender. 2. Add cumin, oregano, and garlic and cook about 1 minute, or until fragrant. 3. Add salt and pepper to season. Then pour in the broth. Add chicken and green chilis. Bring to a boil over low heat. Cover and cook until softened and fully cooked, about 10 to 12 minutes. 4. When cooked, transfer the chicken to a platter and use two forks to shred. 5. Add the chicken to the saucepan again. Add corn and white beans and stir. Simmer for about 10 minutes. 6. Use a wooden spoon to mash ¼ of the beans and then turn off the heat. 7. Add sour cream and mix well. 8. In serving bowls, ladle chili and then divide the cooked chicken. Add cheese, chips, and cilantro on the top, as you like. 9. Serve and enjoy!
Per Serving: Calories 729; Fat 28.5g; Sodium 1716mg; Carbs 55g; Fiber 19g; Sugar 8g; Protein 74g

Crusted Chicken Cutlets with Parmesan

Prep time: 15 minutes | Cook time: 15 minutes | Serves: 4

4 boneless skinless chicken breasts	½ teaspoon cayenne pepper
Kosher salt	Vegetable oil
Freshly ground black pepper	Lemon wedges, for serving
3 large eggs, beaten	1 cup all-purpose flour
2 teaspoon lemon zest	2 ¼ cup panko
	¾ cup freshly grated Parmesan

1. Cut crosswise the chicken breasts into half. And then arrange the cut halves on a chopping board between 2 pieces of plastic wrap. 2. Use a meat tenderizer and flatten the chicken into ¼-inch thick. Toss salt and pepper on both sides of the chicken. 3. In a small basin, beat the eggs. In a separate second basin, add the flour. 4. In a third shallow dish, add the lemon zest, cayenne, Parmesan, and panko and mix well. Then add salt and pepper to season. 5. Coat the chicken with flout, and then dip in the egg liquid. Finally add into the breadcrumb mixture and coat well by pressing. 6. In a large pan, add 2 tablespoons of oil and heat over medium heat. When heated, add the chicken and cook until brown and fully cooked, about 5 to 6 minutes or more. 7. Add lemon slices to serve. Enjoy!
Per Serving: Calories 758; Fat 15g; Sodium 777mg; Carbs 74.5g; Fiber 4g; Sugar 4g; Protein 75g

Creamy Chicken Tortillas

Prep time: 15 minutes | Cook time: 15 minutes | Serves: 4

1 tablespoon extra-virgin olive oil	1 ripe avocado, sliced
2 bell peppers, thinly sliced	1 tablespoon vegetable oil
½ teaspoon chili powder	2 scallions, thinly sliced
½ teaspoon ground cumin	Sour cream, for serving
½ teaspoon dried oregano	½ onion, thinly sliced
4 medium flour tortillas	Kosher salt
2 cups shredded Monterey jack	Freshly ground black pepper
2 cups shredded cheddar	1-pound boneless skinless chicken breasts, sliced into strips

1. In a large pan, heat the olive oil over medium-high heat. Add onion and pepper and cook for 5 minutes. Add salt and pepper to season. Then transfer to a platter. 2. Add the rest vegetable oil in the pan and heat over medium-high heat. 3. Add salt, pepper, and spices to season the chicken. Cook for 8 minutes, or until the chicken is browned and completely cooked. Transfer to a serving plate. 4. Add the cheeses, cooked chicken mixture, and onion and pepper on top of a flour tortilla. 5. Fold together. Cook for 3 minutes and flip to the other side. Cook again for 3 minutes or more until the tortilla becomes golden. Repeat the steps with remaining tortillas. 6. Cut the tortillas into wedges to serve and drizzle sour cream on top. 7. Serve and enjoy!
Per Serving: Calories 942; Fat 62g; Sodium 1222mg; Carbs 32.8g; Fiber 5g; Sugar 4g; Protein 63g

Garlic Beef Loin

Prep time: 15 minutes | Cook time: 20 minutes | Serves: 2

10 ounces beef loin, strips	2 tablespoons margarine
1 garlic clove, diced	1 teaspoon dried sage

1. Toss margarine in the skillet. 2. Add dried sage and diced garlic

and roast them for 2 minutes on low heat. 3. Add beef loin strips and roast them for 15 minutes on medium heat. Stir the meat occasionally.
Per Serving: Calories 422; Fat 33g; Sodium 78mg; Carbs 1g; Fiber 0.2g; Sugar 0g; Protein 29g

Inspired Chicken Gnocchi Soup with Spinach

Prep time: 15 minutes | Cook time: 40 minutes | Serves: 6

2 tablespoons butter	2 celery stalks, chopped
1 medium onion, chopped	1 medium carrot, julienned or shredded
2 cups half and half	
2 cups cooked chicken, shredded	3 cloves garlic, minced
1 (16-ounces) package gnocchi, fresh or thawed from frozen	6 cups low sodium or homemade chicken stock
2 cups baby spinach	3 sprigs thyme

1. In a large saucepan, heat the butter to melt over medium-low heat. 2. Add carrot, onion, and celery and cook for 5 minutes. 3. Then add the garlic and cook until fragrant, for about 30 seconds to 1 minute. 4. Pour in the chicken and scrape off any caramelized bits from the bottom. Add the thyme and bring together to boil. 5. Reduce the heat and simmer until the flavor emerges, about 20 minutes. 6. Add the half-and-half and bring to a boil again. Discard the thyme sprigs and add salt and pepper to season. 7. Then cook the gnocchi according to the package instruction over medium-low heat until al dente. 8. Add the spinach and cook until wilted. 9. Transfer to a serving dish. 10. Serve and enjoy!
Per Serving: Calories 334; Fat 17g; Sodium 410mg; Carbs 26g; Fiber 2g; Sugar 6g; Protein 21g

Garlic Lemon-Pepper Chicken

Prep time: 15 minutes | Cook time: 20 minutes | Serves: 2

½ cup all-purpose flour	Freshly chopped parsley for garnish
1 tablespoon lemon-pepper seasoning	
1 teaspoon kosher salt	2 lemons, divided
½ cup chicken broth	1-pound boneless skinless chicken breasts halved
2 tablespoons butter	
2 cloves garlic, minced	2 tablespoons extra-virgin olive oil

1. Preheat the oven to 400 degrees F. Combine flour, lemon pepper, salt, and one lemon zest in a medium mixing bowl. Toss the chicken breasts in the flour mixture until they are well covered. Cut the rest of the lemon into thin rounds. 2. Heat the oil carefully in a large oven-proof skillet over medium-high heat. Cook until the bottom of the chicken is browned, about 5 minutes, then turn the chicken breasts. 3. Add stock, butter, garlic, and lemon slices to the pan and bake until the chicken is completely cooked and the sauce has slightly reduced, about 5 minutes. 4. Place the chicken on top of the sauce and decorate it with parsley. 5. Combine flour, lemon pepper, salt, and one lemon zest in a medium mixing bowl. Toss the chicken breasts in the flour mixture until they are well covered. Cut the rest of the lemon into thin rounds. 6. Heat the oil carefully in a large oven-proof skillet over medium-high heat. Cook until the bottom of the chicken is browned, about 5 minutes, then turn the chicken breasts. 7. Add stock, butter, garlic, and lemon slices to skillet and heat until chicken is cooked through and the sauce has slightly reduced about 3 minutes. 8. Place the chicken on top of the sauce and decorate it with parsley.
Per Serving: Calories 727; Fat 35g; Sodium 1515mg; Carbs 31g; Fiber 2g; Sugar 1g; Protein 68g

Pork Steak with Tomatoes and Tarragon

Prep time: 10 minutes | Cook time: 22 minutes | Serves: 4

4 medium pork steaks
Black pepper to the taste
1 tablespoon olive oil

8 cherry tomatoes, halved
A handful chopped tarragon

1. Over medium-high heat, add the oil to a pan. 2. Add steaks, season with black pepper, cook them for 6 minutes on each side, and divide between plates. 3. In the same pan, add the tomatoes and the tarragon, and then cook for 10 minutes. Divide next to the pork and serve. 4. Enjoy!
Per Serving: Calories 536; Fat 36g; Sodium 110mg; Carbs 2.7g; Fiber 0.6g; Sugar 1.5g; Protein 47g

Simple Chicken and Rice Casserole

Prep time: 20 minutes | Cook time: 1 hour 40 minutes | Serves: 4

extra-virgin olive oil, for baking dish
2 cups white rice rinsed well and drained
1 large onion, chopped
2 cups low-sodium chicken broth
2 cans cream of mushroom soup

1 clove garlic, finely minced
1 tablespoon freshly chopped parsley for garnish
kosher salt
freshly ground black pepper
4 large bone-in, skin-on chicken thighs (about 2 pound)
2 tablespoons melted butter
2 teaspoons fresh thyme

1. Preheat the oven carefully to 350°F and oil a 9"x13" baking dish. Stir in the rice, onion, broth, and soup until well incorporated. Season with salt and pepper to taste. 2. Brush the melted butter over the skin side of the chicken thighs before placing them in the rice mixture—season with salt and pepper and top with thyme and garlic. 3. Bake for 1 hour, covered with foil. Carefully uncover the foil and bake for another 30 minutes, or until the rice is soft and the chicken is cooked through—Preheat the oven to broil and broil the chicken for 3 to 5 minutes, or until brown. 4. Before serving, garnish with parsley.
Per Serving: Calories 746; Fat 27g; Sodium 542mg; Carbs 88g; Fiber 4g; Sugar 4g; Protein 35g

Lamb and Bean Sprouts Mix

Prep time: 10 minutes | Cook time: 10 minutes | Serves: 4

1 garlic clove, minced
2 red chilies, chopped
1 cucumber, sliced
2 tablespoons balsamic vinegar
1 carrot, sliced
1 radish, sliced

½ cup mint leaves, chopped
½ cup coriander leaves, chopped
Black pepper to the taste
2 tablespoons olive oil
3 ounces bean sprouts
2 lamb fillets

1. Put the chilies in a pan, add garlic and vinegar, bring to a boil, stir well and take off the heat. 2. In a bowl, mix cucumber with radish, carrot, coriander, mint, and sprouts. 3. Heat up your kitchen grill over medium-high heat, and brush lamb fillets with the oil. 4. Add pepper to season and cook for 3 minutes on each side. Slice the meat, add over the veggies, also add the vinegar mix, toss and serve. 5. Enjoy!
Per Serving: Calories 437; Fat 30g; Sodium 110mg; Carbs 6.5g; Fiber 1.5g; Sugar 3g; Protein 34g

Chicken Curry

Prep time: 15 minutes | Cook time: 15 minutes | Serves: 4

2 tablespoons extra-virgin olive oil
1 medium yellow onion, chopped
2 pounds boneless skinless chicken breasts, cut into 1" pieces
3 cloves garlic, minced
1 tablespoon minced ginger
1 ½ cups low-sodium chicken broth
½ cup heavy cream

Kosher salt
Freshly ground black pepper
Basmati rice or naan, for serving
1 tablespoon freshly chopped cilantro for garnish
1 ½ teaspoons paprika
1 ½ teaspoons ground turmeric
1 ½ teaspoons ground coriander
1 teaspoon ground cumin
1 (15-ounce) can crushed tomatoes

1. In a suitable saucepan, add the oil and heat over medium-high heat. Cook until the onion is tender, about 5 minutes. Sear the chicken for 5 minutes, or until no pink remains. Cook until the garlic and ginger are fragrant, about 1 minute. 2. Cook it carefully until the spices are aromatic, about 1 minute. Bring the tomatoes and broth to a boil—season with salt and pepper after adding the heavy cream. And then simmer them until the chicken is done and tender, for about 15 to 20 minutes. 3. Sprinkle with cilantro to garnish and serve over rice or with naan.
Per Serving: Calories 421; Fat 16g; Sodium 339mg; Carbs 13g; Fiber 3g; Sugar 6g; Protein 55g

Buttery Parmesan Chicken

Prep time: 15 minutes | Cook time: 25 minutes | Serves: 3

½ cup all-purpose flour
¾ cup freshly grated Parmesan, divided
1 teaspoon garlic powder
Zest of ½ lemon
2 cloves garlic, minced
2 cups baby spinach
1 cup heavy cream
2/3 cup low-sodium chicken broth

1 lemon, sliced in rounds and halved
¼ cup thinly sliced fresh basil
Kosher salt
Freshly ground black pepper
3 boneless skinless chicken breasts
2 tablespoons extra-virgin olive oil
1 tablespoon butter

1. Combine flour, ¼ cup Parmesan, garlic powder, and lemon zest in a large mixing bowl. Season liberally with salt and pepper and fully combine with a fork. Coat each chicken breast evenly with the flour mixture on all sides. Place aside. 2. Add the oil to a suitable pan and heat over medium-high heat until it shimmers but is not smoking. Sear the chicken for 6 minutes, or until browned. Cook until the opposite side is golden, about 6 minutes more. Set aside after removing from the pan. 3. Adjust the heat to medium. Then add the butter to the pan and heat until melted. Add the garlic and simmer for 1 minute, or until fragrant. Cook it until the spinach is wilted, 1 to 2 minutes. 4. Season with salt and pepper after adding the chicken stock, cream, and remaining ½ cup Parmesan. To blend, stir everything together. Bring to a boil with the lemon slices and cook until slightly thickened, 3 to 4 minutes. 5. Return the chicken to the skillet and cook for another 5 to 6 minutes, or until cooked through. 6. When the chicken is completely cooked, take it from the skillet and sprinkle it with basil before serving.
Per Serving: Calories 666; Fat 30g; Sodium 491mg; Carbs 31g; Fiber 3g; Sugar 3g; Protein 66g

Buttermilk Fried Chicken

Prep time: 15 minutes | Cook time: 30 minutes | Serves: 2

2-pound bone-in skin-on chicken pieces (mix of cuts)	¼ teaspoon cayenne pepper
2 cups buttermilk	3 teaspoons kosher salt, divided
½ cup hot sauce	2 cups all-purpose flour
½ teaspoon oregano	1 teaspoon garlic powder
½ teaspoon freshly ground black pepper	1 teaspoon onion powder

1. Remove the extra fat from the chicken and throw it in a large mixing dish. Combine buttermilk, spicy sauce, and 2 tablespoons of salt in a medium mixing basin. 2. Pour the buttermilk mixture over the chicken, ensuring that all pieces are covered. Refrigerate for at least 1 hour and marinate up to overnight. 3. Combine the flour, 1 teaspoon of salt, and spices in a shallow basin or pie plate. Remove the chicken from the buttermilk mixture piece by piece, brushing off excess buttermilk. Turn to coat in the flour mixture. 4. Place breaded chicken carefully in the air fryer basket, working in batches as needed to avoid overcrowding. Cook the breaded chicken in your oven at 400°F for 20 to 25 minutes, or until the chicken is brown. The internal temperature should reach 165°F, turning halfway through. 5. Repeat with the remaining chicken.
Per Serving: Calories 770; Fat 13g; Sodium 6476mg; Carbs 137g; Fiber 6g; Sugar 22g; Protein 26g

Pork and Sweet Potatoes

Prep time: 10 minutes | Cook time: 1 hour 20 minutes | Serves: 8

½ teaspoon garlic powder	1 cup low-sodium veggie stock
½ teaspoon oregano, chopped	½ cup cilantro, chopped
½ teaspoon cinnamon powder	

1. Heat up a pan with the oil over medium-high heat, add sweet potatoes and onion, stir, cook for 15 minutes and transfer to a bowl. 2. Heat up the pan again over medium-high heat, add pork, stir and brown for 5 minutes. 3. Add black pepper, cumin, garlic powder, oregano, chili powder, cinnamon, stock, return potatoes and onion, stir and cook for 1 hour over medium heat. 4. Add the cilantro, toss, divide into bowls and serve. 5. Enjoy!
Per Serving: Calories 300; Fat 5.5g; Sodium 281mg; Carbs 26g; Fiber 4g; Sugar 3g; Protein 35g

Baked Chicken and Broccoli

Prep time: 15 minutes | Cook time: 40 minutes | Serves: 4

1 tablespoon extra-virgin olive oil	1 cup shredded cheddar
	¼ cup panko breadcrumbs
1 cup small yellow onion, chopped	Kosher salt
2 cloves garlic, minced	2 ½ cup low-sodium chicken broth
1-pound boneless, skinless chicken breasts, cut into 1-inch pieces	Freshly ground black pepper
	1 cup white rice
2 cup broccoli florets	1 cup heavy cream

1. Add the oil to a suitable oven-safe skillet and heat it over medium-high heat. Cook, constantly stirring, until the onion is tender, about 5 minutes. Cook until the garlic is aromatic, about 1 minute more. Season the chicken with salt and pepper. Cook, stirring periodically, for another 6 minutes, or until golden. 2. Combine the rice, heavy cream, and 1 cup of broth in a mixing bowl. Bring them together to a simmer and cook for 15 minutes, or until the rice is cooked. Cook them until the broccoli is soft and the cheese is melted, approximately 10 minutes, with the remaining 1 ½ cups broth. 3. Preheat the broiler. Season the breadcrumbs and chicken mixture with salt and pepper. Broil until they are just golden and crispy, for about 2 minutes.
Per Serving: Calories 648; Fat 31g; Sodium 389mg; Carbs 48g; Fiber 2.5g; Sugar 2.6g; Protein 42g

Garlic Pork with Peanuts

Prep time: 10 minutes | Cook time: 16 minutes | Serves: 4

2 tablespoons lime juice	1 yellow onion, cut into wedges
2 tablespoons coconut aminos	1 ½ pound pork tenderloin, cubed
1 ½ tablespoons brown sugar	
5 garlic cloves, minced	3 tablespoons peanuts, chopped
3 tablespoons olive oil	2 scallions, chopped
Black pepper to the taste	

1. In a bowl, mix lime juice with aminos and sugar and stir very well. 2. In another bowl, mix garlic with 1 and ½ teaspoon oil and some black pepper and stir. 3. Heat up a pan with the rest of the oil over medium-high heat. 4. Add meat and cook them for 3 minutes on each side and transfer to a bowl. 5. Then heat the same pan over medium-high heat. Then add in onion, stir and cook for 3 minutes. 6. Add the garlic mix, return the pork, also add the aminos mix, toss, cook for 6 minutes, divide between plates, sprinkle scallions and peanuts on top, and serve. 7. Enjoy!
Per Serving: Calories 431; Fat 21g; Sodium 182mg; Carbs 11.6g; Fiber 1.7g; Sugar 4g; Protein 49g

Grilled Beef in Tomato Sauce

Prep time: 10 minutes | Cook time: 17 minutes | Serves: 2

2 chuck shoulder steaks	1 tablespoon olive oil
¼ cup tomato sauce	

1. Brush the tomato sauce and oil over the steaks and transfer to the preheated 390 degrees F grill. 2. Grill the meat for 9 minutes. 3. Then turn the meat to the other side and cook for 8 minutes more.
Per Serving: Calories 447; Fat 22g; Sodium 607mg; Carbs 7g; Fiber 2g; Sugar 4g; Protein 51g

Herbed Turkey Skewers

Prep time: 15 minutes | Cook time: 15 minutes | Serves: 4

1-pound boneless, skinless turkey breasts, cut into cubes	1 teaspoon dried thyme
	1 teaspoon dried oregano
1 lemon, juiced	½ teaspoon fine sea salt
2 tablespoons avocado oil	¼ teaspoon ground black pepper
2 tablespoon garlic, crushed	

1. Combine the turkey cubes, lemon juice, avocado oil, crushed garlic, dried thyme, ground black pepper, dried oregano, and fine sea salt in a large mixing bowl. Mix until well coated, and allow to rest for 30 minutes. 2. Spear the turkey cubes onto 8 skewers. 3. Over medium-high heat, heat a non-stick frying pan. 4. Place the skewers in the pan, and cook for 5 to 7 minutes. Flip, and cook for 5 to 8 minutes, or until fully cooked and browned. Remove from the heat, and serve.
Per Serving: Calories 187; Fat 9g; Sodium 525mg; Carbs 3g; Fiber 0.3g; Sugar 0.4g; Protein 25g

Baked Pork and Eggplants

Prep time: 15 minutes | Cook time: 1 hour 10 minutes | Serves: 6

4 eggplants, cut into halves lengthwise
4 ounces olive oil
2 yellow onions, chopped
4 ounces pork meat, ground
2 green bell peppers, chopped
1 pound chopped tomatoes

4 tomato slices
2 tablespoons tomato paste, low-sodium
½ cup chopped parsley
4 garlic cloves, minced
½ cup hot water
Black pepper, to the taste

1. In a suitable pan, add the olive oil and heat over medium-high heat. 2. Then add the eggplant and cook for 5 minutes. Transfer them to a plate. 3. In the same pan, add the chopped onion and heat up over medium-high heat. Cook and stir for 3 minutes. 4. Add pork, pepper, bell peppers, tomato paste, chopped tomatoes, and parsley, stir together and cook for 7 minutes. 5. In a baking tray, arrange the cooked eggplant halves, divide garlic into each eggplant half, spoon over with the meat filling, and top with a tomato slice. 6. Pour the water over them, cover with foil, and bake in the oven at 350 degrees F for 40 minutes. 7. Then divide them among plates and serve. 8. Enjoy!
Per Serving: Calories 354; Fat 23.5g; Sodium 71mg; Carbs 30g; Fiber 13g; Sugar 16g; Protein 11g

Basil Pesto Chicken with Asparagus

Prep time: 10 minutes | Cook time: 15 minutes | Serves: 4

8 ounces uncooked rotini pasta
1 pound asparagus, woody ends removed, cut into bite-size pieces
1 tablespoon coconut oil
12 ounces chicken breasts,

boneless and skinless, cut into bite-size cubes
2 medium Roma tomatoes, chopped
½ cup basil pesto
¼ cup Parmesan cheese, grated

1. With the instruction on the package, cook the rotini pasta until al dente. Scoop out ½ cup of the cooking water, and keep to one side. Add the asparagus pieces to the pasta; when it lasts for 4 minutes until left a mark. Allow it to boil. 2. In a large, heavy-bottom pan, heat the coconut oil over medium-high heat. Fry the cubed chicken breasts for 5 to 10 minutes or until cooked through. Stir in the chopped tomatoes, and remove the pan from the heat. 3. Drain the pasta and asparagus in a colander, and return them to the stockpot. 4. Toss the pasta and asparagus with the basil pesto and ¼ cup of the reserved cooking water. Add the cooked chicken mixture and more cooking water if needed. 5. Top with the grated Parmesan cheese, and serve hot.
Per Serving: Calories 473; Fat 31g; Sodium 451mg; Carbs 25g; Fiber 6g; Sugar 4g; Protein 27g

Garlic Pineapple Chicken

Prep time: 15 minutes | Cook time: 30 minutes | Serves: 4

Aluminum foil
1 pound chicken breasts, boneless and skinless
2 tablespoons olive oil, and more for frying

1 (20-ounce) can crush pineapple, drained
1 tablespoon garlic, minced
Ground black pepper

1. Heat your broiler in advance to high heat, and place the oven rack 4 to 5 inches from the broiler. Line a baking sheet with aluminum foil. 2. Slice each chicken breast in half horizontally to make 2 thin cutlets. Place the cut chicken breasts in a large mixing bowl. 3. Add the olive oil, crushed pineapple, minced garlic, and ground black pepper, and mix to combine. Let the chicken marinate for 10 minutes. 4. Transfer the chicken cutlets and the crushed pineapple to the baking sheet. Broil for 4 to 5 minutes per side, turning once, until the chicken is lightly browned on both sides and fully cooked. 5. Let the chicken cool for 5 minutes before cutting and serving it.
Per Serving: Calories 512; Fat 17g; Sodium 76mg; Carbs 63g; Fiber 1g; Sugar 62g; Protein 26g

Herbed Pumpkin Pork Chili

Prep time: 10 minutes | Cook time: 1 hour 30 minutes | Serves: 6

1 green bell pepper, chopped
2 cups yellow onion, chopped
1 tablespoon olive oil
6 garlic cloves, minced
28 ounces canned tomatoes, no-salt-added and chopped
1 ½ pounds pork, ground
6 ounces low-sodium tomato

paste
14 ounces pumpkin puree
1 cup low-sodium chicken stock
2 ½ teaspoons oregano, dried
1 ½ teaspoons cinnamon, ground
1 ½ tablespoons chili powder
Black pepper to the taste

1. Heat up a pot with the oil over medium-high heat, add bell peppers and onion, stir and cook for 7 minutes. 2. Add garlic and the pork, toss and cook for 10 minutes. 3. Add tomatoes, tomato paste, pumpkin puree, stock, oregano, cinnamon, chili powder, and pepper, stir, cover, cook over medium heat for 1 hour and 10 minutes, and divide into bowls and serve. 4. Enjoy!
Per Serving: Calories 370; Fat 19g; Sodium 312mg; Carbs 18g; Fiber 7g; Sugar 9g; Protein 33g

Turkey Oat Patties with Black Olives

Prep time: 15 minutes | Cook time: 15 minutes | Serves: 2

Aluminum foil
1-pound lean ground turkey
½ cup rolled oats
¼ cup sliced black olives, chopped
¼ cup white onion, finely chopped

¼ cup parsley, finely chopped
1 tablespoon garlic, minced
6 whole-wheat hamburger buns
1 ripe avocado, peeled, pitted, and sliced
6 iceberg lettuce leaves
6 beefsteak tomato slices

1. Heat the broiler, and carefully set an oven rack about 3 inches from it. Line a baking sheet with aluminum foil. 2. In a large mixing bowl, add together the ground turkey, rolled oats, chopped black olives, chopped onion, chopped parsley, and minced garlic. Mix well until combined. Shape into 6 equal patties. 3. Place the turkey patties on the baking sheet, and broil for 6 to 8 minutes, flipping once halfway through cooking or until the juices run clear. 4. Meanwhile, on a serving platter, place the whole-wheat buns, sliced avocado, iceberg lettuce, and tomato slices. Allow diners to assemble their own burgers.
Per Serving: Calories 1487; Fat 88g; Sodium 814mg; Carbs 127g; Fiber 14g; Sugar 53g; Protein 59g

Savory Spiced Beef

Prep time: 10 minutes | Cook time: 1 hour 20 minutes | Serves: 2

1-pound beef sirloin	1 bay leaf
1 tablespoon five-spice seasoning	2 cups of water
	1 teaspoon peppercorn

1. Rub the five-spice seasoning over the beef sirloin and put it in the saucepan. 2. Add bay leaf, water, and peppercorns. 3. Simmer it for 80 minutes with the lid closed on medium heat. 4. Place the cooked meat over a cutting board and then chop it. Sprinkle with the hot spiced water from the saucepan.
Per Serving: Calories 451; Fat 27g; Sodium 149mg; Carbs 2g; Fiber 0.5g; Sugar 0g; Protein 47g

Chicken and Asparagus Bake

Prep time: 15 minutes | Cook time: 30 minutes | Serves: 4

2 tablespoons avocado oil	1 (15-ounce) can low-sodium diced tomatoes, drained
4 bone-in chicken thighs, skins removed	¼ cup water
¾ teaspoon fine sea salt, divided	1 (15-ounce) can asparagus, drained
½ teaspoon ground black pepper, divided	¼ cup black olives pitted
	¼ cup cilantro, chopped

1. Heat the oven to 350°F, gas mark 4. 2. In a large cast iron or oven-safe pan, heat the avocado oil over medium-high heat. 3. Season the chicken thighs with ¼ teaspoon of fine sea salt and ¼ teaspoon of ground black pepper. Place the chicken into the pan, and cook for 2 to 3 minutes per side, or until browned. Transfer to a plate. 4. Mix the diced tomatoes and water in the pan, and deglaze by scraping the bottom. 5. Add the asparagus, pitted olives, ½ teaspoon fine sea salt, and ¼ teaspoon ground black pepper. Mix to combine. 6. Transfer the thighs back into the pan, and turn the heat off. 7. Place the oven-proof pan into the oven, and bake for 20 minutes, or until the chicken is fully cooked. Carefully remove the chicken from the oven, sprinkle with chopped cilantro, and serve hot.
Per Serving: Calories 352; Fat 17g; Sodium 1087mg; Carbs 9g; Fiber 3g; Sugar 5g; Protein 41g

Almond Butter Gingered Chicken

Prep time: 15 minutes | Cook time: 10 minutes | Serves: 2

2 teaspoons olive oil	1 teaspoon ginger, grated
1 tablespoon garlic, crushed, divided	3 tablespoons unsalted almond butter
½ cup brown onion, finely chopped	4 tablespoons water
8 ounces lean ground chicken	6 large iceberg lettuce leaves

1. Heat the olive oil in a heavy bottom pan over medium heat until hot. Add half of the crushed garlic and the chopped onion, and cook for 1 to 2 minutes, until translucent. 2. Add the ground chicken, breaking it up with a fork, and allow to cook for 5 minutes, until golden and cooked through. 3. In a small mixing bowl, add together the grated ginger, remaining crushed garlic, almond butter, and water, and mix to combine. Add the almond butter mixture to the chicken mixture, and cook for 1 minute until the flavors have combined. 4. Divide the chicken mixture into the

iceberg lettuce cups, and serve.
Per Serving: Calories 377; Fat 27g; Sodium 82mg; Carbs 11g; Fiber 4g; Sugar 4g; Protein 26g

Glazed Vegetable Turkey Loaf

Prep time: 15 minutes | Cook time: 55 minutes | Serves: 4

For the meatloaf:	1 tablespoon oregano, chopped
2 cups vegetable medley, cut smaller if needed	1 tablespoon cilantro, finely chopped
12 ounces lean ground turkey	Cooking spray
½ cup whole-wheat breadcrumbs	For the glaze:
¼ cup fat-free evaporated milk	1 tablespoon ketchup
¼ teaspoon ground black pepper	1 tablespoon organic honey
2 tablespoons ketchup	1 tablespoon whole-grain mustard

For the meatloaf: 1. Heat your oven to 350°F. 2. Steam the vegetable medley until fully cooked. 3. In a large mixing bowl, add together the steamed vegetables, ground turkey, whole-wheat breadcrumbs, evaporated milk, ground black pepper, ketchup, chopped oregano, and chopped cilantro. Mix to combine. 4. Prepare a loaf pan and spritz it with non-stick cooking spray, and press the meatloaf mixture evenly into the pan.
For the glaze: 1. In a small mixing bowl, add together the ketchup, organic honey, and whole-grain mustard, and mix to combine. Brush the turkey meatloaf with the glaze on the top. 2. Bake it in your oven for 45–55 minutes, or until the juices run clear when you press the top. Allow standing for 5 minutes. 3. Cut into eight even slices. Serve two slices on each plate.
Per Serving: Calories 1162; Fat 117g; Sodium 325mg; Carbs 20g; Fiber 2g; Sugar 9g; Protein 19g

Italian Chicken and Veggie Rice

Prep time: 15 minutes | Cook time: 20 minutes | Serves: 4

1 pound chicken breasts, bone and skin removed, halved lengthwise	2 tablespoons avocado oil, divided
½ teaspoon Italian seasoning	4 cups broccoli rice
½ teaspoon fine sea salt	1 (15-ounce) can artichoke hearts, drained
¼ teaspoon ground black pepper	¼ cup capers

1. Season the chicken with Italian seasoning, fine sea salt, and ground black pepper. 2. Warm 1 tablespoon of avocado oil in a large, heavy-bottom pan, over medium-high heat. 3. Add the seasoned chicken breasts, and cook for 3 to 5 minutes, or until browned. 4. Flip them to the other side. 5. Cook the chicken for 3 to 5 minutes, or until fully cooked. Transfer onto a cutting board and thinly slice the chicken. 6. Heat the remaining 1 tablespoon avocado oil in the same pan. Add the broccoli rice, and cook for 5 to 8 minutes, frequently stirring, until tender. 7. Add the artichoke hearts and capers, and mix until fully incorporated. Remove from the heat. 8. Serve the broccoli rice and vegetables, and top with the sliced chicken breasts.
Per Serving: Calories 591; Fat 30g; Sodium 1535mg; Carbs 44g; Fiber 9g; Sugar 8g; Protein 38g

Turkey and Green Beans Fry

Prep time: 15 minutes | Cook time: 15 minutes | Serves: 2

2 teaspoons olive oil
3 teaspoons garlic, minced
1½ cups green beans, cut into pieces
1 tablespoon unsalted cashew nuts, roughly chopped
8 ounces turkey breast, cut into 6 strips
¼ teaspoon ground black pepper
1 tablespoon parsley, finely chopped

1. Over medium heat, add the olive oil to a suitable frying pan and heat up. Add the minced garlic, and fry for 1 to 2 minutes, until fragrant and translucent. 2. Add the cut green beans and chopped cashews, and cook for 3 minutes until the green beans begin to soften. 3. Add the turkey strips, and season with ground black pepper and chopped parsley. Cook them for 10 minutes, occasionally stirring, until the turkey is white and cooked through. 4. Divide the mixture between two plates, and serve with steamed or roasted vegetables. Serve warm.
Per Serving: Calories 276; Fat 15g; Sodium 72mg; Carbs 8g; Fiber 2.5g; Sugar 1g; Protein 27g

Berry-But Chicken

Prep time: 15 minutes | Cook time: 30 minutes | Serves: 2

Aluminum foil
½ cup blueberries
2 tablespoons pine nuts
¼ cup basil, finely chopped
2 tablespoons balsamic vinegar
¼ teaspoon ground black pepper
2 (4-ounce) chicken breasts, butterflied

1. Heat the oven to 375°F. Line a medium-sized baking dish with aluminum foil. 2. In a medium-sized mixing bowl, add together the blueberries, pine nuts, chopped basil, balsamic vinegar, and ground black pepper. Mix until well combined. 3. Place the chicken pieces in a suitable baking dish, and pour the blueberry mixture on top. 4. Bake the meal in your oven for 20 to 30 minutes, or until the juices are caramelized and the inside of the chicken is fully cooked. 5. Serve warm with a side dish of your choice.
Per Serving: Calories 268; Fat 11g; Sodium 77mg; Carbs 17g; Fiber 1.2g; Sugar 15.5g; Protein 24g

Sesame Turkey Wraps

Prep time: 15 minutes | Cook time: 20 minutes | Serves: 4

For the sauce:
1 small jalapeno, halved, seeds removed, minced
1 tablespoon garlic, crushed
3 tablespoons organic honey
½ cup water
½ tablespoon low-sodium soy sauce
2 tablespoons lemon juice
For the turkey:
1 tablespoon sesame oil
1 tablespoon ginger, grated
1 tablespoon garlic, crushed
12 ounces boneless, skinless turkey breasts, cut into strips
1 tablespoon low-sodium soy sauce
1 tablespoon sesame seeds
For the wrap:
4 large lettuce leaves
8 basil leaves, roughly chopped
2 cups Napa cabbage, julienned

For the sauce: In a medium-sized stockpot, combine the minced jalapeno, crushed garlic, organic honey, water, soy sauce, and lemon juice. Mix them well, and bring to a boil over high heat. Remove from the heat, and allow to sit for 3 to 5 minutes. Chill the sauce in the fridge for 15 minutes or until cold.
For the turkey: 1. Heat the sesame oil in a large, heavy-bottom pan over medium heat. 2. Fry the crushed garlic and the grated ginger for 30 seconds, until lightly cooked. 3. Add the turkey strips, and fry for 5 to 8 minutes, or until fully cooked. Add the soy sauce and sesame seeds. Allow simmering. Turn off the heat. 4. Cover the pan with a lid.
For the wrap: Arrange a large lettuce leaf on a plate, and add ½ cup of the turkey mixture, 1 teaspoon chopped basil, and ½ cup julienned Napa cabbage. Fold the lettuce wrap together. Divide the sauce between the wraps.
Per Serving: Calories 209; Fat 6g; Sodium 298mg; Carbs 18g; Fiber 1g; Sugar 14g; Protein 22g

Chicken-Courgette Meatballs

Prep time: 15 minutes | Cook time: 15 minutes | Serves: 4

Aluminum foil
1-pound lean ground chicken
1 cup courgettes, shredded
½ cup red onion, finely diced
3 tablespoons black olives,
minced
1 tablespoon Mediterranean seasoning rub blend
1 cup grape tomatoes

1. Heat the oven to broil, and set an oven rack 6 inches from the broiler. Line a baking sheet with aluminum foil. 2. Combine the ground chicken, shredded courgettes, diced onion, minced black olives, and Mediterranean seasoning blend in a medium mixing bowl. Allow marinating for at least 10 minutes. 3. Mold each tablespoon of the chicken mixture into a meatball to make 8 in total, and place them on the baking sheet with the grape tomatoes. 4. Broil for 6 to 12 minutes, until golden brown and fully cooked. The tomatoes should be blistered. 5. Serve with your choice of side.
Per Serving: Calories 264; Fat 15g; Sodium 586mg; Carbs 4g; Fiber 0.8g; Sugar 1.5g; Protein 28g

Sesame Edamame

Prep time: 10 minutes | Cook time: 10 minutes | Serves: 4

1 (14-ounce) package frozen edamame in their shells
1 tablespoon canola or sunflower oil
1 tablespoon toasted sesame oil
3 garlic cloves, minced
½ teaspoon kosher salt
¼ teaspoon red pepper flakes (or more)

1. Bring a large pot of water to a boil over high heat. 2. Add the edamame to the pot, and cook for 2 to 3 minutes. 3. In a large skillet over medium heat, heat the canola oil, sesame oil, garlic, salt, and red pepper flakes for 1 to 2 minutes, and then remove the pan from the heat. 4. Drain the edamame and add them to the skillet and combine all of them. 5. Serve with the staple you like.
Per Serving: Calories 174; Fat 11.51g; Sodium 297mg; Carbs 9.52g; Fiber 4.9g; Sugar 2.63g; Protein 10.37g

Cannellini Bean Dip

Prep time: 10 minutes | Cook time: 5 minutes | Serves: 4

1 (15-ounce) can cannellini beans, rinsed and drained
2 tablespoons extra-virgin olive oil
1 garlic clove, peeled
1 teaspoon finely chopped fresh
rosemary
Pinch cayenne pepper
Freshly ground black pepper
1 (7.5-ounce) jar marinated artichoke hearts, drained

1. In a food processor, blend the beans, oil, garlic, rosemary, cayenne pepper, and black pepper. 2. Add the artichoke hearts, and pulse until roughly chopped.
Per Serving: Calories 63; Fat 3.54g; Sodium 80mg; Carbs 7.59g; Fiber 4.3g; Sugar 0.91g; Protein 1.87g

Pomegranate Chickpea Fatteh

Prep time: 10 minutes | Cook time: 25 minutes | Serves: 8

2 (4-inch) whole-wheat pitas
4 tablespoons extra-virgin olive oil, divided
1 (15-ounce) can no-salt-added chickpeas, rinsed and drained
⅓ cup pine nuts
1 cup plain 1% yogurt
2 garlic cloves, minced
¼ teaspoon salt
½ cup pomegranate seeds (optional)

1. Turn on the oven and preheat it to 375°F. 2. Cut the pitas into 1-inch squares, and toss with 2 tablespoons of oil in a large bowl. Spread onto a rimmed baking sheet and bake, shaking the sheet now and then for 10 minutes. 3. At the same time, in a small saucepan, gently warm the chickpeas and 1 tablespoon of oil for 4 to 5 minutes over medium-low heat. 4. Toast the pine nuts in a skillet with the remaining 1 tablespoon of oil for 4 to 5 minutes over medium heat until golden brown. 5. Combine the yogurt with the garlic and salt in a small bowl. 6. Transfer the toasted pitas to a wide serving bowl and top them with the chickpeas. 7. Drizzle the pitas with the yogurt mixture, then top them with the pine nuts and pomegranate seeds.

Per Serving: Calories 205; Fat 9.58g; Sodium 182mg; Carbs 24.13g; Fiber 5.5g; Sugar 6.65g; Protein 7.59g

Crispy Kale Chips

Prep time: 20 minutes | Cook time: 15 minutes | Serves: 4

1 bunch curly kale
2 teaspoons extra-virgin olive oil
¼ teaspoon kosher salt
¼ teaspoon garlic powder (optional)

1. Turn on the oven and preheat it to 325°F. Line a rimmed baking sheet with parchment paper. 2. Remove the tough stems from the kale, and tear the leaves into squares about the size of big potato chips. 3. Transfer the kale to a large bowl, and drizzle with the oil. Massage with your fingers for 1 to 2 minutes to coat well. Spread out on the baking sheet. 4. Cook for 8 minutes, then toss and cook for another 7 minutes. Take them out after 5 minutes. 5. Sprinkle with salt and garlic powder. Enjoy immediately.
Per Serving: Calories 18; Fat 1.13g; Sodium 171mg; Carbs 1.61g; Fiber 0.6g; Sugar 0.38g; Protein 0.76g

Tortilla Chips

Prep time: 15 minutes | Cook time: 15 minutes | Serves: 4

1 tablespoon canola or sunflower oil
4 medium whole-wheat tortillas
⅛ teaspoon coarse salt

1. Turn on the oven and preheat it to 350°F. 2. Brush the oil onto both sides of each tortilla. 3. Stack them on a large chopping block, and cut the entire stack at once, cutting the stack into 8 wedges of each tortilla. Transfer the tortilla pieces to a rimmed baking sheet. Sprinkle a little salt over each chip. 4. Bake the chips for 10 minutes; flip the chips, and bake for another 3 to 5 minutes. 5. Serve and enjoy.
Per Serving: Calories 157; Fat 7.4g; Sodium 287mg; Carbs 18.81g; Fiber 4g; Sugar 1g; Protein 4g

Spicy Guacamole Sauce

Prep time: 5 minutes | Cook time: 0 minute | Serves: 4

1 ripe avocado, peeled, pitted, and mashed
1½ tablespoons freshly squeezed lime juice
1 tablespoon minced jalapeño pepper, or to taste
1 tablespoon minced red onion
1 tablespoon chopped fresh cilantro
1 garlic clove, minced
⅛ to ¼ teaspoon kosher salt
Freshly ground black pepper

1. Combine all the ingredients in a large bowl. 2. Serve the dish you like with this sauce.
Per Serving: Calories 90; Fat 7.42g; Sodium 82mg; Carbs 6.69g; Fiber 3.8g; Sugar 1.12g; Protein 1.39g

Marinated Berries with Mints

Prep time: 25 minutes | Cook time: 0 minute | Serves: 4

2 cups fresh strawberries, hulled and quartered
1 cup fresh blueberries (optional)
2 tablespoons sugar
1 tablespoon balsamic vinegar

2 tablespoons chopped fresh mint (optional)
⅛ teaspoon freshly ground black pepper

1. In a large nonreactive bowl, gently toss the strawberries, sugar, vinegar, pepper, blueberries (optional), and mint (optional). 2. Let the flavors blend together for more than 25 minutes.
Per Serving: Calories 63; Fat 0.34g; Sodium 2mg; Carbs 15.63g; Fiber 2.4g; Sugar 11.72g; Protein 0.79g

Carrots Black Bean Soup

Prep time: 15 minutes | Cook time: 20 minutes | Serves: 10

8 ounces slab or thick-cut bacon, cut into ¼" pieces
1 large red onion
2 medium carrots, scrubbed, coarsely chopped
6 garlic cloves smashed
2½ teaspoons kosher salt, divided, plus more
3 canned chipotle chiles in adobo,

sliced crosswise, liquid reserved, plus 1 tablespoon adobo sauce
2 teaspoons dried oregano
1 teaspoon ground cumin
1-pound dried black beans, rinsed
2 tablespoons fresh lime juice
Sour cream, corn chips, cilantro leaves, and lime wedges (for serving)

1. Cook bacon in the Instant Pot on the Sauté mode, and cook the bacon for 6 to 8 minutes, turning periodically. 2. At the same time, chop the onion into quarters and keep one aside. Chop the remaining onion coarsely. Add onion, carrots, and garlic to Instant Pot, season with a generous teaspoon of salt, and cook on Sauté, turning periodically, for 6 to 8 minutes. 3. Cook, all the time stirring for about 1 minute. Pour in the beans, 2 teaspoon salt, and 2 quarts of water. Lock the cover and simmer the soup for 20 minutes on high pressure. Manually release the pressure. Add some seasoning according to personal preference. 4. At the same time, slice the saved onion and set it aside in a small bowl. Add the lime juice and the remaining 12 teaspoons salt. 5. Purée the soup in the pot with an immersion blender until smooth (or, working in batches, purée with a standard blender). 6. Divide the soup among the bowls. Sour cream, corn chips, cilantro, and drained pickled onions go on top. Serve alongside lime wedges for squeezing.
Per Serving: Calories 128; Fat 9.39g; Sodium 519mg; Carbs 7.96g; Fiber 1.7g; Sugar 3.54g; Protein 3.89g

Beef Stew with Dijon & Tomato

Prep time: 15 minutes | Cook time: 20 minutes | Serves: 1

2 tablespoons extra-virgin olive oil
3 pounds boneless beef chuck
Coarse salt and freshly ground pepper
2 or 4 cups water
1-pound white mushrooms, trimmed and halved or quartered

if large
2 medium onions, finely chopped
1 medium carrot, finely chopped
1 celery stalk, finely chopped
2 garlic cloves, coarsely chopped
1 can (28 ounces) of whole tomatoes
¼ cup Dijon mustard

1. In a 6- to 8-quart stovetop pressure cooker set, heat the oil to medium-high heat to sauté. Pat dries the beef and season it with 112 tablespoons salt and 34 teaspoon pepper. Working in batches, brown the meat on both sides for 6 to 8 minutes, replace to a platter. 2. Scrape up brown parts with a wooden spoon and add 1 cup of water to the pressure cooker. For the cooktop, add 3 cups additional water, and for electric, add 1 cup more water. Mushrooms, onions, carrots, celery, garlic, tomatoes (with juices), mustard, and 12 teaspoon salt are all good additions. 3. Stovetop: Close the cover. Over medium-high heat, bring to high pressure; lower heat to maintain pressure and cook for 60 minutes. Turn the heat, quickly relieve the pressure, and open the lid. 4. Remove any fat from the surface.
Per Serving: Calories 294; Fat 13.08g; Sodium 280mg; Carbs 6.92g; Fiber 2.1g; Sugar 3.37g; Protein 38.91g

Beef Chuck Roast Stew

Prep time: 15 minutes | Cook time: 20 minutes | Serves: 10

1 pound beef chuck roast
All-purpose flour for coating beef
Kosher salt and freshly ground black Pepper
4 garlic cloves, minced
1 cup halved cremini mushrooms
1 teaspoon Worcestershire sauce, plus more to taste

2 cups beef broth
Fresh flat-leaf parsley, chopped, for garnish
Cooked white rice for serving
2 to 3 potatoes, cut into chunks
3 to 4 carrots
Olive oil
1 stick celery, cut into chunks
12 or so pearl onions, peeled

1. Season the meat well with salt and pepper, and then coat the meat with flour. 2. In a large pan, heat olive oil over medium-high heat and sear steak on both sides for about 5 to 7 minutes. 3. Place the meat in the slow cooker; add Carrots, celery, potatoes, onions, garlic, and mushrooms to the slow cooker. 4. Add Pepper, salt, and Worcestershire sauce to taste. Add the broth and gently whisk everything together. 5. Cook the food for 8 to 10 hours on low. As desired, adjust the spices and gravy consistency. 6. Garnish with parsley and serve over rice.
Per Serving: Calories 183; Fat 4.47g; Sodium 112mg; Carbs 23.5g; Fiber 2.9g; Sugar 3.19g; Protein 14.04g

Kimchi Beef Stew

Prep time: 15 minutes | Cook time: 20 minutes | Serves: 6

1 pound beef (preferably a fatty cut), cut into 2-inch cubes
2 cups prepared kimchi
2 cups water
1 cup chopped yellow onions
1 tablespoon gochutgaru (Korean ground red pepper) or ½ teaspoon cayenne pepper
1 tablespoon gochujang (Korean red chili paste)

½ teaspoon sugar
Salt
½ cup sliced scallions for serving
8 ounces semi-firm tofu
1 cup dried shiitake mushrooms
1 tablespoon minced garlic
1 tablespoon minced fresh ginger
1 tablespoon toasted sesame oil
1 tablespoon dark soy sauce

1. Combine the beef, onions, mushrooms, garlic, kimchi, water, ginger, sesame oil, soy sauce, gochutgaru, gochujang, and sugar in the Instant Pot. 2. Place the pot's lid on. Shut off the pressure release valve. Select MANUAL and set the pressure cooker too HIGH for 15 minutes. Let the pot rest until the pressure has been released. 3. Add some salt and pepper according to personal preference. Stir in the scallions.
Per Serving: Calories 225; Fat 12.42g; Sodium 265mg; Carbs 7.57g; Fiber 2.4g; Sugar 2.44g; Protein 23.28g

Healthy Lentil and Sausage Stew

Prep time: 15 minutes | Cook time: 20 minutes | Serves: 6

2 cups green or brown lentils	1 tablespoon flour
salt, to taste	1 (28-ounce) can have chopped
2 tablespoons butter or olive oil, divided	tomatoes
	cheese, grated (optional)
2 sticks of celery, chopped	4 sausages
1 green bell pepper, chopped	1 onion, chopped
2 cloves of garlic, minced	2 carrots, chopped

1. Boil lentils and 6 cups of water in a pot over medium heat. Add ½ teaspoon of salt to the water containing the lentils. 2. After boiling, reduce to low heat and cook for 20 minutes. Remove from the heat and drain. Taste and adjust the seasoning as required. 3. Preheat your oven to 375° F. 4. When the lentils are cooking, melt one tablespoon of butter in a separate big saucepan over medium heat. 5. Sear the cooked sausages for 5 minutes or the fresh sausage for 15 minutes, turning once to brown on all sides. 6. Transfer the sausages to a dish. 7. Add the onion, carrots, celery, and green pepper to the saucepan and sauté for 5 minutes; sprinkle a pinch of salt over everything, around ½ teaspoon at first. 8. When the veggies are cooked and the onion is transparent, add the garlic and simmer for another 2 minutes, stirring all the time. 9. Finally, sprinkle the flour over everything and toss until the veggies and oil fully absorb it. 10. Stir together the chopped tomatoes and cooked lentils in the saucepan. Allow it to simmer for approximately 5 minutes. 11. Return the sausage to the saucepan and slice it into bite-sized pieces, stir well. 12. Transfer the food to the baking sheet, top them with the cheese, and then bake them in the preheated oven for 20 minutes until the cheese is fully melted. 13. Serve and enjoy.
Per Serving: Calories 137; Fat 6.39g; Sodium 423mg; Carbs 17.79g; Fiber 4.7g; Sugar 5.96g; Protein 5.87g

Tomatillo Stew

Prep time: 15 minutes | Cook time: 20 minutes | Serve: 4

2 medium jalapeños (halved and seeded for less heat, if you prefer)	1 (15-ounce) can of black beans
8 ounces canned diced green chiles	crushed corn chips for serving
	Freshly chopped cilantro, for serving
½-pound (about five medium) tomatillos, husked and washed, quartered	4 cups low-sodium vegetable broth, divided
1 cup fresh cilantro leaves and stems	2 tablespoons olive oil
	1 large yellow onion, diced
Kosher salt	2 garlic cloves smashed and chopped
1 (15-ounce) can of pinto beans	2 teaspoons ground cumin

1. Purée jalapenos, green chiles, tomatillos, and cilantro with ½ cup vegetable broth in a blender. Scrape the mixture into the slow cooker's bowl. 2. Heat the oil in a medium skillet over medium heat. Cook the onion and garlic until soft, then Add some salt and pepper consistent with personal preference. 3. Scrape the mixture into the slow cooker's bowl. 4. Combine the remaining broth and beans in a mixing bowl. Add some salt and pepper according to personal preference. Cook on high for 3 to 4 hours, in a slow cooker with a cover. 5. Remove the cover from the slow cooker and mash the beans with a potato masher to smash them and thicken the stew. Cook for another 15 minutes on high, stirring now and then. 6. Serve the soup in dishes, topped with smashed chips and cilantro. 7. Serve with slices of lime.

Per Serving: Calories 298; Fat 15g; Sodium 880mg; Carbs 36g; Fiber 10.6g; Sugar 9g; Protein 11.11g

Coconut Egg Stew

Prep time: 15 minutes | Cook time: 20 minutes | Serves: 8

8 large eggs	1 lime, finely zested, then juiced
2 tablespoons coconut oil	
1 large onion, diced	sea salt, for serving
1 large red bell pepper, diced	Pinch of each kosher salt and red pepper flakes, plus more to taste
1 (14.5-ounce) can dice or whole tomatoes (cut up into small pieces with kitchen shears)	
	4 large garlic cloves, minced
1 (14-ounce) can of unsweetened coconut milk	1 tablespoon minced fresh ginger
½ to 2 cups long-grain rice	2 teaspoons sweet paprika
½ cup finely chopped cilantro	

1. Bring a large pot of water to a boil, season with 1 tablespoon of salt, and set aside. Carefully lower the eggs into the boiling water. Cook for 6 minutes for soft yolks or 7 minutes for slightly tougher yolks, increasing heat to keep a moderate boil. 2. Transfer eggs to a dish of cold water and freeze for 2 minutes before peeling. 3. Combine the onion, red bell pepper, and a couple of pinches of salt in a mixing bowl. 4. Combine the garlic, ginger, red pepper flakes, and sweet paprika in another mixing bowl. 5. Mix the tomatoes, coconut milk, ½ cup cilantro, and lime zest in the third bowl. 6. Melt the coconut oil over medium heat in a large saucepan to prepare the stew. 7. Add the onion mixture to the saucepan and cook until softened, stirring periodically. 8. Add the garlic mixture to the saucepan and cook for another minute, often stirring, until aromatic. 9. Add the tomato mixture to the saucepan and simmer the food for 10 minutes to let all the flavors mingle. 10. Add some seasoning according to personal preference; add a few red pepper flakes to taste if desired. Cook the food for 1 minute more or so to warm the peeled eggs completely. 11. Turn off the heat and season each egg with a couple of pinches of sea salt. 12. Spoon the eggs and sauce over a mound of rice, and sprinkle with cilantro, then enjoy.
Per Serving: Calories 189; Fat 8.71g; Sodium 77mg; Carbs 23.28g; Fiber 2.6g; Sugar 3.17g; Protein 5.76g

Pumpkin Latte

Prep time: 5 minutes | Cook time: 10 minutes | Serve: 1

½ cup brewed espresso or 1 cup brewed strong coffee	½ teaspoon ground turmeric
	½ teaspoon ground cinnamon, plus more if needed
¼ cup canned pumpkin purée	
1 teaspoon vanilla extract	1 cup 1% milk
1 teaspoon sugar	

1. In a medium saucepan, combine the espresso, pumpkin, vanilla, sugar, turmeric, and cinnamon over medium heat, whisking now and then. 2. In a small pan, warm the milk over low heat. When it is warm whisk it vigorously to make it foamy. 3. Pour the hot coffee mixture into a mug, top them with the frothy milk, and sprinkle with more cinnamon.
Per Serving: Calories 154; Fat 2.63g; Sodium 114mg; Carbs 22.22g; Fiber 2.8g; Sugar 17.76g; Protein 9.24g

Homemade Cassoulet

Prep time: 15 minutes | Cook time: 20 minutes | Serves: 4

4 tablespoons olive oil, divided
4 sweet Italian sausages (about 1 pound total)
1 onion (any color), chopped
2 (15.5-ounce) cans of cannellini or white northern beans (undrained)
1 cup water
1 teaspoon white wine vinegar

1 cup panko, coarse fresh breadcrumbs, or cracker crumbs
⅓ cup chopped fresh parsley
1 stalk celery, thinly sliced
2 garlic cloves smashed and chopped
Kosher salt
Freshly ground black Pepper

1. In a medium pan, heat two tablespoons of the oil over medium-high heat. Prick the sausages all over with the point of a knife. Cook, periodically rotating for 5 to 7 minutes. Place on a chopping board. 2. Season the onion, celery, and garlic with salt and Pepper in the pan. Cook, often stirring, for 5 minutes. Add some salt and pepper according to personal preference and add the beans, liquid, and water. Heat it until it is boiling. Return the sausages to the skillet. Remove it carefully from the heat and stir in the vinegar. 3. Preheat the broiler with the top rack in place. Stir together panko, parsley, and the remaining two tablespoons of olive oil in a small basin. Season the breadcrumbs with salt and pepper and sprinkle over the beans and pork. Place the pan in the oven and broil Allow cooling for a few minutes before serving.
Per Serving: Calories 276; Fat 19.43g; Sodium 688mg; Carbs 16.81g; Fiber 4.5g; Sugar 7.28g; Protein 11.09g

Curry Carrot Soup

Prep time: 10 minutes | Cook time: 30 minutes | Serves: 6

2 tablespoons vegetable oil
2 cups water
1 onion

4 cups vegetable broth
1 tablespoons curry powder
2-pound carrots

1. Take a pot and place in oil over medium heat. 2. Place in the onion and cook until softened. 3. Place in the curry powder by stirring. 4. Add in the carrots and shake them well until carrots are completely rubbed in them. 5. Place in the vegetable broth and let it simmer for about 20 minutes. 6. Move the mixture to the blender and blend until smooth. 7. Again, transfer it to the pot and add water consistent with your consistency.
Per Serving: Calories 119; Fat 5.06g; Sodium 129mg; Carbs 18.53g; Fiber 5.1g; Sugar 8.97g; Protein 1.76g

Creamy Sweet Potato Soup

Prep time: 10 minutes | Cook time: 35 minutes | Serves: 6

2 tablespoons butter
Salt and pepper
1 onion
¾ cup milk
2 celery ribs
¼ cup heavy cream

One medium leek
¼ teaspoon ground nutmeg
½ pound sweet potatoes
1 cinnamon stick
4 cups chicken stock

1. Place the butter in the pot over medium heat—Cook onion for 3 to 4 minutes. 2. Cook in the leeks and celery for 5 minutes. Place in garlic and cook for 1 minute. 3. Place in nutmeg, sweet potatoes, cinnamon sticks, and chicken stock. Boil it to high heat. 4. Now reduce the heat and simmer with an open-top until sweet potatoes are soft. 5. Eliminate the cinnamon stick and blend it well in the blender. 6. Place the cream and milk in the soup. Add some

salt and pepper according to personal preference. To thinner the soup, add more water and serve in the bowls.
Per Serving: Calories 133; Fat 7.98g; Sodium 103mg; Carbs 11.98g; Fiber 3.1g; Sugar 3.87g; Protein 5.84g

Beef and Vegetable Stew

Prep time: 15 minutes | Cook time: 20 minutes | Serves: 8

2 pounds boneless beef chuck, cut into one ½-inch piece
5 or 6 medium green Anaheim chiles, seeded and cut into 1-inch pieces
One large eggplant, cut into one ½-inch piece
7 cups water
¼ cup plus three tablespoons

sweet or hot Turkish pepper paste or tomato paste, or a combination
1 teaspoon sugar
2 teaspoons fine sea salt
1 large onion, coarsely chopped
6 garlic cloves (or to taste), coarsely chopped
1 small carrot, peeled and grated
3 large tomatoes, cut into eighths

1. Turn on the oven and preheat it to 425°F with a rack in the center. 2. Cover the bottom of a large skillet with the meat. Spread the onion, garlic, and carrot over the meat and then add the remaining veggies. 3. Combine the water, pepper and tomato pastes, sugar, and salt in a medium mixing bowl, stirring to dissolve the paste. Pour the sauce over the stew. Bring the liquid to a boil in a saucepan over high heat without stirring. 4. Transfer the pot to the oven and simmer the stew, uncovered, for 3 ½ hours; stir once after 1 ½ hours. If all the ingredients are still immersed in liquid after 3 ½ hours, increase the heat to 450°F and cook for 20 to 30 minutes. 5. Remove the stew from the oven, cover, and let sit for 30 minutes, then heat or cool before placing in the refrigerator or freezer.
Per Serving: Calories 211; Fat 7.65g; Sodium 389mg; Carbs 11.18g; Fiber 2.9g; Sugar 6.1g; Protein 26.13g

Manchego Crackers

Prep time: 15 minutes, plus 1 hour to chill dough | Cook time: 15 minutes | Serves: 40

4 tablespoons unsalted butter, at room temperature
1 cup finely shredded Manchego cheese
1 cup almond flour

1 teaspoon low-sodium salt, divided
¼ teaspoon freshly ground black pepper
1 large egg

1. Using an electric mixer, cream together the butter and shredded cheese until well combined and smooth. 2. In a small bowl, combine the almond flour with ½ teaspoon salt and pepper. Slowly add the almond flour mixture to the cheese, mixing constantly until the dough just comes together to form a ball. 3. Transfer to a piece of parchment or plastic wrap and roll into a cylinder log about 1½ inches thick. Wrap tightly and refrigerate for at least 1 hour. 4. Preheat the oven to 350°F. Line two baking sheets with parchment paper or silicone baking mats. 5. To make the egg wash, in a regular bowl, mix together the egg and remaining ½ teaspoon salt. 6. Slice the refrigerated dough into small rounds, about ¼ inch thick, and place on the lined baking sheets. 7. Brush the tops of the crackers with egg wash and bake for 12 to 15 minutes until the crackers are golden and crispy. Remove from the oven and allow to cool on a wire rack. 8. Serve warm or, once fully cooled, store in an airtight container in the refrigerator for up to 1 week.
Per Serving: Calories 107; Fat 10.06g; Sodium 415mg; Carbs 0.59g; Fiber 0g; Sugar 0.39g; Protein 3.64g

White Bean Stew

Prep time: 15 minutes | Cook time: 20 minutes | Serve: 4

12 ounces navy beans
6 strips thick-cut bacon
¼ cup white onion, diced
6 tablespoons parsley, chopped fine
Salt
Pepper
1 bunch Swiss chard leaves, chopped

Fresh-squeezed lemon juice
Olive oil
Parmesan cheese, grated
28 ounces chopped tomatoes, drained
1 tablespoon black peppercorn (optional)
4 garlic cloves, peeled
3 sprigs thyme

1. Soak beans overnight, more than 6 hours, after rinsing them and removing any stones or dead-looking beans. Rinse and drain. 2. Crisp bacon in a heavy bottom pan or pot. Pour out all except one tablespoon of the bacon grease and drain on a separate dish—sweat onions in the oil for 2 to 3 minutes, or until transparent. 3. Drain most of the liquid from the tomatoes and put it back to the skillet, stirring to be softened. 4. Take the pan off the heat and set it aside. 5. At the same time, combine 8 cups of lukewarm water, whole, peeled garlic cloves, thyme, and peppercorns in a large saucepan. Bring to a boil, lower to low heat, and continue to cook for 20 to 40 minutes. Check periodically and taste more than 5 to 6 beans at a time; add the tomato and onion combination, along with the bacon bean pot. 6. Return to the simmering pot. Remove from fire when beans are cooked through but still firm, and discard thyme sprigs, garlic cloves, and any peppercorns you can reach. 7. Add three tablespoons of minced parsley and combine well—add some salt and pepper according to personal preference. 8. Fill each bowl with 1 cup of chopped Swiss chard and put on the top beans. Squeeze lemon over beans and put on the top remaining parsley, Parmesan, and olive oil.
Per Serving: Calories 123; Fat 4.96g; Sodium 547mg; Carbs 17.53g; Fiber 2.9g; Sugar 5g; Protein 5.76g

Easy Tomato Soup

Prep time: 10 minutes | Cook time: 30 minutes | Serves: 6

1 onion
Red pepper flakes
2 cloves garlic
¼ teaspoon oregano
28-ounce tomatoes

¼ teaspoon Celery seed
1 cup water
Black pepper
1 tablespoon sugar
Salt

1. Place the saucepan over medium heat and place in olive oil and butter. 2. Cook in the garlic and onion until soft for 5 minutes. 3. Bring it to a boil by putting in pepper, oregano, chili flakes, tomatoes, sugar, celery seeds, and water. Please set it to simmer for about fifteen minutes. 4. Remove it from the heat and transfer it to a blender. 5. Warm the soup over the heat and sprinkle some salt and pepper over your desire.
Per Serving: Calories 41; Fat 3.04g; Sodium 106mg; Carbs 9.26g; Fiber 2.1g; Sugar 5.97g; Protein 1.59g

Pie Pumpkin Soup

Prep time: 15 minutes | Cook time: 20 minutes | Serves: 4

2 whole pie pumpkins
16 ounces vegetable or chicken stock
salt to taste

⅓ cup maple syrup
½ cup heavy cream
dash of nutmeg

1. Turn on the oven and preheat it to 300°F. Roast the pumpkins on a baking sheet until they are shriveled and tender. Let it sit to cool before cutting in half and gently scooping out the seeds and pulp. Scoop the delectable meat into a dish. Place aside. 2. Heat the pumpkin flesh, stock, and maple syrup in a saucepan until it simmers. Mash the large lumps out of the mixture, then move to a blender or food processor and purée until silky smooth. Blend in the cream and nutmeg until fully mixed add some salt and pepper according to personal preference. 3. Serve!
Per Serving: Calories 233; Fat 8.08g; Sodium 301mg; Carbs 32.19g; Fiber 2.1g; Sugar 19.91g; Protein 9.45g

Chicken Orzo Soup

Prep time: 10 minutes | Cook time: 30 minutes | Serves: 6

2 tablespoons olive oil
2 tablespoons parsley leaves
1-pound boneless chicken
1 lemon juice
Kosher salt
Black pepper
1 spring rosemary
3 cloves garlic

¾ cup orzo pasta
½ teaspoon dried thyme
1 onion
2 bay leaves
3 carrots
5 cups chicken stocks
3 carrots
2 stalks celery

1. Take a stockpot and place olive oil over medium heat. Rub boneless chicken with black pepper and salt. 2. Place the rubbed chicken in the stockpot. Cook it for 2 to 3 minutes until it becomes golden. 3. Now again, heat the oil in the stockpot and cook celery, carrots, and onion by shaking it for 3 to 4 minutes. 4. Place in the thyme and shake it until fragrant. 5. Place in the water, chicken stock, and bay leaves, blend well, and boil. 6. Place the chicken, orzo, and rosemary until soft for 12 minutes by shaking. 7. Place in the parsley and lemon juice and combine well. Add some salt and pepper according to personal preference. 8. Serve.
Per Serving: Calories 216; Fat 8.11g; Sodium 172mg; Carbs 16.34g; Fiber 3.1g; Sugar 4.23g; Protein 20.82g

Quick and Easy Pot Roast Soup

Prep time: 10 minutes | Cook time: 40 minutes | Serves: 6

2 pounds Chuck roast
Salt and pepper
½ teaspoon kosher salt
1 teaspoon thyme
½ teaspoon black pepper
¼ cup tomato
2 tablespoons olive oil

4 cups low-sodium beef stock
1 onion
⅓ cup faro
3 carrots
4 cloves garlic
1 green pepper
2 stalks celery

1. Slice the beef into pieces with a knife and rub well with pepper and salt. 2. Place the pot over medium heat and place in the olive oil. 3. Place in the beef and sauté it to brown color. 4. Transfer the golden chicken to the plate and place the cooker over the heat. 5. Add celery, onion, green thyme, carrots, garlic, and pepper, and continuously shake and sauté it for 6 to 7 minutes. 6. Remove the veggies from the cooker and place the chicken in it again with barley, tomatoes, thyme, and beef stock. 7. Set the cooker's pressure with shut top and set the timer for 20 minutes. 8. Remove the pressure from the cooker and add the veggies to it back. 9. Set it to simmer to combine the veggies with chicken and sprinkle salt and pepper over them. 10. Transfer the soup into bowls and serve.
Per Serving: Calories 404; Fat 18.35g; Sodium 384mg; Carbs 23.47g; Fiber 2g; Sugar 4.27g; Protein 40.16g

Mustard Parsnip Soup

Prep time: 10 minutes | Cook time: 5 minutes | Serves: 6

1-pound bean salad combine	3 garlic cloves
½ cup cilantro	2 tablespoons white vinegar
1 teaspoon honey	1 tablespoon olive oil
¼ cup red onion	1 tablespoon mustard
½ teaspoon pepper and salt	

1. Wash and drain the legumes. 2. Place it in the bowl with cilantro and onion. 3. Take a bowl and combine garlic, honey, salt, mustard, garlic, and olive oil. 4. Place the dressing over the legume and toss them well. 5. Serve.
Per Serving: Calories 81; Fat 4.07g; Sodium 274mg; Carbs 9.31g; Fiber 2.6g; Sugar 3.03g; Protein 2.39g

Butternut Squash Soup

Prep time: 10 minutes | Cook time: 45 minutes | Serves: 6

One butternut squash	3 cloves garlic
¼ teaspoon cinnamon	15-ounce Coconut milk
2 tablespoons olive oil	¼ tablespoon Ginger
Cilantro	¾ cup onion
2 tablespoons olive oil	¾ teaspoon salt
2 cups vegetable broth	Cayenne pepper

1. Turn on the oven and preheat it. 2. Rub in both halves of the butternut squash with olive oil and salt. 3. Arrange the broth over the baking sheet, folded in the parchment paper. 4. Cook in the preheated oven for fifty minutes. 5. Heat the pot over medium heat. 6. Place in the olive oil and cook onion for 4 minutes. 7. Place in ginger and garlic and cook for more than 2 minutes. 8. Add in the cinnamon. Cayenne, broth, coconut milk, and salt combine them well. 9. Shut the skillet top and set it to simmer for 5 minutes. 10. Once done, remove the skin from the squash. 11. Place in the coconut milk mixture and squash in the blender. 12. Once blended utterly, transfer the soup back to the saucepan to warm the soup again. 13. Serve.
Per Serving: Calories 145; Fat 10.02g; Sodium 556mg; Carbs 12.72g; Fiber 2.8g; Sugar 4.25g; Protein 2.54g

Quick and Easy Pepperoni Pizza Soup

Prep time: 10 minutes | Cook time: 45 minutes | Serves: 6

¾ ounce pepperoni	1 small onion
¼ cup grated parmesan	Salt
16 medium mushrooms	1 teaspoon oregano
12 ounces jar marinara sauce	¼ cup torn fresh basil
3 garlic cloves	1 tablespoon olive oil
6 cups chicken broth	½ cup shredded mozzarella

1. Place the soup pot over medium heat, add the pepperoni, continuously shake and cook for 3 to 4 minutes. 2. Transfer the pepperoni with a slotted spoon, dry it. 3. Reduce the heat and place onions, garlic, oregano, and salt. 4. Sauté by shaking for 6 to 7 minutes. 5. Place in the marinara sauce, parmesan with shut top, and let it to boil. 6. Decrease the heat and sauté for fifteen more minutes. 7. Preheat the broiler over medium heat. 8. Arrange the bread over the baking sheet and apply the salt and oil over it. 9. Cook the bread by flipping it until crispy, spread the mozzarella over it for 2 minutes. 10. Transfer the soup into the bowls and

sprinkle mozzarella over it. 11. Serve.
Per Serving: Calories 147; Fat 6.44g; Sodium 509mg; Carbs 12.1g; Fiber 2g; Sugar 5.09g; Protein 12.48g

Unstuffed Cabbage Roll Soup

Prep time: 10 minutes | Cook time: 45 minutes | Serves:6

2-pound ground beef	1 head cabbage
2 teaspoons low-sodium salt	½ cup water
1 onion	14.5-ounce tomatoes
2 cloves garlic	8-ounce tomato sauce

1. Place the large skillet over medium heat. 2. Place in the onion and beef by stirring and sauté until brown for 5 to 7 minutes. 3. Sewer and remove the grease. 4. Place in the pepper, tomato sauce, cabbage, salt, water, and garlic and let it boil. 5. Slow the heat, shut the lid, and set it to simmer for 30 minutes. 6. Once done. Serve.
Per Serving: Calories 260; Fat 7.98g; Sodium 530mg; Carbs 14.16g; Fiber 3.4g; Sugar 7.71g; Protein 34.89g

Easy Stuffed Pepper Soup

Prep time: 10 minutes | Cook time: 40 minutes | Serves: 6

1 pound ground beef	One small onion
½ teaspoon oregano	14.5-ounce tomatoes
2 tablespoons olive oil	1 cup red chilies
½ teaspoon basil	15-ounce tomato sauce
Salt and black pepper	1 cup green bell pepper
½ tablespoons Chopped fresh parsley	2 garlic cloves
	1 cup brown rice

1. Place the pot over medium heat and place the olive oil in it. 2. Place the beef in it by continuously stirring to brown. 3. Strain the beef, pat dry, and set aside. 4. Now, again, Place the olive oil in the pot. 5. Cook in the green bell peppers, onion, and red bell peppers for 3 minutes. 6. Place in the garlic and sauté for more than 30 minutes. 7. Add the diced tomatoes, beef broth, oregano, basil, tomato sauce, and cooked beef, rub with salt and pepper. 8. Boil the mixture, reduce the heat, and set it to simmer for thirty minutes when continually shaking. 9. Cook the rice consistent with the given over the package. 10. Once done, transfer the soup into the bowls and place in the cooked rice. 11. Serve.
Per Serving: Calories 291; Fat 9.6g; Sodium 74mg; Carbs 32g; Fiber 3.2g; Sugar 3.6g; Protein 20.5g

Bacon Potato Soup

Prep time: 10 minutes | Cook time: 30 minutes | Serves: 6

8-ounce reduced sodium bacon	1 large leek
¼ cup parsley 1 large onion	½ teaspoon thyme
⅓ teaspoon blac k pepper	3 carrots
1 clove garlic	½ teaspoon rosemary
¾ teaspoon low-sodium salt	3 carrots
2 pounds waxy potatoes	6 cups low-sodium chicken broth
½ teaspoon marjoram	2 tomatoes

1. Take a pot and fry in the bacon. Cook in the onion until golden. 2. Cook in the garlic for 1 minute. 3. Place in all the except parsley and boil. 4. Decrease the heat and simmer it with the lid at the top for 30 to 40 minutes. 5. Place in the parsley and set to the simmer for 1 minute. 6. Sprinkle the salt and pepper over it.
Per Serving: Calories 362; Fat 16.75g; Sodium 599mg; Carbs 41.97g; Fiber 6.4g; Sugar 7.44g; Protein 14.15g

Thai Chicken Soup

Prep time: 10 minutes | Cook time: 30 minutes | Serves: 6

1 whole chicken	1 tablespoon fish sauce
3 shallots	½ bunch fresh cilantro
8 cups water	2 new green Thai chilies
4 fresh ginger	2 large lemongrass stalks
Coarse salt	1 strip lemon zest

1. Place a stockpot over medium heat. 2. Place in the chicken, salt, and water. Let it boil. 3. Decrease the heat and set it to simmer by adding ginger, garlic, lemongrass, shallots, lime zest, and cilantro; cook it for thirty minutes. 4. Remove the breast and set it to simmer for 30 minutes. 5. Drain the soup and discard the solids remaining thighs and legs. 6. Place in the soup to the stockpot. Cool the chicken and separate the skin from the bones. 7. Place the lemongrass, chilies, and ginger matchsticks in the soup. 8. Let it to simmer for ten minutes. Shake in the lemon juice and fish sauce. 9. Rub with the salt and apply the garnishing with cilantro. 10. Serve.
Per Serving: Calories 201; Fat 4.49g; Sodium 380mg; Carbs 5.18g; Fiber 0.4g; Sugar 1.5g; Protein 34.09g

Flavorful Veggie Soup

Prep time: 10 minutes | Cook time: 55 minutes | Serves: 6

2 tablespoons olive oil	4 garlic cloves
1 cup fresh peas	2 bay leaves
½ cup yellow onion	14½ ounces low-sodium chicken
½ cup green beans	broth
2 cups carrots	⅓ cup parsley
Black pepper and salt	14½ ounces tomatoes
¼ cup celery	1 cup potatoes
1⅛ teaspoons thyme	

1. Heat the oil in the pot over medium heat. 2. Cook in the celery, onions, and carrot for 4 minutes. 3. Cook in the garlic for 30 seconds. 4. Place salt, pepper, broth, bay leaves, tomatoes, potatoes, and rub. 5. Boil the mixture and place in the green beans. 6. Decrease the heat and simmer with cover top for 30 minutes. 7. Cook in the peas and corn for 5 minutes. 8. Once done, serve and enjoy.
Per Serving: Calories 119; Fat 6.09g; Sodium 87mg; Carbs 14.46g; Fiber 3.2g; Sugar 4.9g; Protein 3.44g

Simple Tuna Croquettes Recipe

Prep time: 40 minutes | Cook time: 25 minutes | Serves: 36

6 tablespoons extra-virgin olive oil, plus 1 to 2 cups	2 teaspoons minced capers
5 tablespoons almond flour, plus 1 cup, divided	½ teaspoon dried dill
1¼ cups heavy cream	¼ teaspoon freshly ground black pepper
1 (4-ounce) can olive oil-packed yellow fin tuna	2 large eggs
1 tablespoon chopped red onion	1 cup panko breadcrumbs (or a gluten-free version)

1. In a big frying pan, heat 6 tablespoons olive oil over medium-low heat. Add 5 tablespoons almond flour and cook, stirring constantly, until a smooth paste forms and the flour browns slightly, 2 to 3 minutes. 2. Increase the heat to medium-high and gradually add the heavy cream, whisking constantly until completely smooth and thickened, and another 4 to 5 minutes. 3. Remove from the heat and stir in the tuna, red onion, capers, dill, and pepper. 4. Transfer the mixture to an 8-inch square baking dish that is well coated with olive oil and allow to cool to room temperature. Cover and refrigerate until chilled, at least 4 hours or up to overnight. 5. To form the croquettes, set out three bowls. In one, beat together the eggs. In another, add the remaining almond flour. In the third, add the panko. Line a baking sheet with parchment paper. 6. Using a spoon, place about a tablespoon of cold prepared dough into the flour mixture and roll to coat. Shake off excess and, using your hands, roll into an oval. 7. Dip the croquette into the beaten egg, then lightly coat in panko. Set on lined baking sheet and repeat with the remaining dough. 8. In a small saucepan, heat the remaining 1 to 2 cups of olive oil, so that the oil is about 1-inch deep, over medium-high heat. The smaller the pan, the less oil you will need, but you will need more for each batch. 9. Test if the oil is ready by throwing a pinch of panko into pot. If it sizzles, the oil is ready for frying. If it sinks, it's not quite ready. 10. Once the oil is heated, fry the croquettes 3 or 4 at a time, depending on the size of your pan, removing with a slotted spoon when golden brown. You will need to adjust the temperature of the oil occasionally to prevent burning. If the croquettes get dark brown very quickly, lower the temperature. 11. Serve warm.
Per Serving: Calories 173; Fat 18.66g; Sodium 347mg; Carbs 0.94g; Fiber 0.1g; Sugar 0.17g; Protein 0.5g

Fried Mushrooms with Fennel and Cod Chowder

Prep time: 20minutes | Cook time: 35 minutes | Serves: 4

1 cup extra-virgin olive oil, divided	pepper
1 small head cauliflower, core removed and broken into florets (about 2 cups)	4 cups fish stock, plus more if needed
1 small white onion, thinly sliced	1-pound thick cod fillet, cut into ¾-inch cubes
1 fennel bulb, white part only, trimmed and thinly sliced	4 ounces' shiitake mushrooms, stems trimmed and thinly sliced (⅛-inch slices)
½ cup dry white wine (optional)	¼ cup chopped Italian parsley, for garnish (optional)
2 garlic cloves, minced	¼ cup plain Greek yogurt, for garnish (optional)
1 teaspoon low-sodium salt	
¼ teaspoon freshly ground black	

1. In large stockpot, heat ¼ cup olive oil over medium-high heat. Add the cauliflower florets, onion, and fennel and sauté for 10 to 12 minutes, or until almost tender. Add the white wine (optional), garlic, salt, and pepper and sauté for another 1 to 2 minutes. 2. Add 4 cups fish stock and bring to a boil. Cover the pot, reduce the heat to medium-low, and simmer for another 8 to 10 minutes until vegetables are very tender. Remove from the heat and allow to cool slightly. 3. Using an immersion blender, purée the vegetable mixture, slowly drizzling in ½ cup of olive oil, until very smooth and silky, adding additional fish stock if the mixture is too thick. 4. Turn the heat back to medium-high and bring the soup to a low simmer. Add the cod pieces and cook, covered, until the fish is cooked through, about 5 minutes. Get away from the heat and keep covered. 5. Heat the remaining ¼ cup olive oil over medium-high heat in a medium skillet. When very hot, add the mushrooms and fry until crispy. Get away from a slotted spoon and transfer to a plate, reserving the frying oil. Besides, toss the mushrooms with a sprinkle of salt. 6. Serve the chowder hot, topped with fried mushrooms and drizzled with 1 tablespoon reserved frying oil. If you are eager to decorate with chopped fresh parsley, adding 1 tablespoon of Greek yogurt may be a good choice.
Per Serving: Calories 437; Fat 28.56g; Sodium 696mg; Carbs 18.1g; Fiber 4.2g; Sugar 6.55g; Protein 29.4g

Easy Granola Bars

Prep time: 70 minutes | Cook time: None | Serves: 14

2 cups raw unsalted almonds, roughly chopped	2 tablespoons sesame seeds (black or white)
1 cup shelled pumpkin seeds	1 teaspoon black pepper
1 cup rolled old-fashioned oats	1 teaspoon dried rosemary
½ cup brown rice syrup	½ teaspoon dried thyme
½ cup dried cranberries	¼ teaspoon freshly ground black pepper
⅓ cup tahini	

1. Combine the pumpkin seeds, oats, brown rice syrup, almonds, tahini, sesame seeds, pepper, rosemary cranberries, black pepper and thyme in a big bowl. Mix well until combined. 2. Line an 8-by-8-inch baking pan with parchment paper and pour the mixture into the pan. 3. Press the mixture down firmly to form a well-packed layer. Refrigerate the mixture for at least 1 hour or freeze for 20 minutes. 4. Once set, get away the bars from the pan by lifting the edges of the parchment paper. Cut into 14 bars. 5. Keep this dish in an airtight container for up to 5 days.
Per Serving: Calories 263; Fat 18.74g; Sodium 203mg; Carbs 21.78g; Fiber 4.4g; Sugar 11.62g; Protein 9.01g

Creamy Potato Soup with Bacon

Prep time: 10 minutes | Cook time: 30 minutes | Serves: 6

6 slices reduced sodium bacon	1 tablespoon all-purpose flour
1 cup cheddar cheese	1 teaspoon salt
1 onion	4 cups low-sodium chicken broth
⅓ cup sour cream	1-pound potatoes
3 garlic cloves	1 cup milk
¼ teaspoon black pepper	

1. Place the saucepan over medium heat and cook in the bacon until brown. 2. Set aside the bacon and pat dry with a towel. 3. Place the oil in the pan and cook in the onion until tender. 4. Cook in the garlic and for 30 seconds. 5. Place in the flour and sauté for 4 minutes. 6. Add the milk, cream, chicken stock, and potatoes, and sprinkle pepper and salt over it. 7. Cook the broth over the simmer until soft. 8. Now, transfer the mixture into the blender and blend completely until smooth. 9. Now, Place in the sour cream and shredded cheese and shake well to combine. Place it back in the pan at medium flame. 10. Once done, serve and enjoy.
Per Serving: Calories 323; Fat 20.34g; Sodium 351mg; Carbs 21.71g; Fiber 2.1g; Sugar 3.94g; Protein 14.7g

Squash and Lentil Soup

Prep time: 10 minutes | Cook time: 40 minutes | Serves: 4

2 tablespoons olive oil	4 cups low-sodium vegetable stock
Natural yogurt	¼ teaspoon hot chili powder
2 onions	½ cup red lentils
1 bunch coriander	1 tablespoon ras el hanout
2 garlic cloves	
1 butternut squash	

1. Place the saucepan over medium heat. Place in the olive oil. 2. Cook in the onion by adding salt for 7 minutes. 3. Cook in the chili, ras el hanout, and garlic for 1 minute. 4. Place in the lentils and squash by shaking and rubbing the stock. 5. Boil the mixture, decrease the heat and simmer it for 25 minutes. 6. Blend and rub the soup and freeze. 7. Transfer the soup into the bowls and garnish with the coriander leaves. 8. Serve.
Per Serving: Calories 248; Fat 8.6g; Sodium 183mg; Carbs 35.64g; Fiber 5.6g; Sugar 10.78g; Protein 10.69g

Bean Soup

Prep time: 10 minutes | Cook time: 30 minutes | Serves: 4

2 tablespoons vegetable oil	10-ounce tomatoes
15-ounce pinto beans	1 yellow bell pepper
1 onion	15-ounce kidney beans
15-ounce black beans	14.5-ounce chicken broth
1 green bell pepper	

1. Take a saucepan and place it over medium heat. 2. Place in the yellow bell pepper, onion, and green bell pepper. 3. Sauté it until soft. 4. Place the chicken, kidney beans, tomatoes, pinto beans, and black beans broth by shaking. 5. Once done, serve and enjoy.
Per Serving: Calories 214; Fat 12.09g; Sodium 44mg; Carbs 22.73g; Fiber 6.1g; Sugar 5.4g; Protein 7.97g

Quinoa Veggie Soup

Prep time: 10 minutes | Cook time: 30 minutes | Serves: 6

2 tablespoons olive oil	3 garlic cloves
1 tablespoon lemon juice	½ teaspoon cumin
1 onion	15½ ounces Cannellini beans
8-ounce ribs removed leaves	1 zucchini
2 stalks celery	1 cup quinoa
8 cups low-sodium vegetable broth	14½ ounces tomatoes

1. Heat the olive oil in a pot over medium heat. 2. Cook in the garlic, celery, and onion and rub with the pepper and salt until tender. 3. Place the tomatoes, zucchini, quinoa, cumin, and beans and sauté for 13 minutes. 4. Place in the kale by shaking and sauté to wilt for one minute. 5. Place in the lemon juice and rub with the pepper, salt, and chili flakes. 6. Serve.
Per Serving: Calories 343; Fat 15.18g; Sodium 247mg; Carbs 39.42g; Fiber 6.2g; Sugar 11.02g; Protein 16.2g

Chicken Mushroom Soup

Prep time: 10 minutes | Cook time: 30 minutes | Serves: 4

1 tablespoon olive oil	¼ cup chopped shallots
¼ teaspoon freshly ground pepper	4 cups low-sodium chicken broth
2 cups mushroom	2 tablespoons parsley
¼ teaspoon salt	1 cup wild rice
¾ cup celery	½ cup sour cream
¼ teaspoon salt	1 cup cooked chicken
¾ cup carrots	
¼ cup all-purpose flour	

1. Heat olive oil in the saucepan over medium heat. 2. Cook in the shallots, mushrooms, and celery for 5 minutes. 3. Cook in pepper, salt, and flour for 1 more minute. 4. Place in the broth and allow it to boil. 5. Place in the rice and simmer with a shut top. 6. Cook until mixture is soft and shake in the parsley, sour cream, and turkey. 7. Sauté the food for 2 minutes. 8. Serve.
Per Serving: Calories 358; Fat 9.7g; Sodium 445mg; Carbs 45.91g; Fiber 4.3g; Sugar 3.94g; Protein 24.64g

Flavorful Sweet Potatoes Fries

Prep time: 10 minutes | Cook time: 35 minutes | Serves: 4

2 sweet potatoes	1 teaspoon low-sodium salt
¼ teaspoon cayenne pepper	1 teaspoon garlic powder
2 tablespoons Canola oil	1 teaspoon paprika

1. Turn on the oven and preheat it to 425°F. 2. Combine all the ingredients in a bowl. 3. Arrange the fries over the baking sheet in a single layer and bake in the oven for 40 minutes. 4. Serve.
Per Serving: Calories 124; Fat 7.14g; Sodium 37mg; Carbs 14.37g; Fiber 2.3g; Sugar 3.07g; Protein 1.26g

Easy Carrot Peach Soup

Prep time: 10 minutes | Cook time: 20 minutes | Serves: 3

1 large carrot	½ tablespoon lime juice
Salt and pepper	2 scallions
1 peach	⅕ cup water
⅕ cup coconut milk	

1. Pour the water into the pot and place it over medium heat. 2. Place in the scallions, carrot, and peach. Sauté it until veggies are soft. 3. Blend the mixture in the blender by adding salt, lime juice, and pepper until tender and thick. 4. Garnish with cilantro and serve.
Per Serving: Calories 76; Fat 4.07g; Sodium 79mg; Carbs 10.39g; Fiber 2.3g; Sugar 7.21g; Protein 1.46g

Onion and Carrot Soup

Prep time: 10 minutes | Cook time: 50 minutes | Serves: 8

1 tablespoon unsalted butter	1 teaspoon fresh thyme
2 cups water	2 garlic cloves
1 tablespoon olive oil	Black pepper
5 cups carrots	4 cups low-sodium chicken broth
1 onion	½ teaspoon salt
1 teaspoon thyme	½ cup fat-free half and half
1 stalk celery	

1. Place the pot over medium heat and place in the butter. 2. Cook in the celery and onion until soft for 6 minutes. 3. Place in the garlic and cook until fragrant. 4. Serve.
Per Serving: Calories 87; Fat 3.77g; Sodium 248mg; Carbs 11.16g; Fiber 2.3g; Sugar 4.76g; Protein 3.73g

Wild Rice Soup

Prep time: 10 minutes | Cook time: 60 minutes | Serves: 8

⅓ cup uncooked wild rice	½ cup unsalted butter
½ teaspoon rosemary	1 onion
1 tablespoon Canola oil	1 carrot
2 cups half and half, fat-free	1 celery rib
2 cups water	1 teaspoon low-sodium salt
½ cup all-purpose flour	

1. Add the oil, rice, and water to the saucepan and bring to a boil. 2. Decrease the heat, cover the pan and simmer the rice for 30 minutes. 3. Sauté the butter, onion, carrot, and butter in the skillet until soft. 4. Shake in the flour and blend by stirring for 2 minutes.

5. Minimize the heat and shake in the salt, cream, and rosemary. 6. Set it to simmer with an open-top until soft for 20 minutes.
Per Serving: Calories 213; Fat 14.25g; Sodium 68mg; Carbs 18.34g; Fiber 1.1g; Sugar 4.18g; Protein 3.64g

Lemon and Cannellini Bean Hummus

Prep time: 10 minutes | Cook time: 15 minutes | Serves: 10

15-ounce Cannellini beans	2 garlic cloves
⅛ teaspoon salt	¼ cup chives
1 tablespoon olive oil	⅛ teaspoon pepper
1 lemon zest	¼ cup parsley

1. Place all the ingredients in a food processor, start the food processor and combine the mixture. 2. Move the mixture to the bowl and place in the chopped chives and parsley. 3. Serve.
Per Serving: Calories 24; Fat 1.58g; Sodium 33mg; Carbs 2.57g; Fiber 0.9g; Sugar 0.5g; Protein 0.6g

Cheese Cupcakes

Prep time: 10 minutes | Cook time: 60 minutes | Serves: 12

12 gingersnaps	¼ cup sugar
1 teaspoon vanilla extract	6-ounce fat-free vanilla yogurt
8-ounce low-fat cream cheese	2 eggs
¼ cup sugar	2 teaspoons orange zest
1 teaspoon all-purpose flour	

1. Turn on the oven and preheat it to 350°F and spot the muffin cups over the muffin pan. 2. Spot the gingersnap in each muffin cup. 3. Take a bowl and combine vanilla, cream cheese, and sugar. 4. Place in the orange zest, egg whites, yogurt until mixed. 5. Fill the cupcake filler and bake in the oven for 25 minutes. 6. Once done, allow it to cool before serving.
Per Serving: Calories 208; Fat 6.78g; Sodium 244mg; Carbs 31.17g; Fiber 0.7g; Sugar 12.15g; Protein 5.67g

Black Beans Brownie Bites

Prep time: 10 minutes | Cook time: 30 minutes | Serves: 16

¾ cup low sodium black beans	1 teaspoon vanilla extract
½ cup packed brown sugar	⅓ teaspoon salt
¼ cup unsweetened apple sauce	¼ cup cocoa powder
1 egg	½ teaspoon baking soda
2 egg whites	⅓ cup whole wheat flour
¼ cup oil	
½ cup chocolate chips	

1. Turn on the oven and preheat it to 300 Fahrenheit. And brush the oil in the baking pan. 2. Blend applesauce, eggs, canola oil, and black beans in a bowl, Place the vanilla, sugar, and egg whites in it, and combine them well. 3. Take a bowl and whisk in the salt, cocoa powder, cocoa powder, flour, and baking powder in it. 4. Place the chocolate chips and sauté in the oven for 25 minutes. 5. Once done, allow it to cool and serve.
Per Serving: Calories 91; Fat 4.14g; Sodium 149mg; Carbs 12.24g; Fiber 1.5g; Sugar 7.31g; Protein 2.18g

Edamame Vegetable Hummus

Prep time: 10 minutes | Cook time: 15 minutes | Serves: 4

1 package frozen shelled edamame	¼ cup fresh mint
rice crackers	⅓ cup lemon juice
½ cup tahini	¼ cup olive oil
fresh vegetables	2 garlic cloves
½ cup water	1 teaspoon low-sodium salt

1. Microwave the edamame for 3 minutes on high until soft. 2. Place it in the food processor and blend all the ingredients for 2 minutes. 3. Served with rice crackers and vegetables.
Per Serving: Calories 451; Fat 34.89g; Sodium 55mg; Carbs 23.2g; Fiber 9.6g; Sugar 4.7g; Protein 17.41g

Easy-to-Make Kale Chips

Prep time: 10 minutes | Cook time: 20 minutes | Serves: 6

1 bunch kale	2 tablespoons olive oil
¼ teaspoon salt	

1. Turn on the oven and preheat it to 275°F. 2. Cut the kale into the slice by removing the stems and transferring it to a bowl. 3. Coat with oil and salt and arrange on the oiled baking sheet. 4. Fried the food in the oven for 20 minutes. 5. Once done, allow it to cool. 6. Serve.
Per Serving: Calories 93; Fat 7.4g; Sodium 112mg; Carbs 5.87g; Fiber 1.5g; Sugar 1.65g; Protein 1.18g

Roasted Chickpeas

Prep time: 10 minutes | Cook time: 30 minutes | Serves: 6

15-ounce low sodium chickpeas	¼ teaspoon black pepper
⅛ teaspoon salt	¼ teaspoon onion powder
1 tablespoon olive oil	¼ teaspoon paprika

1. Turn on the oven and preheat it to 350°F., Grease the baking tray with oil or cooking spray. 2. Washed the chickpeas and patted dry with a towel in the bowl. 3. combine all the ingredients with chickpeas in the bowl. 4. Arrange the chickpeas over the baking sheet evenly. 5. Sauté for 30 minutes in the oven. 6. Serve.
Per Serving: Calories 83; Fat 3.65g; Sodium 145mg; Carbs 9.77g; Fiber 3.2g; Sugar 1.85g; Protein 3.52g

Pineapple-Banana-Spinach Smooth

Prep time: 10 minutes | Cook time: 5 minutes | Serves: 2

1 cups spinach	½ cup pineapple
½ lemon juice	1 tablespoon ground flaxseeds
2 cups water	½ cup banana
1 teaspoon fresh ginger	

1. Place all the ingredients in a blender, and blend them until smooth. 2. Serve.
Per Serving: Calories 122; Fat 2.5g; Sodium 20mg; Carbs 25.66g; Fiber 3.8g; Sugar 16.34g; Protein 2.31g

Roasted Sweet Potatoes with Cinnamon and Honey

Prep time: 15 minutes | Cook time: 45 minutes | Serves: 4

Pepper, to taste	more for drizzling onto cooked potatoes
2 teaspoon ground cinnamon	
¼ cup honey	4 sweet potatoes (peeled and cut into 1-inch cubes)
¼ cup extra-virgin olive oil +	

1. Ensure oven is heated to 375 degrees F ahead of time. 2. Fetch sweet potato cubes in a roasting tray. Shower them in oil and honey, and then top them with cinnamon, pepper, and salt. 3. Roast the sweet potato cubes for 25 to 30 minutes until tender. 4. Pull out from the oven and pour onto a serving platter. 5. Drizzle with additional olive oil before enjoying the meal.
Per Serving: Calories 237; Fat 5.92g; Sodium 232mg; Carbs 45.79g; Fiber 4.9g; Sugar 23.67g; Protein 2.38g

Yummy Garlic Mashed Cauliflower

Prep time: 10 minutes | Cook time: 20 minutes | Serves: 4

Freshly chopped rosemary, for garnish	1 tablespoon extra-virgin olive oil
Freshly ground black pepper	2 tablespoon grated Parmesan cheese
1 smashed and chopped small clove of garlic	¼ cup low-sodium chicken stock
	Low-sodium salt
1 tablespoon non-fat Greek yogurt	1 medium head of cauliflower, chopped

1. Raise water up to the point of boiling in a big pot. 2. Add salt and chopped cauliflower, cook the cauliflower for 10 minutes until it's tenderized. 3. Allow time to get away from liquid and then dry with a paper towel. 4. In a food processor, pour in hot cauliflower with garlic, yogurt, chicken stock, cheese and olive oil. Process components until they are smooth in texture. 5. Stir in a dash of salt and pepper if needed. Proceed in adding in chopped rosemary. 6. Serve!
Per Serving: Calories 48; Fat 2.52g; Sodium 246mg; Carbs 4.6g; Fiber 1.5g; Sugar 1.41g; Protein 2.77g

Easy Strawberry Oatmeal Bars

Prep time: 10 minutes | Cook time:80 minutes | Serves: 4

10-12 ounces jar of strawberry preserves	1 ½ cup rolled oats
½ teaspoon black pepper	1 ½ cup regular white baking flour
1 teaspoon low-sodium baking powder	1 ¾ sticks of unsalted butter (cut into pieces)
1 cup packed brown sugar	

1. To make sure oven is heated to 350 degrees F ahead of time. 2. Butter up a rectangular pan. 3. Mix baking powder, pepper, oat, white baking flour, brown sugar, and butter in a bowl. 4. Press half of the oat mixture into pan, then lay out the strawberry preserves over it. 5. Top the other half of oat mixture over preserve layer and pat down gently. 6. Bake the food for 30 to 40 minutes until color turns light brown. 7. Let cool completely before cutting them into squares.
Per Serving: Calories 392; Fat 4.32g; Sodium 6mg; Carbs 90.87g; Fiber 8.4g; Sugar 28.91g; Protein 11.57g

Pretty Fresh Corn Salad

Prep time: 10 minutes | Cook time: 13 minutes | Serves: 4

½ cup julienned fresh basil leaves
½ teaspoon black pepper
½ teaspoon low-sodium salt
3 tablespoons olive oil

3 tablespoon cider vinegar
½ cup small-diced red onion
5 ears of shucked corn

1. Warm a salted pot of water up to a boil over immense warmth, then cooking up corn for 3 minutes to decrease starchiness. Get away from the liquid. 2. Pour into ice water to prevent cooking in order to set the bright, and the color turns into yellow. 3. Once corn is cooled, cut kernels from the cob. 4. In a big bowl, pour kernels into salt, pepper, onions, oil of olive and vinegar. 5. Before eating, mix with fresh basil, sprinkle with seasonings of choice until you reach desired taste. 6. Enjoy your meal at room temperature or even cold.
Per Serving: Calories 251; Fat 12.26g; Sodium 28mg; Carbs 35.33g; Fiber 5.1g; Sugar 6.31g; Protein 5.9g

Quinoa Pilaf

Prep time: 15 minutes | Cook time: 45 minutes | Serves: 4

½ cup toasted slivered almonds
Black pepper (or plus low-sodium salt)
1 teaspoon sugar
1 teaspoon fresh lemon zest
½ a lemon's juice
1 tablespoon flat leaf parsley, chopped

½ cup scallions (diagonally sliced)
½ cup pomegranate seeds
2 cups low-sodium chicken broth
1 cup quinoa
½ medium onion (diced)
2 tablespoons olive oil

1. In a pan over intermediate to immense warmth, warm up a tablespoon of oil. Sauté the onion until translucent in color and fragrant. Pour in your quinoa and mix to ensure an even coating. 2. Add chicken broth and warm up over immense warmth until it reaches the point of boiling. Decrease warmth and simmer for 20 minutes until quinoa soaks up liquid, and is nice and tender. 3. Mix parsley, scallions, lemon juice, sugar, lemon zest, oil and pomegranate seeds in a bowl until they put together. Pour in quinoa and sprinkle with pepper to season until you get what you want. Decorate with toasted slivered almonds.
Per Serving: Calories 281; Fat 10.26g; Sodium 43mg; Carbs 39.09g; Fiber 5.2g; Sugar 6.66g; Protein 9.51g

Healthy Cauliflower Rice with Onion

Prep time: 10 minutes | Cook time: 20 minutes | Serves: 4

Juice of ½ lemon
2 tablespoons finely chopped parsley leaves
Low-sodium salt

Black pepper
1 finely diced medium onion
3 tablespoons olive oil
A head of cauliflower

1. First and foremost, adorn cauliflower florets, then cutting as much of the stem off as possible. Next, in a food processor, divide florets and pulse into 3 batches until mixture is similar to couscous. 2. Within a pan over intermediate to immense warmth, warm up oil. When you find the oil is going to smoke a bit, add onions, and stirring to coat. Cook the onions for 8 minutes, stirring constantly, until the color turns into golden brown on the edges and soft in texture. 3. Add cauliflower, combining well, then add 1 teaspoon of salt and cook for 3 to 5 minutes until cauliflower is tender. Take way from the heat. 4. Pour in cauliflower in a large serving bowl. Decorate with lemon juice, parsley, pepper and salt. Serve warm!
Per Serving: Calories 119; Fat 10.37g; Sodium 61mg; Carbs 6.41g; Fiber 1.9g; Sugar 2.6g; Protein 1.65g

Fresh Vanilla Almonds

Prep time: 5 minutes | Cook time: 20 minutes | Serves: 4

½ teaspoon ground cinnamon
¼ teaspoon low-sodium salt
¾ cup sugar

4 cups whole almonds
1 teaspoon pure vanilla extract
1 beaten egg white

1. To make sure oven is heated to 300 degrees F ahead of time. 2. Combine egg white with vanilla extract, then pour in almonds and stir to ensure even coatings. 3. Combine salt, sugar and cinnamon, then add to egg white mixture, stirring together well. 4. Pour mixture into solitary layer onto a sheet meant for baking that has been liberally greased. 5. Bake the food for 20 minutes. 6. Remove the food from the oven, keep cool on the waxed paper as soon as possible and then tear into clusters.
Per Serving: Calories 16; Fat 0.62g; Sodium 14mg; Carbs 0.94g; Fiber 0.3g; Sugar 0.44g; Protein 1.17g

Crisp Whole-Wheat Seed Crackers

Prep time: 10 minutes | Cook time: 20 minutes | Serves: 4

1 cup whole wheat flour
2 tablespoons ground flaxseed
2 tablespoons hemp seeds

1 tablespoon za'atar
2 teaspoons garlic powder
½ cup water

1. Heat the oven to 400°F. Line a baking sheet with parchment paper. 2. Mix the flaxseed, flour, za'atar, garlic powder, hemp seeds, and water in a large mixing bowl until it is dough-like and slightly sticky. 3. Using a floured wine bottle or rolling pin, then spread the dough to a thickness of about one-tenth of an inch. To use sharp tools, such as knife or fork, to divide the dough into bite-size crackers (about 1-by-1-inch), and separate them to allow crispy edges to form on each cracker. 4. Bake for 20 minutes until lightly browned and the edges are crispy. Keep in an airtight container for as many as 1 weeks.
Per Serving: Calories 165; Fat 5.4g; Sodium 5mg; Carbs 26g; Fiber 5.7g; Sugar 0.53g; Protein 6.31g

Roasted Cannellini Bean "Chips"

Prep time: 5 minutes | Cook time: 20 minutes | Serves: 6

2 cups low-sodium cannellini beans, drained and rinsed
2 tablespoons avocado oil
1 tablespoon lemon juice

½ teaspoon smoked paprika
½ teaspoon ground cumin
½ teaspoon ground cinnamon

1. Heat the oven to 425 degrees F ahead of time. Line a baking sheet with parchment paper. 2. In a medium mixing bowl, combine the beans, oil, lemon juice, paprika, cumin, and cinnamon. 3. Spread the beans onto the prepared baking sheet in one even layer, and roast for 20 minutes until the beans become crispy and flaky.
Per Serving: Calories 109; Fat 5.19g; Sodium 117mg; Carbs 12.68g; Fiber 3.9g; Sugar 0.91g; Protein 3.76g

Yummy Cheesy Kale Chips

Prep time: 10 minutes | Cook time: 15 minutes | Serves: 4

4 tablespoons unsalted tahini
4 heaping tablespoons nutritional yeast
½ teaspoon garlic powder
½ cup water
1 large bunch of kale, cut into 2-inch chunks (about 5 tightly packed cups)

1. Heat the oven to 400 degrees F ahead of time. Line a baking sheet with parchment paper. 2. Combine the nutritional yeast, garlic powder, tahini, as well as water in a large mixing bowl. The consistency should be runny enough to spread evenly over the kale. 3. Put the tahini mixture into the kale, thinly coating each kale piece, in the meanwhile, avoiding any clumpy chunks of sauce. Then, transfer the dipped kale to the prepared baking sheet; Next, spread them and ensure the pieces don't touch. 4. Bake for 10 to 15 minutes, until the edges become slightly browned and the kale turns into a crispy chip. Eat alongside your favorite main dish or enjoy as a crunchy snack. 5. Keep in a large container for as many as 3 days; the crispiness starts to fade in 24 hours.
Per Serving: Calories 138; Fat 11.72g; Sodium 537mg; Carbs 4.33g; Fiber 1.4g; Sugar 0.4g; Protein 4.66g

Easy Edamame-Guacamole Dip

Prep time: 10 minutes | Cook time: None | Serves: 6

2 medium avocados, ripe
½ cup frozen cooked edamame, thawed
½ medium red bell pepper, diced (½ cup)
2 tablespoons lime juice
¼ cup packed cilantro, leaves only
½ teaspoon freshly ground black pepper

In an average bowl for a food processor, edamame, bell pepper, black pepper, pulse the avocados, lime juice, as well as cilantro until the desired consistency is achieved, 10 to 15 seconds.
Per Serving: Calories 127; Fat 10.52g; Sodium 6mg; Carbs 7.96g; Fiber 5.3g; Sugar 1.01g; Protein 2.88g

Turkey Burgers with Cauliflower

Prep time: 10 minutes | Cook time: 15 minutes | Serves: 4

2 cups cauliflower florets (about ½ medium cauliflower head)
1 small yellow onion, quartered
8 ounces frozen spinach, thawed
1-pound lean ground turkey
1½ teaspoons Mediterranean Seasoning Rub Blend

1. Set a 6-inch oven rack from the broiler, and heat the oven to broil ahead of time. Line a baking sheet with parchment paper. 2. Pulse the onion and cauliflower for 1 to 2 minutes in a blender, until they are minced. 3. In a large mixing bowl, put the cauliflower and onion mixture, turkey, spinach, and the spice together. On the baking sheet, mix well and form into 8 medium patties and place them. 4. First and foremost, broil for 10 minutes on one side, flip when lightly golden and juicy, and then broil for 3 minutes on the other side until golden brown. 5. Serve on a whole wheat bun with lettuce and on top of a salad, tomato, or in a collard green wrap. The burgers can be kept in the refrigerator in an airtight container for as many as 3 days or frozen for up to 3 months.
Per Serving: Calories 210; Fat 9.95g; Sodium 214mg; Carbs 7.3g; Fiber 3.2g; Sugar 2.25g; Protein 24.57g

Delicious Kale Chips

Prep time: 10 minutes | Cook time: 85 minutes | Serves: 4

Low-sodium salt
1 teaspoon za'atar spice
1 teaspoon dried Mexican oregano
Olive oil
10 kale leaves (washed, dried, stems discarded)

1. To make sure oven is heated to 225 degrees F ahead of time. 2. Add leaves of kale to a bowl, and then lightly put olive oil over kale until leaves are thoroughly glistening and coated. 3. Scatter za'atar and oregano over the top of kale. Flavor with salt and toss gently. 4. Transfer kale to baking sheet. 5. Bake the kale for 45 minutes to 1 hour until crispy. 6. Keep cool before enjoy your meal.
Per Serving: Calories 14; Fat 1.25g; Sodium 12mg; Carbs 0.83g; Fiber 0.5g; Sugar 0.16g; Protein 0.28g

Olive Tapenade with Anchovies

Prep time: 10 minutes, plus 1 hour to marinate | Cook time: None | Serves: 2 Cups

2 cups pitted black olives
2 anchovy fillets, chopped
2 teaspoons chopped capers
1 garlic clove, finely minced
1 cooked egg yolk
1 teaspoon Dijon mustard
¼ cup extra-virgin olive oil
Vegetables, for serving (optional)

1. Rinse the olives in cold water and drain well. 2. In a food processor, blender, or a large jar (if using an immersion blender), place the drained olives, anchovies, capers, garlic, egg yolk, and Dijon. Process until it forms a thick paste. 3. With the food processor running, slowly stream in the olive oil. 4. Transfer to a small bowl, cover, and refrigerate at least 1 hour to let the flavors develop. Serve with Seedy Crackers, atop a Versatile Sandwich Round, or with your favorite crunchy vegetables.
Per Serving: Calories 201; Fat 14.73g; Sodium 764mg; Carbs 14.44g; Fiber 5.1g; Sugar 0.05g; Protein 4.39g

Marinated Artichokes and Feta

Prep time: 250 minutes | Cook time: None | Serves: 1

½ cups
4 ounces' traditional Greek feta, cut into ½-inch cubes
4 ounces drained artichoke hearts, quartered lengthwise
⅓ cup extra-virgin olive oil
Zest and juice of 1 lemon
2 tablespoons roughly chopped fresh rosemary
2 tablespoons roughly chopped fresh parsley
½ teaspoon black peppercorns

1. Combine the feta and artichoke hearts in a glass bowl or large glass jar. Add the lemon juice, rosemary, olive oil, parsley, lemon zest, peppercorns and toss gently to coat, ensure not to crumble the feta. 2. Cover and refrigerate for at least 4 hours, or as many as 4 days. Take out the refrigerator 30 minutes before enjoy your meal.
Per Serving: Calories 164; Fat 13.88g; Sodium 432mg; Carbs 5.72g; Fiber 2.7g; Sugar 1.78g; Protein 5.05g

Smoked Salmon Crudités

Prep time: 10 minutes | Cook time: None | Serves: 4

6 ounces smoked wild salmon
2 tablespoons avocado mayonnaise
1 tablespoon Dijon mustard
1 tablespoon chopped scallions, green parts only

2 teaspoons chopped capers
½ teaspoon dried dill
4 endive spears or hearts of romaine
½ English cucumber, cut into ¼-inch-thick rounds

1. Roughly chop the smoked salmon and place in a small bowl. Add the avocado mayonnaise, Dijon, scallions, capers, and dill and mix well. 2. Top endive spears and cucumber rounds with a spoonful of smoked salmon mixture and enjoy chilled.
Per Serving: Calories 153; Fat 2.74g; Sodium 181mg; Carbs 28.42g; Fiber 17.1g; Sugar 2.33g; Protein 8.5g

Citrus-Marinated Olives

Prep time: 10 minutes | Cook time: None | Serves: 2

Cups
2 cups mixed green olives with pits
¼ cup red wine vinegar
¼ cup extra-virgin olive oil
4 garlic cloves, finely minced

Zest and juice of 2 clementines or 1 large orange
1 teaspoon red pepper flakes
2 bay leaves
½ teaspoon ground cumin
½ teaspoon ground allspice

1. In a large glass bowl or jar, combine the olives, vinegar, oil, garlic, orange zest and juice, red pepper flakes, bay leaves, cumin, and allspice. 2. Cover and refrigerate for at least 4 hours or up to a week to allow the olives to marinate, tossing again before serving.
Per Serving: Calories 143; Fat 6.27g; Sodium 282mg; Carbs 19.87g; Fiber 2.7g; Sugar 10.41g; Protein 3.08g

Homemade Guacamole

Prep time: 10 minutes | Cook time: None | Serves: 4

2 large avocados, halved, peeled, and roughly chopped
Juice of ½ lime
2 teaspoons olive oil
¼ red onion, finely diced
½ teaspoon minced garlic (1 clove)

½ teaspoon ground cumin
1 tablespoon freshly chopped cilantro
½ Roma tomato, diced
Pinch salt
Freshly ground black pepper

1. Mash the avocados to the desired consistency in a medium-size bowl. 2. Add the lime juice and oil. Stir in the red onion, garlic, cumin, cilantro, and tomato, then season with salt and pepper.
Per Serving: Calories 189; Fat 17g; Sodium 14mg; Carbs 10g; Fiber 7g; Sugar 1g; Protein 2g

Cilantro Salsa

Prep time: 10 minutes | Cook time: None | Serves: 4

2 cups chopped tomatoes
½ cup diced yellow onion
2 tablespoons minced cilantro
Juice of ½ lime, plus more for seasoning (optional)

1 jalapeño pepper, seeded and chopped
½ teaspoon ground cumin
Pinch salt
Freshly ground black pepper

1. Combine the tomatoes, onion, cilantro, lime juice, jalapeño, and cumin. In a regular bowl, mix well. 2. Add salt and pepper, and more lime juice (if using).
Per Serving: Calories 31; Fat 1g; Sodium 6mg; Carbs 5g; Fiber 1g; Sugar 3g; Protein 1g

Greek Deviled Eggs

Prep time: 15 minutes, plus 30 minutes to chill | Cook time: 15 minutes | Serves: 4

4 large hardboiled eggs
2 tablespoons plain Greek yogurt
½ cup finely crumbled feta cheese
8 pitted Kalamata olives, finely chopped
2 tablespoons chopped sun-dried

tomatoes
1 tablespoon minced red onion
½ teaspoon dried dill
¼ teaspoon freshly ground black pepper

1. Slice the hardboiled eggs in half lengthwise, remove the yolks, and place the yolks in an average bowl. Reserve the egg white halves and set aside. 2. Smash the yolks well with a fork. Add the aioli, feta, olives, sun-dried tomatoes, onion, dill, and pepper and stir to combine until smooth and creamy. 3. Spoon the filling into each egg white half and chill for 30 minutes, or up to 24 hours, covered.
Per Serving: Calories 142; Fat 10.11g; Sodium 268mg; Carbs 3.02g; Fiber 0.5g; Sugar 2.05g; Protein 9.7g

Yummy Goat Cheese–Mackerel Pâté

Prep time: 10 minutes | Cook time: None | Serves: 4

4 ounces' olive oil-packed wild-caught mackerel
2 ounces' goat cheese
Zest and juice of 1 lemon
2 tablespoons chopped fresh parsley
2 tablespoons chopped fresh arugula

1 tablespoon extra-virgin olive oil
2 teaspoons chopped capers
1 to 2 teaspoons fresh horseradish (optional)
Crackers, cucumber rounds, endive spears, or celery, for serving (optional)

1. In a food processor, add the lemon zest and juice, parsley, mackerel, goat cheese, olive oil, arugula, capers, and horseradish (optional). Process or blend until smooth and creamy. 2. Serve with cucumber rounds, endive spears, crackers, or celery. 3. Store covered in the refrigerator for as many as 1 week.
Per Serving: Calories 190; Fat 18.02g; Sodium 344mg; Carbs 2.42g; Fiber 0.5g; Sugar 1.34g; Protein 4.88g

Burrata Caprese Stack

Prep time: 5 minutes | Cook time: None | Serves: 4

1 large organic tomato, preferably heirloom
½ teaspoon low-sodium salt
¼ teaspoon freshly ground black pepper
1 (4-ounce) ball burrata cheese

8 fresh basil leaves, thinly sliced
2 tablespoons extra-virgin olive oil
1 tablespoon red wine or balsamic vinegar

1. Slice the tomato into 4 thick slices, removing any tough center core, and sprinkle with salt and pepper. Place the tomatoes, seasoned-side up, on a plate. 2. On a separate rimmed plate, slice the burrata into 4 thick slices and place one slice on top of each tomato slice. Top each with one-quarter of the basil and pour any reserved burrata cream from the rimmed plate over top. 3. Drizzle with olive oil and red wine (or vinegar), and serve with a fork and knife.
Per Serving: Calories 122; Fat 9.86g; Sodium 276mg; Carbs 2.93g; Fiber 0.6g; Sugar 1.99g; Protein 5.61g

Herbed Potato Mash

Prep time: 20 minutes | Cook time: 5 to 6 hours | Serves: 6

3 ½ pounds red or creamer potatoes, rinsed
2 onions, minced
12 garlic cloves, peeled and sliced
½ cup store-bought vegetable broth
3 tablespoons olive oil
1 teaspoon dried thyme leaves
1 teaspoon dried dill leaves
½ teaspoon salt
⅓ cup grated Parmesan cheese

1. Mix the onion, potatoes, garlic, vegetable broth, olive oil, thyme, dill, and salt in a suitable slow cooker. Cover and cook on low for 5 to 6 hours, or until the potatoes are tender. 2. Mash the potatoes in the slow cooker, leaving some chunky pieces. Stir in the Parmesan cheese and serve.
Per Serving: Calories 293; Fat 9g; Sodium 422mg; Carbs 49g; Fiber 5g; Sugar 5g; Protein 7g

Salmon-Stuffed Cucumbers

Prep time: 10 minutes | Cook time: None | Serves: 4

2 large cucumbers, peeled
1 (4-ounce) can red salmon
1 medium very ripe avocado, peeled, pitted, and mashed
1 tablespoon extra-virgin olive oil
Zest and juice of 1 lime
3 tablespoons chopped fresh cilantro
½ teaspoon low-sodium salt
¼ teaspoon freshly ground black pepper

1. Slice the cucumber into 1-inch-thick segments and using a spoon, scrape seeds out of center of each segment and stand up on a plate. 2. In an average bowl, add the salmon, avocado, olive oil, lime zest and juice, cilantro, salt, and pepper, and mix until creamy. 3. Spoon the salmon mixture into the center of each cucumber segment and serve chilled.
Per Serving: Calories 212; Fat 12.73g; Sodium 275mg; Carbs 8.55g; Fiber 4.5g; Sugar 2.59g; Protein 18.19g

Zucchini-Ricotta Fritters with Lemon-Garlic Aioli

Prep time: 10 minutes | Cook time: 25 minutes | Serves: 4

1 large or 2 small/medium zucchinis (about 2 cups drained, shredded)
1 teaspoon low-sodium salt, divided
½ cup whole-milk ricotta cheese
2 scallions, both white and green parts, chopped
1 large egg
2 garlic cloves, finely minced
2 tablespoons chopped fresh mint
(optional)
2 teaspoons grated lemon zest
¼ teaspoon freshly ground black pepper
½ cup almond flour
1 teaspoon baking powder
8 tablespoons extra-virgin olive oil
8 tablespoons avocado oil mayonnaise

1. Place the shredded zucchini in a colander or on several layers of paper towels. Sprinkle with ½ teaspoon salt and let sit for 10 minutes. 2. Using another layer of paper towels, press down on the zucchini to release any excess moisture and pat dry. 3. In a big bowl, combine the drained zucchini, ricotta, scallions, egg, garlic, mint (optional), lemon zest, remaining ½ teaspoon salt, and pepper. 4. In a regular bowl, mix together the almond flour and baking powder. Stir the flour mixture into the zucchini mixture and let rest for 10 minutes. 5. In a big frying pan, working in four batches, fry the fritters. For each batch of four, heat 2 tablespoons

olive oil over medium-high heat. Add 1 heaping tablespoon of zucchini batter per fritter, pressing down with the back of a spoon to form 2- to 3-inch fritters. Cover and let fry 2 minutes before flipping. Fry another 2 to 3 minutes, covered, or until crispy and golden and cooked through. You may need to reduce heat to medium to prevent burning. Remove from the pan and keep warm. 6. Repeat for the remaining three batches, using 2 tablespoons of the olive oil for each batch. 7. Serve fritters warm with mayonnaise.
Per Serving: Calories 263; Fat 22.9g; Sodium 308mg; Carbs 10.38g; Fiber 1.1g; Sugar 3.83g; Protein 5.64g

Mediterranean Fat Bombs

Prep time: 15 minutes | Cook time: None | Serves: 6

1 cup crumbled goat cheese
4 tablespoons jarred pesto
12 pitted Kalamata olives, finely chopped
½ cup finely chopped walnuts
1 tablespoon chopped fresh rosemary

1. Combine the pesto, and olives, goat cheese, and mix well using a fork in an average bowl. Place in the refrigerator for at least 4 hours to harden. 2. Form the mixture into 6 balls, about ¾-inch diameter. The mixture will be sticky. 3. Place the walnuts and rosemary and roll the goat cheese balls in a small bowl in the nut mixture to coat. 4. In the refrigerator, store the fat bombs for as many as 1 weeks or in the freezer for up to 1 month.
Per Serving: Calories 191; Fat 17.72g; Sodium 312mg; Carbs 1.76g; Fiber 0.8g; Sugar 0.4g; Protein 7.51g

Classic Cashew Cream

Prep time: 5 minutes plus 7 hours for soaking | Cook time: None | Serves: 4

1 cup raw cashews, soaked overnight for at least 7 hours and drained
½ cup water
¼ teaspoon salt
Freshly ground black pepper

1. Place the soaked cashews, water, and salt in a high-speed blender or food processor; blend until completely smooth. 2. Season with pepper.
Per Serving: Calories 197; Fat 16g; Sodium 154mg; Carbs 11g; Fiber 1g; Sugar 2g; Protein 5g

Yummy Caprese Grilled Cheese

Prep time: 10 minutes | Cook time: 10 minutes | Serves: 4

4 versatile sandwich rounds
8 tablespoons jarred pesto
4 ounces' fresh mozzarella cheese, cut into 4 round slices
1 Roma tomato or small slicing tomato, cut into 4 slices
4 tablespoons extra-virgin olive oil

1. On a large cutting board, slice each sandwich round in half horizontally and cut-side up, and spread 1 tablespoon pesto over each half. Top 4 of the rounds with a mozzarella slice and tomato slice and close with the remaining sandwich rounds. 2. Heat 2 tablespoons of olive oil over medium-high heat in a big frying pan. Brush the remaining 2 tablespoons of olive oil over the tops of the sandwiches. 3. When the skillet is hot, add each sandwich, unoiled-side down, pressing down with the back of a spatula to grill. Cook 3 to 4 minutes, or until cheese begins to melt, before flipping and pressing down with the back of a spatula. Grill on second side another 3 to 4 minutes, or until golden and cheese is much melted. 4. Serve hot.
Per Serving: Calories 274; Fat 24.06g; Sodium 651mg; Carbs 2.87g; Fiber 1g; Sugar 1.01g; Protein 12.5g

Delicious Good Morning Grits

Prep time: 15 minutes | Cook time: 7-8 hours | Serves: 4

Cooking spray or neutral-flavored oil, such as canola
1½ cups stone-ground grits
6 cups water

2 teaspoons low-sodium salt
4 to 6 tablespoons vegan butter
Freshly ground black pepper

1. Grease the inside of a slow cooker with cooking spray or oil. 2. Add the water, salt as well as grits, and then mix well. 3. Cover and cook on low for 7 to 8 hours. 4. Take out of the lid. Sprinkle the vegan butter on top of it. Possess a whisk to stir the grits until they can get an even consistency and make the vegan butter melted. 5. Season with pepper and enjoy your meal.
Per Serving: Calories 135; Fat 8.83g; Sodium 384mg; Carbs 13.06g; Fiber 0.9g; Sugar 0.38g; Protein 1.97g

Well-Cooked Artichoke-Basil Hummus

Prep time: 15 minutes | Cook time: None | Serves: 8

1 (15-ounce) can low-sodium chickpeas, drained and rinsed
¼ cup unsalted tahini
2 garlic cloves
3 tablespoons lemon juice
3 tablespoons extra-virgin olive

oil
1 cup frozen artichoke pieces, defrosted
3 tablespoons chopped fresh basil
4 tablespoons water
Freshly ground black pepper

In a blender, blend the tahini, garlic, lemon juice, chickpeas, olive oil, basil, water, artichoke, as well as pepper until smooth.
Per Serving: Calories 127; Fat 7.52g; Sodium 139mg; Carbs 11.96g; Fiber 4.3g; Sugar 1.83g; Protein 4.85g

Lemony Beets and Onions

Prep time: 20 minutes | Cook time: 5 to 7 hours | Serves: 8

10 medium beets, peeled and sliced
3 red onions, chopped
4 garlic cloves, minced
⅓ cup honey

⅓ cup lemon juice
1 cup water
2 tablespoons melted coconut oil
3 tablespoons cornstarch
½ teaspoon salt

1. In a 6-quart slow cooker, mix the beets, onions, and garlic. 2. In an average bowl, mix the honey, lemon juice, water, coconut oil, cornstarch, and salt until well combined. Pour this mixture over the beets. 3. Cover and cook on low for 5 to 7 hours, or until the beets are tender and the sauce has thickened.
Per Serving: Calories 148; Fat 4g; Sodium 229mg; Carbs 29g; Fiber 4g; Sugar 20g; Protein 2g

Awesome Risotto with Cinnamon

Prep time: 5 minutes | Cook time: 6 hours | Serves: 4

4 cups non-dairy milk
1½ cups Arborio rice
1 cup finely diced tart apples such as Granny Smith
⅓ cup packed brown sugar

2 tablespoons vegan butter, melted
2 teaspoons ground cinnamon
½ teaspoon salt
¼ teaspoon ground nutmeg
dried fruit for garnishment, optional

1. Combine the non-dairy milk, Arborio rice, apples, brown sugar, vegan butter, cinnamon, salt, and nutmeg in a slow cooker; mix thoroughly. 2. Cover the lid and cook for 6 hours with low pressure or for 4 to 5 hours with high pressure. 3. Garnish with dried fruit (if using), and serve.
Per Serving: Calories 392; Fat 20g; Sodium 478mg; Carbs 57g; Fiber 11g; Sugar 33.6g; Protein 10g

Simple Nacho Cheese Sauce

Prep time: 10 minutes | Cook time: 15 minutes | Serves: 4

2 cups peeled chopped russet potatoes
1 cup chopped carrots
½ to ¾ cup water
1 tablespoon freshly squeezed lemon juice

½ cup nutritional yeast
½ teaspoon onion powder
½ teaspoon garlic powder
1 teaspoon salt
¼ cup store-bought salsa

1. Boil the chopped potatoes and carrots for about 15 minutes, or until soft. 2. Put ½ cup of water into a blender, followed by the lemon juice, nutritional yeast, onion powder, garlic powder, salt, and salsa (if using). Blend until completely smooth. 3. Pour in the remaining water to thin it out as needed.
Per Serving: Calories 145; Fat 0.5g; Sodium 1786mg; Carbs 25g; Fiber 4.5g; Sugar 3g; Protein 11g

Garlicky Mushroom Gravy

Prep time: 10 minutes | Cook time: 10 minutes | Serves: 4

1 tablespoon oil
1 small yellow onion, diced
1 cup finely chopped button mushrooms
1½ teaspoons minced garlic (3 cloves)

4 tablespoons flour
1¼ cups water
1 tablespoon soy sauce
½ teaspoon dried oregano
2 bay leaves
Freshly ground black pepper

1. In a medium saucepan, add the oil. When heated, add the onion, mushrooms, and garlic. Sauté until just softened. 2. Mix in the flour and form it into a thick paste. 3. Add the water, soy sauce, oregano, and bay leaves, and bring to a simmer over medium heat. Season with pepper. 4. Remove the bay leaves. Use a whisk to gently mix the gravy until it thickens. Add more water if you prefer a thinner gravy.
Per Serving: Calories 88; Fat 4g; Sodium 64mg; Carbs 11g; Fiber 1g; Sugar 2g; Protein 2g

Garlicky Hummus

Prep time: 10 minutes | Cook time: None | Serves: 4

1 (14-ounce) can chickpeas, drained and rinsed
1 teaspoon minced garlic (2 cloves)
3 tablespoons tahini
2 tablespoons freshly squeezed lemon juice

½ teaspoon ground cumin
1 to 2 teaspoons extra-virgin olive oil, as needed
Pinch salt
Freshly ground black pepper
Pinch paprika for garnish
¼ cup toasted pine nuts (optional)

1. Place the chickpeas, garlic, tahini, lemon juice, and cumin in a blender or food processor and process into creamy hummus. For a thinner consistency, add olive oil by the teaspoon. 2. Season with salt and pepper. 3. Then place them in a serving bowl and sprinkle with paprika and pine nuts (if using).
Per Serving: Calories 477; Fat 19g; Sodium 78mg; Carbs 64g; Fiber 19g; Sugar 11g; Protein 22g

Roasted Potatoes and Carrots

Prep time: 20 minutes | Cook time: 6 to 8 hours | Serves: 8

6 carrots, cut into 1-inch chunks
2 yellow onions
2 sweet potatoes
6 Yukon Gold potatoes, cut into chunks
8 whole garlic cloves, peeled
4 parsnips, peeled and cut into
chunks
3 tablespoons olive oil
1 teaspoon dried thyme leaves
½ teaspoon salt
⅛ Teaspoon freshly ground black pepper

1. For the sweet potatoes, peel them and then cut them into chunks. 2. Cut each yellow onion into 8 wedges and place them on a plate for later use. 3. In a 6-quart slow cooker, mix all of the ingredients. Cook on low, covered, for 6 to 8 hours, or until the vegetables are tender.
Per Serving: Calories 370; Fat 6g; Sodium 210mg; Carbs 75g; Fiber 11.5g; Sugar 10g; Protein 8g

Potato Gratin Mix

Prep time: 20 minutes | Cook time: 7 to 9 hours | Serves: 8

6 Yukon Gold potatoes, thinly sliced
3 sweet potatoes, peeled and thinly sliced
2 onions, thinly sliced
4 garlic cloves, minced
3 tablespoons whole-wheat flour
4 cups 2% milk, divided
1½ cups store-bought vegetable broth
3 tablespoons melted butter
1 teaspoon dried thyme leaves
1½ cups shredded Havarti

1. Grease a 6-quart slow cooker with plain vegetable oil. 2. In the slow cooker, layer the potatoes, onions, and garlic. 3. Mix the flour with ½ cup of the milk in a large bowl until well combined. Gradually add the remaining milk, stirring with a wire whisk to avoid lumps. Stir in the vegetable broth, melted butter, and thyme leaves. 4. Pour the milk mixture over the potatoes in the slow cooker and top with the cheese. 5. Cook on low covered for 7 to 9 hours, or until the potatoes are tender when pierced with a fork.
Per Serving: Calories 249; Fat 7.6g; Sodium 726mg; Carbs 40g; Fiber 3.3g; Sugar 9g; Protein 8g

Stewed Prunes, Pears, and Apple

Prep time: 15 minutes | Cook time: 6 to 8 hours | Serves: 12

2 cups dried apricots
2 cups prunes
2 cups dried unsulfured pears
2 cups dried apples
1 cup dried cranberries
¼ cup honey
6 cups water
1 teaspoon dried thyme leaves
1 teaspoon dried basil leaves

1. In a 6-quart slow cooker, mix all of the ingredients. Cook on low, covered, for 6 to 8 hours, or until the fruits have absorbed the liquid and are tender. 2. Store in the refrigerator for up to 1 week. You can freeze the fruit in 1-cup portions for longer storage.
Per Serving: Calories 202; Fat 0.4g; Sodium 9mg; Carbs 53g; Fiber 3g; Sugar 29g; Protein 2g

Butternut Squash and Acorn Squash Purée

Prep time: 20 minutes | Cook time: 6 to 7 hours | Serves: 8

1 (3-pound) butternut squash
3 (1-pound) acorn squash, peeled, seeded, and cut into 1-inch pieces
2 onions, chopped
3 garlic cloves, minced
2 tablespoons olive oil
1 teaspoon dried marjoram leaves
½ teaspoon salt
⅛ teaspoon freshly ground black pepper

1. Peel the butternut squash and remove the seed. Then cut into 1-inch pieces. 2. In a 6-quart slow cooker, mix all of the ingredients. 3. Then cook on low, covered, for 6 to 7 hours, or until the squash is tender when pierced with a fork. 4. Mash the squash right in the slow cooker with a potato masher.
Per Serving: Calories 142; Fat 4g; Sodium 155mg; Carbs 29g; Fiber 5g; Sugar 5g; Protein 2.5g

Tasty Herbed Veggies

Prep time: 20 minutes | Cook time: 3 to 4 hours | Serves: 8

2 bunches Swiss chard, washed and cut into large pieces
2 bunches collard greens, washed and cut into large pieces
2 bunches kale, washed and cut into large pieces
3 onions, chopped
1½ cups store-bought vegetable stock
¼ cup honey
2 tablespoons lemon juice
1 teaspoon dried marjoram
1 teaspoon dried basil
¼ teaspoon salt

1. In a 6-quart slow cooker, mix the Swiss chard, collard greens, kale, and onions. 2. In an average bowl, mix the vegetable broth, honey, lemon juice, marjoram, basil, and salt. Pour into the slow cooker. 3. Cover and cook on low for 3 to 4 hours, or until the greens are very tender.
Per Serving: Calories 79; Fat 0.6g; Sodium 215mg; Carbs 18g; Fiber 2.5g; Sugar 11.7g; Protein 2.5g

Spiced Black Bean Hummus

Prep time: 10 minutes | Cook time: None | Serves: 2

1 (15.5-ounce) can low-sodium black beans, drained and rinsed
½ avocado, peeled
¼ cup tahini
¼ cup freshly squeezed lemon juice
2 tablespoons soy sauce
1 teaspoon chopped fresh cilantro
1 teaspoon garlic powder
1 teaspoon onion powder
1 teaspoon chili powder
1 teaspoon ground cumin

1. Combine the black beans, avocado, tahini, lemon juice, soy sauce, cilantro, garlic powder, onion powder, chili powder, and cumin in a food processor. Blend them together into smooth and creamy, about 1 to 2 minutes or more. 2. Serve with the veggies of your choosing, such as carrots, celery, cucumber rounds, or bell pepper strips. 3. Put the hummus in an airtight container in the refrigerator for up to 5 days. Store the veggies in a separate storage container or bag in the refrigerator for up to 5 days.
Per Serving: Calories 540; Fat 28g; Sodium 642mg; Carbs 58g; Fiber 23.5g; Sugar 5g; Protein 22g

Balsamic Onions and Garlic

Prep time: 20 minutes | Cook time: 8 to 10 hours | Serves: 12

10 large yellow onions, peeled and sliced
20 garlic cloves, peeled
¼ cup olive oil
¼ teaspoon salt
2 tablespoons balsamic vinegar
1 teaspoon dried thyme leaves

1. In a 6-quart slow cooker, mix all of the ingredients. Cover and cook on low for 8 to 10 hours, stirring once or twice if you have the time. 2. Refrigerate the onions for up to 1 week, or divide them into 1-cup portions and freeze for up to 3 months.
Per Serving: Calories 100; Fat 5g; Sodium 55mg; Carbs 14g; Fiber 2g; Sugar 6g; Protein 2g

Classic Tex-Mex Kale

Prep time: 20 minutes | Cook time: 4 to 5 hours | Serves: 8

4 bunches kale, washed, stemmed, and cut into large pieces
2 onions, chopped
8 garlic cloves, minced
2 jalapeño peppers, minced
4 large tomatoes, seeded and chopped
1 tablespoon chili powder
½ teaspoon salt
⅛ teaspoon freshly ground black pepper

1. In a 6-quart slow cooker, mix the kale, onions, garlic, jalapeño peppers, and tomatoes. 2. Sprinkle with the chili powder, salt, and pepper, and stir to mix. 3. Cover and cook on low for 4 to 5 hours, or until the kale is wilted and tender.
Per Serving: Calories 42; Fat 0.5g; Sodium 185mg; Carbs 9g; Fiber 2.5g; Sugar g; Protein 2g

Refried Beans and Onions

Prep time: 10 minutes | Cook time: 9 hours | Serves: 8

4 cups dried pinto beans, rinsed and drained
2 onions, minced
4 garlic cloves, minced
1 jalapeño pepper, minced
1 teaspoon dried oregano leaves
1 teaspoon salt
9 cups store-bought vegetable broth, low-sodium
⅓ cup olive oil

1. In a 6-quart slow cooker, mix the beans, onions, garlic, jalapeño pepper, oregano, salt, and vegetable broth. Cover and cook on low for 8 hours, or until the beans have absorbed most of the liquid and are tender. 2. Remove the lid and then add the olive oil. Mash the beans right in the slow cooker with the potato masher. 3. Cover and cook on low for another 30 to 40 minutes, then serve. If the beans aren't thick enough, remove the cover and cook on high for 40 to 50 minutes longer, stirring occasionally.
Per Serving: Calories 522; Fat 11.4g; Sodium 856mg; Carbs 81g; Fiber 19g; Sugar 9g; Protein 24g

Peanut Butter Banana Sushi

Prep time: 10 minutes | Cook time: None | Serves: 4

Per sushi roll:
1 whole-wheat tortilla
2 tablespoons peanut butter
1 tablespoon mini dark chocolate chips
1 small banana

1. Lay 1 tortilla on a cutting board. Spread evenly over the tortilla with 2 tablespoons of peanut butter and sprinkle this layer with the chocolate chips. Lay the banana close to one of the edges of the tortilla and then roll it up into the tortilla. Use a bit of extra peanut butter to create a seal, then cut into ½-inch pieces à la sushi. 2. Repeat with the remaining 3 tortillas and bananas. 3. Store in airtight containers, sandwich bags, or eco-friendly food wraps in the refrigerator for up to 3 days.
Per Serving: Calories 463; Fat 16g; Sodium 835mg; Carbs 73g; Fiber 8g; Sugar 31g; Protein 9g

Citrusy Herbed Cauliflower

Prep time: 20 minutes | Cook time: 4 hours | Serves: 8

2 heads cauliflower
2 onions, chopped
½ cup orange juice
1 teaspoon grated orange zest
1 teaspoon dried thyme leaves
½ teaspoon dried basil leaves
½ teaspoon salt

1. Clean the cauliflower and rinse. Then cut them into florets. 2. In a 6-quart slow cooker, mix the cauliflower and onions. 3. Top with the orange juice and orange zest, and drizzle with thyme, basil, and salt. 4. Then cook on low with the lid covered for about 4 hours, or until just tender. 5. Serve and enjoy your meal.
Per Serving: Calories 36; Fat 0.2g; Sodium 167mg; Carbs 8g; Fiber 2g; Sugar 4g; Protein 1.7g

Breakfast Mushroom Risotto

Prep time: 20 minutes | Cook time: 3½ to 4½ hours | Serves: 8

8 ounces button mushrooms, sliced
8 ounces cremini mushrooms, sliced
8 ounces shiitake mushrooms, stems removed and sliced
2 onions, chopped
5 garlic cloves, minced
2 cups short-grain brown rice
1 teaspoon dried marjoram leaves
6 cups store-bought vegetable broth, low-sodium
3 tablespoons unsalted butter
½ cup grated Parmesan cheese

1. In a 6-quart slow cooker, mix the mushrooms, onions, garlic, rice, marjoram, and vegetable broth. 2. Cover and cook on low for 3 to 4 hours, or until the rice is tender. 3. Stir in the butter and cheese. Cover and let cook on low for 20 minutes, then serve.
Per Serving: Calories 338; Fat 7g; Sodium 548mg; Carbs 59g; Fiber 6g; Sugar 6g; Protein 11g

Carrot and Potato Gratin

Prep time: 20 minutes | Cook time: 7 to 9 hours | Serves: 8

2 cups hulled barley
2 onions, chopped
5 garlic cloves, minced
3 large carrots, peeled and sliced
2 sweet potatoes, peeled and cubed
4 Yukon Gold potatoes, cubed
7 cups store-bought vegetable broth, low-sodium
1 teaspoon dried tarragon leaves
½ cup grated Parmesan cheese

1. In a 6-quart slow cooker, mix the barley, onions, garlic, carrots, sweet potatoes, and Yukon Gold potatoes. Add the vegetable broth and tarragon leaves. 2. Cook on low, covered, for 7 to 9 hours, or until the barley is tender and the vegetables are tender too. 3. Stir in the cheese and serve.
Per Serving: Calories 444; Fat 3g; Sodium 315mg; Carbs 94g; Fiber 16g; Sugar 14g; Protein 13g

Thai-style Roasted Carrots

Prep time: 20 minutes | Cook time: 6 to 8 hours | Serves: 8

4 large carrots	⅓ cup canned coconut milk
2 onions, peeled and sliced	3 tablespoons lime juice
6 garlic cloves, peeled and sliced	2 tablespoons grated fresh ginger
2 parsnips, peeled and sliced	root
2 jalapeño peppers, minced	2 teaspoons curry powder
½ cup Roasted Vegetable Broth	

1. Peel the large potatoes and cut them into chunks. 2. In a 6-quart slow cooker, mix the carrots, onions, garlic, parsnips, and jalapeño peppers. 3. In a small bowl, mix the vegetable broth, coconut milk, lime juice, ginger root, and curry powder until well blended. Pour this mixture into the slow cooker. 4. Cook on low, covered, for 6 to 8 hours, or until the vegetables are tender when pierced with a fork.
Per Serving: Calories 86; Fat 3g; Sodium 91mg; Carbs 15.5g; Fiber 4g; Sugar 5.5g; Protein 2g

Pecan-Berry Pilaf

Prep time: 20 minutes | Cook time: 8 to 10 hours | Serves: 10

3 cups wheat berries, rinsed and drained	1½ cups dried cranberries
2 leeks, peeled, rinsed, and chopped	1 teaspoon dried thyme leaves
	¼ teaspoon salt
7 cups store-bought vegetable broth, low-sodium	1 cup chopped pecans
2 tablespoons lemon juice	1½ cups shredded baby Swiss cheese

1. In a 6-quart slow cooker, mix the wheat berries, leeks, vegetable broth, lemon juice, cranberries, thyme, and salt. Cover and cook on low for 8 to 10 hours, or until the wheat berries are tender but still slightly chewy. 2. Add the pecans and cheese. Cover and let stand for 10 minutes, then serve.
Per Serving: Calories 396; Fat 15g; Sodium 473mg; Carbs 56g; Fiber 8g; Sugar 16g; Protein 14g

Carrot-Cranberry Muffins

Prep time: 15 minutes | Cook time: 13 minutes | Serves: 12

Butter, for greasing	1 tablespoon plus 2 teaspoons grated orange zest
1¾ cups whole-wheat flour, plus 1 teaspoon	½ cup maple syrup
1½ teaspoons baking powder	⅓ cup melted coconut oil
1 teaspoon ground cinnamon	⅔ cup dairy-free milk (almond, soy, oat)
½ teaspoon baking soda	
½ teaspoon salt	2 tablespoons ground flaxseed
½ teaspoon ground ginger	2 teaspoons apple cider vinegar
½ cup dried cranberries	1 teaspoon vanilla extract
2 cups grated carrots	

1. Preheat the oven to 425°F. Prepare a 12-cup muffin tin and grease with butter or nonstick cooking spray or fill with liners. 2. In a big bowl, whisk together 1¾ cups of flour, the baking powder, cinnamon, baking soda, salt, and ginger. Toss the cranberries with the remaining 1 teaspoon of flour in a separate small bowl, so they don't stick together. Add the grated carrots, floured cranberries, and orange zest to the other ingredients and stir to combine. 3. In an average bowl, whisk together the maple syrup and oil. Add the dairy-free milk, flaxseed, vinegar, and vanilla, and mix well. 4.

Mix the wet ingredients with the dry ingredient until combined. Divide the batter evenly between the muffin cups. Bake them in your oven for 13 minutes, or until the muffins are golden on top and toothpick-inserted-clean. 5. Put them in an airtight container and move to the pantry for 2 days, then move to the refrigerator and can be stored for up to 5 days.
Per Serving: Calories 173; Fat 7g; Sodium 172mg; Carbs 26g; Fiber 3g; Sugar 11g; Protein 3g

Cucumber Caprese Boxes with Olives

Prep time: 15 minutes | Cook time: None | Serves: 4

Per snack box:	¼ cup fresh mozzarella pearls
¼ cup cherry tomatoes	¼ cup pitted Kalamata olives
½ medium Kirby cucumber halved lengthwise and cut into ½-inch bites	Red pepper flakes
	Dried basil

1. In a small container, combine the tomatoes, cucumber, mozzarella, and olives. Add red pepper flakes and basil to taste. 2. Repeat to make 3 more snack boxes. 3. Store the airtight containers in the refrigerator for up to 4 days.
Per Serving: Calories 246; Fat 4.5g; Sodium 258mg; Carbs 47g; Fiber 10g; Sugar 4g; Protein 7g

Mexican-style Jicama and Mango

Prep time: 15 minutes | Cook time: None | Serves: 6

1 medium jicama (about 1 pound), peeled and cut into ½-by-3-inch-long matchsticks	1 teaspoon chili powder
	Pinch salt
	2 medium mangos, cut into ¼-inch wedges
Juice of 1 lime	

1. In an average bowl, combine the jicama, lime juice, chili powder, and salt. Toss to coat well. 2. Store the seasoned jicama and mango wedges together in an airtight container in the refrigerator for up to 4 days.
Per Serving: Calories 112; Fat 1g; Sodium 115mg; Carbs 27g; Fiber 7g; Sugar 17g; Protein 2g

Gingered Pumpkin Yogurt Dip

Prep time: 10 minutes | Cook time: None | Serves: 3

2 cups plain Greek yogurt	1 teaspoon ground cinnamon
1 cup canned pumpkin purée	½ teaspoon ground nutmeg
1 tablespoon maple syrup	½ teaspoon ground ginger

1. In an average bowl, combine the Greek yogurt, pumpkin purée, maple syrup, cinnamon, nutmeg, and ginger. Stir to combine well. Taste and adjust the seasonings if desired. 2. Place them in an airtight container and cool in the refrigerator for up to 1 week.
Per Serving: Calories 348; Fat 25g; Sodium 177mg; Carbs 19g; Fiber 3g; Sugar 12g; Protein 17g

Stuffed Dates with Nut Butter

Prep time: 10 minutes | Cook time: None | Serves: 6

12 Medjool dates
12 teaspoons nut butter (almond, peanut, or cashew)
Ground cinnamon, for garnish (optional)
Unsweetened coconut flakes,
for garnish (optional)
Flaky sea salt, for garnish (optional)
Crushed nuts, for garnish (optional)

1. Make a small slit into each date and carefully remove the pits. 2. Spoon 1 teaspoon of your desired nut butter into the opening of each date. 3. Sprinkle with the optional toppings. 4. Add them to an airtight container to store for up to 3 to 4 days.
Per Serving: Calories 197; Fat 6g; Sodium 24mg; Carbs 38g; Fiber 4g; Sugar 33g; Protein 3g

Garlic Roasted Chickpeas

Prep time: 5 minutes | Cook time: 50 minutes | Serves: 4

2 (15.5-ounce) cans low-sodium chickpeas, drained, rinsed, and dried
2 tablespoons extra-virgin olive oil
1 teaspoon ground cumin
1 teaspoon garlic powder
1 teaspoon brown sugar
½ teaspoon sweet paprika
½ teaspoon chili powder
½ teaspoon salt

1. Preheat the oven to 400°F. 2. In a big bowl, combine the chickpeas, olive oil, cumin, garlic powder, brown sugar, paprika, chili powder, and salt. Gently toss the mixture to coat the chickpeas well. 3. Transfer the mixture to a baking sheet lined with parchment paper and roast in the oven for 40 to 50 minutes. Shake the pan every 10 minutes to prevent the chickpeas from burning. The chickpeas are done when they are lightly browned, and the texture is more crisp than soft. 4. Add them to an airtight container or food storage bag in the pantry for up to 5 days.
Per Serving: Calories 275; Fat 11g; Sodium 610mg; Carbs 34g; Fiber 11g; Sugar 7g; Protein 12g

Chapter 7 Desserts and Smoothies

Easy Peach Cobbler

Prep time: 10 minutes | Cook time: 25 minutes | Serves: 10

2 tablespoons baking powder
1 cup flour
4 teaspoons light rub margarine
1 cup skim milk
⅓ cup sugar
18 ounces cans of sliced peaches
⅔ cup Splenda

1. Melt margarine in the saucepan over medium heat. 2. Cover the sides of the dish to avoid the sticking of the cobbler. 3. Mix baking powder, Splenda, flour, and sugar in a bowl. 4. Mix skim milk and blend. 5. Transfer the blend to the baking dish, and add peaches to the baking dish. 6. Cook the dish in the oven at 400 degrees F for 20 minutes. 7. When done, serve and enjoy.
Per Serving: Calories 181; Fat 0.95g; Sodium 29mg; Carbs 42.51g; Fiber 1.3g; Sugar 30.43g; Protein 2.39g

Cream Berry Cake

Prep time: 60 minutes | Cook time: 0 | Serves: 12

1 (8 ounces) container Cool Whip Lite
2 tablespoon rum extract
12 packets of Splenda or equal
1 10-ounce package frozen unsweetened raspberries
1 angel food cake
1 tablespoon orange juice
1 envelope of unflavored gelatin
1 cup frozen unsweetened cherries
Raspberry-cherry filling

1. Add raspberries to the blender, and blend them well. 2. Mix raspberries, cherries, orange juice, and rum extract in another bowl. 3. Add hot water to a saucepan, pour gelatin in the pot, and stir. 4. Add Splenda, raspberry, and cherry mixture to the blender, and blend them well. 5. Transfer the raspberry mixture to the third bowl, and then put the bowl in the refrigerator to refrigerate the mixture for 50 minutes. 6. Take angel food cake and cut it into three layers. 7. Put the first layer and add ½ of filling. 8. Put another layer on the top and add the filling. 9. Frost cake. 10. Serve and enjoy.
Per Serving: Calories 91; Fat 1.72g; Sodium 67mg; Carbs 16.97g; Fiber 0.6g; Sugar 13.68g; Protein 1.42g

No-Bake Strawberry Cheesecake

Prep time: 60 minutes | Cook time: 10 minutes | Serves: 8

1 teaspoon vanilla extract
1 cup nonfat Greek yogurt
2 tablespoon lemon juice
¼ cup water
For strawberry compote
½ cup Splenda
16 ounces fat-free cream cheese
4 cup strawberries
1¼ cups Kashi Go Lean Crunch cereal

1. Take a blender and Add yogurt, Splenda, cream cheese, and vanilla extract to the blender, and blend them well. 2. Transfer the yogurt mixture to separate serving dishes. 3. Place the dishes in refrigerator for 1 hour. 4. To make the strawberry compote, add all the compote to the saucepan. 5. Cook the mixture for 10 minutes. 6. Remove cake from refrigerator and coat with compote and Kashi

Go Lean Crunch cereal. 7. Serve and enjoy!
Per Serving: Calories 157; Fat 1.1g; Sodium 420mg; Carbs 24.08g; Fiber 2.1g; Sugar 18.89g; Protein 13.26g

Cool Berry Cucumber Drink

Prep time: 10 minutes | Cook time: 0 | Serves: 1

5 to 6 fresh strawberries
5 slices of fresh cucumber
Ice
Water

1. Add the ice and water to a bowl. 2. Add about five slices of cucumber. 3. Wash 5 to 6 strawberries and add them to the bowl of water. 4. Stir the mixture. 5. Serve and enjoy!
Per Serving: Calories 23; Fat 0.24g; Sodium 1mg; Carbs 5.36g; Fiber 1.4g; Sugar 3.42g; Protein 0.61g

Almond Pumpkin Pie

Prep time: 10 minutes | Cook time: 55 minutes | Serves: 9

For Crust
1 tablespoon water
¼ teaspoon salt
¼ cup ground almonds
1 cup quick-cooking oats
3 tablespoons vegetable oil
2 tablespoons brown sugar
¼ cup whole wheat flour
For Filling
⅔ cup evaporated skim milk
4 teaspoons vanilla
1½ teaspoons low-sodium salt
½ teaspoon ground cinnamon
1 cup canned pumpkin
1 egg
¼ teaspoon ground nutmeg
¼ cup brown sugar

1. Preheat the oven to 425 degrees F. 2. Mix sugar, salt, oats, flour, and almonds in the bowl. 3. Mix oil and water, and put it into a bowl containing dry fruits. 4. Transfer the mixture into the baking pan and bake for 8 minutes. 5. Mix cinnamon, salt, egg, sugar, nutmeg, vanilla, milk, and pumpkin in a large mixing bowl. 6. Transfer the filling to the pan and bake for 45 minutes at 350 degrees F. 7. Serve and enjoy!
Per Serving: Calories 186; Fat 11.78g; Sodium 471mg; Carbs 16.21g; Fiber 1.9g; Sugar 9.1g; Protein 6.39g

Vanilla Huckleberry Cake

Prep time: 10 minutes | Cook time: 60 minutes | Serves: 10

1 teaspoon ground cinnamon
Cooking spray
1 teaspoon vanilla extract
1 cup all-purpose flour
1 cup sugar
½ cup Heart Healthy soft tub margarine
2 tablespoons sugar
2 cups fresh or frozen huckleberries
½ teaspoon salt
1 teaspoon baking powder
1 egg
4 ounces nonfat cream cheese

1. Preheat the oven to 350 degrees F. 2. Add cream cheese and margarine to an electric mixer, and mix them well. 3. Add egg, 1 cup of sugar, flour, salt, and baking powder to the mixer, and beat well. Add vanilla in it along with berries. 4. Take a cooking pan and coat it with cooking spray. Pour the batter in it and bake in the oven at 350 degrees F for 1 hour. 5. Let it cool before serving.
Per Serving: Calories 264; Fat 14.68g; Sodium 202mg; Carbs 29.71g; Fiber 0.5g; Sugar 18.83g; Protein 4.07g

Homemade Kiwi Smoothie

Prep time: 10 minutes | Cook time: None | Serves: 8

6 to 8 cups cold water
7 to 8 ripe kiwis, peeled and
quartered
Sweetener as desired

1. Add kiwis, water, and sweetener to the blender, and blend them for 30 seconds on high speed. 2. Pour the smoothie to glasses and serve. 3. Decorate glasses with sliced kiwis on top.
Per Serving: Calories 30; Fat 0.23g; Sodium 7mg; Carbs 6.95g; Fiber 1.3g; Sugar 5.25g; Protein 0.95g

Fruit Party Punch

Prep time: 5 minutes | Cook time: 0 | Serves: 8

3 tablespoons Kool-Aid Tropical Punch Liquid Drink Mix
1 cup pineapple juice
2 cups fruit, diced small
1 can of lemon-lime soda
½ cup peach or pineapple
schnapps
Ice
½ cup coconut rum
3 tablespoons lemonade starter liquid drink mix
1 cup orange juice

1. Add lemonade drink mix, tropical punch drink mix, 2 cups of water to large bowl, and stir well. 2. Add pineapple juice, diced fruit, lemon-lime soda, and orange juice to the bowl, and stir them well. 3. Serve the mixture with ice.
Per Serving: Calories 104; Fat 0.41g; Sodium 30mg; Carbs 25.63g; Fiber 1.3g; Sugar 20.36g; Protein 1.07g

Summer Strawberry-Banana Smoothie

Prep time: 10 minutes | Cook time: 0 | Serves: 3

4 ice cubes
1 medium banana
6 medium strawberries
1 teaspoon vanilla extract
1 cup pineapple
1 cup fat-free, plain yogurt

1. Add all the ingredients to the blender, and blend them thoroughly. 2. Serve and enjoy!
Per Serving: Calories 103; Fat 0.39g; Sodium 23mg; Carbs 19.04g; Fiber 1.3g; Sugar 14.83g; Protein 6.74g

Vanilla Apple Cake

Prep time: 10 minutes | Cook time: 30 minutes | Serves: 20

2 teaspoons ground cinnamon
2 cups all-purpose flour
2 teaspoons vanilla
½ cup pecans
1 cup sugar
1 teaspoon baking soda
1 egg, beaten
¼ cup vegetable oil
1 cup dark raisins
5 cups tart apples

1. Preheat the oven to 350 degrees F. 2. Grease the baking pan with oil. 3. Mix raisins, apples, sugar, and pecans in the bowl. 4. Add oil, egg, vanilla, flour, soda, cinnamon, and apple mixture to another bowl, and mix them well. 5. Transfer the batter to the baking pan, bake the batter in the oven for 30 minutes. 6. Serve and enjoy!
Per Serving: Calories 125; Fat 4.89g; Sodium 67mg; Carbs 18.93g; Fiber 1.4g; Sugar 7.94g; Protein 1.88g

Orange Peel Cake with Icing

Prep time: 20 minutes | Cook time: 40 minutes | Serves: 16

For Cake
¾ cup skim milk
1 teaspoon vanilla
1 ¼ cup sugar
2¼ teaspoon baking powder
1 tablespoon orange peel
4 eggs
4 tablespoon margarine
2¼ cups cake flour
For Icing
½ teaspoon vanilla extract
6 tablespoons cocoa
3 ounces low fat cream cheese
2 cups confectioners' sugar
2 tablespoons skim milk

To make the cake: 1. Preheat the oven to 325 degrees F. 2. Grease the baking pan with oil., and sprinkle some flour. 3. Sift flour and baking powder together. 4. Mix sugar and margarine in a bowl. 5. Add orange peel, vanilla, and eggs to the bowl, and beat them together. 6. Add flour and milk to the bowl, and mix well. 7. Pour the mixture into the pan and bake in the preheated oven for 40 minutes. 8. When cooked, remove the cake from the pan and let it cool.
To make the icing: 1. Mix milk and cream cheese and add cocoa. 2. Add sugar and vanilla and mix well. 3. Coat the icing over the cake and serve.
Per Serving: Calories 232; Fat 4.57g; Sodium 59mg; Carbs 43.84g; Fiber 0.5g; Sugar 27.34g; Protein 4.07g

Fruits Salad with Honey-Orange Sauce

Prep time: 10 minutes | Cook time: 0 | Serves: 12

For Fruit Salad
1 Kiwi fruit
2 cups seedless grapes
2 bananas
1 large mango
2 nectarines
2 cups fresh strawberries
2 cups fresh blueberries
For Honey-Orange Sauce
Dash nutmeg
1 ½ tablespoons honey
⅓ cup unsweetened orange juice
¼ teaspoon ground ginger
2 tablespoons lemon juice

1. Add all the fruits to the serving bowl. 2. Mix all the sauce in another bowl. 3. Pour the sauce over the fruit, and enjoy.
Per Serving: Calories 126; Fat 0.71g; Sodium 4mg; Carbs 31.44g; Fiber 2.7g; Sugar 25.89g; Protein 1.32g

Banana-Pineapple Compote

Prep time: 10 minutes | Cook time: 2 hour 5 minutes | Serves: 8

Fresh mint leaves
2 mangoes
½ teaspoon vanilla extract
2 teaspoons fresh lemon juice
¾ cup water
3 bananas
1 pineapple
One-piece lemon peel
½ cup sugar

1. Add lemon peel, lemon juice, sugar and ¾ cup water to the saucepan over medium high, bring to a boil. 2. When boiled, add the fruits to the saucepan, and cook the fruits for 5 minutes. 3. Pour the fruit mixture into the cup. 4. Take lemon rind off the saucepan and cook for 2 hours. 5. Serve and enjoy
Per Serving: Calories 172; Fat 0.61g; Sodium 3mg; Carbs 44.01g; Fiber 4.2g; Sugar 34.24g; Protein 1.8g

Cucumber-Infused Drink

Prep time: 10 minutes | Cook time: 0 | Serves: 1

½ cup fresh cucumber | Ice cubes
½ fresh Orange | Water

1. Cut oranges and cucumber into thin slices. 2. Fill a glass with water, and then add the cucumber and orange slices to it. 3. Add ice to it. 4. Serve and enjoy the flavor!
Per Serving: Calories 38; Fat 0.17g; Sodium 1mg; Carbs 9g; Fiber 2g; Sugar 7g; Protein 1g

Bread Pudding with Apple-Raisin Sauce

Prep time: 10 minutes | Cook time: 35 minutes | Serves: 9

For Bread Pudding | 3 egg whites
Vegetable oil spray | For Apple-Raisin Sauce
¼ teaspoon nutmeg | ½ teaspoon orange zest
1 teaspoon vanilla extract | ¼ teaspoon ground cinnamon
2 teaspoons white sugar | 2 tablespoons molasses
1½ cups skim milk | 1¼ cups apple juice
10 slices of whole wheat bread | ¼ teaspoon ground nutmeg
¼ teaspoon clove | ½ cup raisins
½ teaspoon cinnamon | ½ cup apple butter
¼ cup brown sugar |

To make the bread pudding: 1. Preheat the oven to 350 degrees F. 2. Grease the baking dish with vegetable oil. 3. Whisk milk, brown sugar, egg whites, vanilla, and white sugar in a bowl. 4. Mix clove, nutmeg, white sugar, and cinnamon in another bowl. 5. Places bread slices in the baking dish, and pour the mixtures over the bread. 6. Bake the food in the preheated oven for 30 minutes.
To prepare apple-raisin sauce: 1. Put all the sauce in the saucepan, and simmer them for 5 minutes. 2. Serve and enjoy!
Per Serving: Calories 199; Fat 6.35g; Sodium 196mg; Carbs 38.01g; Fiber 2.6g; Sugar 22.32g; Protein 6.35g

Sweet Potato Pie

Prep time: 10 minutes | Cook time: 60 minutes | Serves: 16

For Crust | milk
2 tablespoons vegetable oil | ¼ teaspoon nutmeg
¼ teaspoon sugar | ¼ cup brown sugar
⅓ skim milk | 1 teaspoon vanilla extract
1¼ cups flour | 3 large eggs
For Filling | ½ teaspoon salt
3 cups sweet potatoes | ¼ cup white sugar
¼ cup canned evaporated skim |

1. Preheat the oven to 350 degrees F. 2. Mix flour, milk, sugar, and oil in a bowl. 3. Form the mixture into pastry, and roll it into the waxed paper. 4. Remove the paper from the top and turn it downwards on the pie plate 5. Mix vanilla, eggs, nutmeg, salt, milk, sweet potatoes, and sugar in another bowl. 6. Transfer the filling into a pie shell. 7. Bake the pie in the oven for 1 hour. 8. Let the pie cool before serving.
Per Serving: Calories 94; Fat 3.35g; Sodium 92mg; Carbs 13.11g; Fiber 0.7g; Sugar 4.91g; Protein 2.73g

Cranberry-Oat Crisp

Prep time: 10 minutes | Cook time: 40 minutes | Serves: 6

For Filling | For Topping
1 cup cranberries | 1 tablespoon soft margarine
¾ teaspoon lemon juice | ¼ cup whole wheat flour
3 tablespoons all-purpose flour | ⅔ cup rolled oats
5 cups apples | 2 teaspoons ground cinnamon
1 teaspoon lemon peel | ⅓ cup brown sugar
½ cup sugar |

1. Mix lemon peel, sugar, and flour in a bowl. 2. Add cranberries, lemon juice, and apples, and mix well. 3. Transfer the mixture to a baking dish containing 6 cups. 4. Combine cinnamon, brown sugar, flour, melted margarine, and oats in another bowl. 5. Pour the topping over the filling. 6. Cook the food in the oven for 40 minutes at 375 degrees F. 7. Serve and enjoy!
Per Serving: Calories 225; Fat 3.01g; Sodium 7mg; Carbs 52.77g; Fiber 4.9g; Sugar 34.56g; Protein 3.18g

Cinnamon Rice Pudding

Prep time: 10 minutes | Cook time: 45 minutes | Serves: 5

½ teaspoon salt | ⅔ cup sugar
3 cups skim milk | 1 cup rice
2 sticks cinnamon | 6 cups water

1. Add water and cinnamon sticks to the saucepan over medium heat, bring to a boil. 2. Add rice and cook for 30 minutes. 3. Add skim milk, salt, and sugar, and cook for 15 minutes more. 4. Serve and enjoy!
Per Serving: Calories 291; Fat 1.25g; Sodium 304mg; Carbs 63.54g; Fiber 3g; Sugar 32.3g; Protein 7.71g

Banana Vanilla Mousse

Prep time: 5 minutes | Cook time: 0 | Serves: 4

Eight sliced banana | 1 cup plain low-fat yogurt
1 medium banana | 1 teaspoon vanilla
4 teaspoons sugar | 2 tablespoons low-fat milk

1. Add banana, milk, sugar, and vanilla to a blender, and blend them until smooth. 2. Transfer the mixture into dessert dishes, add yogurt, and decorate with two banana slices. 3. Enjoy.
Per Serving: Calories 90; Fat 1.23g; Sodium 47mg; Carbs 16.36g; Fiber 1g; Sugar 12.12g; Protein 3.9g

Banana Mango Shake

Prep time: 5 minutes | Cook time: 0 | Serves: 4

1 small banana | 4 tablespoons frozen mango
2 cup low-fat milk | juice
2 ice cubes |

1. Add all the ingredients to the blender, and blend them thoroughly. 2. Serve and enjoy!
Per Serving: Calories 98; Fat 2.5g; Sodium 59mg; Carbs 15.08g; Fiber 0.7g; Sugar 12.24g; Protein 4.38g

Matzo Almond and Apricot Macaroons

Prep time: 10 minutes | Cook time: 20 minutes | Serves: 16

3 large egg whites
1 teaspoon grated orange rind
¾ cup sugar
¾ cup whole blanched almonds

½ teaspoon almond extract
½ cup chopped dried apricots
¾ cup matzo cake meal, plus some of spreading

1. Preheat the oven to 325 degrees F. 2. Line the baking sheet with parchment paper. Dust matzo cake meal. 3. In a blender, blend almond, sugar, ¾ cup matzo cake meal, and the rest of the ingredients. 4. Spread some matzo cake meal, and make 16 portions of dough. 5. Make small balls with the dough, and bake them in the preheated oven for 20 minutes at 325 degrees F. 6. Serve and enjoy!
Per Serving: Calories 115; Fat 3.81g; Sodium 60mg; Carbs 18.27g; Fiber 1.2g; Sugar 12.59g; Protein 2.69g

Banana Yogurt Parfaits

Prep time: 10 minutes | Cook time: 0 | Serves: 4

2 teaspoons hot water
1 tablespoon cocoa
¼ cup low-fat granola
1 cup sliced strawberries
1 tablespoon confectioner's

sugar
1 large banana
12 ounces fat-free pineapple Greek yogurt

1. Add yogurt, sliced strawberries, and sliced bananas to a small dish. 2. Dust with 1 tablespoon of granola. 3. Take a small cup mix of hot water, cocoa, and confectioner's sugar. 4. Pour the syrup over parfait. 5. Serve and enjoy! **Per Serving:** Calories 143; Fat 2.26g; Sodium 104mg; Carbs 20.89g; Fiber 1.9g; Sugar 15.51g; Protein 10.77g

Simple Blueberry Peach Crisp

Prep time: 10 minutes | Cook time: 20 minutes | Serves: 8

3 tablespoons corn oil margarine
1 tablespoon cinnamon
⅓ cup plus ¼ cup light brown sugar

6 cups fresh peaches
1 cup quick-cooking oats
2 tablespoons all-purpose floor
2 cups fresh blueberries

1. Preheat the oven to 350 degrees F. 2. Mix blueberries and peaches in the baking dish. 3. Mix cinnamon with flour and brown sugar in a bowl. 4. Spread the cinnamon mixture over fruits in the baking dish, and mix well. 5. Mix brown sugar with cinnamon in a separate bowl, add margarine, and spread this over fruits. 6. Cook the food in the oven for 20 minutes. 7. Serve and enjoy!
Per Serving: Calories 110; Fat 3g; Sodium 36mg; Carbs 22.42g; Fiber 3.9g; Sugar 13.65g; Protein 2.58g

Tartar Cocoa Cake

Prep time: 10 minutes | Cook time: 40 minutes | Serves: 12

1½ teaspoons vanilla extract
1 teaspoon cream of tartar
¼ cup sugar
¾ cup flour

1 cup sugar
1¼ cups egg whites
¼ cup cocoa

1. Preheat the oven to 350 degrees F. 2. Mix ¼ cup of sugar, cocoa, and flour in a bowl. 3. Whisk egg whites in another bowl, add cream of tartar, and whisk. 4. Add sugar, vanilla, and flour mixture, and mix them well. 5. Spread the batter in the baking pan. 6. Bake the food for 40 minutes. 7. Serve and enjoy!
Per Serving: Calories 88; Fat 0.44g; Sodium 43mg; Carbs 17.67g; Fiber 0.7g; Sugar 10.52g; Protein 3.9g

Cocoa Pudding

Prep time: 10 minutes | Cook time: 5 minutes | Serves: 4

⅛ teaspoon ground cinnamon
6-8 packets sugar substitute
2 tablespoons cornstarch
1 teaspoon vanilla

1½ cups 2% milk
¼ cup unsweetened cocoa powder

1. Whisk cornstarch and cocoa powder in a bowl; add milk and mix as well. 2. Put in the microwave first at high for 2 minutes and then at medium for 3 minutes. 3. Add vanilla, sugar, and cinnamon and mix. 4. Set aside for 5 minutes. 5. Serve and enjoy!
Per Serving: Calories 100; Fat 3.76g; Sodium 41mg; Carbs 14.85g; Fiber 1.7g; Sugar 8.34g; Protein 3.87g

Vanilla Cottage Cheesecake

Prep time: 20 minutes | Cook time: 50 minutes | Serves: 8

For Crust
¼ tablespoon cinnamon
1 cup low-fat graham cracker crumbs
¼ cup hard margarine
2 tablespoons white sugar

For Cake
⅔ cup white sugar
3 tablespoons all-purpose flour
2 cups low-fat cottage cheese
1 tablespoon vanilla extract
2 eggs

1. Preheat the oven to 325 degrees F. 2. Add cinnamon, graham cracker crumbs, and sugar with melted butter in a cup, and mix them well. 3. Transfer the mixture to the baking pan. 4. Blend sugar, flour, milk, vanilla, eggs, and cottage cheese in a blender. 5. Spread the mixture over the mixture. 6. Bake the food for 50 minutes. 7. Serve and enjoy!
Per Serving: Calories 198; Fat 12.36g; Sodium 337mg; Carbs 10.43g; Fiber 0.7g; Sugar 4.06g; Protein 10.6g

Healthful Banana Bread

Prep time: 20 minutes | Cook time: 50 minutes | Serves: 1

Nonstick spray
¼ cup hot water
1 teaspoon baking soda
2 teaspoons cinnamon
1 cup mashed ripe banana
¼ cup sugar substitute
⅓ cup cinnamon applesauce

½ cup chopped walnuts
½ teaspoon salt
1¾ cups whole-wheat flour
1½ teaspoons vanilla
½ cup cholesterol-free egg substitute
¼ cup honey

1. Preheat the oven to 325 degrees F. 2. Coat a large baking pan with fat-free nonstick spray. 3. Mix honey, sugar substitute, vanilla, egg substitute, beat applesauce, bananas, whole-wheat flour, cinnamon, and salt in a large bowl. 4. Add soda and hot water to a cup, mix well, and then pour over the mixture in a bowl. 5. Transfer mixture to the baking pan, and bake in the oven for 50 minutes. 6. Serve and enjoy!
Per Serving: Calories 147; Fat 2.76g; Sodium 230mg; Carbs 28.85g; Fiber 2.9g; Sugar 13.39g; Protein 4.08g

Brownie Bites

Prep time: 10 minutes | Cook time: 25 minutes | Serves: 18

½ teaspoon salt
½ cup packed brown sugar
1 tablespoon vegetable oil
¼ teaspoon cinnamon
1 can of garbanzo beans
½ teaspoon baking powder
2 teaspoons vanilla extract
2 tablespoons cocoa powder
2 eggs
1 cup semisweet chocolate chips

1. Preheat the oven to 325 degrees F. 2. Grease a mini muffin with oil. 3. Melt chocolate chips in the saucepan over medium heat. 4. Put garbanzo beans in the blender along with other ingredients, blend them to prepare the batter. 5. Pour the batter in muffin pans, and bake for 20 minutes. 6. Serve and enjoy!
Per Serving: Calories 67; Fat 2.1g; Sodium 108mg; Carbs 10.88g; Fiber 1.1g; Sugar 7.63g; Protein 1.7g

Tasty Strawberry Shortcake

Prep time: 10 minutes | Cook time: 0 | Serves: 12

1 loaf fat-free pound cake
1 tablespoon lemon juice
½ cup strawberry preserves
3 cups fat-free whipped topping
¼ cup honey
2 pints' strawberries

1. Mix strawberries, lemon, and honey in a bowl. 2. Arrange a slice of pound cake over a dessert plate. 3. Spread strawberry mixture and whipped topping. 4. Place a few strawberries for garnishing. 5. Serve and enjoy!
Per Serving: Calories 167; Fat 0.54g; Sodium 135mg; Carbs 37.72g; Fiber 4.2g; Sugar 21.77g; Protein 3.49g

Hot Cocoa

Prep time: 10 minutes | Cook time: 10 minutes | Serves: 4

1 teaspoon vanilla extract
2 tablespoons unsweetened cocoa powder
4 cups skim milk
2 tablespoons honey

1. Add all ingredients to the saucepan over medium heat, and cook them for 5 to 10 minutes. 2. Add the mugs before serving.
Per Serving: Calories 167; Fat 5.68g; Sodium 72mg; Carbs 25.57g; Fiber 1.2g; Sugar 22.98g; Protein 4.86g

No-Oil Carrot Muffins

Prep time: 10 minutes | Cook time: 20 minutes | Serves: 10

½ cup raisins
¼ cup molasses
1½ cups whole-wheat flour
½ cup skim milk
2 teaspoons baking powder
¼ cup brown sugar
⅓ cup shredded carrots
Two egg whites

1. Preheat the oven to 400 degrees F. Line muffin tins with paper liners. 2. Mix milk and carrots with egg whites in a bowl. 3. Add flour, molasses, brown sugar, baking powder, and raisins to the bowl, and mix well. 4. Pour batter into the tins, and bake them in the preheated oven for 20 minutes. 5. Serve warm!
Per Serving: Calories 119; Fat 0.49g; Sodium 19mg; Carbs 27.1g; Fiber 2.1g; Sugar 13.49g; Protein 3.17g

Almond Apple Crisp

Prep time: 10 minutes | Cook time: 40 minutes | Serves: 6

¼ cup brown sugar
6 apples
1 teaspoon vanilla extract
2 tablespoons honey
2 tablespoons sliced almonds
¾ old-fashioned rolled oats
¼ cup plus 2 tablespoon
water
2 tablespoons raisins
1 tablespoon vegetable oil
1½ teaspoons ground cinnamon
2 tablespoons raw sunflower seeds

1. Preheat the oven to 325 degrees F. Line the baking sheet with parchment paper. 2. Mix vanilla, honey, almonds, oats, oil, cinnamon, and sunflower seeds in a large bowl. 3. Arrange granola mixture on the baking sheet, and bake for 30 minutes. 4. Remove the sheet and add raisins. 5. Cook cinnamon, diced apples, and brown sugar in the saucepan for 10 minutes over medium heat, and remove apples. Mash the apples. 6. On a serving plate, add ½ cup cooked apples and ¼ cup granola, and serve.
Per Serving: Calories 117; Fat 4.08g; Sodium 4mg; Carbs 20.85g; Fiber 1.5g; Sugar 18.1g; Protein 0.96g

Carrot Oat Cake

Prep time: 10 minutes | Cook time: 15 minutes | Serves: 24

1 large apple
¼ cup unsalted butter
1 large egg
1 cup unsweetened applesauce
½ teaspoon baking soda
2 teaspoons cinnamon
1 cup whole wheat flour
2 medium carrots
2 teaspoon vanilla extract
½ cup honey
½ teaspoon salt
½ teaspoon nutmeg
½ cup ground flaxseed
2¼ cups old-fashioned oats

1. Preheat the oven to 350 degrees F. Line the baking sheet with parchment paper. 2. Mix salt, nutmeg, flaxseed, oats, baking soda, cinnamon, and flour in a bowl. 3. Mix vanilla extract, applesauce honey, melted butter, and egg in another bowl. 4. Combine the egg mixture with the nutmeg mixture. 5. Take ¼ cup of batter and pour in the baking sheet. 6. Bake the food for 15 minutes. 7. Serve and enjoy!
Per Serving: Calories 106; Fat 3.78g; Sodium 83mg; Carbs 19.2g; Fiber 3.4g; Sugar 8.1g; Protein 3.29g

Grilled Peaches with Yogurt Drizzle and Almonds

Prep time: 10 minutes | Cook time: 10 minutes | Serves: 4

¼ cup sliced almonds
1½ cups plain, fat-free yogurt
1 tablespoon brown sugar
2 tablespoons honey
2 teaspoons vanilla extract
Four ripe peaches

1. Whisk sugar, peaches, and vanilla in a large bowl, then let them sit for 15 minutes. 2. Mix vanilla, yogurt, and honey in another bowl, and set aside for later use. 3. Transfer peaches to the grill and grill them for 4 minutes at high. 4. Cook almonds in the small pan for 3 minutes over low heat. 5. Transfer peaches to the bowl, top them with yogurt and roasted almonds on the top. 6. Enjoy!
Per Serving: Calories 163; Fat 1.84g; Sodium 65mg; Carbs 31.71g; Fiber 2.3g; Sugar 29.9g; Protein 6.24g

Oat Pumpkin Smoothie

Prep time: 10 minutes | Cook time: 0 | Serves: 4

3-4 ice cubes	½ teaspoon pumpkin pie spice
2 tablespoons honey	2 tablespoons rolled oats
⅓ cup skim milk	⅓ cup fat-free plain yogurt
½ cup canned pumpkin	

1. Add ice cubes, honey, yogurt, pumpkin pie spice, oats, pumpkin, and milk to a blender, and then blend them until frothy. 2. Transfer the smoothie to the serving glass, and enjoy.
Per Serving: Calories 150; Fat 7.8g; Sodium 61mg; Carbs 16.98g; Fiber 1.5g; Sugar 12.88g; Protein 6.66g

No Bake Prunes Cashew Energy Bites

Prep time: 65 minutes | Cook time: 0 | Serves: 12

1 tablespoon water	⅓ cup cashews
½ cup unsweetened shredded coconut	1 tablespoon coconut oil
	10 dried prunes

1. In the blender, blend the cashews, water, coconut flakes, prunes, and coconut oil to form a paste. 2. Take 1 tablespoon of the mixture from the blender, and make small balls. 3. Take shredded coconut in the bowl, and coat balls with coconut. 4. Refrigerate the balls for 1 hour. 5. Serve and enjoy!
Per Serving: Calories 70; Fat 4.92g; Sodium 32mg; Carbs6.49g; Fiber 0.9g; Sugar 0.9g; Protein 1.05g

Pecan Phyllo Tarts

Prep time: 10 minutes | Cook time: 15 minutes | Serves: 15

15 mini phyllo shells	½ cup pecans
¼ teaspoon vanilla extract	2 tablespoons honey
4 teaspoons brown sugar	One large egg
1 tablespoon melted butter	

1. Preheat the oven to 350 degrees F. 2. Mix all the ingredients in a bowl. 3. Place the baking sheet with mini pie shells. 4. Fill the shells with pecan mixture, and bake them for 15 minutes. 5. Serve and enjoy!
Per Serving: Calories 101; Fat 4.58g; Sodium 99mg; Carbs 13.47g; Fiber 0.7g; Sugar 3.13g; Protein 1.85g

Blueberry Muffins

Prep time: 10 minutes | Cook time: 20 minutes | Serves: 24

Raw sugar	¾ cups fresh blueberries
½ cup milk	2 cups all-purpose flour
2 teaspoons baking powder	1¼ teaspoons vanilla
2 eggs	1 cup sugar
1 stick of unsalted butter	

1. Preheat the oven to 375 degrees F. 2. Mix sugar and butter in a bowl. 3. Add eggs, baking powder, flour, milk, and vanilla, and stir well. 4. Add blueberries to the mixture, and mix well. 5. Pour the batter into muffin cups, and bake for 20 minutes. 6. Serve and enjoy!
Per Serving: Calories 78; Fat 1.02g; Sodium 8mg; Carbs 15.54g; Fiber 0.4g; Sugar 7.2g; Protein 1.68g

Easy-to-Make Green Juice

Prep time: 10 minutes | Cook time: 0 | Serves: 2

Juice of ½ lemon	1 teaspoon grated fresh ginger
1 tablespoon ground flaxseeds	½ banana
½ cup pineapple	2 cups water
3 cups spinach	

1. Blend all the ingredients in the blender. 2. Serve and enjoy!
Per Serving: Calories 105; Fat 2.53g; Sodium 43mg; Carbs 20.64g; Fiber 3.7g; Sugar 13.19g; Protein 2.87g

Rolled Biscuits

Prep time: 15 minutes | Cook time: 10 minutes | Serves: 4

⅓ cup low-fat milk	1 cup low-sodium baking mix

1. Preheat the oven to 450 degrees F. 2. Mix 1 cup of low-sodium baking mix with milk in the bowl. 3. Knead the dough gently. 4. Take a biscuit cutter, and cut the dough. 5. Transfer the food to the baking sheet, and bake for 10 minutes. 6. Serve and enjoy!
Per Serving: Calories 68; Fat 0.64g; Sodium 63mg; Carbs 29.11g; Fiber 1.3g; Sugar 1.02g; Protein 0.72g

Cheesecake Cupcakes

Prep time: 10 minutes | Cook time: 20 minutes | Serves: 12

1 tablespoon all-purpose flour	2 egg whites
2 teaspoons orange zest	6 ounces fat-free vanilla Greek yogurt
1 teaspoon vanilla extract	¼ cup sugar
8 ounces reduced-fat cream cheese	12 Gingersnap cookies

1. Preheat the oven to 350 degrees F. Line the 12-cup muffin pan with cupcake liners. 2. Arrange a gingersnap in each cupcake liner. 3. Mix cream cheese, vanilla, and sugar. Add flour, orange zest, yogurt, and egg whites in an electric mixer. 4. Transfer the mixture to cupcake liners, and bake the food for 20 minutes. 5. Serve and enjoy!
Per Serving: Calories 93; Fat 3.59g; Sodium 135mg; Carbs 12.52g; Fiber 0.2g; Sugar 6.81g; Protein 2.53g

Cherry and Caramel Biscuits

Prep time: 10 minutes | Cook time: 10 minutes | Serves: 6

⅓ cup low-fat milk	1 cup cherry
1 tablespoon vanilla essence	½ cup caramel
2 tablespoons baking powder	1 cup low-sodium baking mix
3 cups flour	

1. Preheat the oven to 450 degrees F. 2. Mix all the ingredients in the bowl to get a smooth mixture. 3. Take a baking sheet and pour a spoonful onto it. 4. Cook the food in the oven for 10 minutes. 5. Serve and enjoy!
Per Serving: Calories 321; Fat 1.58g; Sodium 66mg; Carbs 77.91g; Fiber 3.1g; Sugar 8.09g; Protein 7.53g

Banana Ice-cream

Prep time: 20 minutes | Cook time: 0 | Serves: 1

A very ripe medium-sized banana

1. Peel the banana and cut it into pieces. 2. Place chunks in the freezer for 1 hour. 3. Take out frozen banana pieces, and blend in a blender till it becomes creamy. 4. Enjoy.
Per Serving: Calories 105; Fat 0.39g; Sodium 1mg; Carbs 26.95g; Fiber 3.1g; Sugar 14.43g; Protein 1.29g

Sweet Vanilla Cookies

Prep time: 10 minutes | Cook time: 15 minutes | Serves: 12

1 cup milk	1 teaspoon vanilla essence
2 teaspoons sugar	½ cup unsalted butter
2 cups flour	1 tablespoon reduced sodium
2 tablespoons cocoa powder	baking powder

1. Preheat the oven to 450 degrees F. 2. Mix all the ingredients except milk and butter in a bowl. 3. Add butter and then milk to the bowl, mix them well. 4. Drop a spoonful of mixture onto the baking pan. 5. Bake the food for 15 minutes. 6. Serve and enjoy!
Per Serving: Calories 141; Fat 6.13g; Sodium 14mg; Carbs 18.44g; Fiber 0.9g; Sugar 1.55g; Protein 3.26g

Orange-Strawberry Smoothie

Prep time: 10 minutes | Cook time: 0 | Serves: 2

½ cup ice cubes	1 cup soy milk
1 cup papaya	1 orange
½ cup blueberries	1 cup strawberries

1. Blend all the ingredients in the blender. 2. Serve and enjoy!
Per Serving: Calories 155; Fat 0.82g; Sodium 62mg; Carbs 33.88g; Fiber 4.4g; Sugar 26.05g; Protein 5.73g

Carrot-Apple Juice

Prep time: 10 minutes | Cook time: 0 | Serves: 3

Juice of one orange	Juice of one lime
1-inch piece of fresh ginger	1 large granny smith apple
1 large carrot	2 medium beets
2 cups water	

1. Peel the beets and chop off the ends. Cut them into pieces. 2. Peel the ginger. 3. Rinse apples, and cut them into chunks. 4. Chop carrots, and cut lime and orange in half. 5. Use a juicer to juice away. 6. Serve and enjoy!
Per Serving: Calories 79; Fat 0.31g; Sodium 42mg; Carbs 18.6g; Fiber 3.5g; Sugar 12.24g; Protein 1.24g

Spinach and Fruit Smoothie

Prep time: 10 minutes | Cook time: 0 | Serves: 4

1 tablespoon honey	juice
1 cup fat-free milk	One banana
1 cup fresh baby spinach	1 cup frozen blueberries
½ cup calcium-fortified orange	

1. Blend all the ingredients in a blender. 2. Serve and enjoy!

Per Serving: Calories 100; Fat 0.52g; Sodium 40mg; Carbs 22.55g; Fiber 2.1g; Sugar 16.81g; Protein 3.03g

Banana-Avocado Smoothie

Prep time: 5 minutes | Cook time: 0 | Serves: 1

1 cup ice cubes	1 large ripe banana
1 tablespoon chia seeds	2 teaspoon honey
1 cup unsweetened vanilla almond milk	¼ ripe avocado
	1 cup packed baby kale

1. Add all the ingredients to the blender, and blend them until smooth. 2. Serve and enjoy!
Per Serving: Calories 392; Fat 13.51g; Sodium 164mg; Carbs 68.36g; Fiber 11.9g; Sugar 43.91g; Protein 5.86g

Strawberry Cocoa Smoothie

Prep time: 5 minutes | Cook time: 0 | Serves:2

1 tablespoon honey	cocoa powder
1 tablespoon unsalted butter	1 cup chilled unsweetened
1 ½ cups frozen strawberries	chocolate almond milk
1 tablespoon unsweetened	

1. Add all the ingredients to the blender, and blend until smooth. 2. Serve and enjoy!
Per Serving: Calories 220; Fat 5.53g; Sodium 62mg; Carbs 41.32g; Fiber 4.3g; Sugar 32.05g; Protein 5.34g

Peanut Strawberry Smoothie

Prep time: 10 minutes | Cook time: 0 | Serves: 1

2-4 ice cubes	1 teaspoon vanilla extract
1 tablespoon honey	1 tablespoon natural peanut
1 cup chopped kale	butter
1 cup unsweetened soy milk	1 cup frozen strawberries

1. Add all the ingredients to the blender, and blend them until creamy. 2. Serve and enjoy!
Per Serving: Calories 291; Fat 3.47g; Sodium 355mg; Carbs 55.53g; Fiber 5.6g; Sugar 43.76g; Protein 11.09g

Almond Butter Banana-Pumpkin Smoothie

Prep time: 5 minutes | Cook time: None | Serves: 2

2 heaping tablespoons. almond butter	1 teaspoon ground nutmeg
	1 teaspoon pure maple syrup
1 banana	1 teaspoon vanilla extract
½ cup unsweetened canned pumpkin	1 cup nut milk of choice
	2 or 3 ice cubes
1 teaspoon ground cinnamon	

1. In a blender, blend the almond butter, banana, pumpkin, cinnamon, nutmeg, maple syrup, vanilla extract, nut milk, and the ice cubes together until smooth. 2. Then serve in tall glasses. 3. Garnish as you desired. Serve and enjoy!
Per Serving: Calories 620; Fat 53g; Sodium 131mg; Carbs 31g; Fiber 9g; Sugar 15g; Protein 16g

Strawberry-Pineapple Smoothie

Prep time: 5 minutes | Cook time: 0 | Serves: 1

1 tablespoon almond butter
1 cup chopped fresh pineapple
1 cup frozen strawberries
¾ cup chilled unsweetened almond milk

1. Add all the ingredients to the blender, and blend them well. 2. Serve and enjoy!
Per Serving: Calories 352; Fat 14.21g; Sodium 135mg; Carbs 58.72g; Fiber 7.7g; Sugar 42.09g; Protein 3.1g

Cinnamon Fruit and Oat Bran Smoothie

Prep time: 5 minutes | Cook time: 5 minutes | Serves: 1

¾ cup unsweetened vanilla almond or cashew milk
2 tablespoons oat bran
¼ teaspoon apple pie spice or ground cinnamon
½ teaspoon vanilla extract
1 cup baby spinach or ⅓ cup frozen
½ cup nonfat plain Greek
yogurt
1 tablespoon avocado
½ medium banana, sliced and frozen
½ cup green apple, unpeeled, chopped and frozen
¼ cup cooked or canned white beans, rinsed and drained
½ cup ice

1. In a high-powered blender, add oat bran, spinach, yogurt, apple pie spice, vanilla, yogurt, milk, spinach, banana, avocado, ice, and apple and blend until smooth. 2. Transfer to a serving glass. 3. Serve and enjoy!
Per Serving: Calories 690; Fat 38g; Sodium 304mg; Carbs 82g; Fiber 26g; Sugar 33g; Protein 22g

Peanut Jelly Smoothie

Prep time: 5 minutes | Cook time: 0 | Serves: 1

1-2 tablespoon pure maple syrup
½ cup frozen strawberries
1 cup baby spinach
½ cup low-fat milk
1 tablespoon natural peanut butter
1 cup frozen banana slices
⅓ cup nonfat plain Greek yogurt

1. Add all the ingredients to a blender, and pulse them until smooth. 2. Serve and enjoy!
Per Serving: Calories 273; Fat 3.57g; Sodium 351mg; Carbs 47.9g; Fiber 3.6g; Sugar 38.62g; Protein 14.8g

Easy Apricot-Strawberry Smoothie

Prep time: 5 minutes | Cook time: 0 | Serves: 1

2 fresh apricots
¾ cup unsweetened almond
1 cup frozen strawberries

1. Put all the ingredients in a blender, and blend them until smooth. 2. Serve and enjoy!
Per Serving: Calories 116; Fat 0.97g; Sodium 5mg; Carbs 28.16g; Fiber 6.2g; Sugar 16.58g; Protein 2.12g

Coconut Berry Bowl

Prep time: 10 minutes | Cook time: 0 | Serves: 1

1 teaspoon chia seeds
1 tablespoon sliced almonds
¼ cup pineapple chunks
1 cup frozen mixed berries
1 tablespoon unsweetened
coconut flakes
½ kiwi
½ cup unsweetened soymilk
1 large banana

1. Add soymilk, banana, and berries to the blender, and blend until smooth. 2. Transfer the smoothie to the serving bowl, and garnish with kiwi, coconut, pineapple, almonds, and chia seeds. Enjoy.
Per Serving: Calories 355; Fat 5.56g; Sodium 79mg; Carbs 77.04g; Fiber 11.4g; Sugar 50.94g; Protein 6.55g

Mango-Almond Smoothie

Prep time: 10 minutes | Cook time: 0 | Serves: 1

½ teaspoon honey
⅛ teaspoon ground allspice
¼ cup plain unsweetened almond milk
½ cup nonfat plain Greek yogurt
¼ cup raspberries
5 tablespoons unsalted almonds
¼ cup frozen sliced banana
½ cup frozen chopped mango

1. Add allspice, almond milk, yogurt, almonds, banana, and mango to the blender, blend them well. 2. Transfer smoothie to the bowl and garnish with raspberries, almonds, and honey. Enjoy.
Per Serving: Calories 465; Fat 26.85g; Sodium 93mg; Carbs 42.12g; Fiber 11.2g; Sugar 27.67g; Protein 22.03g

Fruity Spinach-Kale Smoothie

Prep time: 15 minutes | Cook time: 5 minutes | Serves: 2

¾ cup water
2 cups spinach
1 tablespoon ground flaxseeds
1 large frozen banana, chopped
1 tablespoon almond butter or
peanut butter, optional
2 large kale leaves, chopped (about 1½ cups)
½ cup frozen peach
½ cup frozen mango

1. Add water, spinach, and kale in a blender and mix on low speed until the mixture is just decomposed. 2. Then turn to medium speed and mix until it is fully decomposed and smooth. 3. Add nut butter, banana, mango, peach, and the ground flaxseeds and blend on medium-high until it reaches your desired consistency. 4. Transfer to serving glasses. 5. Serve and enjoy!
Per Serving: Calories 252; Fat 8g; Sodium 69mg; Carbs 45g; Fiber 8g; Sugar 30g; Protein 7g

Healthy Fruit Smoothie

Prep time: 5 minutes | Cook time: 0 | Serves: 2

1 tablespoon ground chia seeds
½ cup unsweetened refrigerated coconut milk beverage
½ cup chopped ripe mango
1 tablespoon cashew butter
½ medium ripe banana
½ cup frozen strawberries

1. Add all the ingredients to the blender. 2. Blend the food until smooth 3. Serve and enjoy!
Per Serving: Calories 290; Fat 23.26g; Sodium 57mg; Carbs 22.09g; Fiber 5.5g; Sugar 13.09g; Protein 3.09g

Cocoa Almond Butter Smoothie

Prep time: 5 minutes | Cook time: None | Serves: 1

1 cup almond milk
2 tablespoons almond butter
1 tablespoon cocoa powder
1 teaspoon espresso powder (or to taste)

1 to 2 (1-gram) packets stevia (or to taste)
¼ teaspoon almond extract
½ cup crushed ice

1. In a blender, add all the ingredients and blend together until smooth. 2. To puree the mixture, let the blender run. 3. Serve and enjoy!
Per Serving: Calories 351; Fat 24g; Sodium 262mg; Carbs 22g; Fiber 5g; Sugar 14.5g; Protein 18g

Lemony Tzatziki Smoothie

Prep time: 5 minutes | Cook time: None | Serves: 2

2 English cucumbers, cut into chunks
1 cup 2 percent plain Greek yogurt

1 apple, unpeeled, cored and chopped
Juice of 1 lemon
3 ice cubes

1. Add the yogurt, cucumbers, apple, ice cubes, and lemon juice in a blender and process to puree until smooth. 2. Then transfer the mixture into 2 serving glasses. 3. Serve and enjoy!
Per Serving: Calories 149; Fat 1g; Sodium 49mg; Carbs 23g; Fiber 4g; Sugar 17g; Protein 14g

Peanut Blackberry Smoothie

Prep time: 5 minutes | Cook time: 5 minutes | Serves: 4

2 cups frozen blackberries
1 cup plain low-fat Greek yogurt

1 cup unsweetened peanut milk
½ cup natural peanut butter

1. In a food processor, add yogurt, almond milk, almond butter, and berries and then blend together. More peanut milk can be added to thin the mixture. 2. Transfer to serving glasses. Serve and enjoy!
Per Serving: Calories 381; Fat 15g; Sodium 267mg; Carbs 50g; Fiber 6g; Sugar 36g; Protein 16g

Spinach Smoothie with Berries and Banana

Prep time: 15 minutes | Cook time: 5 minutes | Serves: 2

2 cups spinach
1 tablespoon almond butter
¾ cup frozen blackberries

1 cup water
1 small frozen banana, chopped
¾ cup frozen blueberries

1. Add water and spinach in a blender and mix on low speed until decompose. 2. Then stir on medium speed until smooth and thoroughly decomposed. 3. Add the chopped banana, blueberries, blackberries, and almond butter and combine again on medium-high speed until it achieves the desired consistency. 4. Remove from the blender and transfer to 2 serving glasses. 5. Serve and enjoy!
Per Serving: Calories 167; Fat 5g; Sodium 28mg; Carbs 30g; Fiber 7g; Sugar 18g; Protein 4g

Blueberry-Banana Smoothie

Prep time: 5 minutes | Cook time: 5 minutes | Serves: 1

1 cup blueberries, frozen
½ cup silken tofu
1 banana

½ cup (120 ml) low-fat cow's or rice milk, unsweetened

1. In a blender, blend all the ingredients together until smooth. 2. Serve and enjoy!
Per Serving: Calories 462; Fat 7g; Sodium 66mg; Carbs 97g; Fiber 8g; Sugar 74g; Protein 11g

Spinach Smoothie with Berries and Banana

Prep time: 15 minutes | Cook time: 5 minutes | Serves: 2

2 cups spinach
1 tablespoon almond butter
¾ cup frozen blackberries

1 cup water
1 small frozen banana, chopped
¾ cup frozen blueberries

1. Add water and spinach in a blender and mix on low speed until decompose. 2. Then stir on medium speed until smooth and thoroughly decomposed. 3. Add the chopped banana, blueberries, blackberries, and almond butter and combine again on medium-high speed until it achieves the desired consistency. 4. Remove from the blender and transfer to 2 serving glasses. 5. Serve and enjoy!
Per Serving: Calories 167; Fat 5g; Sodium 28mg; Carbs 30g; Fiber 7g; Sugar 18g; Protein 4g

Coconut Veggie-Fruit Smoothie

Prep time: 10 minutes | Cook time: None | Serves: 1

½ cup fresh blueberries
½ banana
1 cup packed spinach

1 cup coconut milk
½ teaspoon vanilla extract

1. In a blender, add the banana, blueberries, coconut milk, vanilla, and spinach and blend until smooth. 2. Transfer in serving glasses. 3. Garnish as you desired. Serve and enjoy!
Per Serving: Calories 256; Fat 9g; Sodium 130mg; Carbs 37g; Fiber 4g; Sugar 27g; Protein 10g

Lychee-Blueberry Smoothie with Raisins

Prep time: 10 minutes | Cook time: 10 minutes | Serves: 1

½ cup chopped frozen blueberries
½ cup frozen lychee, peeled and seeded

1½ cups unsweetened peanut milk, plus more as needed
½ cup raisins

1. In a food processor, add blueberries, lychee, peanut milk, and raisins together and process until creamy and smooth. More peanut milk can be added as needed to achieve a desired smooth. 2. Transfer to a serving glass. 3. Serve and enjoy!
Per Serving: Calories 368; Fat 8g; Sodium 388mg; Carbs 61g; Fiber 3g; Sugar 56g; Protein 16g

Cauliflower and Fruit Smoothie

Prep time: 5 minutes | Cook time: 0 | Serves: 1

1 tablespoon granulated sugar
½ cup frozen strawberries
¼ cup low-fat plain yogurt
½ cup frozen peaches
½ cup frozen cauliflower rice
½ cup apple juice

1. Blend all the ingredients in a blender until smooth. 2. Serve and enjoy!
Per Serving: Calories 209; Fat 1.58g; Sodium 66mg; Carbs 46.4g; Fiber 4.8g; Sugar 36.59g; Protein 5.55g

Chai Spiced Banana Smoothie

Prep time: 10 minutes | Cook time: None | Serves: 1

1 cup unsweetened almond milk
1 date, pitted and chopped
1 banana, sliced into ¼-inch rounds
¼ teaspoon vanilla extract
½ teaspoon chai spice blend
Pinch salt
Ice cubes

1. In a blender, blend together date, banana, chai spice blend, salt, ice cubes, vanilla, and almond milk until smooth. 2. Add toppings as you desired to serve.
Per Serving: Calories 181; Fat 5g; Sodium 259mg; Carbs 46g; Fiber 4g; Sugar 32g; Protein 11.5g

Almond Chocolate-Cherry Spinach Smoothie

Prep time: 5 minutes | Cook time: 5 minutes | Serves: 1

For the smoothie:
½ cup unsweetened vanilla almond or cashew milk
1 teaspoon vanilla extract
1 cup fresh baby spinach
1 tablespoon almond butter
1 tablespoon unsweetened cocoa powder
½ cup nonfat plain Greek yogurt
¾ cup frozen cherries
½ medium banana, sliced and frozen
3 to 4 ice cubes
For serving
¼ cup berries, such as blueberries, raspberries, or strawberries
½ small banana, sliced
1 teaspoon sliced almonds
½ tablespoon cacao nibs

1. In a high-powered blender, combine together milk, almond butter, cocoa, cherries, ice, banana, vanilla, and spinach and blend until smooth. 2. Transfer the mixture into a bowl and add the berries, banana slices, almonds, and cacao nibs on the top. 3. Serve and enjoy!
Per Serving: Calories 546; Fat 16g; Sodium 240mg; Carbs 90g; Fiber 11g; Sugar 67g; Protein 19g

Kiwi Strawberry Smoothie

Prep time: 5 minutes | Cook time: None | Serves: 2

1 cup fresh strawberries
2 kiwi fruits, peeled and cut into quarters
1 cup unsweetened yogurt
1 cup nonfat milk

1. In a blender, add kiwi, yogurt, milk, and strawberries and blend together on high until smooth. 2. Add fresh diced kiwis and strawberries to serve, as desired. 3. Serve and enjoy!

Per Serving: Calories 185; Fat 5g; Sodium 124mg; Carbs 27g; Fiber 3g; Sugar 22g; Protein 10g

Fruit-Veggie Smoothie

Prep time: 10 minutes | Cook time: 5 minutes | Serves: 2

1 cup almond milk
3 cups kale or spinach
1 small green apple
½ cup frozen peaches
¼ cup vanilla Greek yogurt
1 banana, peeled
1 orange, peeled

1. In a blender, add the almond milk, kale or spinach, green apple, peaches, yogurt, banana, and orange and blend completely until smooth. 2. Transfer to serving glasses. 3. Serve and enjoy!
Per Serving: Calories 287; Fat 6g; Sodium 81mg; Carbs 56g; Fiber 7g; Sugar 43g; Protein 8g

Ginger Peat-Carrot Smoothie

Prep time: 10 minutes | Cook time: None | Serves: 2

2 carrots, peeled and grated
1 ripe pear, unpeeled, cored and chopped
2 teaspoons. grated fresh ginger
Juice and zest of 1 lime
1 cup water
½ teaspoon ground cinnamon
¼ teaspoon ground nutmeg

1. Blend pear, ginger, lime juice, water, lime zest, cinnamon, nutmeg, and carrots together in a blender until smooth. To ensure the mixture is pureed, run the blender run long enough. 2. Add the mixture into 2 serving glasses. 3. Serve and enjoy!
Per Serving: Calories 57; Fat 0g; Sodium 30mg; Carbs 15g; Fiber 5g; Sugar 7g; Protein 1g

Banana-Pineapple Oat Muffins with Walnuts

Prep time: 10 minutes | Cook time: 20 minutes | Serves: 8

2 tablespoons ground flaxseed
5 tablespoons water
2 cups oat flour
1 tablespoon cinnamon
1 teaspoon baking powder
1 cup mashed banana (about 3
medium-size ripe bananas)
2 tablespoons pure maple syrup
½ cup crushed pineapple (in 100-percent juice), packed
1 teaspoon pure vanilla extract
¼ cup walnut pieces

1. Before cooking, heat your oven to 375 degrees F. 2. Prepare 8 muffin cups and a muffin tin. Line the cups in the muffin tin. 3. Add water and flaxseed in a small mixing bowl and stir well. Allow it to sit until the mixture congeals, about 5 minutes. 4. Add cinnamon, baking powder, and flour in a large mixing bowl and combine well. 5. Add the bananas, pineapple, vanilla, maple syrup, and the flaxseed mixture in a medium and stir well. 6. Mix together the wet ingredient and the dry ingredient and then stir in the walnut. 7. Divide the mixture evenly into the muffin cups and bake in the preheated oven until the muffins are golden brown on the top. Insert a fork in the center of each muffin and the fork should be clean. 8. Serve warm or store in an airtight container in a refrigerator for up to 5 days.
Per Serving: Calories 205; Fat 5g; Sodium 8mg; Carbs 36g; Fiber 4.5g; Sugar 11.6g; Protein 4.9g

Coconut Green Smoothie Bowl

Prep time: 10 minutes | Cook time: 3 minutes | Serves: 2

1 green apple, thinly sliced, divided
1 banana, cut into chunks
1 cup frozen mango chunks
1 cup chopped kale leaves
1 cup baby spinach
1 cup 1% milk
¼ cup unsweetened coconut flakes
½ lemon, thinly sliced

1. Toast the coconut flakes in a small dry skillet over medium heat until lightly browned, about 2 to 3 minutes. Set it aside. 2. Add banana, mango, spinach, kale, milk, and ¾ of the apple slices in a blender. 3. Then pour the mixture into a storage container. Separately store the smoothie, the remaining apple slices, and lemon slices. 4. To serve, in each serving bowl, add half the smoothie. Then add half the remaining apple slices, half the lemon slices, and coconut flakes for each, 5. Serve and enjoy!
Per Serving: Calories 246; Fat 5g; Sodium 73mg; Carbs 48g; Fiber 7g; Sugar 35g; Protein 7g

Chia Berries Smoothie

Prep time: 5 minutes | Cook time: None | Serves: 2

½ cup mixed berries (blueberries, strawberries, blackberries)
1 tablespoon ground chia seeds
2 tablespoons. unsweetened coconut flakes
½ cup unsweetened plain
almonds milk
½ cup lettuce
¼ cup unsweetened vanilla nonfat yogurt
½ cup ice

1. In a blender, combine together the almond milk, Brazilian nut flakes, lettuce, yogurt, and ice together until completely smooth. 2. Serve and enjoy!
Per Serving: Calories 121; Fat 4g; Sodium 100mg; Carbs 16g; Fiber 3g; Sugar 12g; Protein 5g

Coconut Grape-Kale Smoothie

Prep time: 10 minutes | Cook time: None | Serves: 1

¼ avocado
1 cup fresh grapes
1 cup packed kale leaves, thoroughly washed
1 tablespoon hemp seed
1 or 2 mint leaves
¼ cup cashews (optional)
1 cup coconut milk
Ice (optional)

1. In a blender, add grapes, hemp seed, avocado, kale leaves, mint leaves, coconut milk, cashews (if using), and ice (if using) and blend together until smooth. 2. Transfer the smoothie into a serving glass and add your favorite toppings. 3. Serve and enjoy!
Per Serving: Calories 748; Fat 48g; Sodium 135mg; Carbs 66g; Fiber 8g; Sugar 41g; Protein 24g

Apple Green Smoothie

Prep time: 5 minutes | Cook time: None | Serves: 2

2 cups shredded kale
½ avocado, diced
½ Granny Smith apple, unpeeled, cored and chopped
1 cup unsweetened almond milk
¼ cup 2 percent plain Greek yogurt
3 ice cubes

1. In a blender, process together the shredded kale, diced avocado, apple, ice cubes, yogurt, and almond milk until thick and smooth. 2. Transfer into 2 serving glasses. 3. Serve and enjoy!

Per Serving: Calories 177; Fat 10g; Sodium 100mg; Carbs 21g; Fiber 6g; Sugar 14g; Protein 3g

One-Pot Almond Chocolate-Carrot Cookies

Prep time: 10 minutes | Cook time: 20 minutes | Serves: 8

1¼ cups almond meal
½ teaspoon baking powder
¼ cup dark chocolate chips
½ cup shredded carrots
¼ cup unsweetened applesauce
2 teaspoons pure maple syrup
1 whole egg
1 teaspoon cinnamon

1. Before cooking, heat your oven to 375 degrees F. 2. Prepare a baking sheet and line with a sheet of parchment paper. 3. Add cinnamon, a beaten egg, maple syrup, applesauce, shredded carrots, chocolate chips, baking powder, and almond meal in a large mixing bowl and mix until well combined to reach your desired consistency. 4. Then use a tablespoon scooping out the dough. Form the dough into cookies of your desired shape. 5. Arrange the cookies on the prepared baking sheet and bake in the preheated oven until the cookies are just fluffy and lightly golden brown, about 10 to 15 minutes. 6. A fork should be clean after removing from the center of the cookies. 7. Serve or store in an airtight container in a refrigerator for up to 4 days.
Per Serving: Calories 62; Fat 3g; Sodium 49mg; Carbs 8g; Fiber 1g; Sugar 5g; Protein 1g

Refreshing Green Smoothie

Prep time: 15 minutes | Cook time: 10 minutes | Serves: 2

¾–1 cup water
1 cup chopped kale
3–4 ice cubes
1 small avocado, pitted, peeled, and chopped
1 tangerine, peeled and separated into segments
1 green apple, chopped
2 small kiwifruits, peeled and halved

1. Add water and kale in a blender and process on low. 2. When the kale starts to decompose, increase the speed to medium and stir until it is fully decomposed and smooth. 3. In the blender, add kiwifruit, tangerine, ice cubes, apple, and avocado and mix again on medium-high speed until it reaches your desired consistency. 4. Transfer to serving glasses. 5. Serve and enjoy!
Per Serving: Calories 277; Fat 15g; Sodium 16mg; Carbs 38g; Fiber 12g; Sugar 21g; Protein 4g

Healthy Strawberry Green Smoothie

Prep time: 15 minutes | Cook time: 5 minutes | Serves: 2

2 cups spinach
½ cup frozen strawberries
1½ cups frozen peach
1 cup water
1 tablespoon coconut oil
1 small frozen banana, chopped

1. Add water and spinach in a blender and mix on low speed until the spinach is just decomposed and smooth. 2. Add coconut oil, banana, peaches, and strawberries in the blender and mix on medium-high speed until it reaches your desired consistency, about 1 minute. 3. Transfer to serving glasses. 4. Serve and enjoy!
Per Serving: Calories 306; Fat 7g; Sodium 39mg; Carbs 62g; Fiber 7g; Sugar 50g; Protein 3g

Herbed Mango Grape Smoothie

Prep time: 10 minutes | Cook time: None | Serves: 1

1 cup fresh or frozen mango chunks	½ cup unsweetened almond milk
½ teaspoon fresh thyme leaves	Pinch sea salt
½ cup fresh seedless green grapes	Pinch freshly ground black pepper
¼ fennel bulb	Ice (optional)

1. In a blender, add all the ingredients and blend together until smooth. 2. Transfer to a serving glass. Add toppings to garnish, as you desired. 3. Serve and enjoy!
Per Serving: Calories 343; Fat 3g; Sodium 704mg; Carbs 84g; Fiber 6g; Sugar 76g; Protein 3g

Cinnamon Pistachio-Orange Smoothie

Prep time: 5 minutes | Cook time: None | Serves: 1

½ cup plain whole-milk Greek yogurt	1 tablespoon shelled pistachios, coarsely chopped
½ cup unsweetened almond milk	1 to 2 teaspoons. monk fruit extract or stevia (optional)
Zest and juice of 1 clementine or ½ orange	¼ to ½ teaspoon ground allspice
1 tablespoon extra-virgin olive oil or MCT oil	¼ teaspoon ground cinnamon
	¼ teaspoon vanilla extract

1. Blend all the ingredients in a blender until creamy and smooth. 2. Transfer to a serving glass. 3. Serve and enjoy!
Per Serving: Calories 342; Fat 23g; Sodium 144mg; Carbs 30g; Fiber 3g; Sugar 25g; Protein 7g

Ginger-Pear Smoothie

Prep time: 5 minutes | Cook time: None | Serves: 1

1 pear, cored and quartered	½ cucumber, peeled if wax-coated or not organic
½ fennel bulb	
1 thin slice fresh ginger	½ cup water
1 cup packed spinach	Ice (optional)

1. In a blender, blend together all the ingredients until creamy and smooth. 2. Transfer the smoothie into a serving glass. 3. Serve and enjoy!
Per Serving: Calories 108; Fat 1g; Sodium 89mg; Carbs 25g; Fiber 9g; Sugar 15g; Protein 4g

Plum-Yogurt Smoothie

Prep time: 5 minutes | Cook time: None | Serves: 2

4 ripe plums, pitted	yogurt
1 cup skim milk	4 ice cubes
6 ounces 2 percent plain Greek	¼ teaspoon ground nutmeg

1. Add all the ingredients in a blender and process until a smooth puree is formed. 2. Then divide the smoothie into 2 serving glasses. 3. Serve and enjoy!
Per Serving: Calories 212; Fat 1g; Sodium 101mg; Carbs 40g; Fiber 1g; Sugar 39g; Protein 13g

Savory Banana Smoothie

Prep time: 5 minutes | Cook time: 1 minutes | Serves: 1

1 frozen banana, sliced	1 cup ice
1 tablespoon peanut butter	¼ cup plain nonfat or low-fat Greek yogurt
1 cup nonfat or low-fat milk	

1. In a blender, add peanut butter, milk, yogurt, ice, and bananas and blender about 30 seconds, or until smooth. 2. Transfer to a serving glass. 3. Serve and enjoy!
Per Serving: Calories 276; Fat 5g; Sodium 413mg; Carbs 47g; Fiber 3g; Sugar 34g; Protein 14g

Simple Almond Butter-Banana Smoothie

Prep time: 3 minutes | Cook time: 1 minutes | Serves: 2

1 medium frozen banana, chopped	1½ tablespoons unsweetened cocoa powder
¾ cup unsweetened almond milk	⅛ teaspoon ground cinnamon
1 tablespoon raw, unsalted almond butter	3 drops almond extract
¼ cup water	3–4 ice cubes
	Sprig of fresh mint

1. In a blender, add the chopped banana, almond milk, almond butter, water, cocoa powder, ground cinnamon, almond extract, and ice cubes. 2. Blend together on high until smooth, about 1 minute. 3. Add more ice to make a thicker, slushier smoothie. 4. Pour the mixture into 2 serving glasses. 5. Add mint to garnish. 6. Serve and enjoy!
Per Serving: Calories 257; Fat 10g; Sodium 84mg; Carbs 43g; Fiber 5g; Sugar 30g; Protein 4g

Banana Blueberry Smoothie

Prep time: 15 minutes | Cook time: 5 minutes | Serves: 2

1 teaspoon almond extract	1 cup fresh or frozen blueberries
1 cup unsweetened yogurt	1 cup nonfat milk
1 banana, cut into 4 pieces	

1. In a blender, add yogurt, milk, banana, almond extract, and blueberries and blend together at high speed until it reaches your desired consistency, about 1 to 2 minutes. 2. Transfer to serving glasses. 3. Serve and enjoy!
Per Serving: Calories 216; Fat 5.28g; Sodium 122mg; Carbs 35g; Fiber 2g; Sugar 18g; Protein 10g

Almond Butter and Macadamia Smoothie

Prep time: 5 minutes | Cook time: 20 minutes | Serves: 1

1 cup nonfat milk	almond butter
1 tablespoon all-natural creamy	2 ounces macadamias, shelled

1. In a food processor, add all the ingredients and process until smooth. 2. Transfer to a serving glass. 3. Serve and enjoy!
Per Serving: Calories 596; Fat 52g; Sodium 169mg; Carbs 23g; Fiber 7g; Sugar 16g; Protein 17g

Quick Healthy Peaches and Greens Smoothie

Prep time: 5 minutes | Cook time: 1 minutes | Serves: 1

½ cup nonfat or low-fat milk
2 cups fresh spinach (or ⅓ cup frozen)
½ cup plain nonfat or low-fat Greek yogurt
½ teaspoon vanilla extract

1 cup frozen peaches (or fresh, pitted)
1 cup ice
Optional: no-calorie sweetener of choice

1. Add vanilla extract, milk, ice, yogurt, spinach, and peaches in a blender and blend to form a smooth puree. 2. Transfer the mixture to a serving bowl. 3. Serve and enjoy!
Per Serving: Calories 191; Fat 0g; Sodium 157mg; Carbs 30g; Fiber 3g; Sugar 3g; Protein 18g

Banana Strawberry Smoothie

Prep time: 5 minutes | Cook time: 1 minutes | Serves: 1

1 cup frozen strawberries
½ frozen banana
½ cup nonfat or low-fat milk

½ orange, peeled
1 cup plain nonfat or low-fat Greek yogurt

1. Add orange, milk, yogurt, banana, and strawberries in a blender and blend together to form a smooth puree. 2. Transfer the mixture to a serving bowl. 3. Serve and enjoy!
Per Serving: Calories 305; Fat 1g; Sodium 170mg; Carbs 52g; Fiber g; Sugar 37g; Protein 29g

Banana Kiwifruit Smoothie

Prep time: 5 minutes | Cook time: None | Serves: 1

1 medium banana, cut into chunks
½ cup frozen wild raspberries

½ cup frozen kiwifruit chunks
1 cup almond milk

1. In a small freezer-safe container, add the banana chunks, raspberries, and kiwifruit and put in a freezer to frozen for later use. 2. In a processor, blend all the ingredients until smooth. 3. Serve and enjoy!
Per Serving: Calories 253; Fat 1g; Sodium 184mg; Carbs 59g; Fiber 7g; Sugar 39g; Protein 2g

Cinnamon Banana Smoothie

Prep time: 10 minutes | Cook time: 5 minutes | Serves: 1

1 tablespoon unsalted almond butter
3–4 ice cubes
⅛ teaspoon vanilla extract
1 cup unsweetened almond

milk
⅛ teaspoon ground cinnamon
1 tablespoon wheat germ
1 large banana

1. Add almond butter, ice cubes, vanilla extract, almond milk, ground cinnamon, wheat germ, and banana in a blender and mix together on low speed. 2. Once the mixture is just decomposed, stir on medium speed until fully decomposed and smooth, about 1 minute. 3. Transfer the mixture to a serving bowl. 4. Serve and enjoy!
Per Serving: Calories 338; Fat 13g; Sodium 183mg; Carbs 52g; Fiber 8g; Sugar 25g; Protein 10g

Sweet and Lemony Raspberry Sorbet

Prep time: 5 minutes, plus 2 to 4 hours to chill | Cook time: 15 minutes | Serves: 2

2 cups frozen raspberries
2 teaspoons honey

1 teaspoon lime juice
½ cup warm water

1. Add the lime juice, water, raspberries, and honey in a blender. 2. Blend together until well combined, about 2 to 3 minutes. 3. Then divide the mixture into sorbet moulds. Freeze in a freezer until firm, about 2 to 4 hours. 4. Serve or store in an airtight container in a freezer for up to 1 month.
Per Serving: Calories 280; Fat 0g; Sodium 4mg; Carbs 71g; Fiber 11g; Sugar 60g; Protein 2g

Mango Radicchio Smoothie

Prep time: 10 minutes | Cook time: 10 minutes | Serves: 1

2 cups tightly packed radicchio
1 cup frozen lychee
1 cup frozen mango chunks
1 small orange, peeled and

pitted
1 cup (60mL) apple cider
¼ teaspoon cayenne pepper

1. In a food processor, add radicchio, lychee, mango chunks, orange, apple cider, and cayenne pepper and process together on high until smooth. 2. Serve cold. Enjoy!
Per Serving: Calories 283; Fat 2g; Sodium 304mg; Carbs 68g; Fiber 10g; Sugar 53g; Protein 6g

Ginger Strawberry Yogurt Smoothie

Prep time: 10 minutes | Cook time: 1 minutes | Serves: 4

2 cups frozen strawberries
1½ cups plain whole-milk Greek yogurt
1 cup ice

2 tablespoons. chia seeds
⅛ teaspoon ground nutmeg
¼ teaspoon ground ginger

1. In a food processor, add all the ingredients and process until smooth. 2. Divide the mixture into serving glasses. 3. Serve and enjoy!
Per Serving: Calories 153; Fat 7g; Sodium 64mg; Carbs 18g; Fiber 4g; Sugar 11g; Protein 5g

Tropical Smoothie with Raisins

Prep time: 5 minutes | Cook time: 2 minutes | Serves: 1

1 cup frozen mango chunks
½ cup frozen pineapple chunks
2 frozen guava chunks
½–1 cup plant-based milk
2 tablespoons. chopped nuts of

your choice
¼ cup chopped fruit of your choice
1 tablespoon raisins
1½ tablespoons. pine nuts

1. In a food processor, add the first 4 ingredients and blend until smooth. 2. Pour the mixture into a serving bowl. Add raisins, pine nuts, or other chopped fruit and nuts, as you desired. 3. Serve and enjoy!
Per Serving: Calories 81; Fat 3g; Sodium 20mg; Carbs 6g; Fiber 0.4g; Sugar 6g; Protein 7g

Cantaloupe-Spinach Mix Smoothie

Prep time: 15 minutes | Cook time: 10 minutes | Serves: 2

2 cups spinach
½ cup frozen strawberries
¾ cup chopped honeydew

melon
½–¾ cup water
¾ cup chopped cantaloupe

1. Add water and spinach in a blender and blend at low speed.
2. Once the spinach is about to decompose, increase the speed to medium and process until the mixture is smooth and is fully decomposed. 3. Then add the flaxseeds, ice cubes, strawberries, honeydew melon, and cantaloupe to the blender. Process on high speed, until your desired consistency is reached, about 1 minute. 4. Transfer to 2 serving bowls. 5. Serve and enjoy!
Per Serving: Calories 77; Fat 2g; Sodium 29mg; Carbs 15g; Fiber 3g; Sugar 7g; Protein 3g

Peach Avocado Yogurt Smoothie

Prep time: 15 minutes | Cook time: 5 minutes | Serves: 2

1 cup nonfat plain or vanilla Greek yogurt
1 avocado, peeled and pitted
1½ teaspoons stevia, granulated
1 teaspoon pure vanilla extract

1 to 2 cups ice cubes
1½ cups peaches, frozen
1½ cups nonfat milk
1 tablespoon flaxseed, ground

1. In a blender, add yogurt, avocado, stevia, vanilla extract, ice cubes, peaches, milk, and ground flaxseed and process to form a smooth puree. 2. Pour the mixture into 2 serving bowls. 3. Serve and enjoy!
Per Serving: Calories 323; Fat 15g; Sodium 142mg; Carbs 32g; Fiber 8g; Sugar 21g; Protein 21g

Strawberry-Apple and Nuts Crumble

Prep time: 10 minutes | Cook time: 50 minutes | Serves: 6

¼ cup almond meal
¾ cup quick-cooking oats
2 teaspoons pure maple syrup
1 tablespoon avocado oil
1½ teaspoons ground

cinnamon, divided
¼ teaspoon ground nutmeg
¼ cup pecan pieces
3 Fuji apples, thinly sliced
2 cups strawberries, quartered

1. Before cooking, heat your oven to 400 degrees F. 2. Add 1 teaspoon of cinnamon, pecan, nutmeg, oil, maple syrup, oats, and almond meal in a medium mixing bowl and combine well. 3. Add strawberries, the remaining cinnamon, and apple in an oven-safe dish and stir well to coat. 4. Sprinkle the crumble mixture over the fruit mixture and bake in your preheated oven until the topped crumble mixture is lightly golden and apples are softened, about 45 to 50 minutes. 5. Then transfer into 6 serving bowls. 6. Serve or store in an airtight container in your refrigerator for up to 4 days. As it sits, it will get a bit softer. For a crispy taste, you can put it in an oven on broil for about 5 minutes.
Per Serving: Calories 141; Fat 6g; Sodium 3mg; Carbs 22g; Fiber 4g; Sugar 13g; Protein 2g

Raspberry, Carrot, and Celery Smoothie

Prep time: 10 minutes | Cook time: None | Serves: 1

1 carrot, trimmed
½ cup fresh raspberries
1 celery stalk
1 small beet, scrubbed and

quartered
1 cup coconut water
1 teaspoon balsamic vinegar
Ice (optional)

1. In a blender, add all the ingredients and blend together until smooth. 2. Pour the mixture into a serving glass. Add toppings to garnish as you like. 3. Serve and enjoy!
Per Serving: Calories 212; Fat 1g; Sodium 345mg; Carbs 50g; Fiber 10g; Sugar 39g; Protein 4g

Blueberry, Carrot, and Greens Smoothie

Prep time: 20 minutes | Cook time: 15 minutes | Serves: 2

¼ cup water
2 cups chopped mixed greens (such as kale, collard greens, mustard greens, Swiss chard, and spinach)
4 ice cubes

½ cup frozen blueberries
¼ cup unsweetened almond milk
½ cup coarsely chopped unpeeled cucumber
⅓ cup chopped carrot

1. Add water and the mixed greens in a blender and blend at low speed until the greens is just about to decompose. 2. Then increase the speed to medium and continue stirring until smooth. 3. Add the remaining ingredients in the blender and process on medium-high speed until it reaches your desired consistency, about 1 minute. 4. Serve and enjoy!
Per Serving: Calories 55; Fat 1g; Sodium 44mg; Carbs 12g; Fiber 3g; Sugar 8g; Protein 1g

Refreshing Orange-Carrot Green Smoothie

Prep time: 10 minutes | Cook time: 5 minutes | Serves: 2

1 tablespoon fresh parsley
1 large rib celery, chopped
¾ cup chopped carrot
1 small orange, separated into

segments
½–¾ cup water
½ cup chopped cooked beets

1. Add water, parsley, and celery in a blender and blend on low speed. 2. When the parsley and celery is just about to decompose, increase the speed to medium and process until fully decomposed. 3. Add orange, carrot, and beets in the blender and continue stirring on medium-high speed until the mixture reaches your desired consistency. 4. Pour the smooth mixture into 2 serving glasses. 5. Serve and enjoy!
Per Serving: Calories 64; Fat 0.3g; Sodium 89mg; Carbs 15g; Fiber 4g; Sugar 10g; Protein 2g

Dipped Pear Slices with Walnut Butter

Prep time: 15 minutes | Cook time: 25 minutes | Serves: 4

1 cup raw walnuts
1 teaspoon ground cinnamon

¼ teaspoon pure vanilla extract
4 pears, cored and sliced

1. Before cooking, heat your oven to 425 degrees F. 2. Prepare a baking sheet and line over with parchment paper. Spread the raw walnuts over the paper. 3. Bake the walnuts in your preheated oven until they are golden brown, about 5 minutes. 4. In a food processor, add cinnamon, vanilla, and the baked walnuts and blend until the walnuts are like butter, about 15 to 18 minutes. Scrape down the sides if needed, while processing. 5. Serve the slices of 1 pear with 1 tablespoon of walnut butter. 6. In an airtight container, store the remaining walnut butter in the refrigerator for up to 1 week.
Per Serving: Calories 235; Fat 13g; Sodium 2mg; Carbs 30g; Fiber 7g; Sugar 18g; Protein 4g

Cantaloupe Slices with Blackberry Balsamic Glaze

Prep time: 15 minutes | Cook time: 15 minutes | Serves: 2

1 cup blackberries, mashed
½ cup balsamic vinegar

½ teaspoon pure maple syrup
2 cups cubed cantaloupe

1. Add the mashed blackberries, balsamic vinegar, and pure maple syrup in a small pot and bring together to a boil over medium heat. 2. Then simmer over low heat until the mixture thickens to half as a glaze. 3. Divide the cantaloupe cubes into 2 serving bowls and glaze over with the mixture. 4. Serve and enjoy!
Per Serving: Calories 238; Fat 0.5g; Sodium 47mg; Carbs 56g; Fiber 6g; Sugar 50g; Protein 3.5g

Chocolate-Tofu Mousse

Prep time: 5 minutes | Cook time: 5 minutes | Serves: 6

1 (3.5-ounce) bar 70-percent dark chocolate
1 (14-ounce) package extra-firm tofu, excess water drained and tofu patted dry

1 teaspoon pure vanilla extract
1 teaspoon honey
1 teaspoon cinnamon

1. Add the chocolate bar in a medium microwave-safe bowl and heat for 2 minutes, or until the bar has melted. 2. Blend together the vanilla, cinnamon, melted chocolate bar, honey, and tofu in a blender about 1 minute, or until smooth. Scrape down the sides if needed. 3. Store the mousse in an airtight container in the refrigerator for up to 3 days. It will lightly get thicken as it cools.
Per Serving: Calories 166; Fat 11g; Sodium 9mg; Carbs 10.3g; Fiber 2g; Sugar 5g; Protein 8g

Peanut Butter and Chocolate Black Bean Brownie

Prep time: 10 minutes | Cook time: 15 minutes | Serves: 6

1 (15-ounce) can low-sodium black beans, drained and rinsed
6 small dates, halved
1½ ounces (about half a bar) 70-percent dark chocolate bar, quartered

2 tablespoons quick-cooking oats
2 tablespoons unsalted raw peanut butter
2 tablespoons water

1. Before cooking, heat your oven to 350 degrees F. 2. Add dates, oats, water, peanut butter, chocolate, and black beans in a medium bowl, and then blend for about 2 to 3 minutes, until doughy and smooth. 3. Spread evenly the batter onto an oven-safe baking sheet and bake in the preheated oven until the batter shows a darker brown, about 15 minutes. A fork should come out clean from the middle. 4. Allow it to cool for 5 minutes and cut into 6 squares. 5. Serve or store in an airtight container for up to 3 days.
Per Serving: Calories 153; Fat 5g; Sodium 112mg; Carbs 23g; Fiber 5g; Sugar 9g; Protein 5.5g

Blueberry Yogurt Bark with Pumpkin Seed

Prep time: 5 minutes plus 2 to 4 hours for chilling | Cook time: None | Serves: 6

2 cups nonfat plain yogurt
1¼ cups blueberries, divided
1 tablespoon coarsely chopped fresh mint

1 teaspoon honey
¼ cup raw unsalted pumpkin seeds

1. Prepare a baking sheet and line with parchment paper, making sure the edges are covered. 2. Combine together 1 cup of blueberries, mint, honey, and yogurt in a food processor and process for 2 minutes, or until smooth. 3. Spread the yogurt mixture evenly over the parchment paper with a rubber spatula. 4. Top evenly the yogurt mixture with the remaining blueberries and pumpkin seeds. 5. Then freeze until the bark is fully frozen, about 2 to 4 hours. Use a fork to poke the middle of the pan to check whether it has hardened. 6. Then break into 12 pieces to serve or store in an airtight container in a freezer for up to 1 month.
Per Serving: Calories 129; Fat 5g; Sodium 40mg; Carbs 17g; Fiber 1g; Sugar 16g; Protein 5g

Conclusion

A healthy heart is a central focus of health. By changing your lifestyle, you can stay away heart disease and lower your risk for a heart attack or stroke. You will never be too old to begin making healthier choices. The sooner low-fat foods are embraced, the longer one will reap the benefits.

Be an active participant in your health. How you live on a day-to-day basis, the food you eat, being well-rested, and regular exercise habits – all of these things affect your heart health. Do what work for you to be healthy as well as enjoy your life. Be aware that no one knows your body better than you do. It's up to us [the writers] to help serve up useful information that will enable you to make the right decisions by giving you enough options so that it feels like there are many great ways to achieve positive results while trying out different recipes! That's exactly why we've curated this collection of some of the best books available on heart-healthy diets, recipes, and natural remedies - so that no matter what dietary approach will work best for you, there'll be something here for every other person too!

Appendix 1 Measurement Conversion Chart

WEIGHT EQUIVALENTS

US STANDARD	METRIC (APPROXINATE)
1 ounce	28 g
2 ounces	57 g
5 ounces	142 g
10 ounces	284 g
15 ounces	425g
16 ounces (1 pound)	455 g
1.5pounds	680 g
2pounds	907g

VOLUME EQUIVALENTS (LIQUID)

US STANDARD	US STANDARD (OUNCES)	METRIC (APPROXIMATE)
2 tablespoons	1 fl.oz	30 mL
¼ cup	2 fl.oz	60 mL
½ cup	4 fl.oz	120 mL
1 cup	8 fl.oz	240 mL
1½ cup	12 fl.oz	355 mL
2 cups or 1 pint	16 fl.oz	475 mL
4 cups or 1 quart	32 fl.oz	1 L
1 gallon	128 fl.oz	4 L

VOLUME EQUIVALENTS (DRY)

US STANDARD	METRIC (APPROXIMATE)
⅛ teaspoon	0.5 mL
¼ teaspoon	1 mL
½ teaspoon	2 mL
¾ teaspoon	4 mL
1 teaspoon	5 mL
1 tablespoon	15 mL
¼ cup	59 mL
½ cup	118 mL
¾ cup	177 mL
1 cup	235 mL
2 cups	475 mL
3 cups	700 mL
4 cups	1 L

TEMPERATURES EQUIVALENTS

FAHRENHEIT (F)	CELSIUS (C) (APPROXIMATE)
225 °F	107°C
250 °F	120°C
275 °F	135°C
300 °F	150°C
325 °F	160°C
350 °F	180°C
375 °F	190°C
400 °F	205°C
425 °F	220°C
450 °F	235°C
475 °F	245°C
500 °F	260°C

Printed in Great Britain
by Amazon